Art of Renaissance Florence

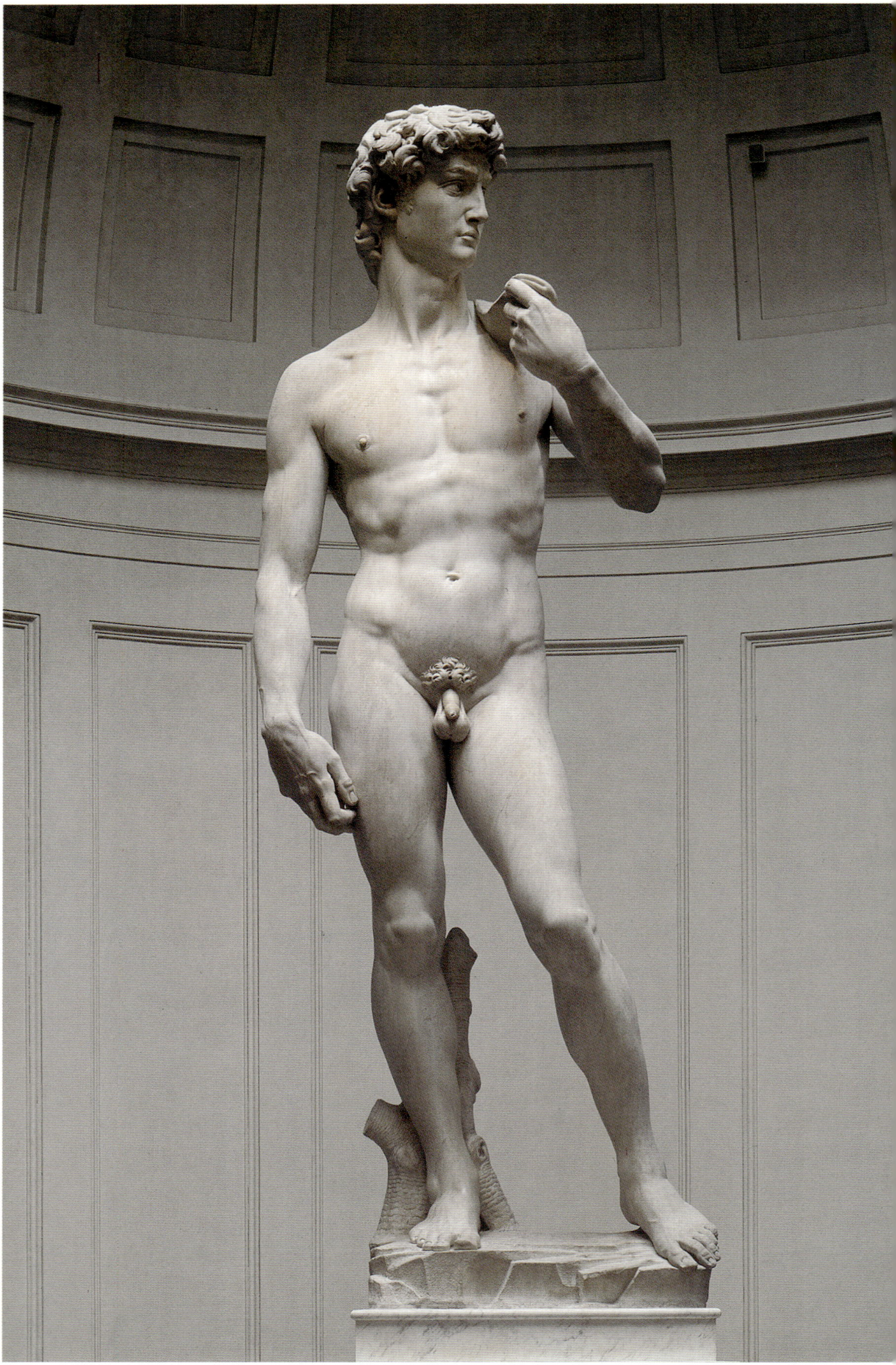

Art of Renaissance Florence:
A City and Its Legacy

Scott Nethersole

Laurence King Publishing

For Andrew

'You will understand what I mean to say in spite of the words which, although factual, might have been put together by an idiot.'

Antonio Manetti, *Life of Brunelleschi*, early 1480s

I would like to thank Joost Joustra, Laura Llewellyn, Paula Nuttall, Guido Rebecchini, Nat Silver, Michael and Susan Smirin, and my family, all of whom read drafts of various chapters. My undergraduate students generously advised me on structure and content. I remain deeply grateful to my dinner companions at 'chapter, chapter', Charles Robertson, Patricia Rubin and Alison Wright, as well as to my editors at Laurence King.

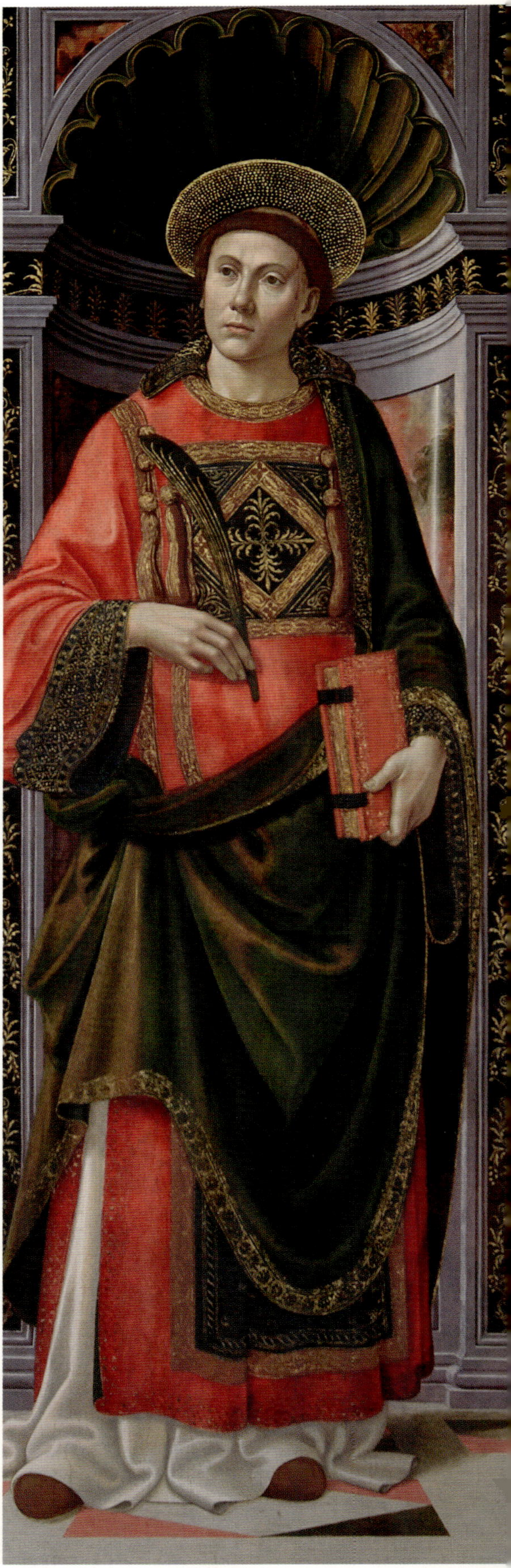

Published in 2019 by
Laurence King Publishing Ltd
361–373 City Road
London EC1V 1LR
e-mail: enquiries@laurenceking.com
www.laurenceking.com

A catalogue record for this book is available from the British Library.

ISBN: 978-1-78627-342-0

Series and cover design by Pentagram
Design: Geoff Fennell
Picture research: Julia Ruxton

Cover: Ghirlandaio, *Visitation* (*see* page 107)
Frontispiece: Michelangelo, *David* (*see* page 24)
This page: Ghirlandaio, *Saints James, Stephen and Peter* (detail; *see* page 87)

Printed in China

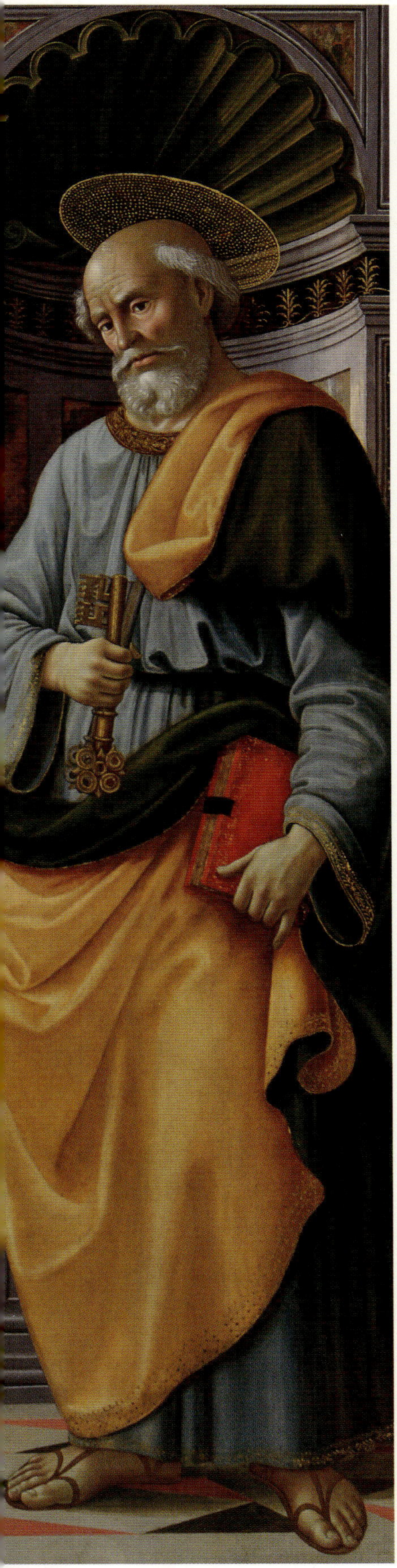

Contents

Map of Florence

1. Mercanzia
2. Ognissanti
3. Orsanmichele
4. Palazzo Medici
5. Palazzo Sassetti
6. Palazzo della Signoria
7. Palazzo Strozzi
8. Palazzo Tornabuoni
9. Santa Croce
10. Santa Felicità
11. San Frediano
12. San Giovanni (the Baptistery)
13. San Lorenzo
14. San Marco
15. San Miniato al Monte
16. San Salvatore al Monte
17. Santa Maria del Carmine
18. Santa Maria del Fiore (the Cathedral or Duomo)
19. Santa Maria Maddalena di Cestello
20. Santa Maria Novella
21. Santa Maria Nuova
22. Santa Trinita
23. Santissima Annunziata
24. Santo Spirito

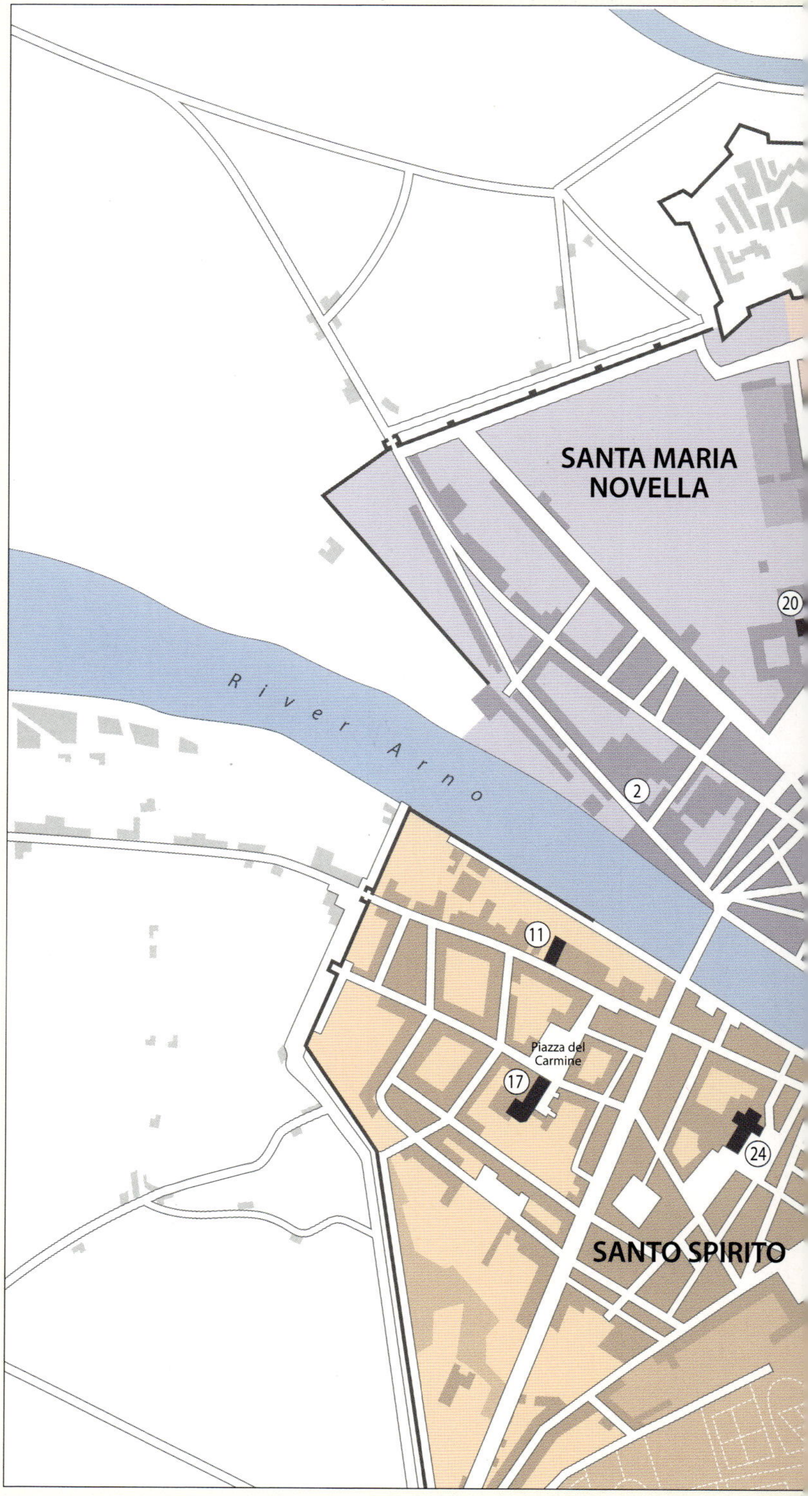

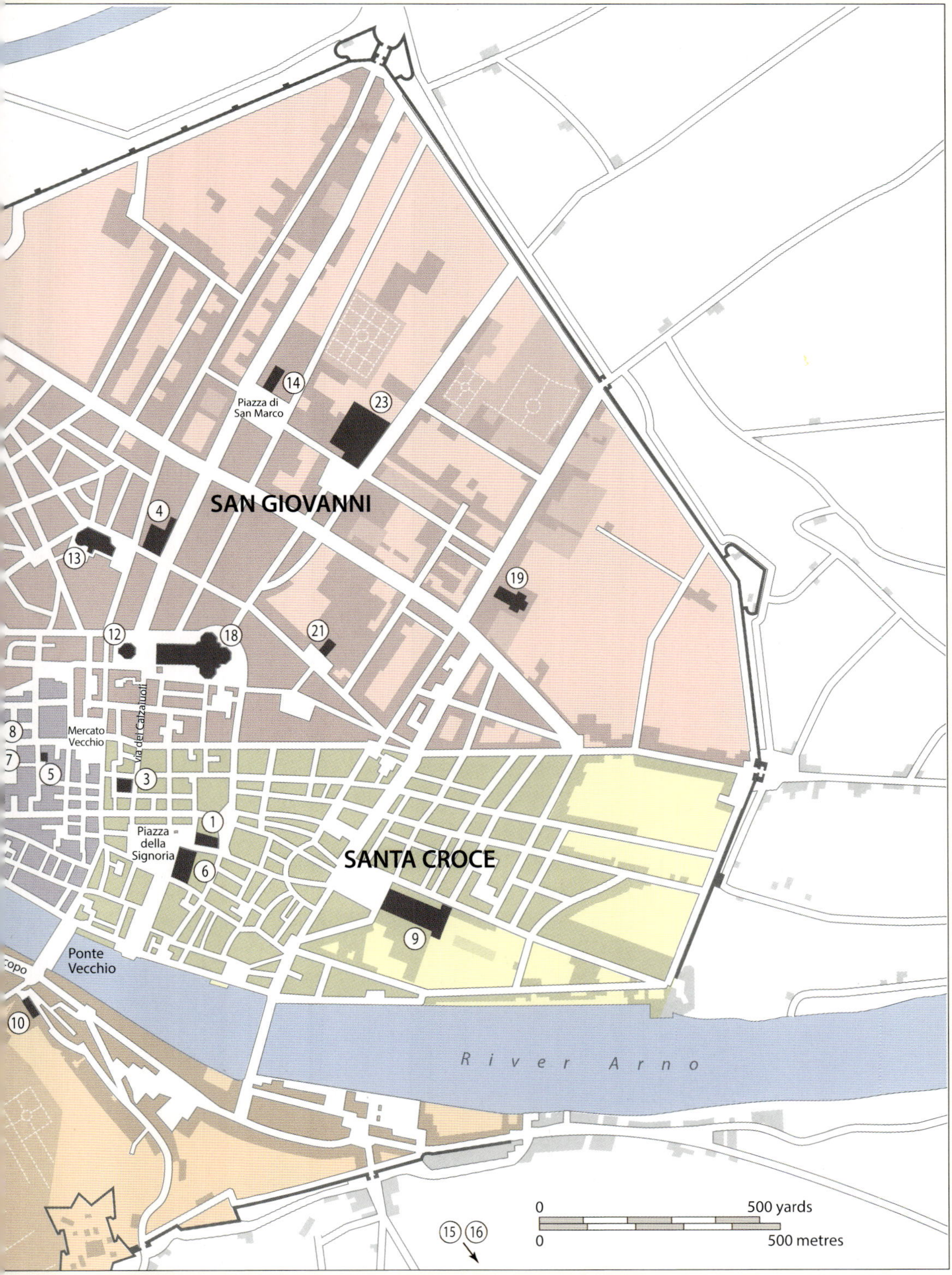

SAN GIOVANNI
SANTA CROCE
Piazza di San Marco
Mercato Vecchio
Via dei Calzaiuoli
Piazza della Signoria
Ponte Vecchio
River Arno
0 500 yards
0 500 metres
1
3
4
5
6
7
8
9
10
12
13
14
15
16
18
19
21
23

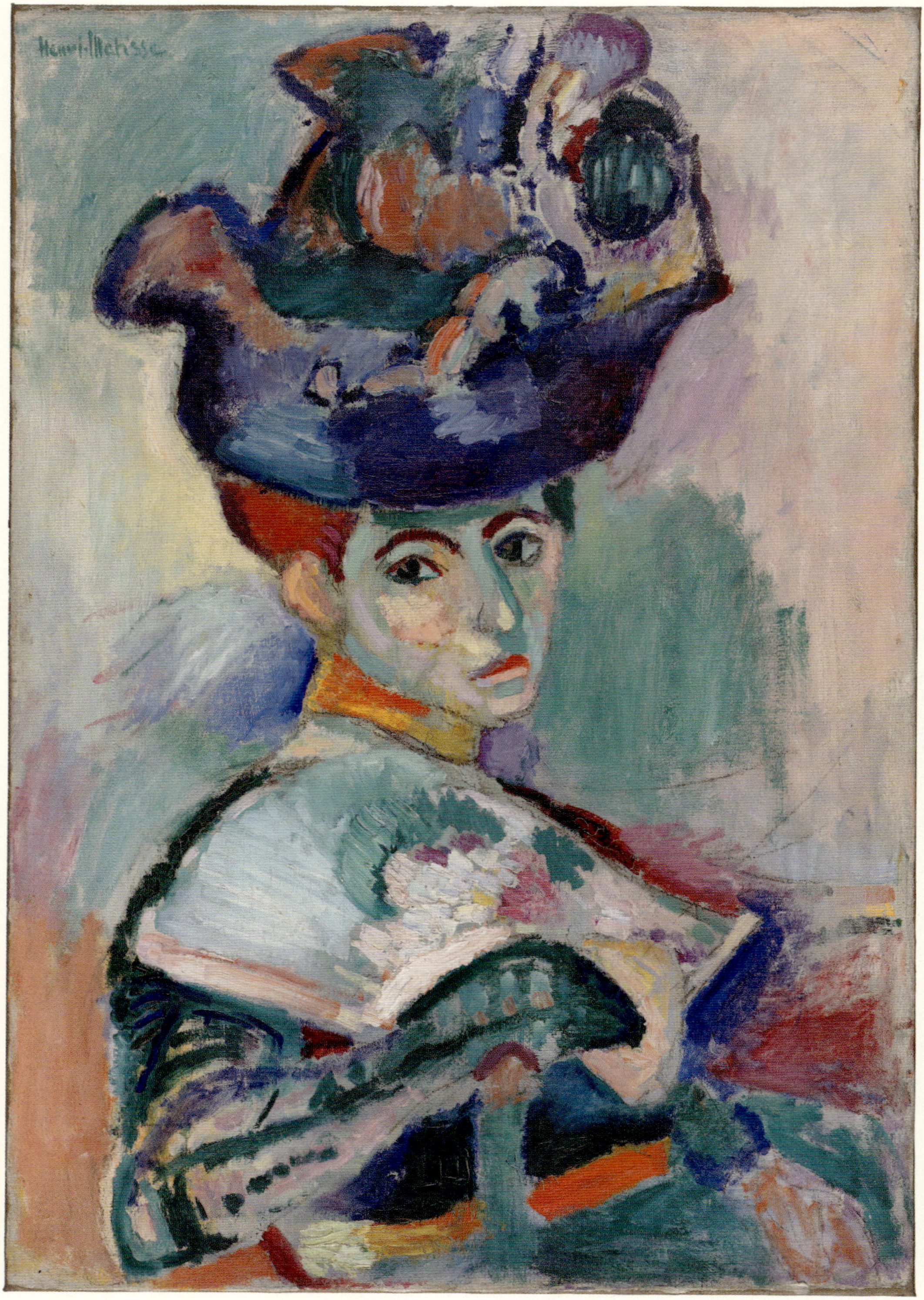
Henri-Matisse

Introduction

The Myth of Florence

Far-reaching claims are made for the art of Florence in the fifteenth and early sixteenth centuries. They are nothing new. Visiting the Salon d'automne in Paris in 1905, the art critic Louis Vauxcelles was struck by a room full of brightly coloured canvases by Henri Matisse, André Derain and their fellow painters (FIG. 1). What made the works especially arresting was the comparison with two classicizing sculptures by Albert Marque (1872–1939) that had been placed in the centre of the gallery. 'The candour of these busts is surprising, amid the orgy of pure tones,' wrote Vauxcelles; 'Donatello among the wild beasts' ('*Donatello chez les fauves*'). Vauxcelles's famous critique is well known, because his description of these painters as 'wild beasts' gave their movement a name, Fauvism. But it is equally illuminating for what it reveals about the status of Donatello, and by extension about the Florentine Renaissance, at the dawn of modernism. Even after 500 years, sculptors and their critics were still looking to Renaissance Florence as a standard against which to judge good art. The avant-garde, by implication, was defined by a rejection of artistic traits established half a millennium earlier. The non-representative colour of Matisse would seem to revolt against Renaissance naturalism; his expressive forms a reaction against clas-

Fig. 1
Henri Matisse
Woman with a Hat

1905, oil on canvas, 80.65 × 59.69cm ($31\frac{3}{4} \times 23\frac{1}{2}$in). San Francisco Museum of Modern Art. Bequest of Elise S. Haas.

sical norms (FIG. 2). Whatever these vague terms might mean – and we shall return to them more than once – 'Donatello' stood for all that was being undone in the art of the early twentieth century.

Fifty years later, Ernst Gombrich addressed an international conference on the history of art in Amsterdam. Gombrich, one of the most respected art historians of his generation, was at the height of his career. His subject was the 'Renaissance idea of progress'. He told his audience that it 'belongs to the class of ideas which act like eating from the tree of knowledge – once you have a notion of good and evil you are forever cast out of the Paradise of Innocence'. He continued by evoking an illustrious predecessor, Giorgio Vasari (1511–1574), the historian and artist who wrote extensively about art:

> When Vasari identified the history of art almost entirely with the history of art in Florence … he was not only prompted by a parochial patriotism. He was writing the history of the new game that had actually sprung up in Florence. And this new conception acted like a vortex with ever widening range and momentum. The Sienese school, for instance, ceased to preoccupy itself with the problems of the centre and it became provincial, a backwater, very charming no doubt, on the surface, but paying for its refusal to go Florentine as Urbino had done, by being unhitched from the train of progress.

For the likes of Gombrich, Florence established a universal standard. It witnessed one of the most remarkable periods of cultural, artistic and intellectual blossoming. Florence saw the birth of the Renaissance and not only delivered this epoch-shifting 'movement', but also nurtured its early development. Within its walls, the shape of European civilization was altered permanently, as the path to an enlightened future was paved with the ideas of the past. The visible and textual remains of classical antiquity became the defining source for the arts, philosophy, public life and more besides, exerting such an all-pervading influence that it has come to define the period: what else does 'Renaissance' mean if not the rebirth of interest in the ancient world?

In the visual arts, the fathers of the Renaissance are accredited with developing a new ideal of beauty, based on skill in drawing and design, which took seed in the city and then grew outwards across Europe. These men wrote theoretically about art for the first time since Pliny or Vitruvius in antiquity; they developed new, often secular, art forms; and they lifted the status of the artist from humble craftsman to learned practitioner, well versed in

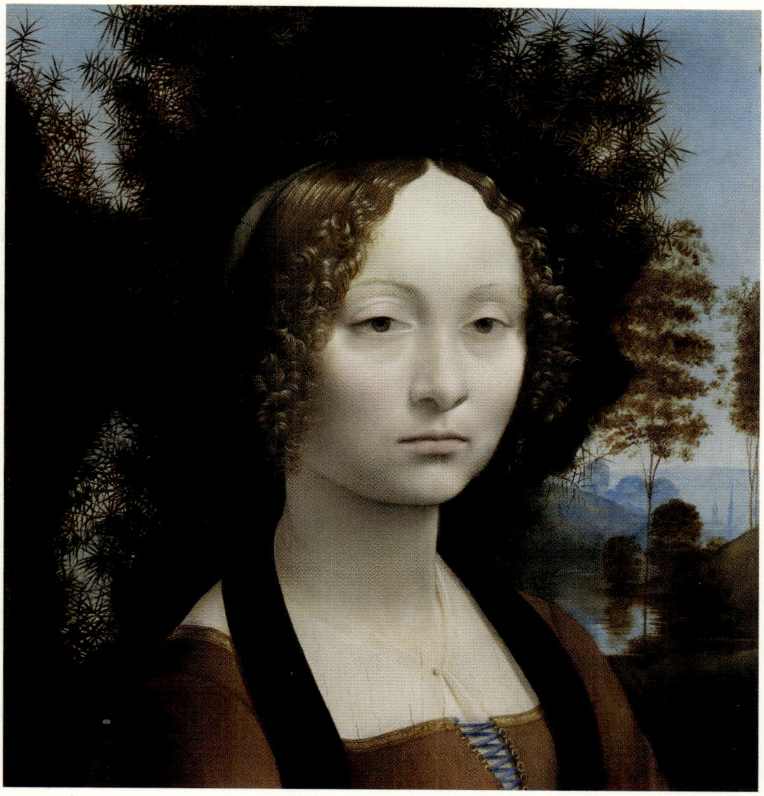

Fig. 2
Leonardo da Vinci
Portrait of Ginevra de' Benci

ca. 1474–8. Oil on panel, 38.1 × 37cm (15 × 14 9/16 in). National Gallery of Art, Washington DC. Ailsa Mellon Bruce Fund (1967.6.1.a).

poetry and humanist thought. In short, they invented the idea of art itself and gave rise to an identifiable type, the artist. Henceforth, painting, sculpture and architecture would constitute a form of knowledge in its own right, one that is intelligible to the mind, even if crafted by the hand. Art came to support complex ideas and sustain extended analysis.

Of course, these exaggerated generalizations have all been challenged in recent decades, and rightly so. Scholars have shifted their attention to other centres in the Italian peninsula, or elsewhere in Europe and beyond, noting that the traits claimed for Renaissance Florence are not unique, as was once thought, and that distinct and influential artistic traditions developed and flourished in other European cities, whether in Venice and Perugia, or Bruges, Prague or Nuremberg. Others, who have continued to study fifteenth-century Florence, have nonetheless suggested that there was greater continuity with the preceding centuries, with the late Middle Ages if you like. They have sought to correct an idea that the Renaissance was predicated on wholesale change. Such continuity is especially evident in devotional practices and in sacred art.

The biggest problem, however, that some have had with the continued attention given to Renaissance Florence is that it somehow established a standard, a universal ideal, against which all art should be measured: *Donatello chez les fauves*. Vasari, whom Gombrich evoked, is sometimes blamed for this bias, but in truth it is a prejudice of more recent making. Had you studied art history sometime between the 1940s and 1970s at the Courtauld Institute of Art in London, where I work, teach and am writing this book, you would have taken 'The Renaissance Course' rather than a general survey course, regardless of whether you intended to go on to study Picasso, Byzantium or Chinese vases. It was as if an understanding of the Renaissance, with Florence at its centre, was essential if one were to comprehend the art of the rest of the world. It is not difficult to see, then, how the nineteenth- and twentieth-century celebration of Florence, and of the Renaissance more generally, has come to be associated with Western Imperialism and all its attendant problems. Why do we keep returning to the art of Renaissance Florence, when cultures – just as developed, instructive and worthy of sustained study – flourished in contemporary Isfahan in present-day Iran, or in Benin in west Africa?

In contrast to these academic misgivings, tourists continue to flock to the city on the river Arno; exhibitions about its artists attract huge crowds; and undergraduates are keen to take courses in it. Tour-company publicity and galleries' marketing departments continue to perpetuate a myth of Florence, 'the cradle of the Renaissance'. RENAISSANCE Inc. is booming and FLORENCE plc is open for business. This book, like so many others, is implicated in this huge commercial venture. A gulf separates the idea of Renaissance Florence sold to tourists, undergraduates and gallery-goers and the sceptical (perhaps too sceptical) reservations of some scholars.

This book advances in the conviction that something important did happen in Florence in the fifteenth and early sixteenth centuries, something that is hard to grasp when examined in detail, but that paradoxically comes into sharper focus when considered in general terms. But it also proceeds from the premise that the art of Florence was no better than, say, that of the Burgundian Netherlands or fifteenth-century Ife in present-day Nigeria. Like most work dedicated to Florence in recent years, it does not try to impose its ideas on other regions of Europe or other parts of the globe. The ideas about art that developed in Florence – about what constituted invention, for example, or how a history of art might be structured – are relevant to the study of that city in that time. In common with so many of my colleagues, I make no claim for their universality.

Often those factors that still make Florence worthy of study are best revealed when its art is compared with that produced in other parts of the world, but without qualitative judgement. Given the degree to which the innovations of Renaissance Florence have been naturalized within the West, rightly or wrongly, it can sometimes be difficult to appreciate just how peculiar they were, until we juxtapose them with the solutions artists found elsewhere. To take an obvious example, for someone within the Western tradition the use of linear perspective to represent space might seem the most obvious solution imaginable, until we realize just how rarely makers of images from around the globe ever had need to use it. A similar point might be made about naturalism, or realism, to which we will return in Chapters 7 and 8.

This book focuses on Florence in the period between about 1400 and the first decade of the sixteenth century, from what is traditionally called the early to the high Renaissance, and therefore includes works from Ghiberti's first doors for the Baptistery to Michelangelo's giant *David*. It aspires to look at Florence afresh, asking how our traditional narratives have been derived, what is good about them and what they leave out. To that end, it begins by analysing the stories we tell about Florentine art and considers how they developed in some of the first writings about art in the West since antiquity. These two chapters on telling tales (Chapters 2 and 3) are preceded by a short introductory chapter on the Sala dei Gigli, which examines different symbols associated with the Renaissance city, as well as the saints that Florentines venerated and the heroes they celebrated. The subsequent chapters are arranged thematically, not chronologically, and address two broad themes. Chapters 4, 5 and 6 are dedicated to institutions and individuals. They consider questions of patronage and the corporations that structured the arts. Chapters 7–10 consider the style of the art produced in Florence, especially the attempt to produce a convincing 'illusion' of space and nature, together with an analysis of the media used to do so and the implications these new stylistic developments had for spectatorship. By returning to some of the major preoccupations of Florentine artists, their patrons and their audiences, I hope to argue, often only implicitly, that it is still important to study the art of Renaissance Florence.

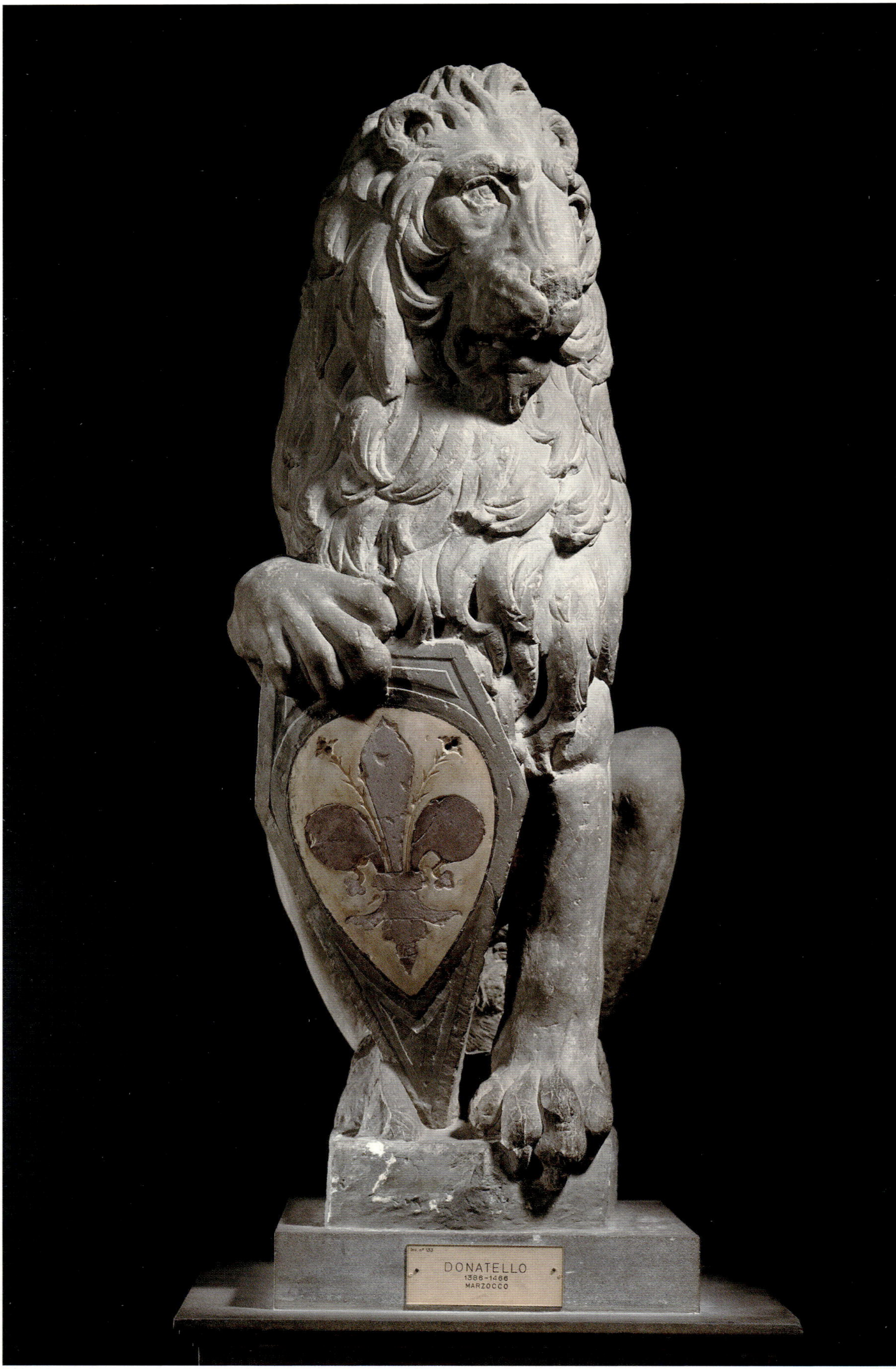
DONATELLO
1386-1466
MARZOCCO

1

Symbols, Saints and Heroes

'The city of Florence was always much more enthusiastic for liberty than other cities – in fact, as you know, the name of Liberty can be seen written in gold letters among her public emblems.' So wrote the humanist Alamanno Rinuccini in his dialogue *On Liberty* (1479). He was quite right. Florentines valued the freedom of their Republic. They celebrated it not only in political speeches, treatises on civic life and polemical dialogues such as Rinuccini's, but also in the images with which they decorated their public buildings, especially the Palazzo della Signoria (now known as the Palazzo Vecchio), the seat of their government (FIG. 4). We learn much about what mattered to Florentines from the symbols, saints and heroes they carved and painted for this building.

By the mid fifteenth century, the Palazzo della Signoria was well over a century old and in need of renovation. These works dragged on into the 1480s and included the Sala dei Gigli (Hall of the Lilies), the redecoration of which will introduce us to the ideas and images that preoccupied fifteenth-century Florentines, at least publicly (FIG. 6). A document dated 17 September 1482 calls the room the '*Aula Dominationum*', or Hall of the Lords, referring to the nine citizens, chosen by lot every two months, who constituted

Fig. 3
Donatello
Marzocco

ca. 1419, *pietra serena* [grey sandstone], 135.5cm (53⅜in) high. Museo Nazionale del Bargello, Florence.

Donatello's *Marzocco* was originally sculpted as a newel post for a staircase in the Papal apartment at Santa Maria Novella.

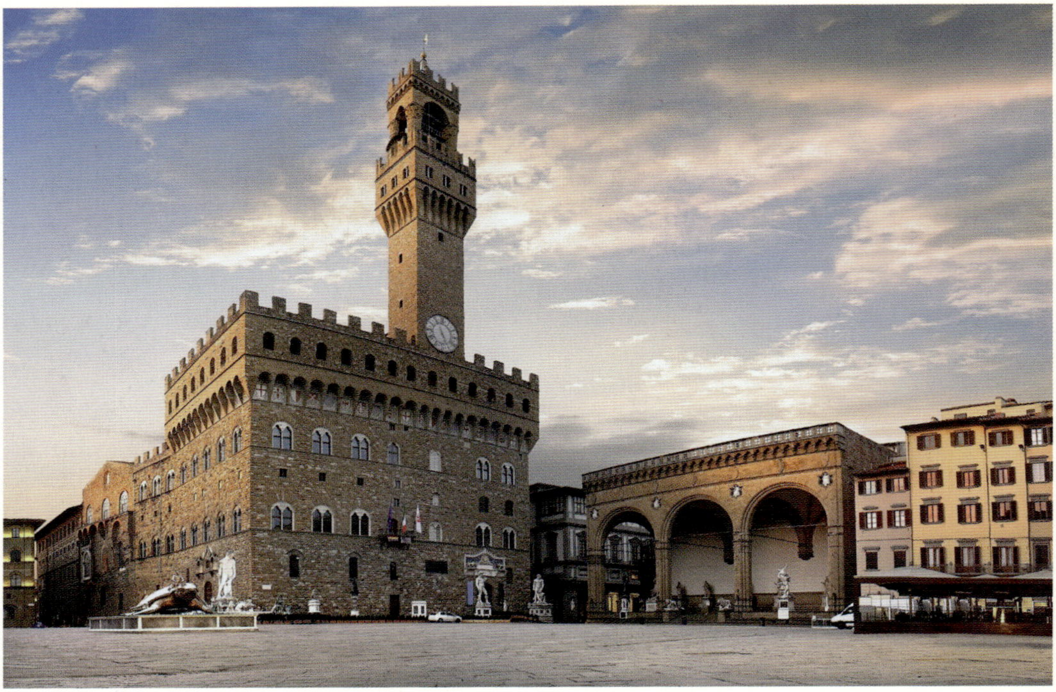

Fig.4
Palazzo della Signoria

From via dei Calzaiuoli, Florence.

the government or Signoria. Here they ate, assembled for large gatherings of the advisory colleges and councils, and performed their official duties. Here, too, visiting dignitaries and foreign ambassadors probably waited to see them. The decoration of the room guided the priors in how to govern justly and reminded their visitors of what was good about Florence and Florentine values. Like those important dignitaries, we can also visit the Sala dei Gigli, imaginatively, to understand how Florentines chose to present themselves to the world.

Symbols

A boldly carved frieze of gilded lions runs around the Sala dei Gigli, just below an imposing coffered ceiling inspired by the vaults of ancient buildings such as the Basilica of Maxentius in Rome. The lions clutch wreathed shields emblazoned with the cross of the people (the *popolo*); the fleur-de-lys of the commune or government; the eagle triumphing over a dragon of the Guelph Party; and the word 'LIBERTAS', as Rinuccini observed. The fleur-de-lys (or *giglio*) is a device generally associated with the French house of Anjou, which notionally protected Florentine liberty, ever since Charles of Anjou had triumphed over the Ghibellines at the Battle of Benevento in 1266, freeing Florence from the control of the Holy Roman Emperor. As a consequence of Charles's victory, the Guelph Party took control of Florentine politics, even though by the second half of the fifteenth century its power was much reduced and largely ceremonial. In the fifteenth century the Valois king, Louis XI, reiterated the relationship and even (in 1465) extended the privilege to the Medici family, who thereafter incorporated three gold fleurs-de-lys on a blue ground into their coat of arms (FIG. 5).

The lions that bear the shields in the Sala dei Gigli are not without meaning themselves. Lions abound in Renaissance Florence. Live ones were even kept in cages behind the Palazzo della Signoria. The heraldic Florentine lion, or *marzocco*, stood on the *ringhiera*, a raised platform in front of the palace, until 1812, when it was replaced by a version carved by Donatello (FIG. 3). The word *marzocco* is etymologically linked to *Marte*, or Mars, the god of war, who also held a particular significance for the Florentines, as we shall see. Florentine troops, or rather the mercenaries whom Florence employed to fight its battles, yelled '*Marzocco*' on the battlefield. For Florentines, it was a symbol of their freedom, but it could equally be a sign of subjugation in territories held by the city. In 1494, for instance, the Pisans were quick to throw down the *marzocco* when rebelling against Florentine rule.

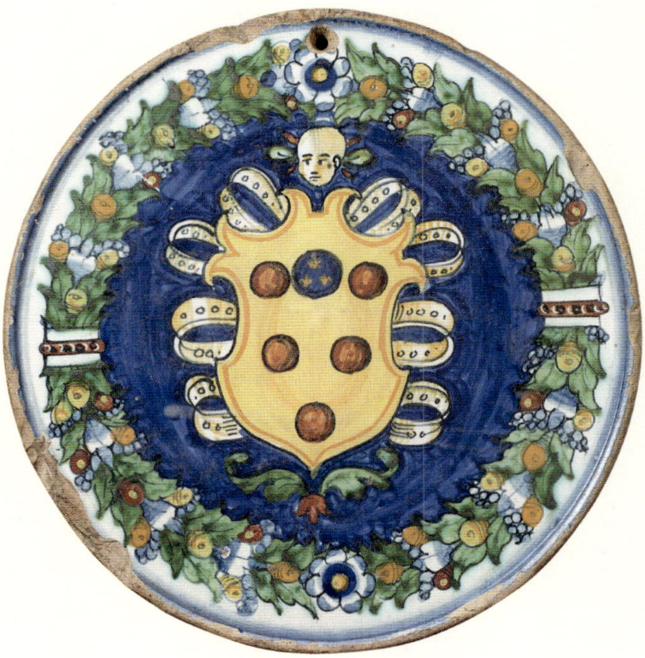

Fig.5
Plate decorated with the Medici coat of arms

16th century, maiolica. Museo Nazionale del Bargello, Florence.

Fig.6
Sala dei Gigli, Palazzo della Signoria

Florence.

The marble doorway was opened in the sixteenth century and is not original.

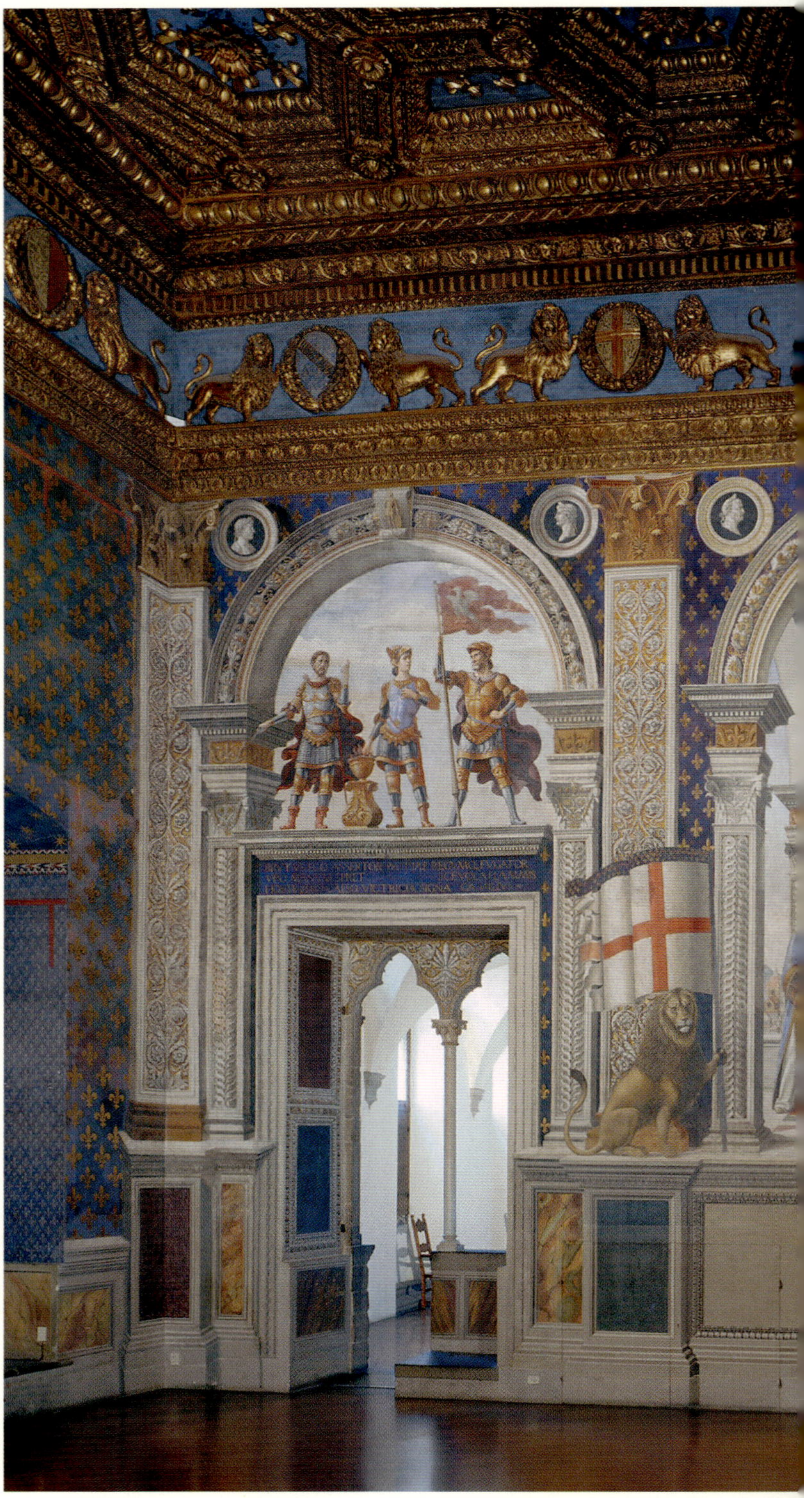

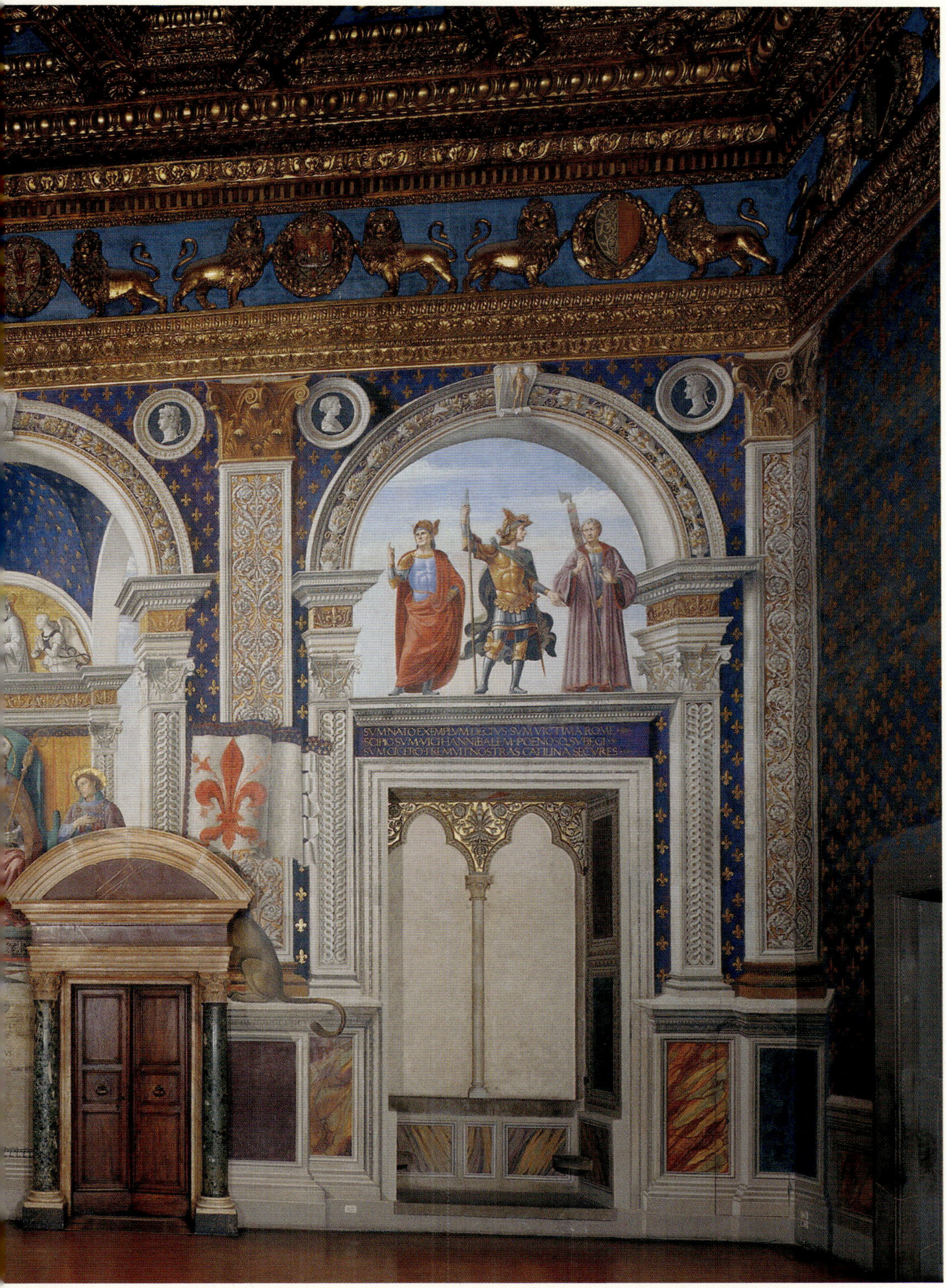

Saints

Below the carved frieze, the walls of the Sala dei Gigli are painted with golden lilies on a blue ground, from which the room derives its name. They were the work of the relatively unknown painter Bernardo di Stefano Rosselli (1450–1526), who completed them in 1490. The only exception is the east wall, which was frescoed by Domenico Ghirlandaio (1448–1494) and his workshop in 1482–3. It is divided by pilasters into three bays, each of which contains an arch, in the manner of Roman triumphal architecture. The arch of Titus in Rome was probably the source. The space behind the central arch is conceived as a chapel punched through the wall. On either side of the space, the *marzocco* appears once again bearing the arms

Fig. 7
Domenico Ghirlandaio
Saints Zenobius, Eugenius and Crescentius

1482–3, fresco. Central bay of the east wall of the Sala dei Gigli, Palazzo della Signoria, Florence.

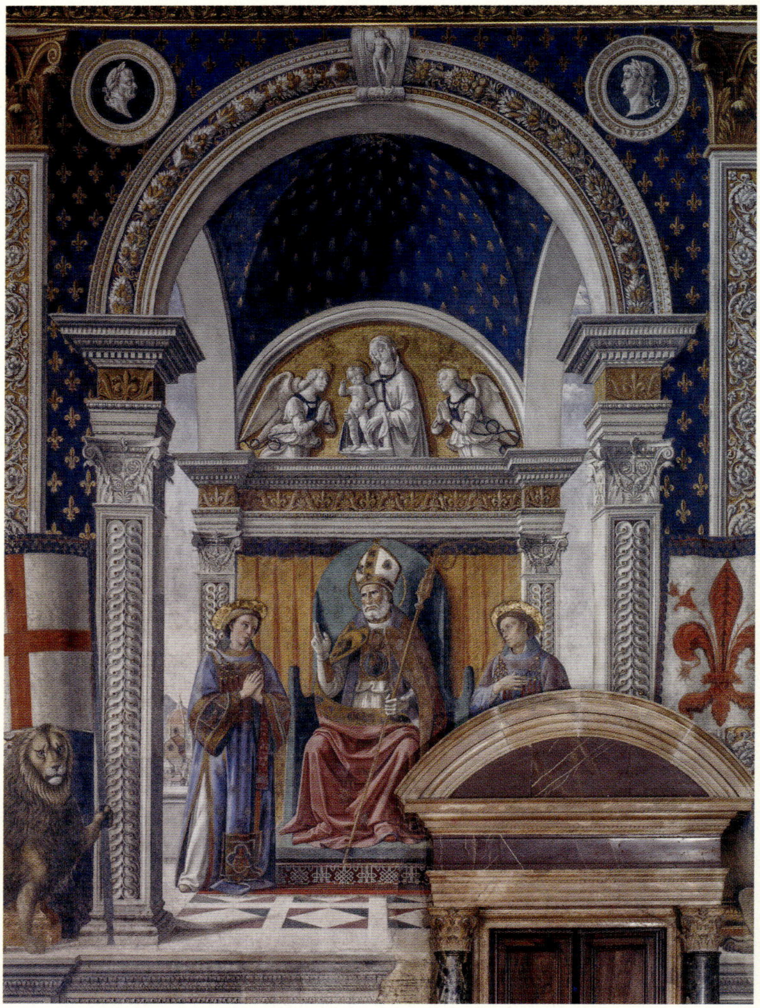

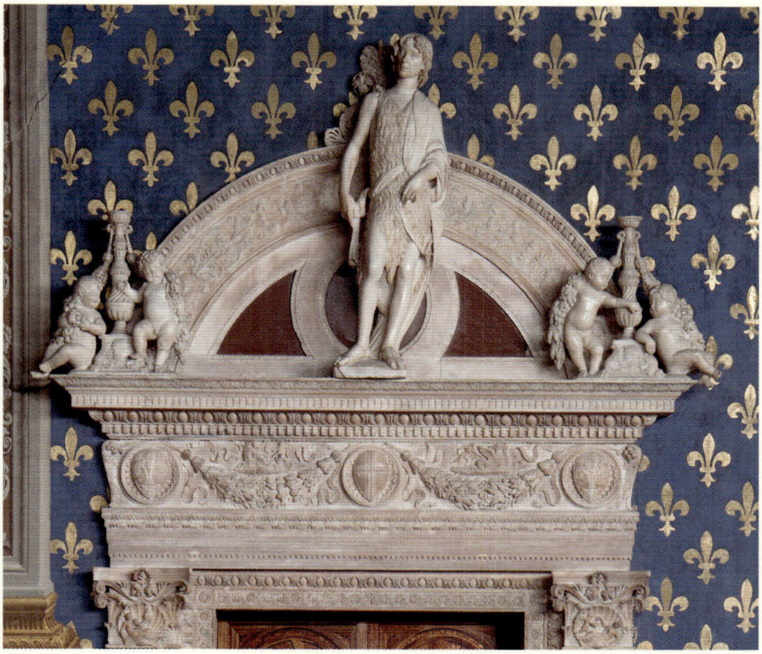

Fig. 8
Benedetto da Maiano
Portal to the Sala dell'Udienza including *St John the Baptist*

Installed 1480, marble, statue approx. 144cm (56⅝in) high. Sala dei Gigli, Palazzo della Signoria, Florence.

of the people and of the commune. Within this breezy, *trompe l'œil* chapel, St Zenobius sits between his two deacons, Saints Eugenius and Crescentius. Zenobius (337–417) was one of Florence's patron saints, second only to John the Baptist in importance. He was the city's first bishop, and, as the fourteenth-century chronicler Giovanni Villani wrote, it was 'because of his merits that [Florence] was liberated from the Goths'. He raises his hand in blessing, while staring out of the north windows of the room towards his episcopal seat, the cathedral, which is clearly visible from the Sala dei Gigli. The cathedral appears in the fresco, too, in a small vignette on the left, with its unfinished facade and the faceted roof of the Baptistery in front of it (FIG. 7).

The cathedral was consecrated in 1436 by Pope Eugenius IV, on the feast of the Annunciation (25 March), which was also the beginning of the Florentine year. It was dedicated to Santa Maria del Fiore, Saint Mary of the Flower. The Roman city was known as 'Florentia', a name that derives from the Latin verb 'to flower' or the genitive 'flowering', from which the archaic Italian name 'Fiorenza' originated. The modern name for the city, 'Firenze', developed subsequently. 'Florence' in English descends from French, but has the same root. The origin of Florence, and its relationship to flowers, was a subject debated by late medieval and Renaissance writers, such as Giovanni Gherardi. In effect, it is a double dedication, for the flower of the Virgin is also the flower of her womb, Christ. In Ghirlandaio's

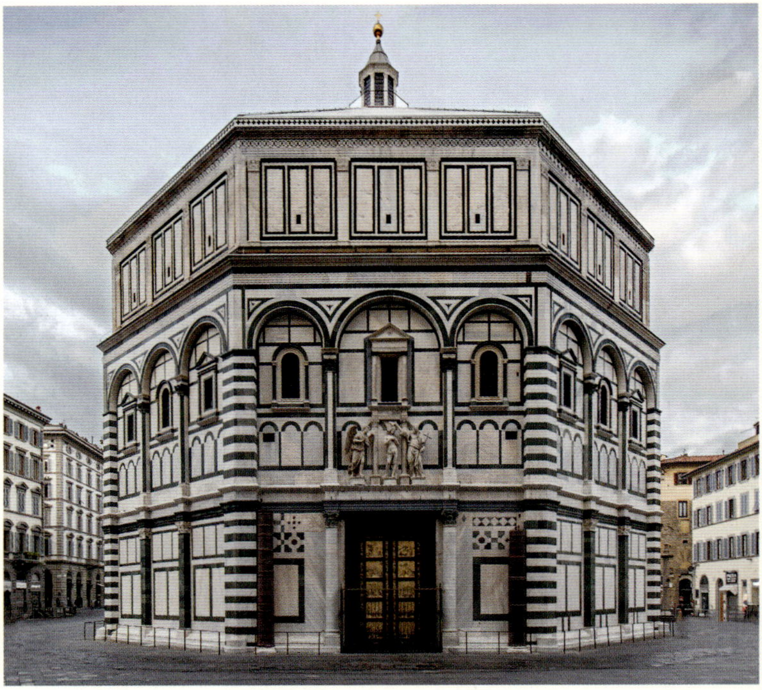

Fig.9
The Baptistery (San Giovanni) from within the door of the cathedral, Santa Maria del Fiore

Florence.

fresco, the Virgin and Child appear in a lunette above Zenobius. They are represented as a glazed-terracotta relief of the type associated with the della Robbia family: the Virgin looks down, protectively, at her city of Florence and at us, visitors to the room, while her son bestows his blessing.

On the other side of the room from Ghirlandaio's fresco is a marble door case carved by Benedetto da Maiano (1442–1497). It is surmounted by a sculpture of St John the Baptist, which was installed in December 1480 (FIG. 8). The Baptist has been venerated in Florence as its patron saint since at least the twelfth century. He is positioned opposite Zenobius, in a configuration that repeats the relationship between the Baptistery, of which John was the dedicatee, and the cathedral, Zenobius's seat and the location of his relics. The Baptistery was a separate building that faced the cathedral (FIG. 9), an arrangement that is not unusual, but which is especially significant in Florence given the sacred and civic importance of the Baptistery (San Giovanni). The present structure is Romanesque, and was begun shortly after the turn of the first millennium, but in the fifteenth century Florentines thought it was an ancient temple dedicated to Mars, or at least that it was on the same site as a building once dedicated to the Roman god. Mars, they believed, preceded the Baptist as protector of the city.

Heroes

Florentines and their government looked to the Virgin and to their patron saints for protection and for guidance in living as good Christians. Increasingly, they also turned to the statesmen and heroes of ancient Rome for examples of upstanding conduct in public life. In the arches that flank the sacred company around Zenobius (*see* FIG. 6), Ghirlandaio painted six ancient heroes of the Roman Republic, above what were once windows. All male, they are a reminder that the halls of government were an exclusively masculine environment. From left to right, Brutus, Mucius Scaevola, Camillus, Decius Mus, Scipio Africanus and Cicero stand proudly against a cloudy sky. Each figure is accompanied by a short Latin *titulus* that records his identity and significance. Their purpose, conveyed through gesture and inscription, was didactic. Thus, the words under Brutus read: 'I am Brutus, the liberator of my country and the bane of kings,' a reminder – spoken as if by Brutus himself – that he led the revolt that overthrew the last Roman king and established the Roman Republic.

Florence, too, was a Republic. Its chancellors, such as Leonardo Bruni (ca. 1370–1444), and its publicly engaged intellectuals extolled its virtues and celebrated its freedom. The 'LIBERTAS' in the frieze of the Sala dei Gigli recalls this constant preoccupation of Florentine oratory, especially when it was directed against those states that threated its sovereignty, such as Milan in the early years of the fifteenth century. Government was to be popular, led by patriots committed to public service, and free from external domination. For all the rhetoric, however, it was an illusion. During the first 30 years of the century, Florence was controlled by a small and tight-knit oligarchy of powerful families. After the banker Cosimo di Giovanni de' Medici (the Elder, 1389–1464) returned from exile in 1434, he and his descendants established themselves as de facto rulers of the city by banishing their competitors and manipulating the electoral processes of the government, its councils and committees. Cosimo's grandson Lorenzo (the Magnificent, 1449–1492), who played a significant role in determining the decoration of the Sala dei Gigli, masked his effective grip on power by emphasizing that he was not 'Lord of Florence'; he was nothing more than a 'citizen with some authority'. The Medici were eventually exiled in 1494, chased from the city as tyrants. The newly liberated Republican government survived until 1512, when the Medici re-entered the city. The Medici well understood how art and visual culture could consolidate their position in the Republic, all the while disguising their assumption of quasi-autocratic power.

Florence's republicanism, as much as the sense that the city needed to be defended from external threat, prompted its leaders to identify with two ancient heroes: the biblical David and the mythological Hercules. The reasons that Florence might compare itself to an adolescent shepherd boy are obvious. David defeated a mighty foe and liberated his people from tyranny. His victory was a reminder that even the defenceless and weak can be triumphant if they are virtuous and favoured by God. Hercules had appeared on the seal of the commune since the thirteenth century, accompanied by an inscription that read 'Florence subdues depravity with a Herculean club'. His association with opposition to tyranny is less obvious, however. Nonetheless, the merchant Goro Dati (1362–1435), who was an important diarist and wrote a history of Florence, interpreted Hercules as a giant who defeated tyrants and evil lords, much like Florence itself.

Hercules appeared in different forms around the Palazzo della Signoria, although he is absent from the Sala dei Gigli, except for a tiny relief in the frieze of the marble door. David, by contrast, was

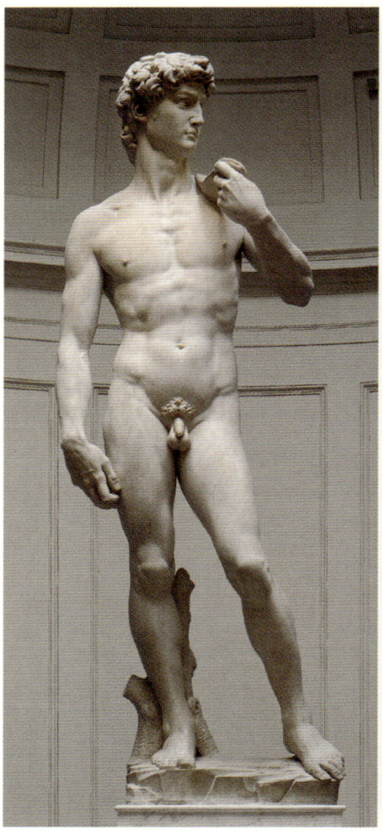

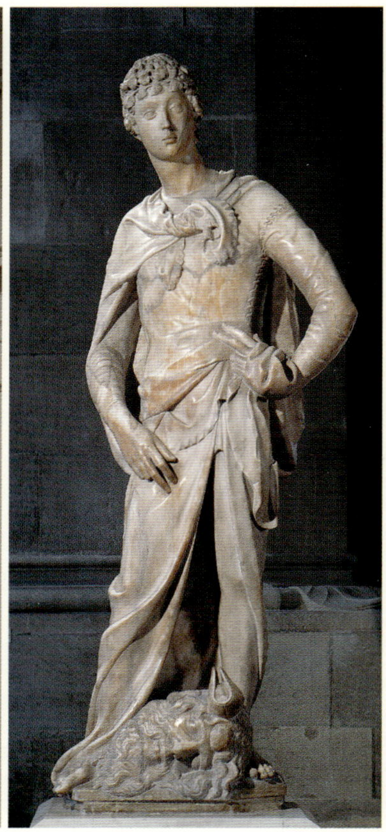

Fig. 10 (left)
Michelangelo Buonarroti
David

Completed 1503, marble, 516cm ($203\frac{1}{8}$in) high. Galleria dell'Accademia, Florence.

Fig. 11 (right)
Donatello
David

1409, marble, 191cm ($75\frac{1}{4}$in) high. Museo Nazionale del Bargello, Florence.

very much present. In 1504 Michelangelo's nude giant was placed outside the entrance to the building as a renewed statement of Florentine liberty (FIG. 10), but already in the fifteenth century several figures of David were inside the palace. Donatello's marble *David*, which (like Michelangelo's) had been commissioned for one of the buttresses of the cathedral in 1408, was transferred to the site of the Sala dei Gigli in 1416, where it was placed on the south wall against a painted backdrop of *gigli* on a blue ground (FIG. 11). The inscription on its pedestal left no doubt as to its meaning: 'God helps those who fight against terrible enemies for the fatherland.' Sixty years later, on 10 May 1476, the Signoria acquired another *David* (FIG. 12), which they placed on the landing at the entrance to the Sala dei Gigli, the so-called Porta della Catena. Based on Donatello's bronze *David* (FIG. 13), which would itself be moved to the Palazzo della Signoria in 1495, it was made by Andrea del Verrocchio and had been sold by Lorenzo de' Medici and his brother Giuliano. Visitors to the Sala dei Gigli could not avoid representations of David. Again and again, they were reminded of the need to protect the Republic from tyranny.

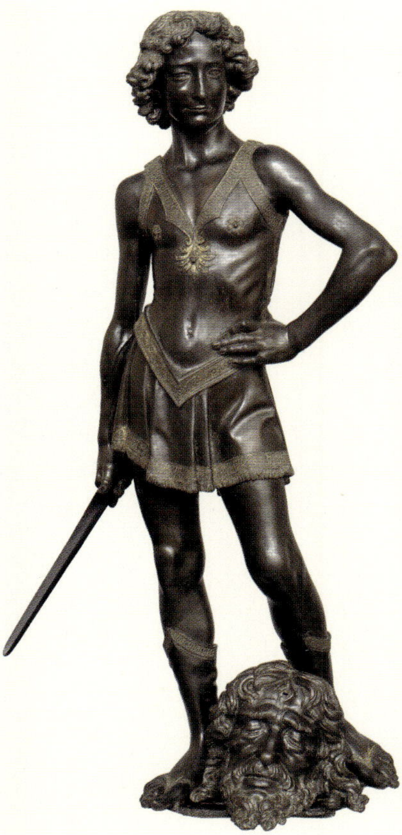

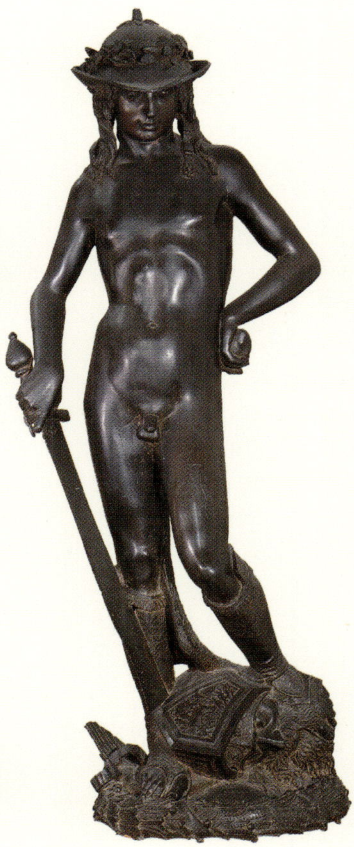

Fig. 12 (left)
Andrea del Verrocchio
David

Before 1476, bronze with some gilding, 126cm (49$\frac{5}{8}$in) high. Museo Nazionale del Bargello, Florence.

Fig. 13 (right)
Donatello
David

Probably 1450s, bronze, 158cm (62$\frac{1}{4}$in) high. Museo Nazionale del Bargello, Florence.

By 1469, this sculpture was recorded in the centre of the courtyard of the Palazzo Medici.

Cultural Heroes

Fig. 14
Giuliano da Maiano and **Francione**, probably after **Sandro Botticelli** and **Filippino Lippi**
Doors to the Sala dell'Udienza including Dante and Petrarch

Completed by 1480, various woods (*intarsia*), approx. 290cm (114⅛in) high. Palazzo della Signoria, Florence.

The building in which the Signoria lived, and from which they governed, reflected the ideals of the Republic; it was covered with symbols associated with the city and its people, and decorated with exemplary figures, both sacred and secular. The architectural vocabulary of a room such as the Sala dei Gigli, as well as the style of the painting, contributed to these ideas. They were *all'antica*, in the style or manner of the ancients. Yet the ancient past was more than just a source of visual or architectural motifs. Style was a choice, and it had meaning. Here, it suggested that Florence was the new Rome and that its citizens were the modern equivalent of civically minded statesmen such as Cicero.

The Sala dei Gigli, however, is not only concerned with the ancient past. After all, to style something *all'antica* implies fashioning it in light of the past, but in the present. It was not an attempt to return to the past. Florence's recent and not-too-distant cultural heroes were also celebrated in the Sala dei Gigli. The fourteenth-century poets Dante and Petrarch are represented in wooden inlay (*intarsia*) on the doors that hang within Benedetto da Maiano's door case (FIG. 14). Completed by June 1480, they were made by the woodworkers Giuliano da Maiano (Benedetto's brother) and Francione, even if they were probably designed by the painters Sandro Botticelli and Filippino Lippi. Dante and Petrarch stand in profile, clutching open manuscripts whose lines are just legible, above shelves with illusionistic renderings of their books. They provide modern complements to the famous ancient heroes on the opposite wall. The skill with which they were executed, and the complexity with which their books were foreshortened in perspective, displayed the invention and ingenuity (*ingegno*) of Florence's living woodworkers and painters. So, too, the complex rendering of space in Ghirlandaio's composition made manifest his mastery of his craft (or *arte*). For visitors, the Sala dei Gigli showcased the artistry for which Florence was famous, and demonstrated the extent to which it valued beauty as an indicator of its worth.

The decoration of the Sala dei Gigli testifies to the importance Florentines placed on sight. The most significant ideas about their Republic were communicated visually. But we must be careful not to accept, blindly, what they have brought before our eyes. It is deceptive. Despite a conspicuous pride in the capacities of government, the period brought a slow erosion of its potency as Lorenzo the Magnificent sought to consolidate his power in a small group of loyal partisans. For all that the visual rhetoric of the room's imagery reinforces a republican ideology, the reality of those who actually held the reins of power was very different.

If we dig deeper, and ask questions about how the decoration of the room was financed, the answers become far less savoury. On 17 July 1444 exorbitant fines of 6,000 florins were imposed on four Jewish moneylenders, who were alleged to have violated usury legislation, as a means of raising money to pay for the building works in the Palazzo della Signoria. Twenty years later, on 3 October 1468, further funds were extracted from a certain Isaac, again a Jewish banker, who was forced to pay a further 4,100 florins, part of which was earmarked for work in the Sala dei Gigli. The money was almost immediately redirected to repair the walls of two towns within the Florentine dominion, Castrocaro and Facciano, and funds were subsequently sought from taxes levied on foreigners who traded in Florence. The Signoria was explicit that, 'considering that the works in the palace are not finished … and not wanting to touch the wallets of our citizens', they would increase the tax on foreign artisans and merchants, which was after all minimal in their opinion, 'considering the great profit they made from the places in which they live' – in other words, from Florence. For all that we might marvel at the Sala dei Gigli, its decoration was ultimately the result of anti-Semitism and xenophobia.

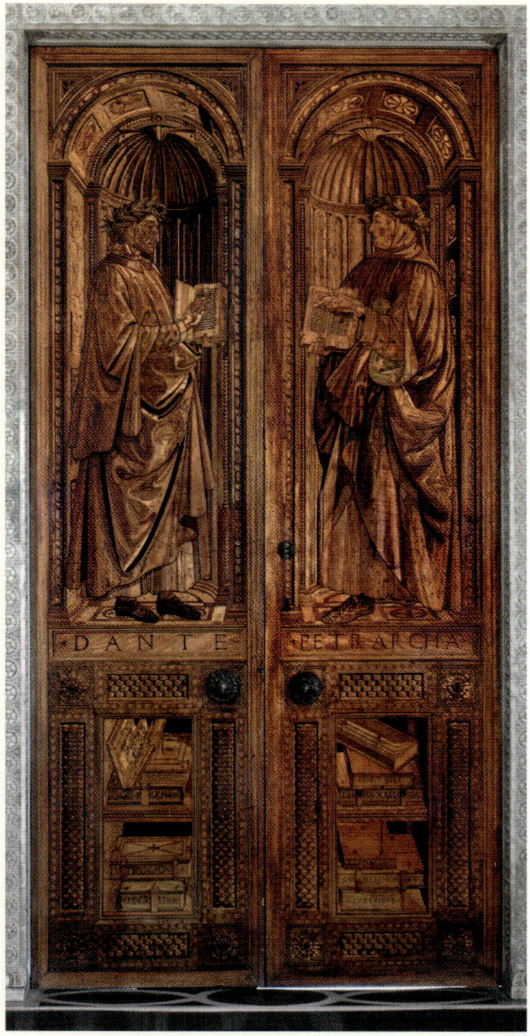

As it must have done for foreign dignitaries visiting the city in the fifteenth century, a visit to the Palazzo della Signoria tells us a good deal about what Florentines thought of themselves, their collective achievements and good government. It also reminds us of the role played by beauty in Florence, as a marker of accomplishment and an indicator of self-worth. We should wonder at the beauty of the Sala dei Gigli, and ponder the republican politics and propagandistic manoeuvring that created it, but we should also remember that it was ultimately based on an ideology and forms of exploitation that we now find abhorrent. The Renaissance had a darker side.

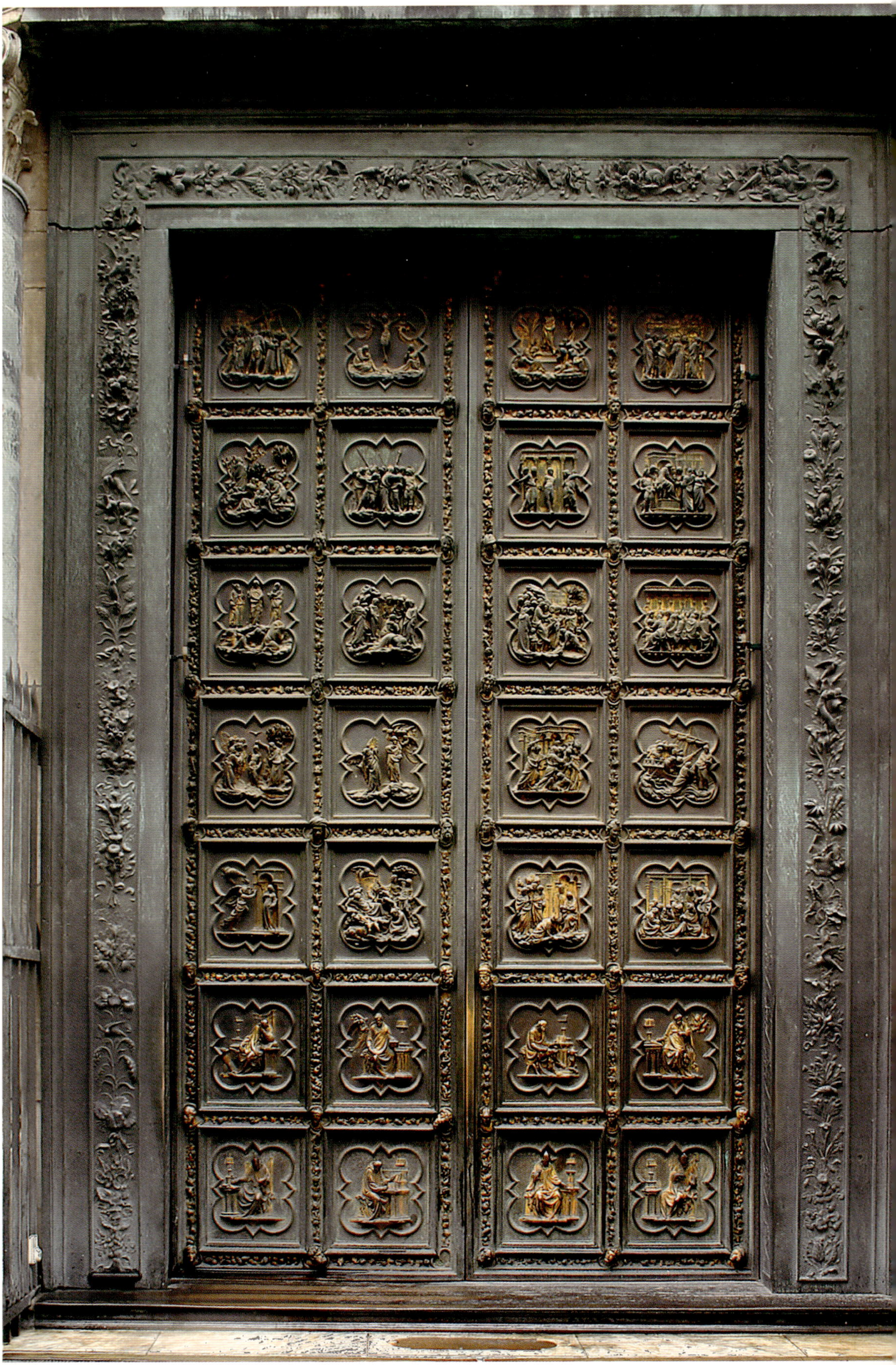

2

Telling Tales: The Story of Florentine Art

Florentine art has a story. It has evolved over 500 years or more, and is based on an idea of progress – an idea that developed within the Renaissance itself. Since at least the sixteenth century, if not earlier, this narrative has favoured painting, sculpture and architecture over goldsmiths' work, prints or objects of the so-called decorative or minor arts. This chapter tells that story. It outlines the basic plot and introduces the key characters. But for all that it will set the scene for what follows, there are problems with this approach, and we shall consider them, too. Telling tales is a dubious endeavour. The century that separates Ghiberti's Baptistery doors (FIG. 15), commissioned in about 1403, from Leonardo and Michelangelo's lost cartoons for the Palazzo della Signoria of about 1503–4 (FIGS. 16, 17) was not a seamless development of continuous artistic improvement, however much we would like it to be. Narratives are comforting and a useful framework to structure knowledge, but they are artificial and must be recognized as such. There is nothing natural about them.

Fig. 15
Lorenzo Ghiberti
North doors, originally for the Baptistery and shown when still in situ

1403–24, gilded bronze, 457 × 251 cm (180 × 98⅞ in). Museo dell'Opera del Duomo, Florence.

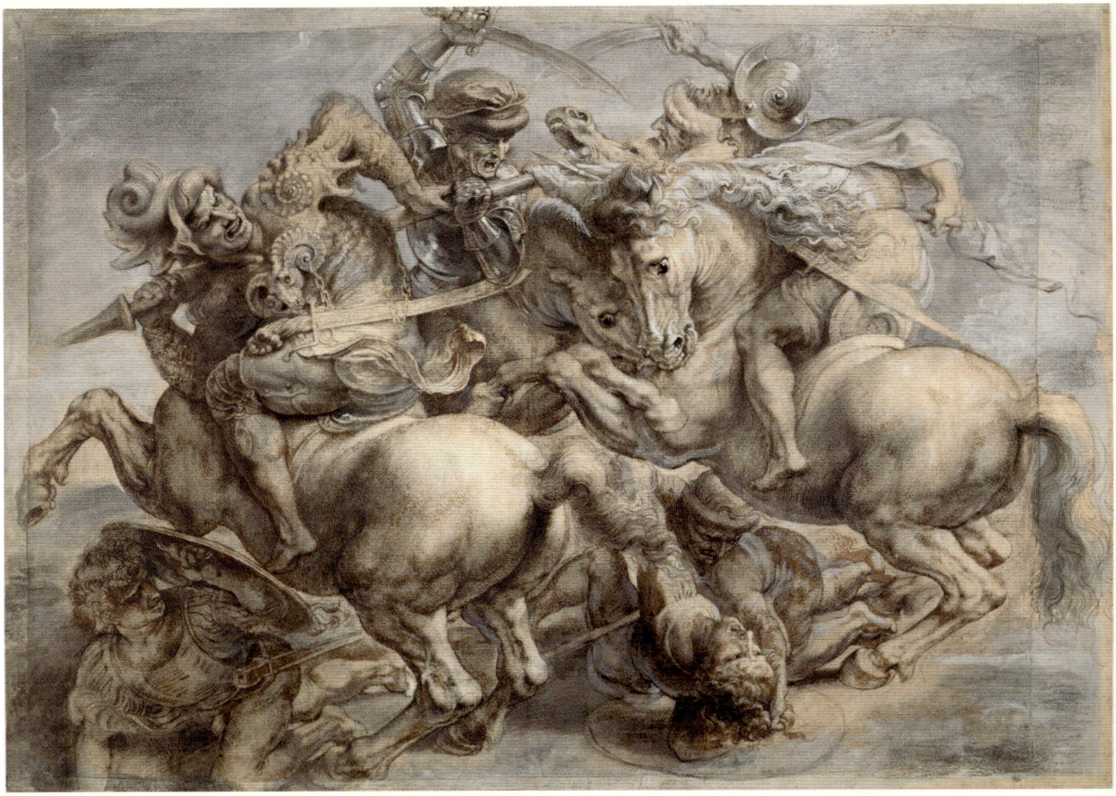

Fig. 16
Paul Peter Rubens, reworking an earlier drawing after **Leonardo**
Battle of Anghiari

Late 16th or early 17th century after an original of 1503–4, mixed media including black chalk, pen and ink, wash and white heightening on paper, 45.3 × 63.6cm (17⅞ × 25in). Musée du Louvre, Paris.

Neither Leonardo's nor Michelangelo's mural for the Sala del Gran Consiglio was ever completed. The fame of their compositions derives from the cartoons (or full-scale drawings) that each artist completed, but which have been lost.

Once Upon a Time …

Our story is best known from the narrative told by Giorgio Vasari (1511–1574), an artist and writer from Arezzo, a town to the south of Florence that had been part of its territory since 1384. It is his narrative that we shall follow in this chapter. In 1550 he published *Le vite de' più eccellenti pittori scultori e architettori* (*Lives of the Most Excellent Painters, Sculptors and Architects*), with a press run by Lorenzo Torrentino (hence its name in Italian, the *Torrentiniana*). Almost 20 years later, in 1568, Vasari released a second edition with the Giunti family (the so-called *Giuntina*), which was much expanded with 30 new biographies. That is the version most often consulted today, and the one generally translated into English.

In common with others before him, and many since, Vasari charted a growing interest in nature and classical antiquity that had begun in the late thirteenth century. In his opinion, the 'sister' arts of painting, sculpture and architecture had achieved perfection in the ancient world, only to enter a period of decline during the rule of the Emperor Constantine (ca. 272–337), from which they sank into a deep and sustained torpor, prompted by the destruction of ancient art by the barbarians and the early Church.

All stories need a good beginning. For Vasari, it was the reawakening of the arts after this long slumber, which he described as a '*rinascita*', or rebirth. The idea of a rebirth had been around for a while, since Petrarch in the fourteenth century, but Vasari was the first to connect it to art explicitly. His rebirth did not occur simultaneously in painting, sculpture and architecture. Architecture was the first to stir. He discerned early signs of a revival in the building campaigns initiated shortly after the turn of the first millennium, such the cathedral at Pisa or the Florentine church of San Miniato al Monte, which was begun in about 1013. Their builders were interested in 'good antique order [*ordine buono antico*]', which they knew from buildings such as the Baptistery in Florence, a structure that was once considered ancient, but which Vasari recognized as of more recent construction. Despite the premature promise of these buildings, designed in a manner that we would now call 'Romanesque', architecture remained relatively dormant until the time of Filippo Brunelleschi (1377–1446) – in Vasari's opinion, at least.

The art of painting, Vasari wrote, began to emerge from the darkness later than architecture, sometime in the final decades of the thirteenth century. Cimabue (ca. 1240–1302) 'originated the new way [*nuovo modo*] of drawing and painting', followed by Giotto

Fig. 17
Aristotile da Sangallo, after **Michelangelo**
Battle of Cascina

ca. 1542 after an original of 1505, oil on panel, 76.5 × 129cm (30⅜ × 51⅛in). Holkham Hall, Norfolk.

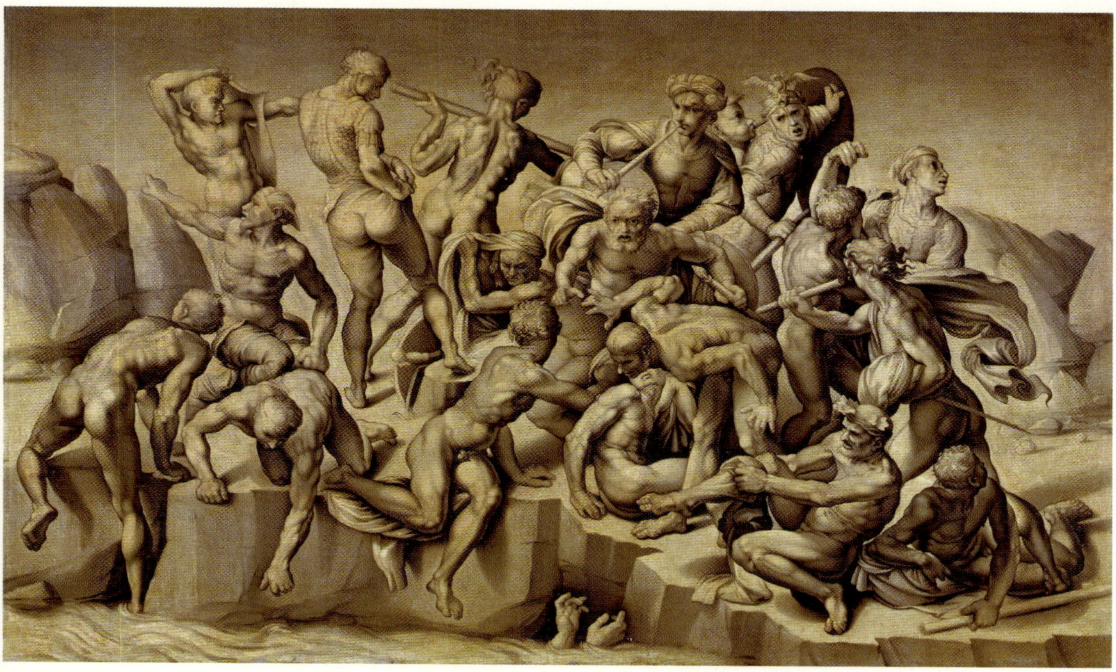

(ca. 1267–1337). During the preceding period, local painters had been indebted to the manner of the 'Greeks', by which Vasari intended Byzantine artists, from whom the Italians learned an awkward style. Giotto abandoned the Greek manner ('*maniera greca*'). He marked a new beginning, even if Vasari was cautious in his praise and observed that he fell a long way short of perfection. Vasari praised Giotto for his judgement ('*giudizio*') and his interest in nature ('*natura*'). It is striking that in painting it was the example of nature that prompted change, not classical antiquity, as it had been for the first architects to show promise.

In Vasari's narrative, the art of sculpture also improved around the time of Giotto, especially in its design. Vasari singled out Andrea Pisano, who was responsible for the first doors on the Florentine Baptistery, for particular praise. However, fourteenth-century sculpture continued to show defects and, like painting, was a long way from perfection. The problem, or so Vasari contended, was a lack of 'good works to imitate', by which he meant both works of antiquity and those of modern masters who had taken nature as their example. During the next century, however, sculpture made 'so many great improvements that there was little left for the [next] generation'. These improvements were attributed to various sculptors, but especially to Lorenzo Ghiberti (1378–1455) and Donatello (ca. 1386–1466). The former made strides in invention, order, style and design ('*invenzione, ordine, maniera e disegno*'), but it was really Donatello who combined the perfect examples of both nature and antiquity. For Vasari, Donatello was equal to the ancients: 'He imparted movement to his figures, giving them such vivacity and animation that they are worthy to rank both, as I said, with the work of the ancient world and also with that of the modern.'

Although the rebirth had begun early in architecture, it had to wait until the time of Brunelleschi before the order and proportion found in antique buildings were properly realized. In sculpture and painting, by contrast, the first signs appeared with Giotto in the early fourteenth century, in which the example of nature was the catalyst. But, once again, it was not until Donatello in the fifteenth century that a new standard was set. The metaphors with which this process is described are slippery. Sometimes they are about sleep and awakening; on other occasions about light and darkness (such as when the medieval period is described as the 'dark' ages, a metaphor as old as Petrarch). For Vasari, it was biological. The arts, he wrote, 'like human beings themselves, are born, grow up, become old, and die [*come i corpi umani, hanno il nascere, il crescere, lo invecchiare et il morire*]'. Vasari's *Lives* was divided into three sections, or ages, which roughly correspond to the fourteenth, fifteenth and sixteenth centuries, and reflect the birth, youth and maturity of the arts. Each of these ages was introduced by a preface, which provided the basis for the account given above, after which follow the biographies proper. Thus, in the second edition of 1568, the First Age includes artists from Cimabue to Lorenzo di Bicci (ca. 1350–1427); the Second from Jacopo della Quercia (ca. 1374–1438) to Luca Signorelli (ca. 1445–1523); and the Third from Leonardo da Vinci (1452–1519) to Vasari himself. The model that linked these three ages was cyclical and progressive. It culminates in the lives of Michelangelo (1475–1564) and Raphael (1483–1520), in whose art perfection was achieved. Vasari wrote in the preface to the second section: 'Having very carefully turned all this over in my mind, I have come to the conclusion that it is inherent in the very nature of these arts to progress step by step from modest beginnings, and finally to reach the summit of perfection.'

This book focuses in large part on Vasari's Second Age, together with a few artists from the beginning of the Third. In Anglo-German scholarship of the past century and a half, the stylistic development that occurred in this period has traditionally been described using the terms 'Early' (1400–1500) and 'High' Renaissance (*Hochrenaissance*; 1500–20). These terms are value-laden and are much criticized. They do not exist in Italian scholarship, nor in Vasari's text, for that matter; he described the style of the Third Age as the 'modern manner', '*maniera moderna*', not the 'High Renaissance'. The sense of progress – and the idea that one period was somehow better than another – is nonetheless present in either scheme. We shall return to the biases of his account, but for the moment it is necessary to introduce the artists of the Second Age, who will crop up again and again in this book.

The Artists of the Second Age

All stories need protagonists, both heroes and villains. The artists of Vasari's Second Age hailed from various parts of Italy – from Siena to Venice, Perugia to Bologna – but by far the greatest number were Florentine. He introduced them in the preface to the Second Age. The diligent and studious architect Filippo Brunelleschi was one of the heroes of that age, for it was through him that 'architecture rediscovered the proportions and measurements of the antique', qualities exemplified in the cupola of the cathedral, especially its lantern (FIG. 18), and in the churches of Santo Spirito and San Lorenzo. Brunelleschi began work on those buildings in which we notice

Fig. 18
Filippo Brunelleschi
Cupola of the cathedral

Completed 1436. Santa Maria del Fiore, Florence.

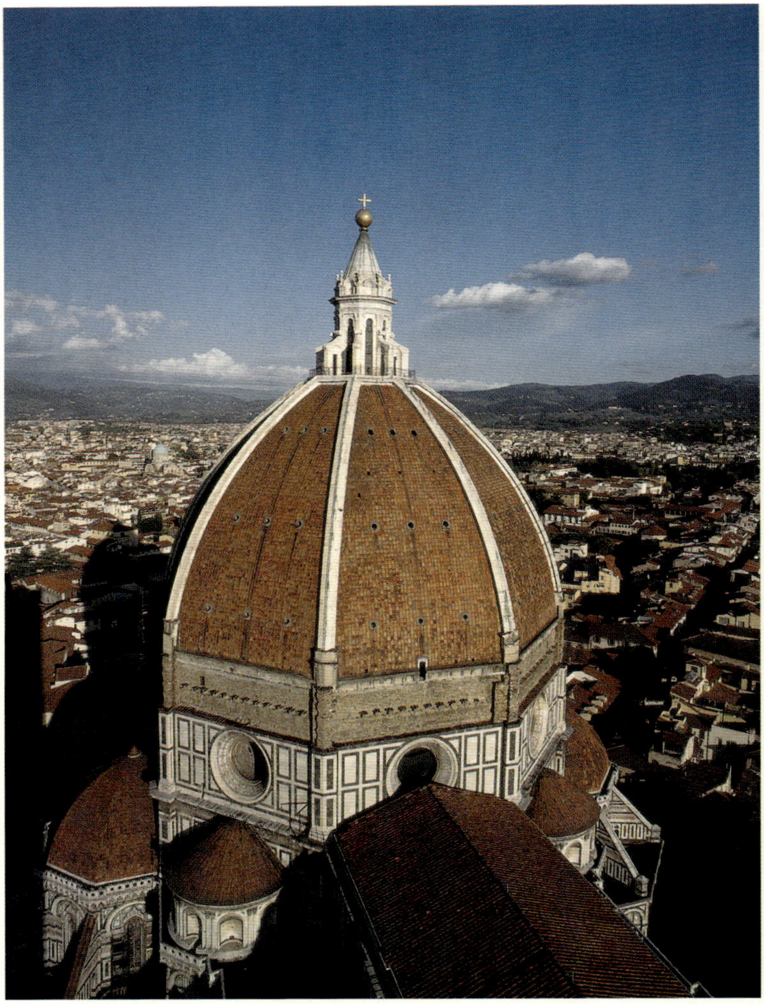

the sudden appearance of a new style in a relatively short period, perhaps even two years, from about 1418 to 1420. He was joined in painting by Masaccio (1401–1428), whose frescoes in the Brancacci chapel in Santa Maria del Carmine include the 'figure of a man shivering with cold, as well as other lifelike and spirited pictures [*pitture vivezze e spiriti*]' (FIG. 19). In a career spanning little more than six years during the 1420s, the 'superb Masaccio completely freed himself from Giotto's style', adopting a new manner of depicting heads, draperies, buildings and even nudes. He understood colouring and foreshortening, 'and brought into existence the modern style [*maniera moderna*] which, beginning in their period, had been employed by all our artists until the present day'. Modern scholars would add that he mastered linear perspective, a technique for the representation of space developed by Brunelleschi.

But while Brunelleschi and Masaccio are undoubted heroes of the age, Vasari's real praise was reserved for the sculptors Ghiberti and Donatello, who – as we have seen – achieved the 'greatest progress'. Vasari was even uncertain whether to include Donatello in the Second Age at all, for although he was contemporary with these artists, his works were the equal of the ancients, a quality characteristic of the Third Age. Donatello was more fortunate than Masaccio in that he was active for almost six decades, right up to his death in 1466.

The generation following the premature death of Masaccio developed a style which Vasari characterized as 'dry, crude and cutting', or perhaps 'harsh' and 'linear' is a better translation. Although some of the artists were not Florentine, many did live and work in the

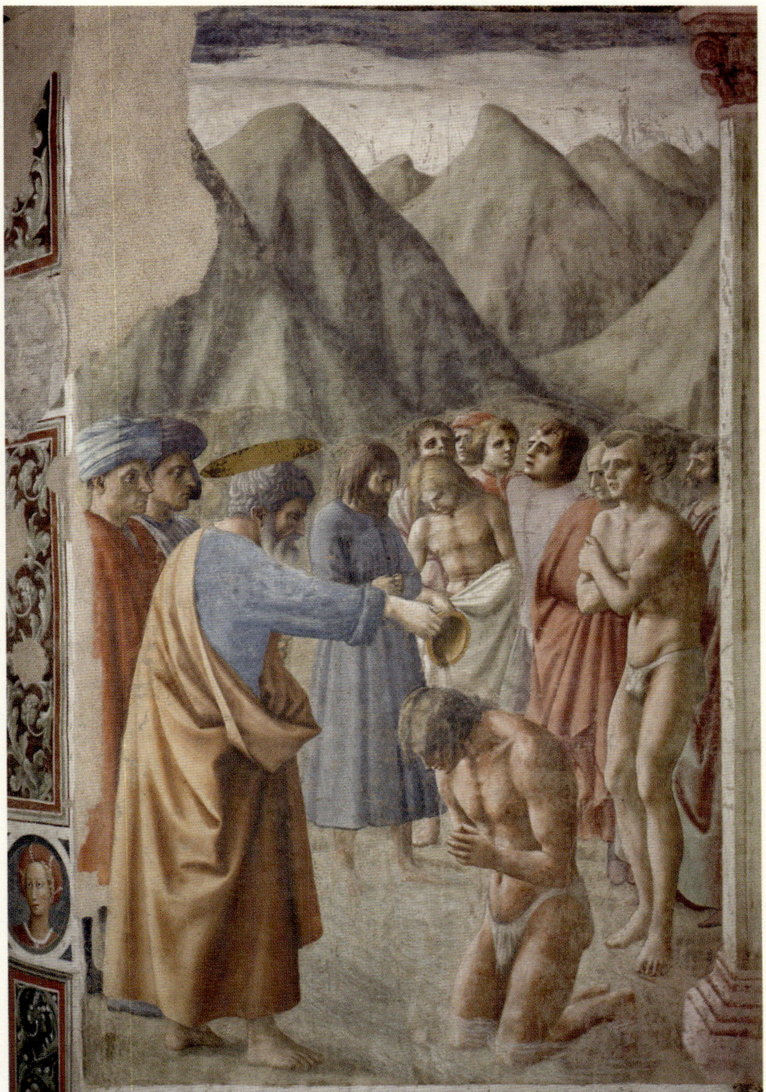

Fig. 19
Masaccio
Baptism of the Neophytes
from the Brancacci chapel

ca. 1426–7, fresco. Santa Maria del Carmine, Florence.

city, including Alesso Baldovinetti (1425–1499), Andrea del Castagno (before 1419–1457), Giuliano d'Arrigho, known as Pesello (ca. 1367–1446), Cosimo Rosselli (1439–1507), Domenico Ghirlandaio, Sandro Botticelli (1445–1510), Filippino Lippi (ca. 1457–1504) and Luca Signorelli, who was originally from Cortona. These are only the names that appear in Vasari's prefaces, but many more were admired by him and received full biographies in the Second Age, including Paolo Uccello (1397–1475) and Fra Angelico (ca. 1395–1455). At this point, the reader of this book could do no better than put it down and read Vasari's biographies.

These names represent several generations of painters from the 1430s to the early years of the sixteenth century, among whom Vasari perceived a certain stylistic affinity. Nowadays, we tend to see this group as more stylistically diverse. Some, such as Gentile da Fabriano (ca. 1370–1427), Masolino (1383–after 1435) or Uccello, are thought to have tendencies associated with artistic developments north of the Alps and are consequently bundled together as representatives of the 'International Gothic', a problematic term that was born in the nineteenth century and has little fifteenth-century valence. Others are appreciated for the quality of light in their work, especially a group of painters around mid century, who have consequently come to be labelled the '*pitture di luce*', 'painters of light', in more recent Italian scholarship. For Vasari, however, they were brought together by what they lacked – that is, the example set by antique sculpture – which would only be revealed to a subsequent generation.

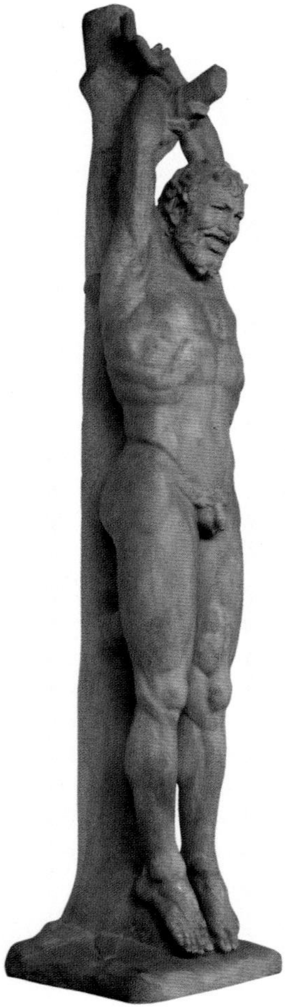

Fig. 20
Hanging Marsyas

2nd century CE with later restorations attributed to Mino da Fiesole, marble, 245cm (96½in) high. Galleria degli Uffizi, Florence.

The seated *Marsyas* that Verrocchio restored for Lorenzo de' Medici is lost. This hanging *Marsyas* was acquired by Cosimo de' Medici, his grandfather, who had it restored, probably by Mino da Fiesole.

In the preface to the Third Age, Vasari named the artists from the second half of the fifteenth century who had laid the way for the perfection to come in the work of Michelangelo. Andrea del Verrocchio (1435–1488) and Antonio del Pollaiuolo (1432–1498) 'endeavoured to make figures more studied', with good drawing or design ('*disegno*') and the imitation of 'natural things'. They nevertheless fell short of perfection, even if their works did invite comparison with the ancients, especially a marble Marsyas that Verrocchio restored for the Medici (FIG. 20). Vasari's purpose in this section of the preface was to discuss the example of the antique, and he is consequently quiet about the fact that Verrocchio's and Pollaiuolo's workshops of the 1470s break the pattern of a clear division between painting and sculpture. Both of them worked – or at least designed – in both media, and more besides. They received their first commissions in the 1460s and remained the primary Florentine workshops in the 1470s and into the 1480s, when they both moved away, Verrocchio to Venice and Pollaiuolo to Rome.

According to Vasari's tale, it took the discovery of certain free-standing antique sculptures in the final decades of the fifteenth century, and the early years of the sixteenth, for there to be an example that could lead artists to perfection. A multi-figure sculpture of *Laocoön and his Sons* was unearthed in January 1506 and achieved almost immediate fame, not least because it was associated with a celebrated marble mentioned by Pliny. Together with other sculptures displayed in the courtyard of the Belvedere at the Vatican, such as the *Apollo Belvedere* (FIG. 21), it prompted the disappearance of 'a certain dry, crude and cutting style [*una certa maniera secca e cruda e tagliente*]' by providing a model of 'most gracious grace [*una*

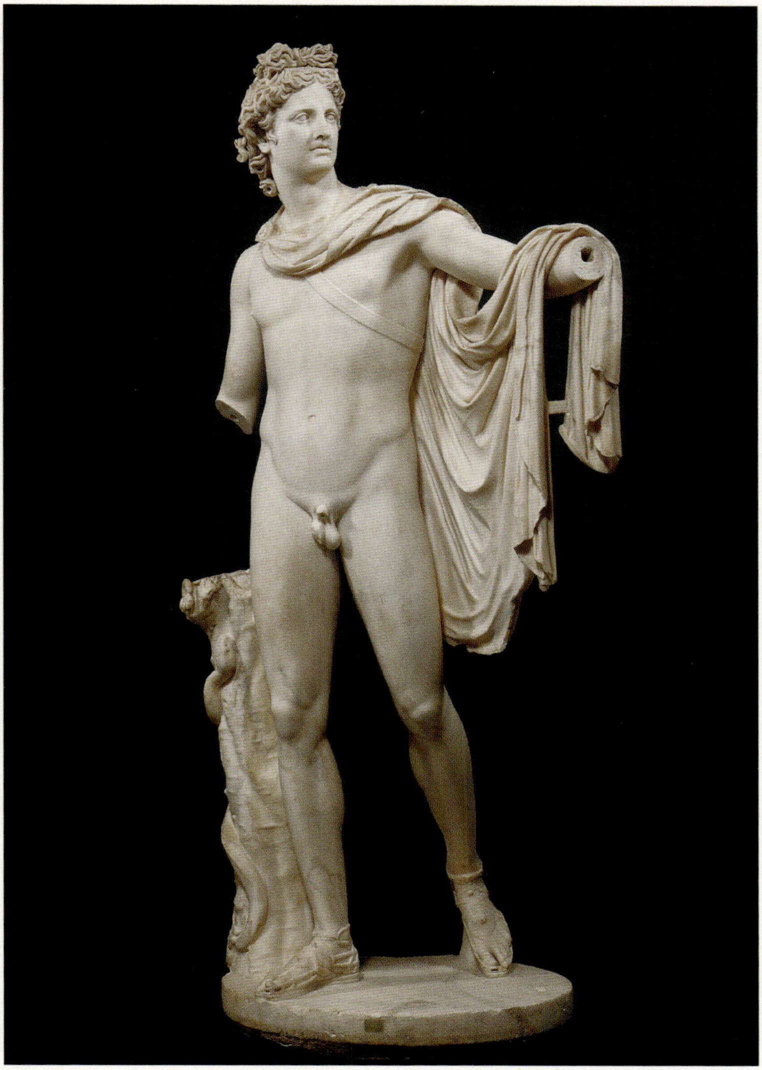

Fig. 21
Apollo Belvedere

ca. 120–40 CE, marble, 224cm ($88\frac{1}{8}$in) high. Museo Pio-Clementino, Vatican City.

graziosissima grazia]' through natural movements and the 'beauty of the living [*bellezze del vivo*]'. It is significant that these discoveries were made in Rome. While the story of the rebirth and youthful development of the visual arts is centred on Florence, its maturity for Vasari – and many since – was in Rome under Pope Julius II and Leo X (the latter a Florentine and a Medici). Traditionally, then, there is understood to be a shift in scene from the city on the Arno to the ancient *caput mundi* on the river Tiber, even if there were various preludes to the *maniera moderna* in Florence – notably Leonardo's cartoon for Santissima Annunziata (lost, 1500), Michelangelo's *David* (1503, *see* FIG. 10) and the two artists' ill-fated mural projects for the Sala di Gran Consiglio (1503–4; *see* FIGS. 16, 17).

The first sign of change from the style of the Second Age came not from Florentines, according to Vasari, but from Francesco Francia (ca. 1447–1517) and Pietro Perugino (ca. 1446/52–1523), the one from Bologna, the other from a town near Perugia, but who maintained a workshop in Florence. They gave their figures 'liveliness [*prontezza*]' and achieved a 'sweetness' in the blending of their colours ('*una dolcezza ne' colori unita*'). But it was really the Florentine Leonardo da Vinci who changed the course of art: '[He] originated the third style [*terza maniera*], which we like to call the modern age [*moderna*]; for in addition to the force and robustness of his draughtsmanship [*disegno*] and his subtle and exact reproduction of every detail in nature [*natura*], he showed in his works an understanding of rule, a better knowledge of that order, correct proportion, perfect design, and an inspired grace [*buona regola, miglior ordine, retta misura, disegno perfetto e grazie divina*].' These artists, and those who followed them, understood the importance of good rule, order, proportion, design and style, the key characteristics of the *maniera moderna*. Vasari also mentioned two other Florentines in the wake of Leonardo, Fra Bartolomeo (1472–1517) and Andrea del Sarto (1486–1530), the latter much influenced, in Vasari's opinion, by Raphael, 'the most graceful of them all'.

Raphael was not Florentine. He was born in Urbino and came to Florence only about 1504. There he studied from ancient and modern masters, selecting the best qualities in their works, such that he could be compared to Apelles or Zeuxis in antiquity. Vasari wondered whether he 'might even be said to have surpassed them'. When it came to Michelangelo, the third hero of the *maniera moderna*, Vasari was in no doubt about his relationship to the art of the ancient world, or nature for that matter: '[He was] supreme not in one art alone but in all three. He surpasses not only all those whose work can be said to be superior to nature but also the artists of the ancient world, whose superiority is beyond doubt.' Vasari's celebration of Michelangelo implicitly championed those artists to whom Michelangelo was indebted, such as Giotto and Masaccio, all of whom are associated with a particularly sculptural approach to form. Artists who had been interested in qualities of surface, from Gentile to Botticelli, were sidelined.

In the paragraphs above, I have used Vasari's prefaces to name names. The artists between the times of Brunelleschi, Masaccio, Ghiberti and Donatello and the *maniera moderna* receive short shrift in the prefaces, a fact that has less to do with what Vasari thought of their art than with his purpose in writing the prefaces. Vasari concluded the preface to the Second Age with a summary of what had been achieved during the period:

> Artists tried to reproduce neither more nor less than what they saw in nature [*nel naturale*], and as a result their work began to show more careful observation and understanding. This encouraged them to lay down definite rules for perspective and to make their foreshortenings in the exact form of natural relief, proceeding to the observation of light and shade, shadows and other difficult things. They endeavoured to compose their narratives with greater verisimilitude [*con più propria similitudine*], attempting to make their landscapes more truthful [*più simili al vero*], along with the trees, the grass, the flowers, the air, the clouds, and the other natural things [*cose della natura*]. They did this so successfully that these arts were brought to the flower of their youth [*nel fiore della lor gioventù*], holding out the promise that in the near future they would enter the perfect age [*perfetta età*].

Vasari accorded privilege to certain qualities. The first is *disegno*, a word that embraces both drawing and design, combining the actions of the hand and the mind. *Disegno* was associated, above all, with the art of the Florentines, which stood in contrast to the colour and colouring (*colorito*) of the Venetians. The second is 'nature [*natura*]'. Vasari began his first preface to the *Lives* by stating that all previous writers on the arts of sculpture and painting acknowledge that they 'were first derived from nature by the people of Egypt'. In doing so, he revealed that for him good art was that which adheres most closely to nature. Yet nature remains a much misunderstood term, as we shall see in Chapter 8. It relates less to the world 'out there', less to the idiosyncratic and particular quirks of nature than to an ideal, somewhat like that found in ancient art, which is the third factor in Vasari's account. Although intimately linked, the awareness of nature and the rebirth of interest in antiquity happened at different moments in painting, sculpture and architecture, at least in Vasari's reckoning. In painting, they were out of step: an interest in nature appeared before that in antiquity. In sculpture, they came together in the work of Donatello in the fifteenth century, while in architecture, nature was not a quality that Vasari could assess, and he spoke instead about the turn to ancient canons of proportion and languages of ornament. Many of the words and concepts used in Vasari's text, as well as those employed in mine above, are contingent; they are not universal qualities that determine good art (as if such a thing could exist!), but rather ideas that depend on time and place. So, too, are ideas such as originality or inventiveness. They are not innocent.

Fig. 22
Gallery 2 at the Galleria degli Uffizi, including Fig. 79 (left)

Florence, in 2017.

Fig. 23
The 'Donatello Room' at the Museo Nazionale del Bargello, including Figs. 3, 11, 13 and 44

Florence, in 2017.

An Enduring Model

Vasari's model has endured, even if it has not remained static. It can be found readily in textbooks and museum displays. Visitors to the Uffizi Gallery in Florence, which holds the most extensive collection of Florentine painting anywhere, are greeted by Giotto's *Maestà* (left), flanked by Cimabue's rendition of the same subject (FIG. 22). These works provide a starting point, an origin, for all that is to

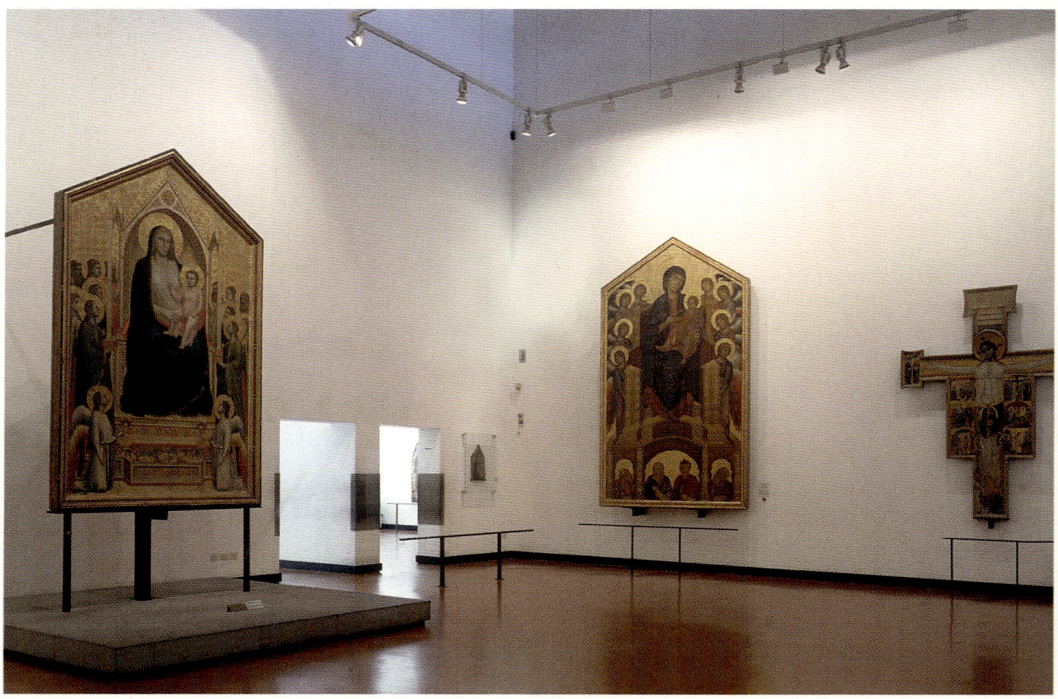

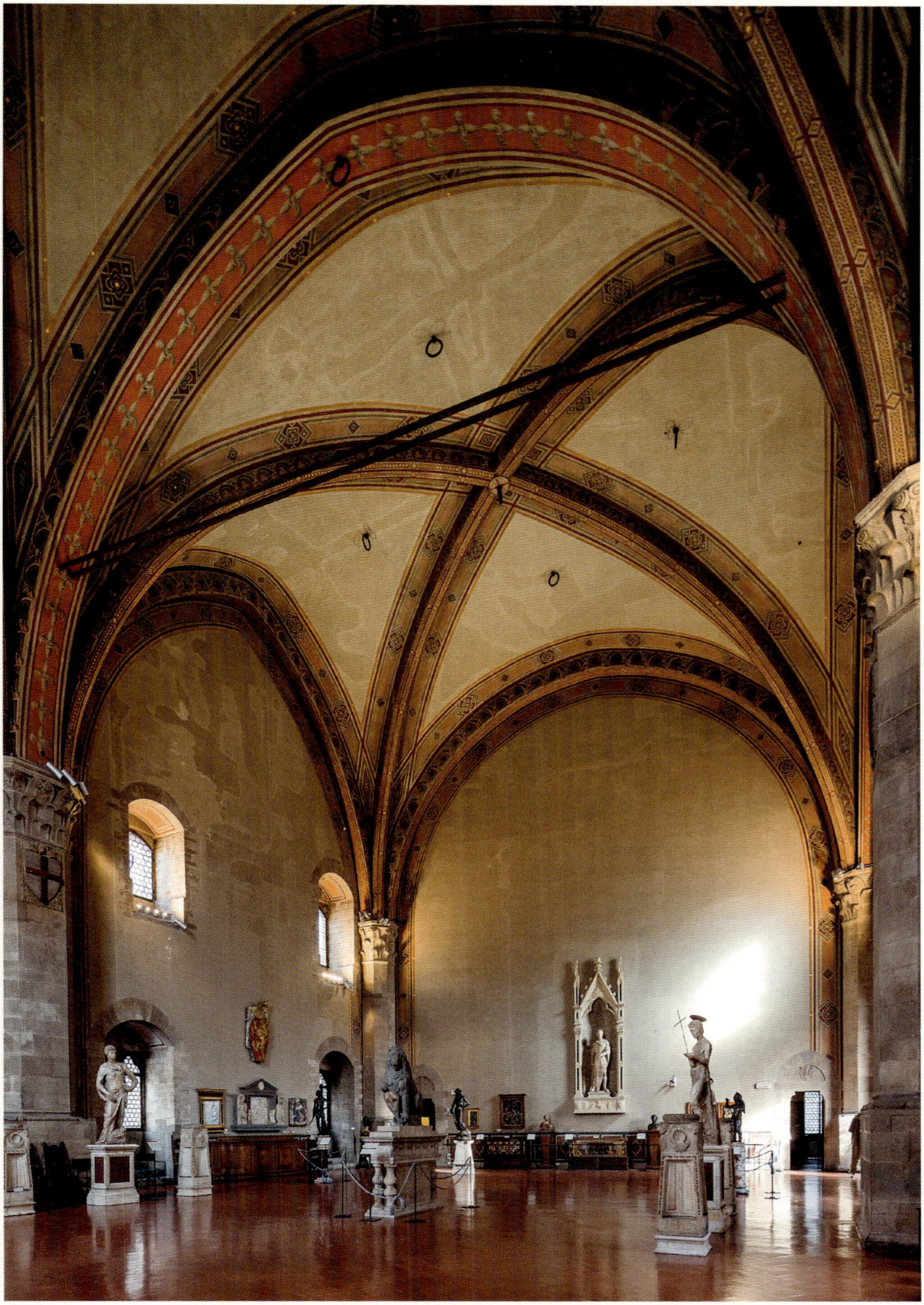

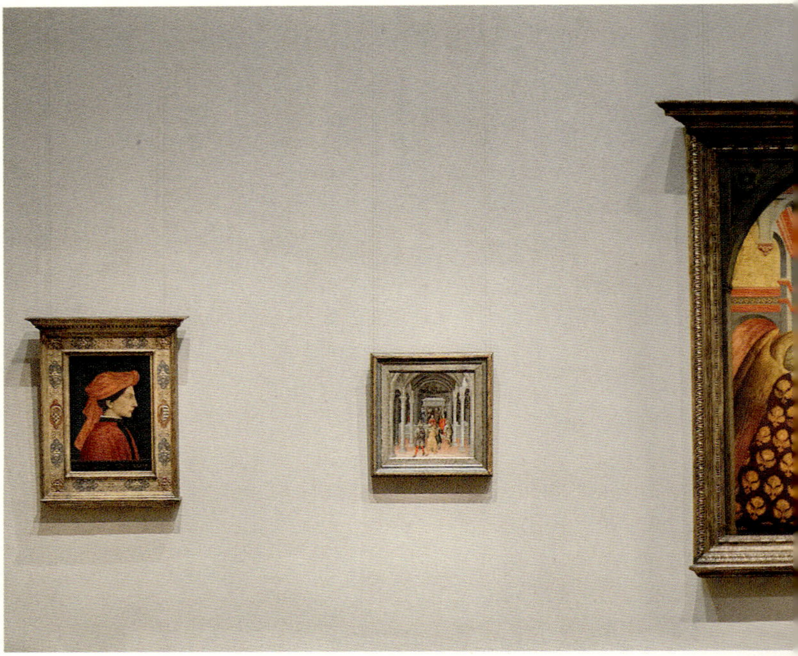

come, much as they do in Vasari's tale. Those arriving on the first floor of the Bargello, the museum that holds the national collection of sculpture in Florence, encounter a space dominated by the work of Donatello (FIG. 23). Donatello's sculptures structure the space, marking out the walls or floors in such a way that all the other works must enter into dialogue with them. Even five centuries on, the role accorded Donatello by Vasari lives on, and with good reason.

For the work of painters from the second quarter of the fifteenth century, the National Gallery of Art in Washington DC is exemplary. Take Room 4, for example. It holds important paintings by Masolino, Domenico Veneziano, Francesco Pesellino, Andrea del Castagno and Fra Angelico, whose works are at the centre of each wall. Others, of equal significance, by Fra Filippo Lippi and Benozzo Gozzoli are placed between them. The canon of artists, established by Vasari, has determined curatorial decisions about which works to include in the gallery and which to consign to store. And where key artists are missing from the collection, substitutes are found. Thus, on the first wall the visitor encounters when entering the gallery from Room 3, artists of Masaccio's generation are shown (FIG. 24). Masolino's *Annunciation* from the Guardini chapel in San Niccolò Oltrarno, painted in the 1420s, hangs beside a painting by Gentile da Fabriano, made for the same church. Masolino was Masaccio's collaborator in the Brancacci chapel, yet Masaccio himself – the most

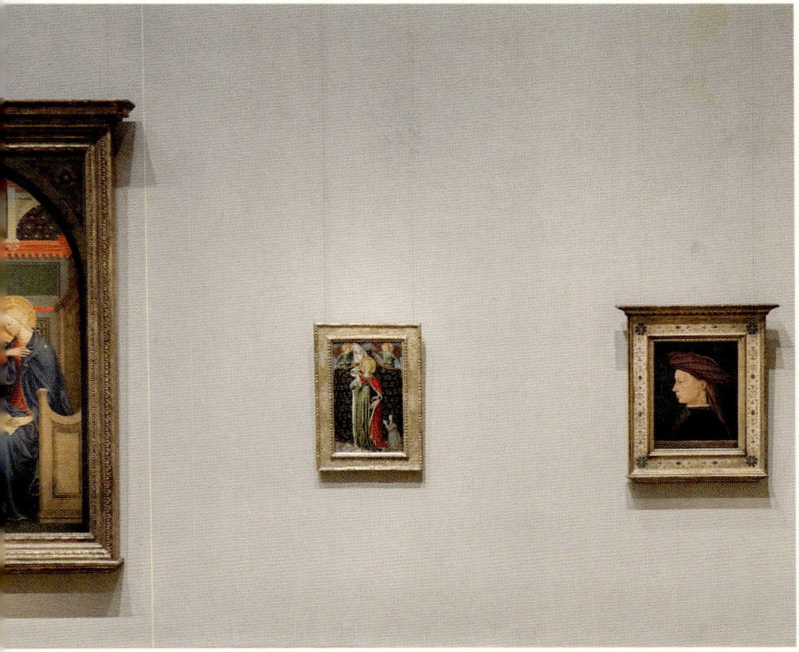

Fig. 24
Room 4 at the National Gallery of Art

Washington DC, in 2018.

important artist of the generation, at least according to Vasari – is missing: the collection in Washington lacks panels by him. He is represented by substitutes in the form of two portraits that frame the hang; one was once thought to be his work. Although in truth we do not know who painted these portraits, they contain stylistic traits – especially their simplified forms, sculpted by light – that are associated with Masaccio, and this association still determines their status and role in the room. They tell a story about origins and progress.

To be clear, I am not critiquing – at least, not in the accepted negative sense – the hang at the National Gallery in Washington, nor do I wish to dismiss the grand narrative that unfolds at the Uffizi. They all tell a story successfully. But that does not mean that it is the only way the tale can be told, or that one telling is more authoritative than another. They are all constructs, much like Vasari's narrative. At the Metropolitan Museum of Art in New York, for instance, objects are grouped by type and function – all the portraits together, or art for the home. The Victoria and Albert Museum in London and the Bode Museum in Berlin have a similar approach. Likewise, Vasari's narrative – in which Brunelleschi, Masaccio, Ghiberti and Donatello are agents of change – could be countered by an examination of the sites on which they worked and the people for whom they toiled, as we will do in Chapter 4. Location and patronage are just two possible alternatives to the narrative of stylistic progress constructed by Vasari.

My purpose is not to do away with these tales. It is rather to point out that Florentine art continues to have a story, even if we recognize its shortcomings and seek alternatives. The drive to construct the history of art as a narrative has been stereotyped above through Vasari, if only to avoid telling you my own, intensely subjective version. Here, however, I must sound a note of caution. Too much blame is laid at his feet, sometimes for claims he never made, and often without understanding of his purpose in writing the *Lives*. The presence of Gentile in Room 4 in Washington is a case in point, even if it is better illustrated by the role that same artist plays in the hang of the National Gallery in London. In Room 53, which contains Florentine works from the first half of the fifteenth century, his *Madonna and Child* hangs to the right of a door (FIG. 25). It comes from the same polyptych as the small predella panel in Washington that was made for the Quaratesi family. On the opposite side of the door is a *Virgin and Child* by Masaccio, likewise removed from a polyptych, made for Santa Maria del Carmine in Pisa (*see* FIG. 80). Only a single year separates these two commissions, but their display suggests that an epochal shift has occurred between Gentile and Masaccio. They are presented as offering two different directions for painting in the 1420s, a perception that is only heightened by hanging them on either side of a door, as if, to pass into the next room – and thus into the future – the visitor must choose between the two artists.

In this conception, Masaccio's panel demonstrates all the progressive qualities that Vasari articulated: an interest in nature and *all'antica* design. Gentile, on the other hand, is considered the representative of a decorative style, excessively interested in surface pattern and ornament, the so-called 'International Gothic' (despite the extraordinary naturalism of his Virgin). This stylistic category is a more recent addition to Vasari's narrative. He had written disparagingly of a 'German' manner in architecture that subsequently came to be called 'gothic', but the notion was applied to painting and sculpture only in the nineteenth century, when it was subdivided into various stages. The 'International Gothic' was only one of its final flowerings, when the 'true way' – the route defined by Masaccio and his followers – was becoming apparent. The juxtaposition of Masaccio and Gentile, which is now axiomatic and a fixed chapter in the story of the Florentine Renaissance, has little to do with Vasari.

Vasari's purpose was not to compile an inventory of artists and their works, as he in fact tells us at the beginning of his second preface. It was, instead, to provide exemplary lives and work that others might take as their model. It was a type of history writing that he inherited from antiquity. He wrote, again in the introduction to

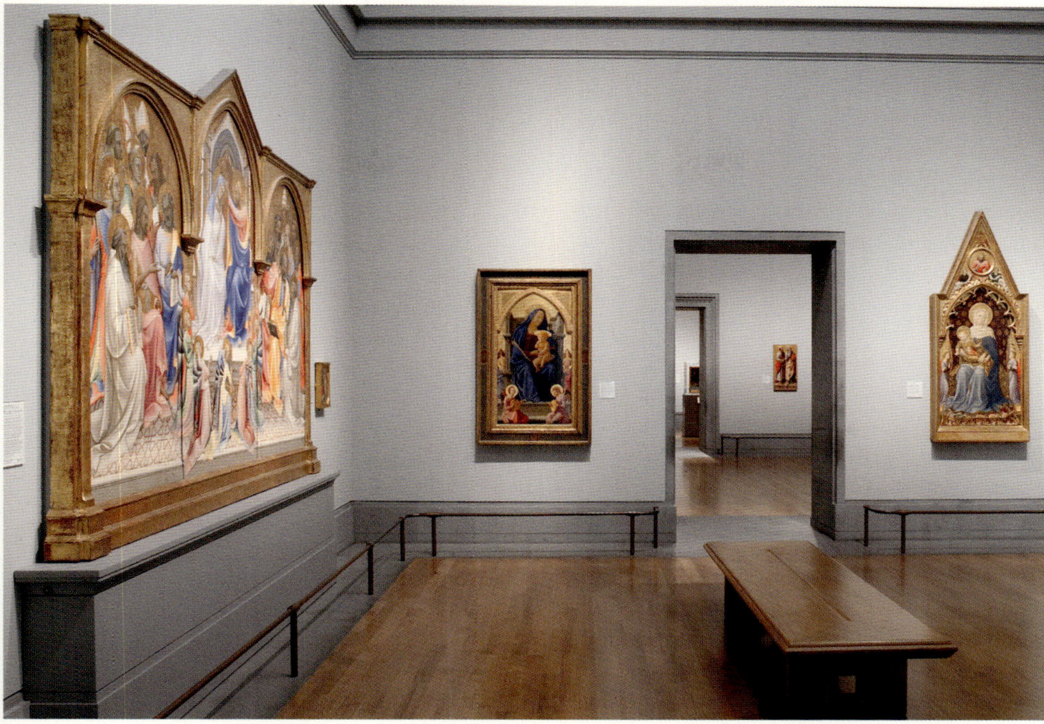

the second preface: 'I have endeavoured not only to record what the artists have done but also to distinguish between the good, the better, and the best,' continuing by recalling that his motivation was 'to help people who cannot find out for themselves'. Vasari has become a punchbag for many scholars. He stands accused of conceiving a partial and parochial art history, one that positioned Florence at the centre of all artistic developments, downplaying innovation elsewhere in the Italian peninsula and almost completely ignoring Northern Europe, except perhaps for the development of oil painting. Such charges, while true in part, do not do justice to his *Lives*, nor do they understand the purpose of history writing in the sixteenth century. They assume that his sole purpose was a comprehensive listing of facts. They also fail to take account of the full historiography of Florentine art since Vasari's time, especially the contributions made by Filippo Baldinucci (1624–1697) in the seventeenth century or Luigi Lanzi (1732–1810) at the end of the eighteenth. Even more seriously, they do not recognize the role Florence assumed for the intellectuals who established the history of art as a new discipline in nineteenth-century Germany, or the connection between narrative histories of twentieth-century modernism and the perception of innovative, 'avant-garde' tendencies in Florentine art 500 years earlier.

Fig. 25
Room 53 at the National Gallery, including Fig. 80 (to left of door)

London, in 2017.

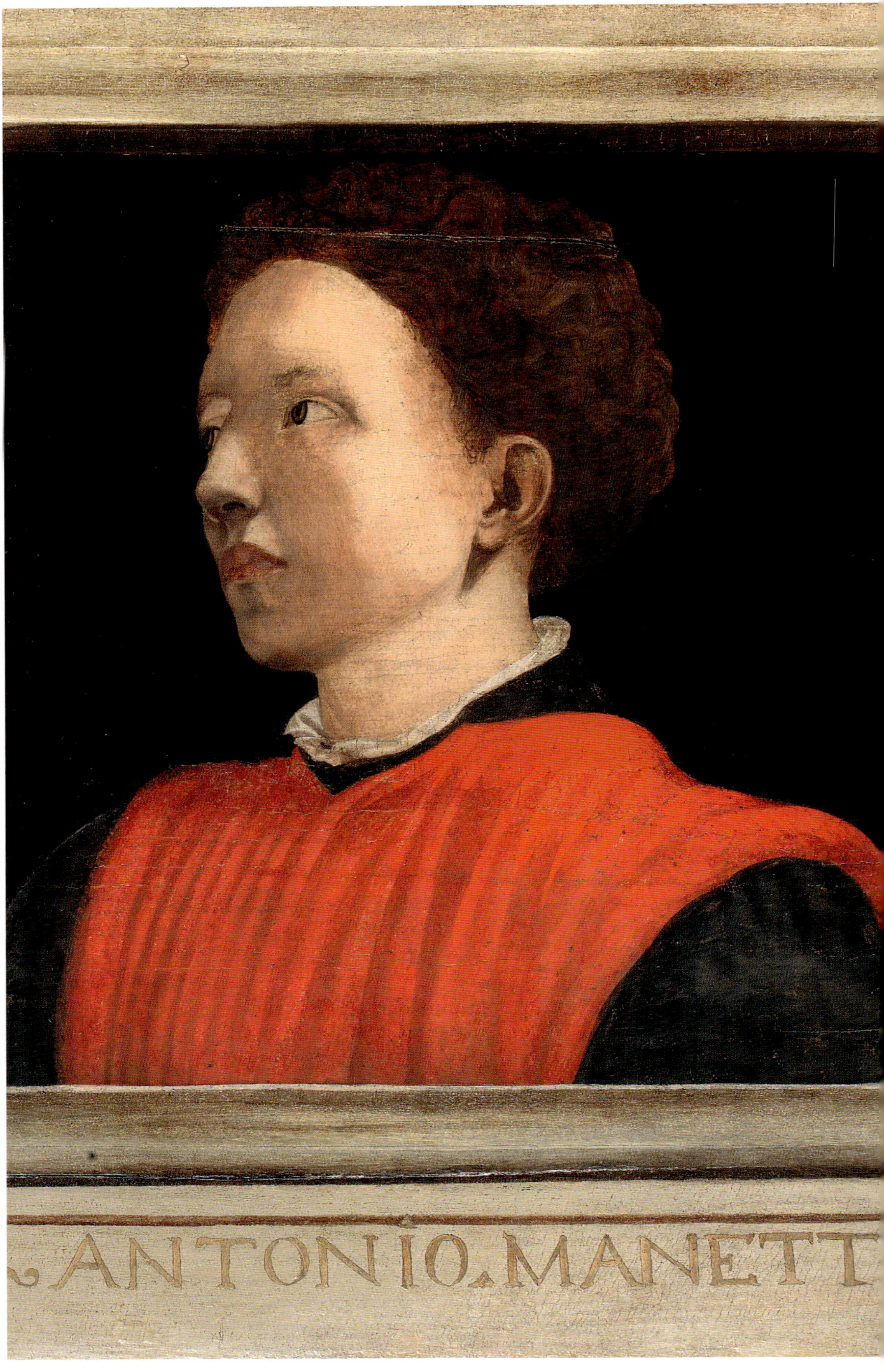
ANTONIO MANETT

3

Writing about Art

As we saw in the previous chapter, our chief source for the lives of Renaissance artists is Giorgio Vasari, who was born in 1511, around the time this survey concludes. While it would be remiss to ignore him in this account of Florentine writings on art, his work did not spring from nowhere, nor was biography the only model for writing about art. By this date, there was already a considerable corpus of writing on art, more than is sometimes realized. We must now turn our attention to the writing of Lorenzo Ghiberti, Antonio di Tuccio di Marabottino Manetti (1423–1497) and Leon Battista Alberti (1404–1472).

The first was a sculptor and was keen to write as one. The second was described as an 'architect' in the fifteenth century, even if he is better understood as a humanist, much like the third, who nonetheless assures his reader that he writes as a painter. All wrote in the Tuscan vernacular, the language that would become modern Italian, although Alberti also translated his text into Latin. He took the first steps towards theorizing art, especially painting and architecture, but also sculpture. He gave it a language, finding words in ancient rhetoric with which to describe its constituent elements, and began the process of elevating its status, such that it could be counted

Fig. 26
Portrait of Antonio Manetti

Detail of Fig. 28.

among the liberal arts. His endeavour transformed the way Western art is discussed and appreciated. Ghiberti produced the first account of Renaissance painting and sculpture, the development of which he conceived in cyclical terms. Its legacy continues to be felt every time we speak of the 'Renaissance', even if he cannot be credited with the notion of rebirth. He also wrote an autobiography, the first of any artist in Western Europe, and paved the way for Manetti, whose biography of Brunelleschi was an important model for Vasari. Beyond texts that are exclusively dedicated to the arts, artists are named in a variety of elevated contexts, from Alamanno Rinuccini's dedication to his translation of Philostratus's *Life of Apollonius* (1473) to Cristoforo Landino's preface to his commentary of 1481 on Dante's *Divine Comedy*.

Ghiberti's *Commentaries*

Towards the end of his life, as the *Gates of Paradise* (the east doors of the Baptistery, *see* FIG. 87) were nearing completion, Ghiberti began writing a book on art, which he left unfinished at his death in 1455. Modern editions divide his text into three broad sections. The first considers the origins of painting and sculpture, together with the art of antiquity ('*arte antica*'). It is derived in large part from Vitruvius and Pliny the Elder. Vitruvius's *De architectura* (or *The Ten Books on Architecture*), written in the first century CE, is the only work on architecture to have survived from antiquity. Pliny's *Natural History* (*Naturalis Historia*) is an encyclopaedic discussion of the natural world written about a century later, and it remains our major source of information about ancient art since it contains an account of ancient painting and sculpture (books 33–7). Ghiberti's second section builds on the first part by examining art from the advent of Christianity until his own time. His account of 'modern art [*arte moderna*]' is by far the most original element of his text, not least because it is entirely his own invention, and we shall focus on it shortly.

The third part of Ghiberti's text breaks with the quasi-historical account of the previous two parts. It is theoretical. Had Ghiberti ever completed this section, it would have provided an important corollary to the work of Alberti, discussed below. Several kinds of information can be gleaned from it even in its unfinished state. It offers evidence of a sculptor's learning, for Ghiberti's education and background could not have been further from the humanist studies of someone like Alberti. In this part of the book, Ghiberti hoped to address questions of anatomy, rules of proportion and, above all, optics. Indeed, his text includes some of the first attempts to find words in the vernacular for certain optical terms. Ghiberti drew on various ancient and medieval authorities, above all on the Arab scholar Ibn al-Haytham (965–ca. 1040, called Alhazen in the West). Alhazen's work on optics was known in Latin as *De aspectibus* and was translated into the Tuscan vernacular in a rare manuscript preserved in the Vatican (MS. Vat. 4595). It was probably known to Ghiberti (and Alberti, for that matter), but if not, Alhazen's ideas were also transmitted to Renaissance scholars through the thirteenth-century students of optics Roger Bacon (ca. 1214–1292), John Pecham (ca. 1230–1292) and Erazmus Ciołek Witelo (ca. 1230–1280/1314). Ghiberti copied sections of both Bacon's *Perspectiva* and Pecham's *Perspectiva communis* in his third section, in addition to the many citations from Alhazen.

Since the early twentieth century, Ghiberti's text has been referred to as his *Commentarii* (*Commentaries*), because he ends the second section with the phrase 'The second commentary [*commentario*] is finished; we come to the third.' A closer reading of the text reveals, however, that he uses the word 'commentary' only in the second section about the art of his own time, and that the two commentaries to which he refers are those of modern painting and modern sculpture. The misunderstanding might not seem serious were it not for the fact that the title 'Commentaries' bestows a systematic order on the book, as if it were a treatise, and disguises its close similarity to *zibaldoni*, or chapbooks, in which Florentines collected passages copied from various authorities, ancient and modern, whether Cicero, Boethius or Dante. Like them, Ghiberti copied texts by Alhazen and Pliny. His preoccupation was with memory, and he preserved *ricordi* of texts as much as he sought to memorialize works of art by describing them.

Ghiberti's account of '*arte moderna*' is entirely concerned with painting and sculpture, despite his promise to write a text on architecture, of which no trace survives. It begins at the time of Constantine in the fourth century, suggesting that, with the arrival of Christianity, the fear of idolatry was such that 'the art of sculpture and painting came to an end'. It is a brave claim, given the time in which he lived, and differs somewhat from other writers, who held the barbarian invaders to account. Ghiberti perceived a cyclical structure to human culture, as Petrarch had done before him, and he was the first to apply it to the history of art. Unlike Vasari later, he did not employ a metaphor of rebirth, but he did adopt a similar structure in which, after a period of decline, the 'Greeks' (Byzantines) began painting crudely, until the time of Giotto, when the example of nature initiated the rival of the arts. Thereafter Ghiberti lists the works of Giotto and his various followers, establishing a model of art-historical writing that is structured around their works, rather than their biographies. First, he recorded painting by Florentine artists, then that of their peers in Siena, followed by the work of sculptors, including the mysterious Gusmin from Cologne. He concluded the second part with an extended account of his own work. It is the first autobiography of an artist.

Ghiberti's interest in the works of artists, and in providing a lasting memory of them, is most apparent in his discussion of Ambrogio Lorenzetti (ca. 1290–1348). He describes him as 'a perfect master, a man of great genius, a very fine draughtsman and most expert in the theory of his art'. His description of Lorenzetti's frescoes at San Francesco in Siena (now largely destroyed) takes its cue from ancient *ekphrases*, vivid descriptions of works of art, imagined or real. It is the longest passage dedicated to any individual work of art in the *Commentarii*, and not only demonstrates his admiration for Lorenzetti, but also shows Ghiberti grappling with the most fundamental problem of art writing: how to translate visual phenomena into words. He reserves his most evocative prose for a description of the lost frescoes of the Franciscan martyrs at Centa that Lorenzetti painted in the cloister of San Francesco:

> The friars set out … but are taken and brought to the Sultan, who straightaway orders them to be tied to a column and beaten with rods. They are immediately tied up and two men begin to beat them. Here it is painted how two men beat them and how, with rods in their hands and having been relieved, another two of them rest, with wet hair, dripping with sweat, with much unease and breathlessness. Additionally, there are all the people with their eyes fixed on the naked friars and there is the Sultan, seated in the Moorish fashion, all with such varied poses and costumes that one would certainly believe them alive. [Lorenzetti showed] how this Sultan sentences them to be hanged on a tree. It is painted how they hanged one of them from a tree, before all the people who are there to see and hear the hanged friar preach … [he showed] how [the sultan] orders the executioner to behead them; and here how these friars are decapitated before a great crowd on horseback and on foot. There is the executioner with many armed men, there are men and women and, as the said friars are beheaded, there appears a dark tempest with hail, lightning, thunder and earthquakes, so that one seems to see painted all the perils of the sky and earth, and it seems that everyone seeks shelter in great trepidation – men and women pull their

> clothes over their heads, the armed men hold their shields over their heads and the hail beats down on them; it really seems that the hail bounces from the shields as if driven by marvellous winds; one sees the trees bend to the earth and split, everyone seems to flee, and one sees them fleeing; one sees the executioner fall beneath his horse and get killed ... For a painted story [*storia picta*] it seems to me a marvellous thing.

Ghiberti's graphic description of violence, whether that of mankind or of nature, reveals the scene in the mind's eye of his reader, like ancient ekphrastic texts. Without the fresco, it is impossible to judge how much was painted by Lorenzetti and how much sprang from Ghiberti's own imagination (or *fantasia*). But that is precisely the point. Ghiberti provided a memory of these frescoes that brings them to life even 300 years after their destruction.

Ghiberti knew Siena well, having worked there on the Baptistery font. His praise for Sienese art might surprise us, who are so used to thinking of Florence as the centre of innovation in the period. But from the perspective of a Florentine sculptor in the late 1440s, the history of art was as much Sienese as it was Florentine. Half of his account of 'modern art' is dedicated to Siena. What is more, the hero of his narrative is Lorenzetti, not Duccio, who – at least since the eighteenth century – has been hailed as the father of Sienese painting.

If through description Ghiberti brings works of art before the eyes, he also reveals himself as sensitive to touch, as one might expect from a sculptor. In addition to texts on optics, the third section records certain ancient sculptures (Ghiberti is known to have had a collection of antiquities). One of them was the lying hermaphrodite (FIG. 27) of which Ghiberti records seeing a version in Rome. He

Fig. 27
Lying hermaphrodite

First quarter of the 2nd century CE, marble, 152 cm (59⅞ in). Galleria degli Uffizi, Florence.

Ghiberti knew a sculpture of this type, although none that currently survives is documented in the fifteenth century. It is unlikely to have been this version, which is first recorded in 1669 in Rome, since Ghiberti records that its head had been broken off.

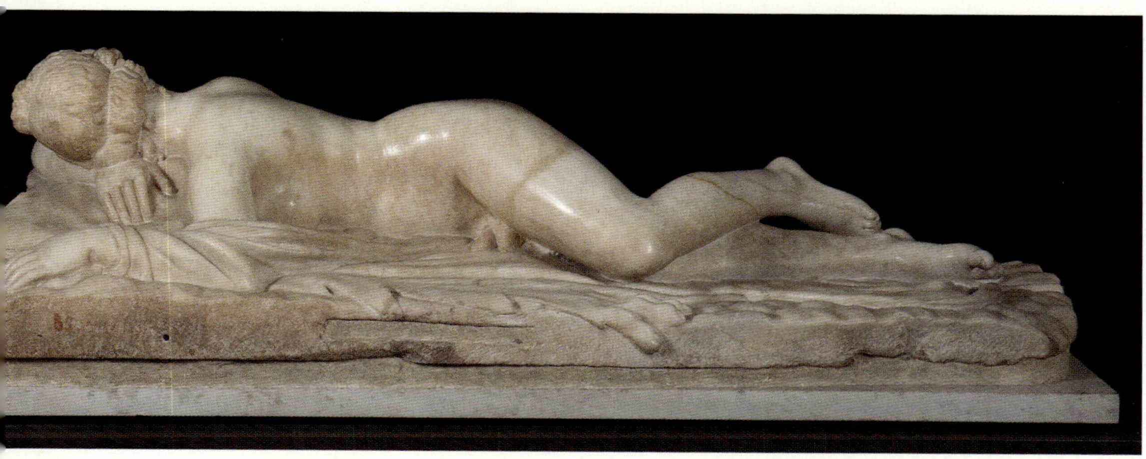

tells of its discovery and restoration, remembering that 'the learning, craftsmanship and mastery were such that no tongue could tell its perfection', and continuing to note that the 'figure was turned in such a way that both the male and female characteristics were shown'. What is most striking, after this careful visual description, is that his appreciation was partially based on touch: 'There were many subtleties to it, although the face [i.e. the eye] espied none of them, but through the touch of the hand.'

Manetti's *Life of Brunelleschi*

Ghiberti might have included an autobiographical passage in his *Commentaries*, but it was his great rival, Brunelleschi, who received the first comprehensive 'life' of an artist. Biography, as a literary form, had a long and venerable history. Plutarch wrote his *Parallel Lives* in Greek in the first century CE, pairing famous Greeks and Romans; Suetonius produced *On the Lives of the Caesars* (*De vita Caesarum*) in the following century; and Diogenes Laërtius wrote the *Lives and Opinions of Eminent Philosophers* in the third century. During the Middle Ages, lives of the saints were written with great regularity,

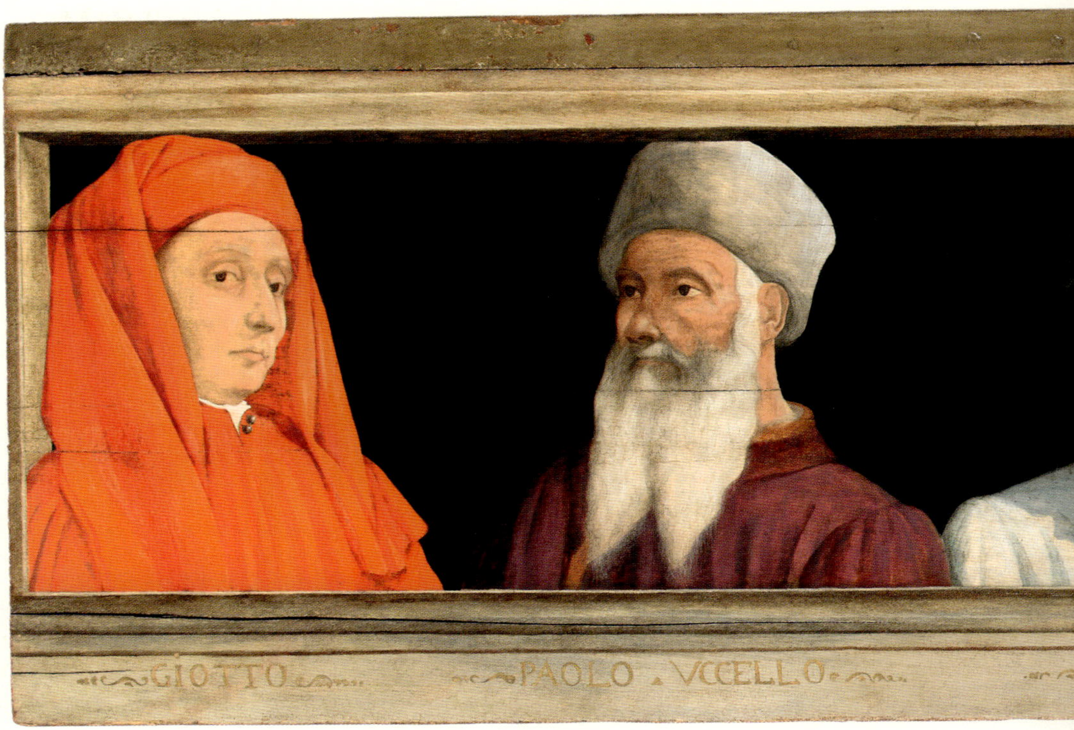

recording their miracles and piety, while rulers such as Charlemagne were sometimes afforded biographies (such as Einhard, *Vita Karoli Magni* from the first half of the ninth century). In the years immediately preceding Manetti's work on his *Life of Brunelleschi*, the papal librarian Bartolomeo Platina (1421–1481) completed his magisterial *Lives of the Popes* (*Vitæ Pontificum*, 1479), while in Florence, the bookseller Vespasiano da Bisticci (1421–1498) was engaged in writing – in the vernacular – 103 biographies of illustrious men (*Uomini illustri del secolo XV*), many of whom he knew or had known. There was nothing novel about writing the lives of famous individuals, especially if they were statesmen and princes, or saints or scholars. But that a biography should be dedicated to an architect was new, and testament to the changing status of the profession. Filippo Villani had written about certain painters in the late fourteenth century, but his comments were brief and they did not employ the painter's life to structure a discussion of his fame and work. Craftsmen were not generally the subject of biographies.

The identity of the author of the *Life of Brunelleschi* was once the cause of some debate. Most scholars would now agree that he was Antonio di Tuccio di Marabottino Manetti (who should not be confused with Antonio di Manetto Ciaccheri, nor with Giannozzo

Fig. 28
Portraits of Giotto, Uccello, Donatello, Manetti and Brunelleschi

Probably early 16th century, oil on wood, 65 × 213cm (25⅝ × 83⅞in). Musée du Louvre, Paris.

This unusual panel, which Vasari attributed to Uccello, shows Manetti in the company of Giotto, Uccello, Donatello and Brunelleschi. It is the visual corollary of a text such as Manetti's *Huomini singhularii*.

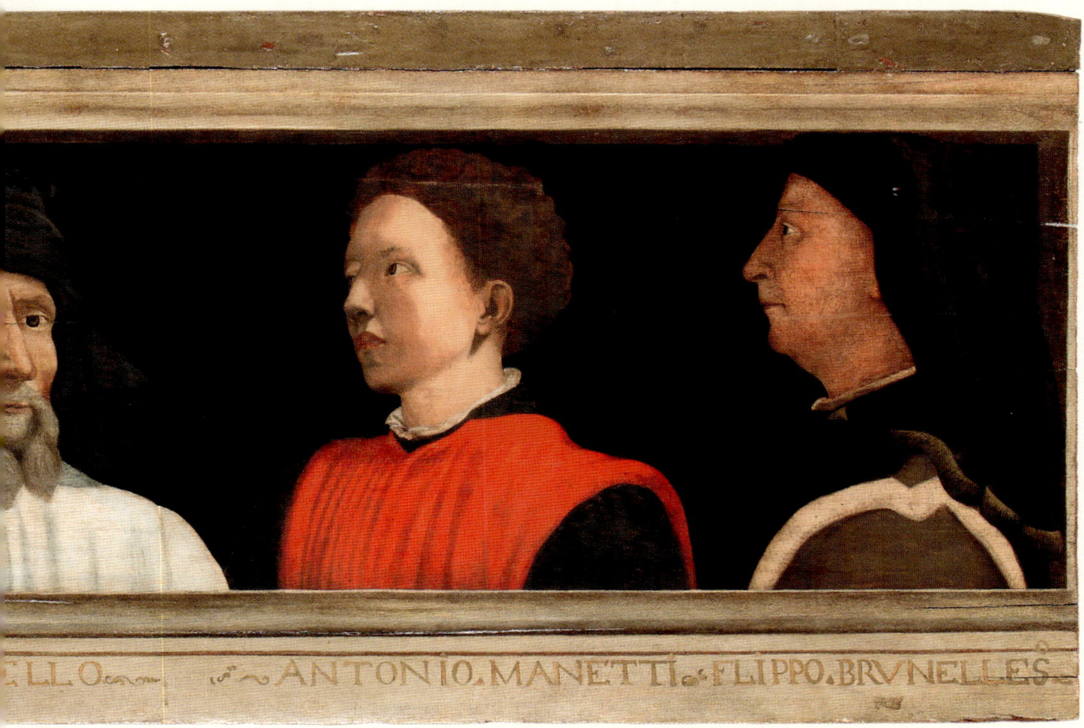

Manetti; FIG. 28). The attribution is based on a manuscript, preserved in the Biblioteca Nazionale in Florence, that would seem to be a draft in his hand; it was probably written in the 1480s, some 40 years after Brunelleschi's death. Manetti was a humanist with diverse interests, from mathematics to astronomy and the work of Dante, and a friend of such luminaries as Marsilio Ficino. Among his many civic duties, he appeared in 1491 on a committee that attempted to resolve the problem of the unfinished facade of the cathedral. In this capacity, he was described as '*civis et architectus*', citizen and architect, an indication if nothing else of the complex meaning of the word 'architect' in the fifteenth century.

Many of the texts Manetti wrote and copied have been preserved, and among them are biographies: a copy of Donato Acciaiuoli's life of Charlemagne and a vernacular version of Villani's *Book on the History of the City of Florence and its Famous Citizens* (*Liber de origine civitatis Florentiae et eiusdem famosis civibus*, 1381–2), which included notes on famous Florentines, among them painters. Manetti is also widely accepted as the author of 14 brief biographies of *Outstanding Men in Florence since 1400* (*Huomini singhularii in Firenze dal MCCCC innanzi*, after 1494), which continued where Villani's *De origine* had left off and included Brunelleschi among biographies of seven other artists (Donatello, Ghiberti, Masaccio, Fra Angelico, Fra Filippo Lippi, Uccello and Luca della Robbia), two theologians and four humanists. Finally, Manetti wrote the comic *Tale of the Fat*

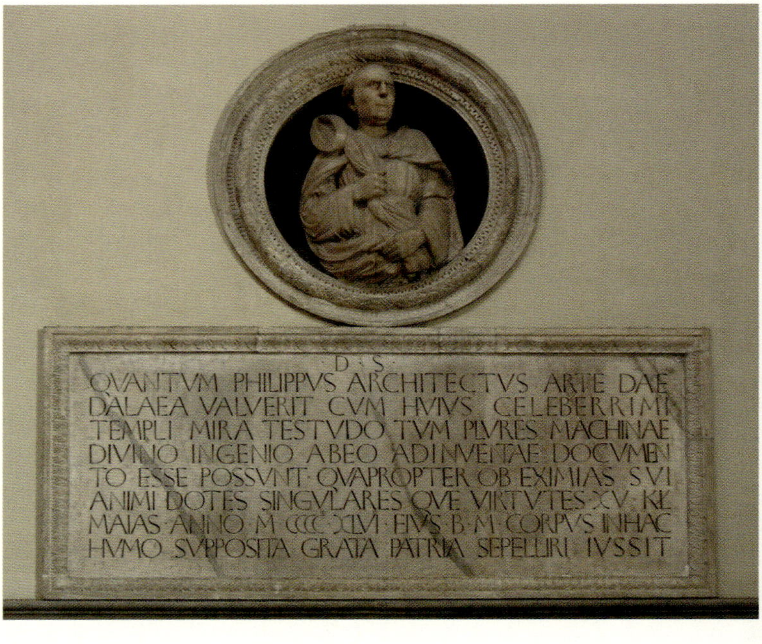

Fig. 29
Andrea di Lorenzo Cavalcanti, called **Il Buggiano**
Monument to Filippo Brunelleschi

1447, marble. Santa Maria del Fiore, Florence.

The bust was carved by Brunelleschi's adopted son. The epitaph was composed by Carlo Marsuppini, chancellor of the Republic, and reads: 'How valiant Filippo the Architect was in the Daedalian art as both the wonderful vault of the celebrated temple [i.e. the cupola of the cathedral] and the many machines invented by his divine genius document. Wherefore because of the excelling unique and virtuous gifts of his mind, a grateful country ordered his body to be buried in this grave on the Kalends of May in the year MCCCCLVI.'

Woodworker (*Novella del grasso legnaiuolo*), in which Brunelleschi and others played an elaborate practical joke on a carpenter, Manetto di Jacopo di Ammannatino, by robbing him of his identity and convincing him that he was, in fact, someone else called Matteo. The appalling *beffa* led not only to his imprisonment, but ultimately to such great shame that he moved to Hungary.

The text of Manetti's biography of Brunelleschi opens by addressing Girolamo (probably the poet Girolamo Benivieni), and by mentioning Brunelleschi's role in the *Novella del grasso legnaiuolo*, which precedes it in the autograph manuscript in the Biblioteca Nazionale. Girolamo, it seems, has asked several questions, prompted by Brunelleschi's bust and epitaph in the cathedral (FIG. 29): 'Why was he granted the great distinction of being buried in Santa Maria del Fiore and why was the marble bust, which they say was carved from life [*al naturale*], placed there in perpetual memory with such a splendid epitaph?' This point is crucial. The honour accorded to Brunelleschi of being buried in the cathedral, a distinction that was reserved for only the most distinguished servants of the state (such as their mercenary captains), attests to his status in the late fifteenth century and therefore to the very reason that someone might wish to write a biography of him. In Manetti's words, he was a man of 'great intellect, great resoluteness [*virtù*], and extraordinary talent [*ingegnio*]'.

It is precisely because of the credit due to Brunelleschi that Manetti wrote his account. He was concerned to protect Brunelleschi's '*fama*', his fame, and digresses more than once to malign those who have caused its flame to flicker. His explicit aim was to purge Brunelleschi's buildings of the errors (or '*manchamento*') that crept in through the work of those who finished them after his death, especially the carpenter and architect Antonio di Manetto Ciaccheri, who had taken over work on buildings such as San Lorenzo (he is never named explicitly, but the focus of the invective is clear). To do so, Manetti needed to establish Brunelleschi's 'correct' intentions, in the process of which he provided criteria by which to judge buildings and a vocabulary with which to describe them.

The text reveals something about Manetti's sources and the nature of his account: where did he come by this information, and what genre of literary text is this *vita*? He claims in the opening paragraph that he will answer Girolamo's questions with an account that he can 'read as a true narrative [*novella*] and not as a fable [*favola*]'. His account of Brunelleschi's earlier life tends to be less accurate than the descriptions of what happened to his buildings after his death. Brunelleschi died in 1446, when Manetti was in his early twenties.

After 40 or 50 years, Manetti's memory must have been cloudy, but it seems likely that colourful episodes, such as Brunelleschi's rivalry with Ghiberti, were remembered from conversations with Brunelleschi himself. Manetti's effective use of anecdote reminds us that he was the author of a *novella*, and at one point he even appropriates witticisms from Poggio Bracciolini's *Facezia* (1438–52). But Manetti was also an early adventurer in the archive. Again and again, he confirms facts from documents in the archive of the Opera del Duomo, or the register of the Priors, sometimes even citing them directly. He had also been an *operaio* at the Ospedale degli Innocenti in 1466, a fact that put him in a privileged position to obtain information about Brunelleschi's commission there. He certainly made good use of Brunelleschi's original design of the facade, which was then in the Audience Chamber of the Silk Guild (of which Manetti was a member), to point out differences between his original intention and the building as it had been completed. Ultimately, Manetti was meticulous in collecting evidence, and he even notes that he has seen all the works of art he mentions. Occasional embellishments or errors of fact are more readily explained as literary devices, a reminder that biography served a different purpose in Renaissance Florence from what it does today.

Manetti's biography reveals other debts, too. At a certain point, he breaks away from his account of Brunelleschi's life to address the subject of *all'antica* buildings, because, as he writes, 'not everyone has information about the origins of these buildings'. Manetti describes the origins of the 'craft of building' in crude huts of wood and dried grass, earth and dry stones, and then recounts how, with new material and technical discoveries – the use of bitumen and lime by means of fire, for instance – buildings improved. His history surveys several civilizations, none of which he would have known firsthand, from Egypt to the Tartars to diverse Asian kingdoms, until it arrives at Greece and the temple of Diana at Ephesus, which allowed him to discuss ratio and proportion, and their relationship to technical improvements (the plumb line, mason's level and T-square). Masters flourished, we are told, even more wondrously in Rome than in Greece, until it happened 'that with the decline in the empire, the architecture and the architects declined'. The revival began, for Manetti as for Vasari, with those Romanesque buildings, such as San Pier Scheraggio (which was largely demolished in the sixteenth century to make way for the Uffizi) and Santi Apostoli, that Manetti thought were the work of Charlemagne's architects, at an even earlier date. Again, as for Vasari, the revival happened only with Brunelleschi, whose manner is described as '*alla antica*' or '*alla Romana*', but not 'modern'. Instead, the architectural style that we would now call gothic, but which he called the '*modi Tedeschi*' or the 'German modes', was for him 'modern', a far cry from Vasari's '*maniera moderna*'.

Here, then, is a history of sorts within a biography. Manetti draws on Alberti, whom he mentions by name, and 'certain writers in pagan times', by which he meant Vitruvius. It was presumably from these two writers that he derived his architectural vocabulary. Manetti deploys a sophisticated lexicon, distinguishing between 'types of columns, bases, capitals, architraves, friezes, cornice and pediments' and their organization in different systems ('Ionic, Doric, Tuscan, Corinthian and Attic'), and also a language for 'the abutments and thrusts of buildings, [their] masses, lines and *invenzioni* according to and in relation with the function'.

Manetti also had a vocabulary for discussing images. It emerges in his account of the panel Brunelleschi prepared for the Baptistery commission, which is discussed in the next chapter. He was principally interested in formal qualities and how they had an effect on the bearing (or *attitudini*) of the figures. It is important to emphasize here the novelty of writing the biography of an artist or architect. Biography would become standard in the next century with Vasari, for whom it was didactic and exemplary. Each of his *Lives* functioned within a broader structure that gave shape to his understanding of history. Manetti's *Life* stands alone, accompanied only by his comic *novella*. While it might share some characteristics with Vasari's *Lives*, especially in the digression on *all'antica* architecture, Manetti's main purpose was to defend Brunelleschi's fame with evidence and *novella*-like anecdote.

Alberti's *On Painting*

If Ghiberti and Manetti both wrote about art in relation to artists and their works, Alberti initiated an entirely new form of art writing, one that established a theory of visual representation based on the study of optics, mathematics and ancient rhetoric. He wrote *On Painting* in both the Tuscan vernacular (*Della pittura*) and Latin (*De pictura*). Although scholars long thought that he wrote the Latin version first, more recent work has suggested that he began the treatise in the vernacular, even if not everyone is agreed. Alberti had completed a draft by August 1435, long before either Ghiberti or Manetti took up a pen.

Alberti's aims were different from those of Ghiberti and Manetti. By arguing that painting was the mistress of all the arts, he made a far bolder claim for the importance of his treatise than did either of theirs. In his own words, 'it is of little concern to us to discover the first painters or the inventors of the art, since we are not writing a history of painting like Pliny, but treating the art in an entirely new way.' Before *De pictura*, the language of art came from the workshop, and was thus limited to technical and practical terms. A good example can be found in the *Libro dell'arte* (literally, the 'book of craft'), a handbook written by the Florentine painter Cennino Cennini in about 1400, when he was in Padua. Cennino gave instructions for all kinds of manual practices, from gessoing a panel to painting it and applying gilding. But beyond a few brief comments about *fantasia* (poetic imagination), there was no vocabulary for artistic criticism in the *Libro dell'arte*. Alberti, instead, looked to ancient literary theory, especially Cicero and Quintilian's books on rhetoric, for concepts with which to theorize visual representation. We have him to thank that such words as 'composition' or 'invention' are now part of our daily discussion of art.

Alberti summarized the three-part structure of *De pictura* in the dedication of the vernacular text:

> You will see that there are three books. The first, which is entirely mathematical, shows how noble and beautiful art arises from roots within Nature herself. The second puts the art into the hands of the artist, distinguishes its parts and explains them all. The third instructs the artist how he may and should attain complete mastery and understanding of the art of painting.

Book I contains the much-studied instructions in linear perspective, the first of their kind in art theory. It includes fundamental ideas about the centric ray and the visual pyramid, to which we shall return in Chapter 7, and draws an analogy between the surface of a painting and an open window, a simile that has resonated down the centuries as a guiding principle of naturalism (it is worth pointing out, however, that Alberti evokes the 'window' as a practical tool for the painter, something like the 'veil' that he described in Book II; it was not intended as a metaphor for understanding the relationship between viewer and representation). The book is deeply indebted to the study of optics and geometry, known on the one hand from Euclid and Aristotle, and on the other from Arab scholars, al-Kindī (ca. 801–873) and especially Alhazen.

Book II opens with a justification of why painting is worthy of study, in which Alberti explores the *virtù* of painting. Thereafter he breaks it down into three parts: circumscription (outline or contour), composition and the reception of light (tone, or modelling in light and shade, and hue, or colour). Here, Alberti's debt to ancient rhetoric is most evident, and the number of references to ancient literature multiplies exponentially. The final book, book III, is the shortest, and the one in which Alberti's pedagogical aims are most apparent. He explains the purpose and requirements of the painter as follows: he must be wise and learned in the liberal arts, keeping the company of poets and intellectuals; he must have *virtù* if he is to achieve fame and avoid the vicissitudes of fortune; but he must also create worthy inventions, forever taking nature as his guide.

Alberti's audience is hard to determine. Who was this polymath who was well versed in humanist Latin and had grappled with Euclid and Arab science, but also dabbled in drawing and painting? The dedication of the vernacular text, from which Alberti's words were quoted above, was addressed to Brunelleschi and mentions Ghiberti, della Robbia, Donatello and Masaccio, whom he praised for their talent ('*ingegno*') and celebrated as worthy of the ancients. Most of them were at work on the cathedral as it neared completion; the only one not so (Masaccio) was also the only painter. The fact

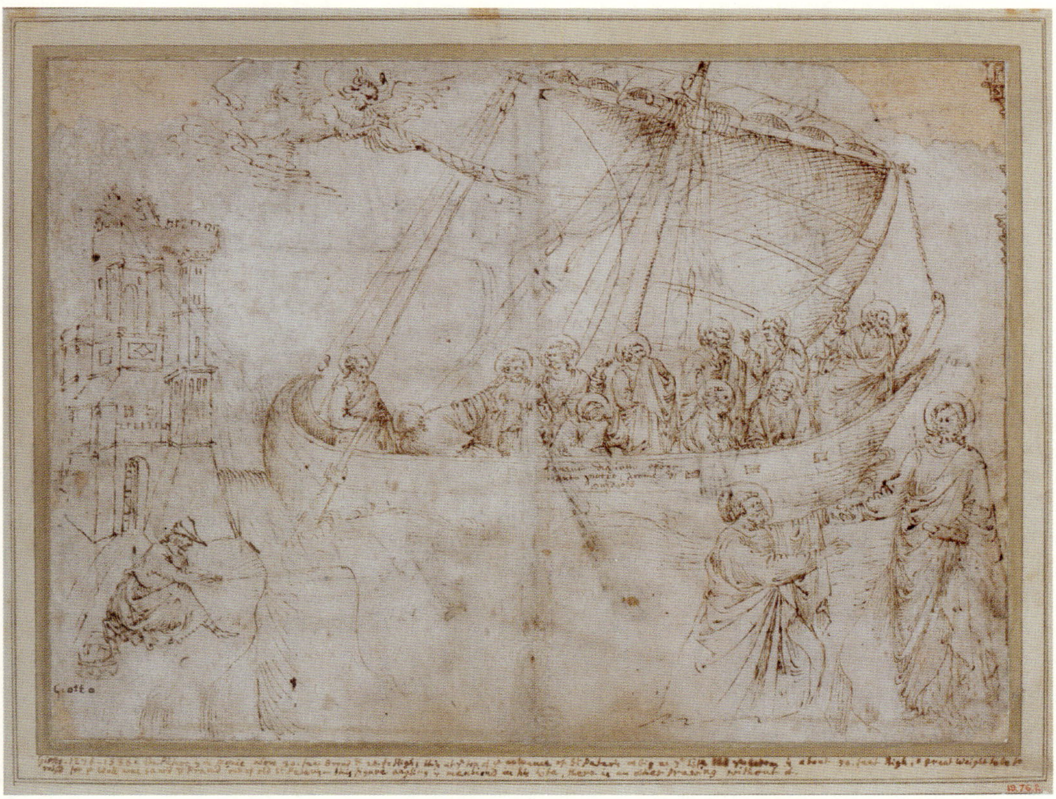

Fig. 30
Parri Spinelli,
after **Giotto**
Navicella

ca. 1420, pen and ink on paper, 27.5 × 39cm ($10^{13}/_{16}$ × $15^{3}/_{8}$in). Metropolitan Museum of Art, New York. Hewitt Fund, 1917 (19.76.2).

Giotto's original mosaic was in the courtyard of Old St Peter's in Rome, and survives only in a very compromised state. It is known from drawings, such as this one, which once belonged to Vasari.

that it was written in the vernacular suggests that the treatise was intended for these artists and craftsmen, but when it is compared to the earlier *Libro dell'arte*, Alberti's practical advice is limited. Even if he claims to write as a painter, there is little more than the instructions on how to use a 'veil' or 'intersection' as a means of tracing nature. The treatise does not appear to have circulated much among artists, either. But three manuscripts of the vernacular version survive today, and only one of them, in the Biblioteca Nazionale, contains the

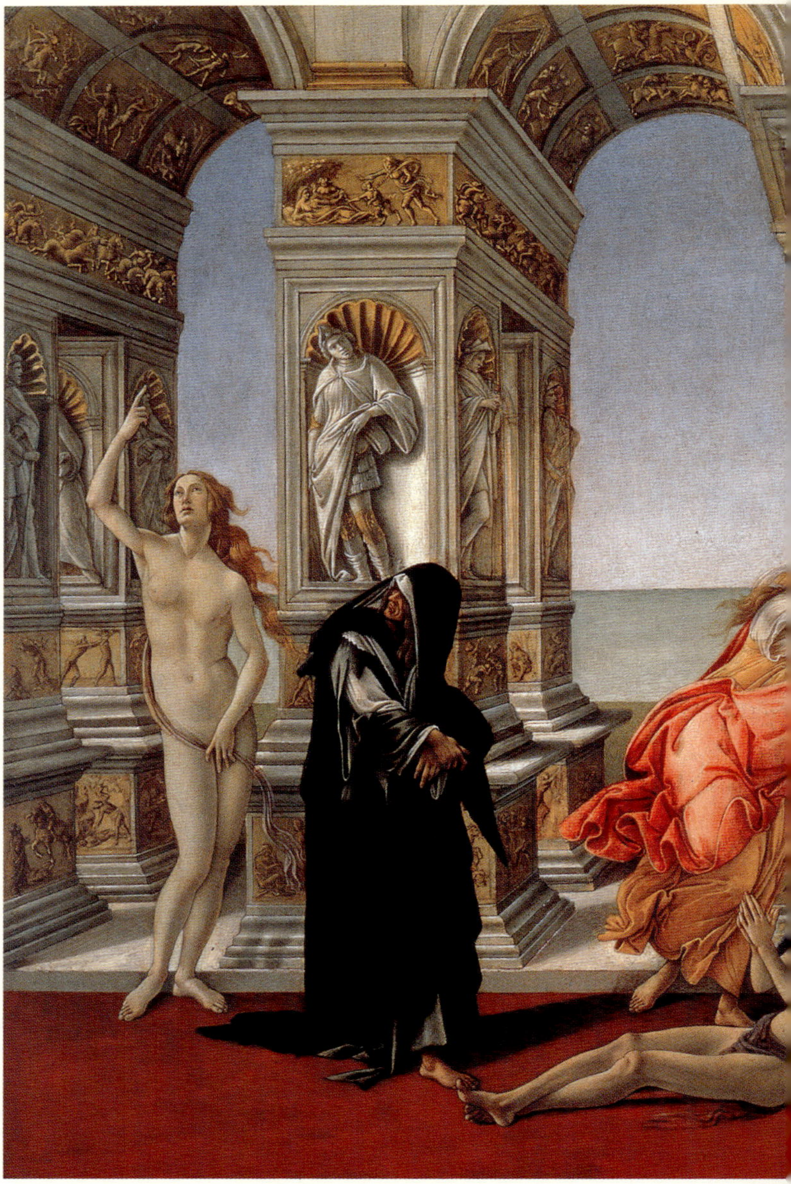

Fig. 31
Sandro Botticelli
Calumny of Apelles

ca. 1494, tempera on panel, 62 × 91 cm (24⅜ × 35⅞ in). Galleria degli Uffizi, Florence.

Alberti illustrated his point that invention would give pleasure with Lucian's description of a lost painting of *Calumny* by Apelles. Half a century after Alberti wrote *De pictura*, Botticelli attempted to recreate the painting.

dedication to Brunelleschi, unlike the 21 surviving versions of the Latin manuscript. Indeed, the vernacular version does not seem to have been widely known until it was printed in the nineteenth century (sixteenth-century vernacular versions are a translation of the Latin, not a printing of Alberti's first version).

If, instead, we return to the vernacular dedication, and the explanation of the structure of the treatise, another audience becomes apparent. Alberti borrowed the three-part division of his text

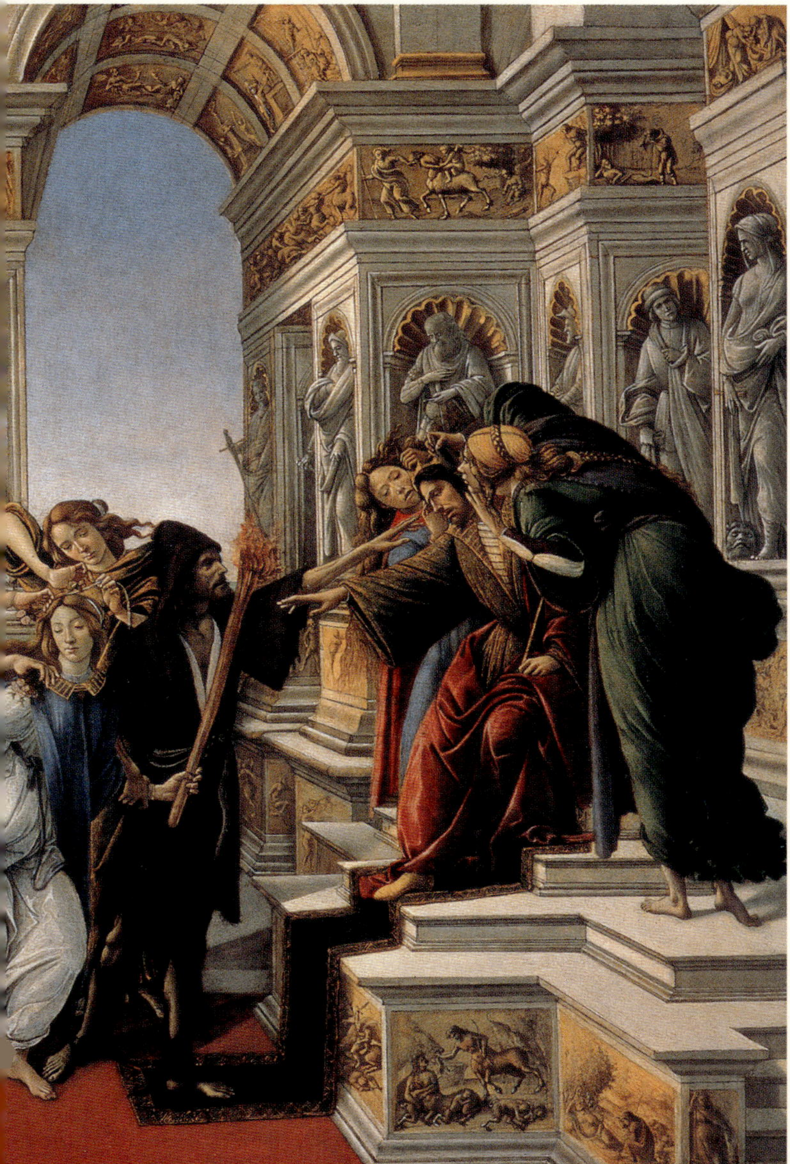

– into the basics of the art, their application in practice and the results they achieve – from Quintilian's *Institutio oratoria* (*Institutes of Oratory*), an ancient textbook on rhetoric written in about 95 CE. There is every reason to assume that Alberti expected his reader to recognize the debt, and he draws attention to the study of letters, to learned men and to scholars, in his dedication of the Latin version to Gianfrancesco Gonzaga, Marquis of Mantua (a dedication that is repeated in 14 of the 21 manuscripts). It is perhaps in the context of humanist education in Mantua – especially that of La Giocosa, the famous school run by Vittorino da Feltre – that *De pictura* finds its most convincing context. That said, it was not written solely for the delectation or pedagogy of humanists and rhetoricians, as the dedication to Brunelleschi makes clear, but neither was it instructional in the vein of the *Libro dell'arte*. The difference is captured well in a phrase Alberti uses towards the end of Book II, in a discussion of the reception of light: 'So now we shall speak of the [kinds of colours], not after the manner of the architect Vitruvius as to where excellent red ochre and the best colours are to be found, but how selected and well-compounded colours should be arranged together in painting.' Alberti was interested not in practical knowledge, born from experience of where pigments might be found, say, or how they should be employed on the panel, but rather in what resulted from the application of that knowledge and how it could be united into a series of precepts, or rules. *De pictura* is perhaps best understood as a bridge between the workshop, the intellectual discussions of the *studia humanitatis* and the scientific study of optics and the eye.

Alberti introduced several important concepts into nascent art theory (such as the visual pyramid, the centric ray and the idea of painting as analogous to a window), to which we will return in later chapters, but '*historia*' (or '*istoria*' in the vernacular) deserves attention here. The word means both 'story' and 'history', and encapsulates many of the themes addressed in the previous chapter. However, Alberti used it in a manner that is true to neither of these translations. 'History painting' is a later idea, although one that develops out of Alberti's *historia*, and 'narrative' is not entirely true to his concept either. It is perhaps best to explain it with the examples that he himself used. The word first crops up in relation to his definition of composition: 'The great work of the painter is the *historia*', which is composed on bodies; 'part of the body is the member, and part of the member is the surface'. It is, in other words, a figurative composition. 'From the composition of surfaces,' he continued, 'arises that elegant harmony and grace in bodies, which they call beauty.'

Alberti praised an *historia* in Rome, a sculpted relief (and not a painting) that showed the dead Meleager (it is now identified with a sarcophagus lid that is only known from a photograph taken in the early twentieth century). What impressed Alberti was how every limb strained to support the weight of the dead body, while Meleager was evidently lifeless to the viewer. From it, he drew a lesson about appropriateness: 'In every painting the principle should be observed that all the members should fulfil their function according to the action performed, in such a way that not even the smallest limb fails to play its appropriate part.' At its core, this passage is about what is appropriate, and relates to ideas of decorum that underscore much of Alberti's idea of beauty and the praiseworthy *historia*.

Decorum re-emerged in Alberti's discussion of the depiction of emotion. 'Everything the people in the painting do among themselves, or perform in relation to the spectators, must fit together and explain the *historia*,' he explained, taking Giotto's *Navicella* as an exemplar. 'They also praise in Rome the boat in which our Tuscan painter Giotto represented the eleven disciples struck with fear and wonder at the sight of their colleague walking on water, each showing such clear signs of his agitation in his face and entire body that their individual emotions are discernible in every one of them' (FIG. 30). But emotion should not only be appropriate – decorous – it should also be varied, another idea that Alberti appropriated from ancient literary theory (*varietas*). Finally, it should give pleasure through its invention (*inventio*), one of Cicero's five divisions of rhetoric, the others being arrangement (*dispositio*), expression (*elocutio*), memory (*memoria*) and delivery (*pronuntiatio*). And, for pleasing inventions, the painter should consult literary men (FIG. 31). For, as Alberti says, if the '*historia* seizes the imagination when described in words, how much beauty and pleasure do you think it presented in the actual painting of [an] excellent artist?'

The idea and importance of *historia* have resonated down the ages, much as *De pictura* itself has done. In the pages that follow we shall come back to Alberti's slim volume time and time again. Its impact on the art of his own time is debated, and rightly so, since few painters seem to have read it, but its importance as a theoretical text is beyond question. Alberti transformed writing about art.

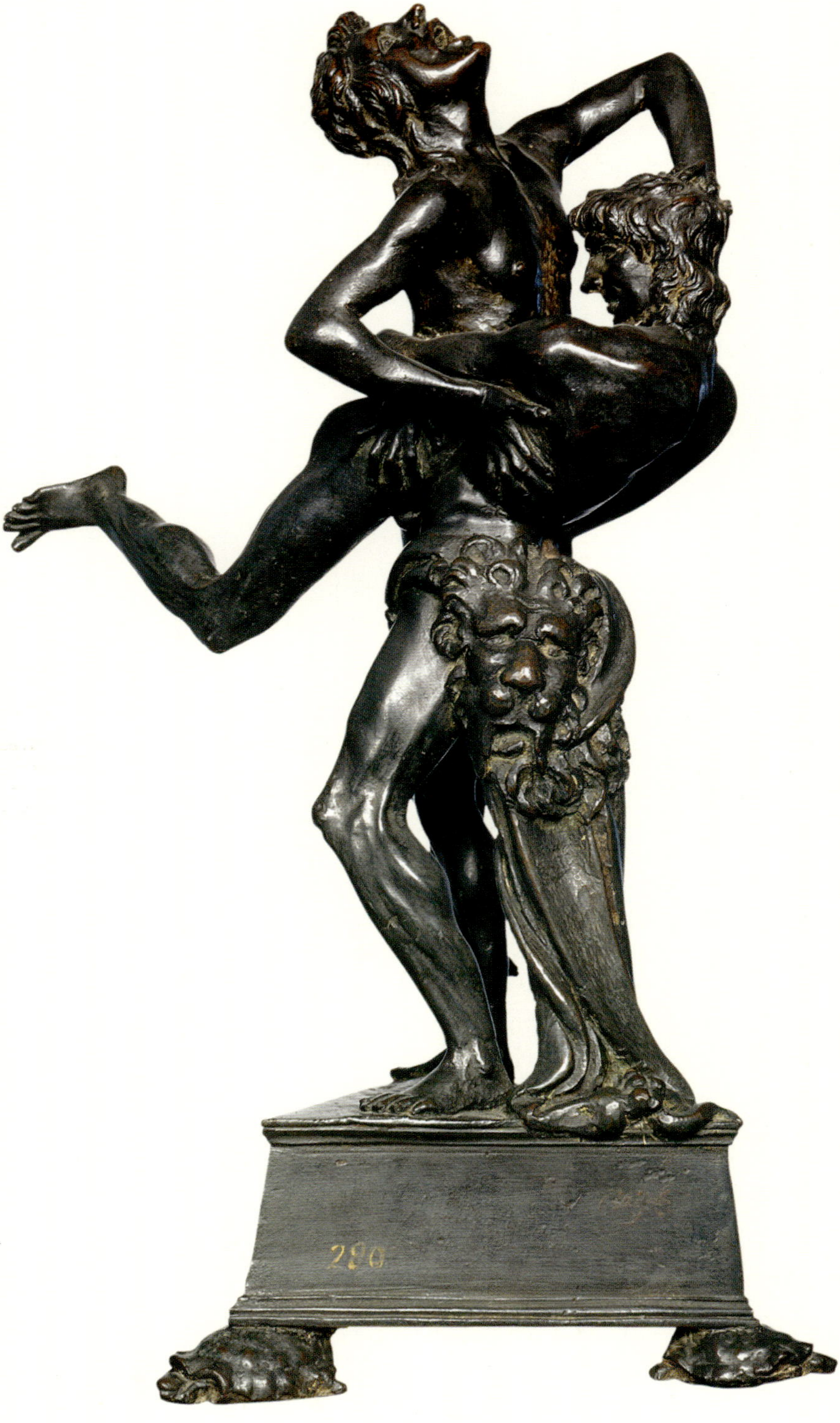
280

4

Guilds, Confraternities and Competition

Vasari, in telling the story of his early life, recalled how he benefited from competition with his peers: 'In those times, the competition between my contemporaries and companions, many of whom have since become most excellent in our art, was also of great help to me.' In his opinion, competition drove progress in art and could only be of benefit, provided it did not turn into envy, as in the case of Andrea del Castagno, who – Vasari believed erroneously – had murdered Domenico Veneziano out of jealousy. Themes of rivalry that run through Vasari's *Lives* rework ideas from classical antiquity, which he knew from Pliny's account of the way artists achieved fame though competition. But competition was more than a literary device; it was also a fact of the Florentine marketplace. By the fourteenth century, competitions had become standard for architectural projects, especially those associated with the nave of the cathedral, initiated between 1355 and 1370. Competitiveness drove up quality, pitting artisans against one another as they vied for work.

Competition was exploited by corporate patrons, who are the subject of this chapter, far more than by their private counterparts. Of course, private patrons benefited from competitiveness among

Fig. 32
Antonio del Pollaiuolo
Hercules and Antaeus

ca. 1470, bronze, 46cm (18⅛in) high. Museo Nazionale del Bargello, Florence.

artists, but they did not employ competitions as systematically as institutions. We like to think that the private patron entered into a sustained exchange with an artist over time, as was the case with Cosimo de' Medici and Donatello, or Lorenzo de' Medici and the sculptor Bertoldo di Giovanni. After all, is it not this long-standing relationship, built in part on trust, that distinguishes private patronage from the single purchase? Competition, by contrast, delivers the one-off: it is a means of achieving the best deal, qualitatively or economically, for the present purpose. We must now turn our attention to institutions and their artists, especially such figures as Ghiberti, who built a career on corporate patronage. Guilds, as we shall discover, not only oversaw artistic practice, but were also patrons of it.

Guilds

Medieval guilds were associations of tradesmen or merchants, who banded together to regulate quality, working conditions and membership of their profession, craft or *arte* (we shall return to the meaning of this last term in the conclusion). Guilds controlled behaviour within the marketplace, setting down rules for production, trade and labour, and overseeing the processes by which individuals were apprenticed. They matriculated 'masters' into their ranks and saw to their social and spiritual needs. Elsewhere, whether in the Italian peninsula or more widely across Europe, guilds were the basic organizational unit for most local economies long into the sixteenth century. Artists, divided according to craft, belonged to specialized guilds, so that there were separate guilds for painters, stoneworkers, goldsmiths and so forth.

The situation in Florence was different and in many ways unique. With the establishment of a mercantile republic in the late thirteenth century, a Priorato delle arti (Government of the Guilds), guild membership became an essential requirement for entry into government and its various advisory councils. Legislation passed in 1320 limited the number of guilds and divided them into six *arti maggiori* (major guilds) and fourteen *arti minori* (minor guilds). Of the nine priors that constituted the Florentine Signoria, six were elected from the major guilds and only two from the minor ones. Florence's richest and most influential men belonged to these major guilds, which oversaw the most profitable industries – the cloth and wool trade, as well as international banking and monetary exchange – that accounted for most foreign capital that flowed into the city. The minor guilds included many in the artisanal classes, whose labour met the needs of the internal market for goods and services. The poorest of the poor, the *popolo minuto*, were denied guild membership and thus political representation, a situation that had prompted the Ciompi (dyers, shirtmakers and wool workers) to revolt in 1378. They were briefly successful in creating a guild for themselves and in achieving political recognition, but by 1382 an oligarchy of powerful families had re-established power and all but squashed them.

With the exception of painters, most of the artisans who worked as artists were members of the minor guilds. From 1315, painters belonged to the Arte dei Medici e Speziali (Doctors and Apothecaries), a major guild, ostensibly because they acquired their pigments from apothecaries. Their membership was determined by the materials they used. Sculptors, who carved in wood and stone, matriculated into the Arte dei Maestri di Pietra e Legname (Masters of Stone and Wood), but furniture-makers, who likewise worked in wood, were represented by the Arte dei Legnaioli (Carpenters). Carving a wooden crucifix for a church was distinguished from joining a *cassone* (chest). In this instance, a commonality of material was insufficient to justify membership of the same guild, when their products were so different. Perhaps the Masters of Stone and Wood are better understood as construction workers, since many were masons, working on major sites, such as the cathedral or any of the many palace projects of the period. Architects, who would probably not have identified themselves as such during the fifteenth century, often began their careers as masons and were frequently members of this guild, even if their most celebrated exponent, Brunelleschi, registered for the Arte della Seta (the Guild of Silk Weavers and Merchants) in 1393 and matriculated into it in 1404. The Silk Guild was sometimes known as Por Santa Maria on account of its location, and it included goldsmiths and other metalworkers among its members. Ghiberti was a member of this guild, as were several other bronze sculptors. Sculptors could, in short, find themselves in any of three guilds, the Masters of Stone and Wood, the Carpenters or the Silk Guild, a fact that suggests a distinction between their professions that has become flattened over time.

From the example of sculptors, it might seem that guild membership in Florence was highly specialized and focused, with crafts subdivided by material, technique and object type. In fact, the opposite was true. One of the consequences of politicizing guild membership, and of limiting their number to 21, was that the guilds became conglomerates of different trades and professions, as they vied for political representation. It comes as some surprise to find Dante's name among those matriculating into the guild of Doctors and

Apothecaries in 1297. Dante was many things, but he was neither of those! In Florence, guilds did not represent a single trade or craft, as in other cities. Only the Arte dei Mercatanti di Calimala (who oversaw the international trade in cloth), the Cambio (Bankers), Giudici e Notai (Judges and Notaries) and Vaiai e Pellicciai (Furriers and Skinners) were relatively homogeneous. Most Florentine guilds assimilated members from other trades and effectively created a two-tier membership between those who constituted its core (or original) business and those who were members of the supplementary crafts appended to it at some time in its history. This point is well illustrated by painters, who were not the core members of the Doctors and Apothecaries, but rather constituted a separate *membrum*, or strand, within the guild, much like the saddle-makers (*sellai*), who were also counted among their number.

As guilds could represent more than one profession, so artisans could belong to more than one guild. Ghiberti matriculated into the Silk Guild as a goldsmith (*aurifex*) on 3 August 1409, but on 20 December 1426 he also became a Master of Stone and Wood, matriculating as a carver (*sculptor* in Latin). Such freedom, which was not always afforded artisans in other cities, created the circumstances whereby Florentine artists could work in more than one medium, and provide designs for many more. In Bruges, a sculptor could not polychrome his sculpture, since that was a right reserved by the painters' guild for their members. In Florence, a sculptor was free to paint his work, and if he turned to a painter to do so, as in the many cases of Neri di Bicci being called on to polychrome sculpture, it was for reasons of expedience or skill. It is doubtful that a *maestro di disegno* (master of drawing and design) such as Antonio del Pollaiuolo could have flourished without a guild system as lax as that in Florence. How else could he have worked as a goldsmith, bronze-caster, woodcarver and painter (FIGS. 32, 33)?

However, it is well not to overstate the case. Brunelleschi was unexpectedly gaoled in 1434, having worked for many years as a mason without becoming a master in Stone and Wood. And, for all that the Florentine guilds did not interfere in the economic and social activities of their members (at least by comparison with those of other European cities), they nonetheless wrote statutes and notionally regulated the trades they oversaw. Among such statutes were rules that pertained directly to artists, which can be exemplified by those applicable to painters. The Doctors and Apothecaries drew up statutes in Latin in about 1313 and again in 1349, when they were accompanied by a vernacular translation. Artisans, including painters, could not practise their craft until they had been judged and matriculated into the guild, at which point they must pay an entrance fee (*tassa d'entratura*). Evidently such regulations were not always followed. Botticelli did not join the Doctors and Apothecaries until 1499, but he never suffered from any lack of work.

In 1349, among the many regulations that applied to all members of the guild, were two that pertained specifically to painters. One reads:

> It is ordered and ruled that if any painter were to paint any room [*sala* or *camera*], ceiling, support, wall, or any other place, and that the payment for that painting were to be a matter of dispute between the painter and him that had ordered such painting, then the consuls of the said guild are required to elect one or more painters, … [who] should decide and conclude this issue by declaring what is due to this painter for such painting.

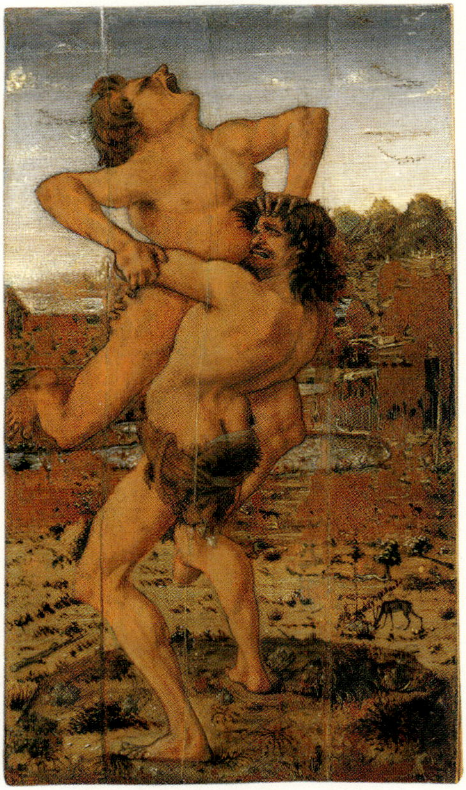

Fig. 33
Antonio del Pollaiuolo
Hercules and Antaeus

ca. 1460, tempera on panel, 16 × 9cm (6¼ × 3½in). Galleria degli Uffizi, Florence.

This small panel is a reduced version of canvases painted by Pollaiuolo for the Palazzo Medici in 1460. He reused the same pose, but in bronze, in Fig. 32.

From such rubrics, it is evident that the guild had a broad understanding of what constituted a painter or *dipintore*, including many whom we would now call decorators or whitewashers. It is also clear that one of the guild's primary roles was in settling disputes. The guild functioned as a court, deciding disagreements that could be escalated to the Mercanzia, or merchants' tribunal, that oversaw all the guilds. There is irony in the fact that Botticelli's first documented commission, the figure of *Fortitude* (now in the Uffizi), was executed for this tribunal in 1470, at which date he does not appear to have been a member of any guild.

The brief regulations set down for painters proved insufficient to their needs, and amendments were passed during the fifteenth and early sixteenth centuries. In 1470, rules for 'valuing painting, and against scheming to take work from other painters' were introduced. In 1506 it was decreed that members were 'not to paint sacred images where you do bad things', which specifically prohibited painters from realizing figures of 'our Lord or our Lady or any saint, male or female, in any location … that is used to piss or do other bad things [*bruttura*]'. The very fact that these revisions, clarifications and corrections continued suggests that the guild had not lost its power completely. All the same, the statutes were often vague, and much valuable guild legislation was incorporated into the communal statutes in

1415, rendering their regulation somewhat redundant. Such statutory oversight was matched by the increasing importance that was given to the Mercanzia as a court, especially in the later part of the fifteenth century. Artisans, in other words, had access to a judicial system beyond the reach of their guild, which consequently did not need to interfere quite as much in their activities as in other cities.

Compagnia di San Luca

One particular amendment to the statutes of the Doctors and Apothecaries, approved in 1406, is worth exploring further. It obliged all painters to attend mass at Santa Maria Nuova at least twice a month as members of the Compagnia di San Luca (Confraternity of Saint Luke). They were also obliged to pay 10 *soldi* annually, on pain of a fine. The brethren of the Compagnia di San Luca were in large part artists, especially painters. The confraternity is sometimes mistaken for a guild – especially since artists' guilds in Northern Europe (in Antwerp, for example) were often dedicated to St Luke, who was thought to have painted the Virgin – but it was not. It attended to the social and spiritual needs of its members, a role that was generally taken on by guilds elsewhere. Confraternities were lay organizations, often attached to religious orders, that performed acts of mercy and charity as diverse as helping the poor or accompanying the condemned to the scaffold. They were divided into those that sung lauds (*laudesi*) and those in which the brethren also flagellated together (*disciplinati*). The confreres met frequently, often to perform paraliturgical ceremonies, and sometimes to parade through the streets, hooded and anonymous, as part of a yearly cycle of religious festivities.

The Compagnia di San Luca was no different. In common with other confraternities, it drew up '*capitoli e ordinamenti*' (chapters and ordinances, or regulations), the oldest of which survive in a vernacular version of 1386, even though they were probably first written in the 1340s. They were revised in 1395. They provide essential information about the history of the confraternity, noting that it was formed in the year 'XXXVIIII' (most likely 1339), on 17 October, the feast of St Luke. The *ordinamenti* begin with instructions for the religious life of its members, and then move on to their governance. For example, the confraternity had four *capitani* (captains), four *consiglieri* (advisors) and two *camerlighi* (treasurers). Unlike the guild, it was not concerned with professional conduct. Just how different the two institutions were can be appreciated from the following requirement:

Competition

From what we have seen of guilds so far, it might seem that they had very little effect on the visual arts. Notionally, they regulated the market, but in practice artisans formed companies, or took apprentices, according to their own commercial needs. Competition, rather than guild regulation, was thus an important driver of the market. In other European cities, medieval guilds typically limited the degree of competition among their members. As such, they were a hindrance to the development of pre-Industrial capitalism and a spanner in the works of a free market. But, as we have seen, these restrictions were not characteristic of Florence, where the guilds, although politically significant, appear to have exercised little control over the behaviour of their members. And when acting as patrons, they actively promoted competition, rather than suppressing it.

Having examined the institutional organization of the arts, we must now turn our attention to how those corporate institutions employed competition in the works of art they commissioned. They used the mechanism in different ways, many of which are exemplified in sculptural commissions for the Baptistery, cathedral and Orsanmichele in the first few decades of the fifteenth century (a pattern that would repeat itself in the period between 1494 and 1512, when the sculptural programme on the Baptistery again attracted attention). It was at these sites that new styles emerged in the second decade of the fifteenth century, one informed by classical antiquity, the other by Northern European art (the so-called International Gothic). Competition, then, played an important role in stylistic development. All these commissions involved guilds in some capacity, and they can be divided into competitions to win work; competitiveness between artists working on the same commission; and rivalry between their patrons. Naturally, they all overlap, but we shall examine each in turn.

Around 1401, the Calimala ran a competition for a new pair of bronze doors for the Baptistery, which was ultimately awarded to Ghiberti (*see* FIG. 15). The guild had long administered the fabric of the building, assisted by two subcommittees: the Officiali del Musaico (Mosaic Officials) and the Opera di San Giovanni (Board of Works of the Baptistery). The records of the Calimala were lost to fire in the eighteenth century, and, although some were copied in the seventeenth century by the bibliophile and scholar Carlo Strozzi, we have no documentation that pertains directly to the competition. Instead, our chief source is Ghiberti's own account, in the autobiographical section of his *Commentaries*. It is necessarily biased, and differs somewhat from the account provided by Manetti in the *Life of Brunelleschi*, but it does provide crucial information about how the competition was run.

Ghiberti takes up the story in about 1400, when he was called to Florence by his friends because the governors of the Baptistery were looking for well-qualified masters to make a test piece in order to win the commission, which he describes as a battle (*combattimento*). They were each to make the same scene, the sacrifice of Isaac. Ghiberti named the other competitors: Simone da Colle, about whom little is known; Niccolò di Luca Spinelli (1397–1477); Francesco di Valdambrino (1363–1435); Niccolò di Piero Lamberti (ca. 1370–probably before 1434); Brunelleschi; and Jacopo della Quercia. At least two of them were Sienese, and another Aretine. 'We were six to take the test,' wrote Ghiberti, excluding himself from the number, 'a test which was a demonstration of a large part of the art of sculpture.'

Evidently each contestant was given the necessary bronze, which Ghiberti correctly calls *ottone* or brass, in the form of plates or panels (*tavole*). Manetti was more explicit than Ghiberti about how the process worked: 'The following method was employed to choose the best one,' he wrote. 'They selected the shape of one of the compartments from the bronze doors that had been made by non-Florentine masters in the last century … Each of them was given a scene to sculpt in bronze within such a form with the principal intention of commissioning the doors to the one who came out the best in the aforesaid test.' The shape of the panel was prescribed and based on the quatrefoil shape employed on the previous set of doors, cast by Andrea Pisano in the fourteenth century. Likewise the scene was agreed in advance. We can be relatively certain that they also determined the characters, since the two competition reliefs that survive – those by Ghiberti and Brunelleschi (FIGS. 34, 35) – contain an identical cast of characters and animals, which are not typically found in representations of the sacrifice of Isaac. The guild needed to create a level playing field if they were going to judge the relative merits of each panel. They therefore established criteria that would enable them to compare the panels.

Ghiberti also provides a sense of who was involved in adjudicating the competition:

> The palm of victory was conceded to me by all the experts [*periti*] and by all those who took the test with me. The glory was conceded to me universally, without exception. Everyone felt I had gone beyond the others in that time, without a single exception, with

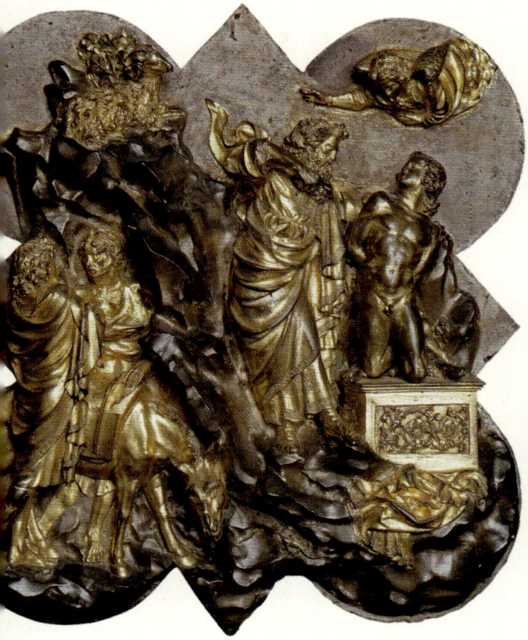

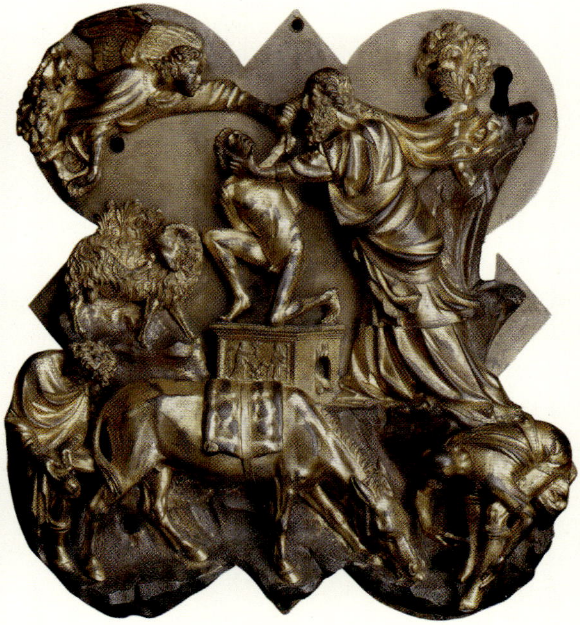

> a great consultation and examination by learned men [*uomini dotti*]. The board of the temple [*operai di detto governo*] wanted to have their decisions written by their own hand; they were very expert men [*homini molti periti*], including painters and sculptors in gold and silver and marble. The judges [*giudicatori*] were thirty-four, counting those of the city and the surrounding areas; the endorsement in my favour of the victory was given by all, and by the consuls and board and the whole body of the merchants' guild [*e consoli et operai et tutto il corpo dell'arte mercatoria*], which has the temple of St John the Baptist in its charge.

Fig. 34 (left)
Lorenzo Ghiberti
The Sacrifice of Isaac

1401, partly gilt bronze, 44 × 38 × 10.5cm ($17\frac{3}{8}$ × 15 × $4\frac{1}{8}$in). Museo Nazionale del Bargello, Florence.

Fig. 35 (right)
Filippo Brunelleschi
The Sacrifice of Isaac

1401, partly gilt bronze, 41.5 × 39.4 × 9cm ($16\frac{3}{8}$ × $15\frac{1}{2}$ × $3\frac{1}{2}$in). Museo Nazionale del Bargello, Florence.

In essence, this procedure was no different from what had become routine on the construction sites of the cathedral over the past century, even if the various committees and subcommittees might differ slightly in their composition and remit. A jury of 34 experts that found Ghiberti to be the victor was different from consuls of the Guild and the *operai* (as the members of an *opera*, or board of works, were called), to whom they had to submit a written report of their decision. This process established a pattern for competitions, so that when the Wood Guild wanted to commission a shrine for the remains of St Zenobius, to be housed in the cathedral (which they oversaw in much the same way as the Calimala looked after the Baptistery), they followed a similar procedure.

Fig. 36 (left)
Nanni di Banco
St Luke

1408–15, marble, 208cm (81⅞in) high. Museo dell'Opera del Duomo, Florence.

Fig. 37 (right)
Bernardo Ciuffagni
St Matthew

1410–15, marble, 224cm (88⅛in.) high. Museo dell'Opera del Duomo, Florence.

In the *Life of Brunelleschi*, Manetti confused the matter. He wrote that the commission had been awarded to Ghiberti and Brunelleschi together, but that Brunelleschi, indignant at the idea of partnership, had refused to collaborate, and so the officials decided on Ghiberti alone. On the whole, Manetti is less well informed about the competition than Ghiberti, and his account has been contested, even if it does give a good sense of the emotional stakes involved. Some scholars, however, have interpreted the survival of both Ghiberti and Brunelleschi's competition panels, and none of the other competitors', as compelling evidence that corroborates Manetti's tale. If Manetti was correct – and the evidence is too slight to resolve the issue either way – then the officials were hoping to keep the two goldsmiths in competition with each other right through the commission. As it turned out, the result of awarding the commission to a

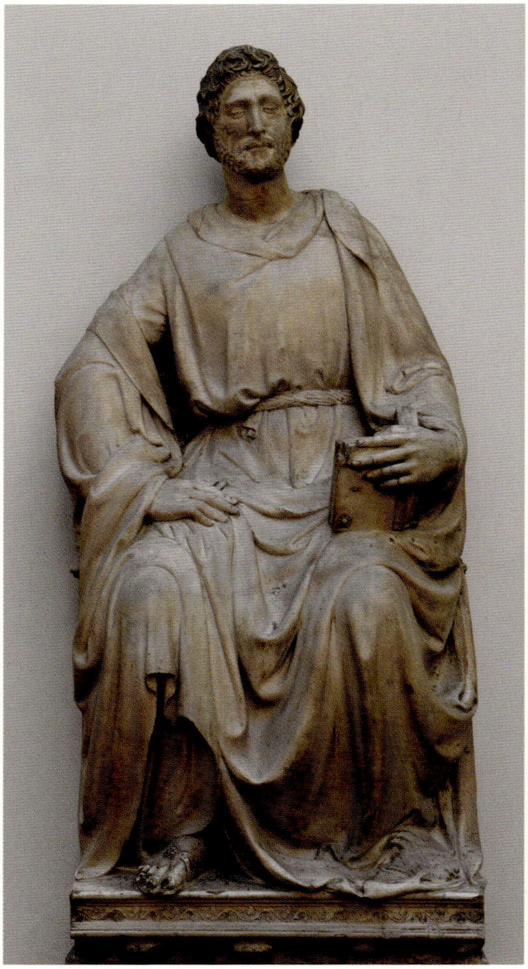

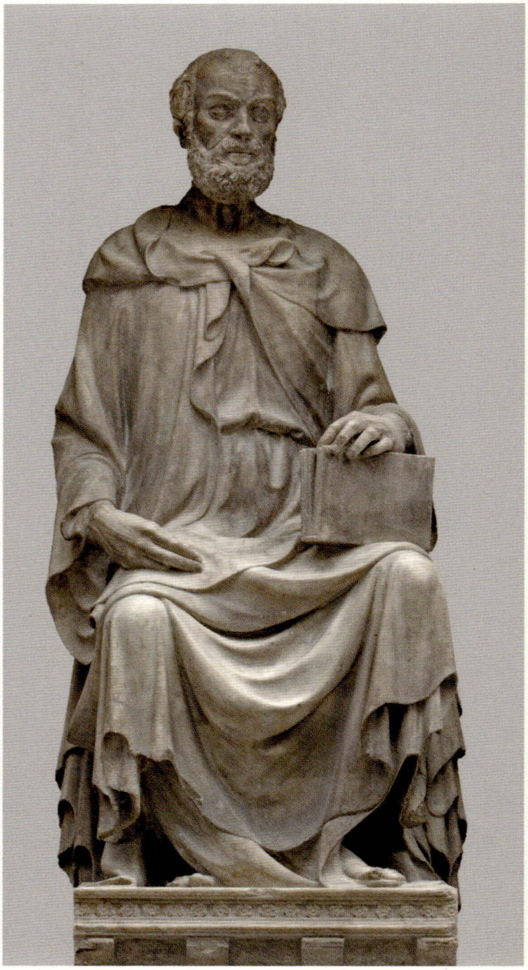

single craftsman was that he would no longer be compelled by competitiveness to produce the work on time. Of course, other factors would come into play, such as Ghiberti's reputation and his desire to earn new work on the back of the Baptistery commission. But the fact remains that although he signed a contract with the guild on 25 November 1403, followed by a revised contract on 1 June 1407, the north doors would not be hung until 1424, despite clauses intended to compel him to finish promptly.

A different approach was adopted by the Opera del Duomo (the board of works for the cathedral) when, only a few years later, the *operai* commissioned figures of the Evangelists for the facade of the cathedral. The sculptures survive today in the Cathedral Museum (FIGS. 36, 37, 38, 39), but they were originally destined for niches on either side of the main portal, where they can be seen in a drawing

Fig. 38 (left)
Donatello
St John the Evangelist

1408–15, marble, 210cm (82⅝in) high. Museo dell'Opera del Duomo, Florence.

Fig. 39 (right)
Niccolò di Pietro Lamberti
St Mark

1408–15, marble, 217cm (85⅜in). Museo dell'Opera del Duomo, Florence.

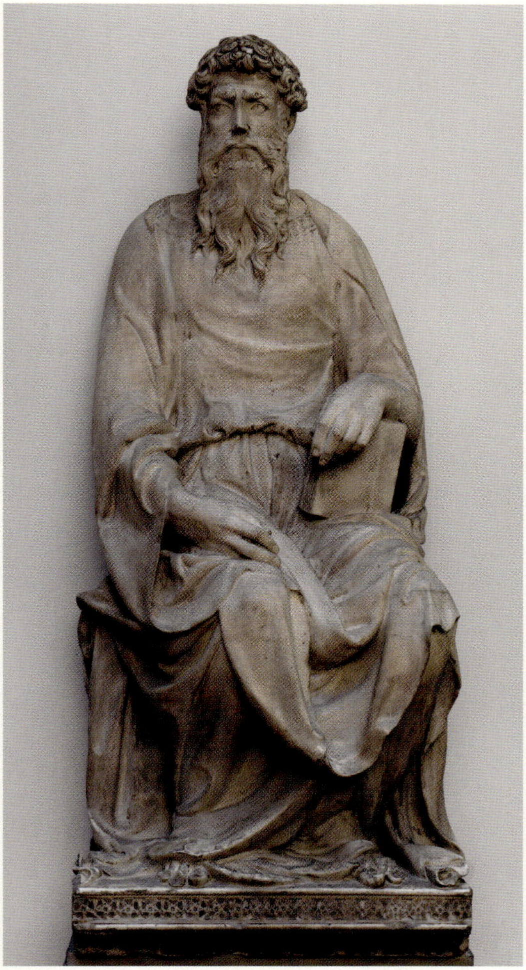

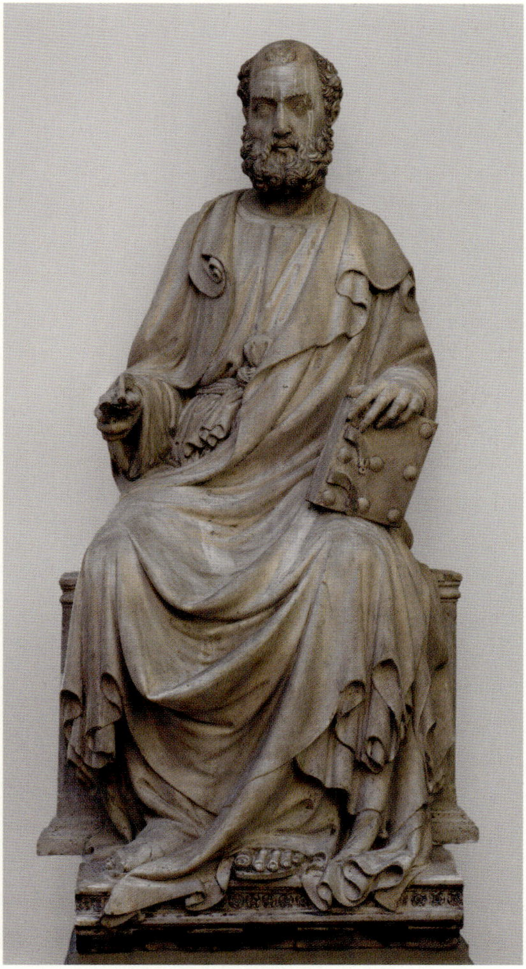

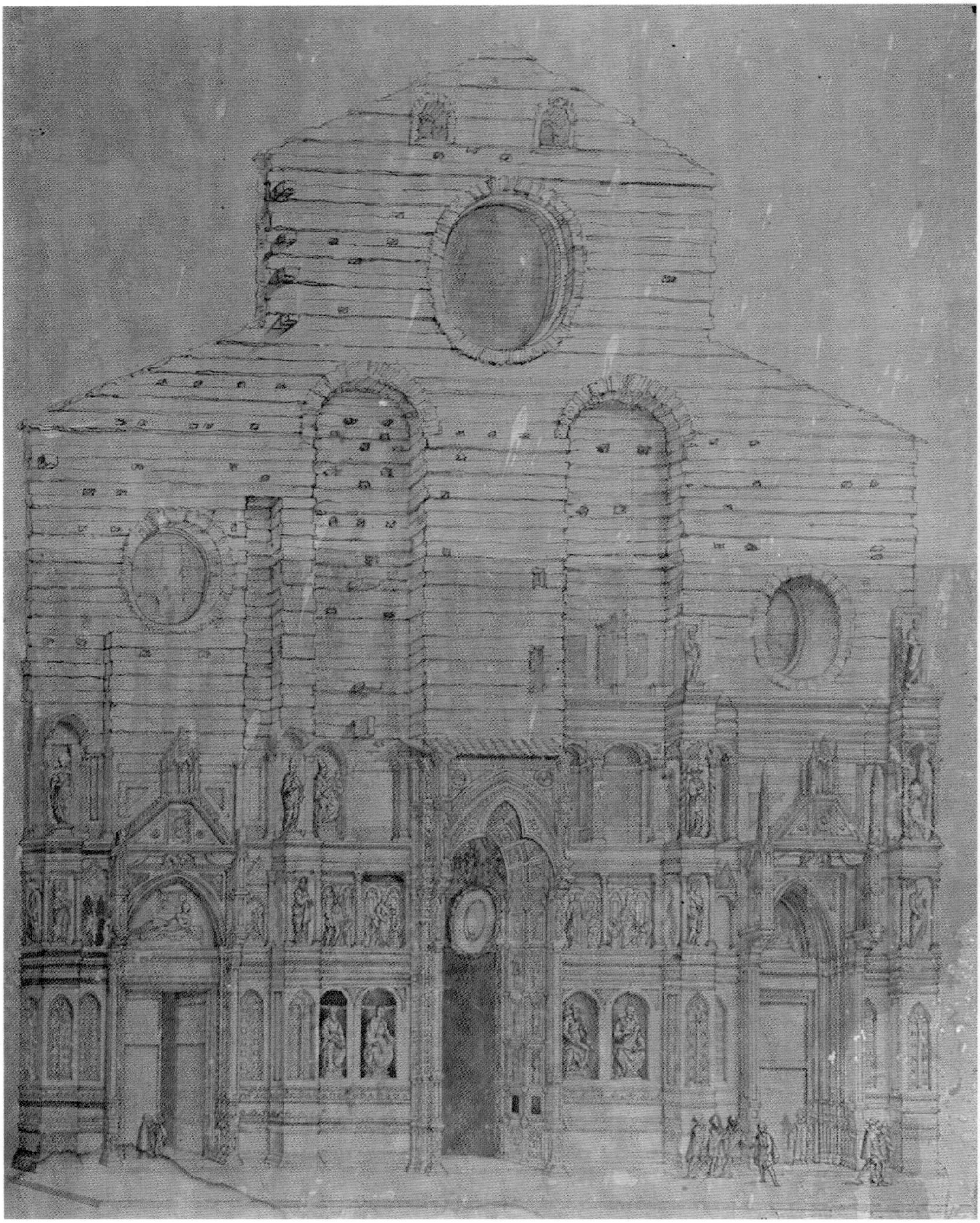

Fig. 40
Bernardino Poccetti
Facade of the Cathedral

Before 1587, pen and ink and watercolour on paper applied to canvas, 101 × 58cm (39¾ × 22⅞in). Museo dell'Opera del Duomo, Florence.

made by Bernardino Poccetti before the old facade was demolished, in 1587 (FIG. 40). The *operai* aimed to keep the sculptors in competition with one another right up until the work was completed. In a meeting on 19 December 1408, they agreed to assign a single figure and the necessary marble to three artisans: Niccolò di Pietro Lamberti (1370–1451), who had been a competitor for the Baptistery doors; Nanni di Banco (ca. 1374–1421); and Donatello. There were, of course, four Evangelists – Matthew, Mark, Luke and John – but only three sculptors had been named. In their deliberations, the *operai* were explicit in their reasons for doing so, because 'the fourth block is to be granted to one of the three that is said to have made the better figure'. Rather than award the commission to a single sculptor on the basis of a competition, they wanted Lamberti, Nanni di Banco and Donatello to compete for the fourth figure. They must have reasoned that such a strategy would ensure the best work. It is even possible that they contrived to have the sculptors work in close

Fig. 41 (left)
Lorenzo Ghiberti
St Matthew

1419–23, bronze, 270cm (106⅜in) high. Orsanmichele, Florence.

Commissioned by the Arte del Cambio (the Bankers' Guild).

Fig. 42 (right)
Lorenzo Ghiberti
St John the Baptist

1412–16, bronze, 254cm (100in) high. Orsanmichele, Florence.

Commissioned by the Arte dei Mercatanti di Calimala (the Cloth Merchants' Guild).

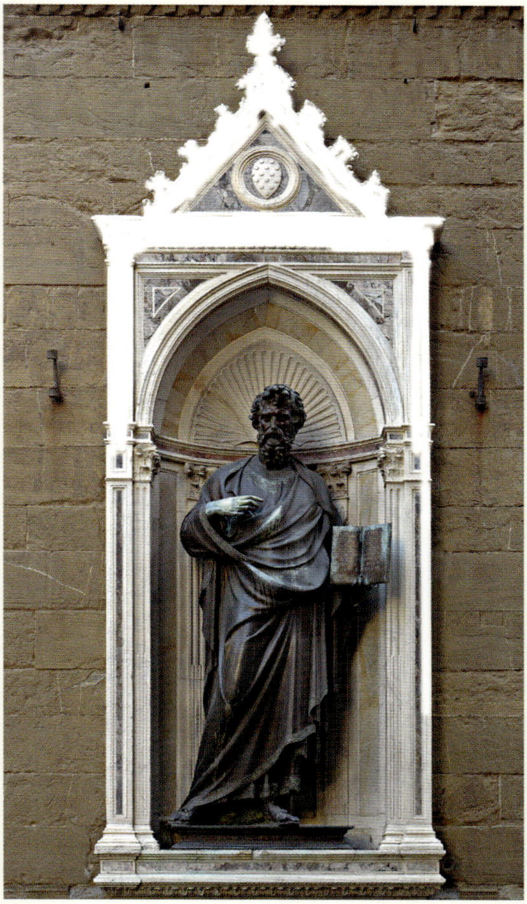

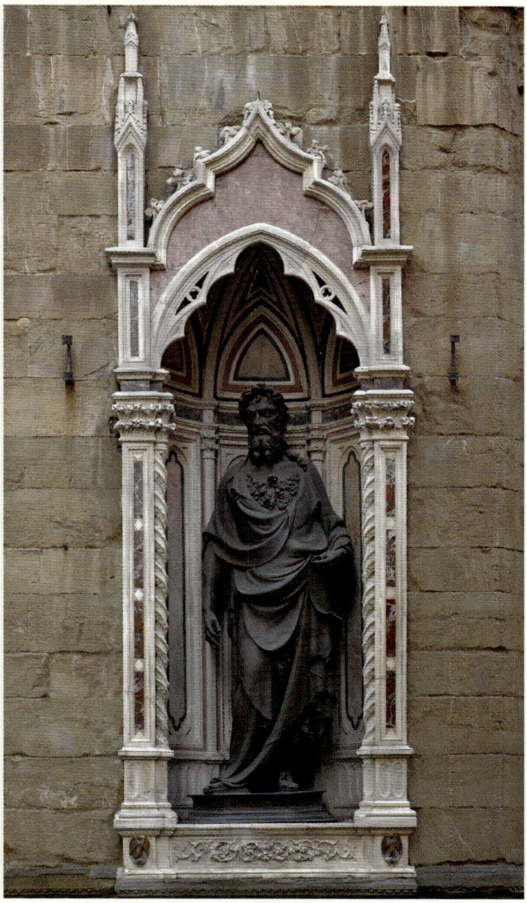

proximity, since we know that they were occupied within various chapels in the cathedral itself, as if the sight of one another's work would spur them on to greater things. As an additional incentive, full payment was delayed until completion, when the worth of the sculptures would be evaluated (indeed, all sculptures were evaluated in 1415).

In the end, however, the tactic was unsuccessful. Three sculptors simply took too long and, on 29 May 1410, the *operai* commissioned Bernardo Ciuffagni (1381–1458) to execute the remaining figure of St Matthew. While on this occasion competition had not produced the desired result, nonetheless the *operai* would use it again when commissioning designs for stained-glass windows from Ghiberti and Donatello in 1434, or in ordering two *cantorie* (singing galleries) from Nanni di Banco and Donatello at about the same time.

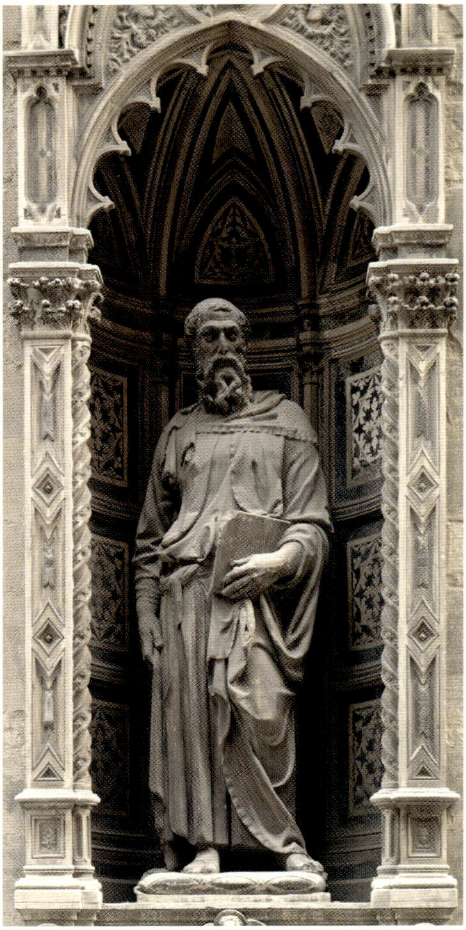

Fig. 43
Donatello
St Mark

1411–ca. 1415, marble, 236cm (93in) high. Orsanmichele, Florence.

Commissioned by the Arte dei Linaiuoli e Rigattieri (the Linen Weavers' and Pedlars' Guild).

At both the Baptistery and the cathedral, artisans jostled with one another for commissions and then competed to produce the best work. The beauty and prestige of the objects they made reflected well on the guilds that administered these important sites, and were a source of pride for all Florentines. They cared that their cathedral and Baptistery were bigger and more beautiful than those in rival cities, such as Pisa or Siena. At Orsanmichele, however, the situation was somewhat different. Thirteen of the guilds were represented on the exterior niches, leading naturally enough to one-upmanship. Ghiberti does not appear to have been in competition with other sculptors when, on 26 August 1419, he signed a contract with the Bankers' Guild for a sculpture of St Matthew (their patron saint) that was to be set in their niche, which he was also to design (FIG. 41). Instead, it was his patrons, the members of the guild itself, who were competing with the Calimala.

The Bankers established a four-man subcommittee to oversee the work, and recorded their deliberations, agreements and expenses in a special account book, the *Libro del pilastro* (*Book of the Pilaster*). Its survival has ensured that Ghiberti's *St Matthew* is one of the best-documented sculptures of the fifteenth century. It allows us to follow the entire process from commission to completion (although, annoyingly, it does not provide the date on which the sculpture was positioned in the niche, which is generally thought to have occurred in March 1423). The contract is particularly revealing for our present purposes. Its first clause states that the statue was to be as large as, if not bigger, than the figure of St John the Baptist that Ghiberti had made previously for the Calimala (FIG. 42). Evidently, size mattered. This small, seemingly inconsequential stipulation reveals that the consuls and *operai* of the guild (among them the young Cosimo de' Medici) were keen to equal, and ideally better, the sculpture of another guild of similar standing and prestige. Like the *St John*, the *St Matthew* is made from the most expensive of materials and is set on one of the primary facades of the building; the *St John* on the main festival route linking the Piazza della Signoria to the cathedral, and the *St Matthew* on the entrance facade. Although art history has tended to think that the competition at Orsanmichele was between Ghiberti and Donatello, or between their respective styles, the true rivalry was between their patrons.

There is also an important distinction to make between the guilds for which Donatello and Ghiberti were working. With the exception of his *St Louis of Toulouse*, which was made for the Guelph party, Donatello's sculptures for Orsanmichele were commissioned by minor guilds. The *St Mark* (FIG. 43) was destined for the niche of the Arte dei Linaiuoli e Rigattieri (Linen Weavers and Pedlars), and the *St George* (FIG. 44) for the Arte dei Spadai e Corazzai (Swordsmiths and Armourers). By contrast, Ghiberti was working for the major guilds: the Calimala, the Bankers and the Wood Guilds, for which he produced a figure of St Stephen. While Donatello's sculptures were carved in marble and decorated the flanks of the building, Ghiberti's were set in prestigious positions and cast in costly bronze. We want to think of Donatello's *all'antica* art as more progressive than Ghiberti's, but it was Ghiberti's style that, in its time, attracted powerful institutions, corporations that controlled the Florentine economy and ensured the quality of its products through competition.

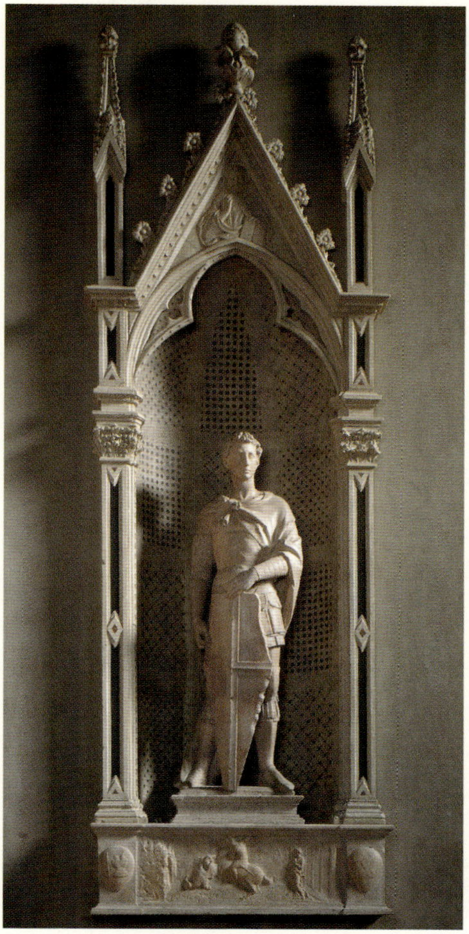

Fig. 44
Donatello
St George

ca. 1417, marble, 209cm (82¼in) high. Museo Nazionale del Bargello, Florence.

Commissioned by the Arte dei Spadai e Corazzai (the Swordsmiths' and Armourers' Guild).

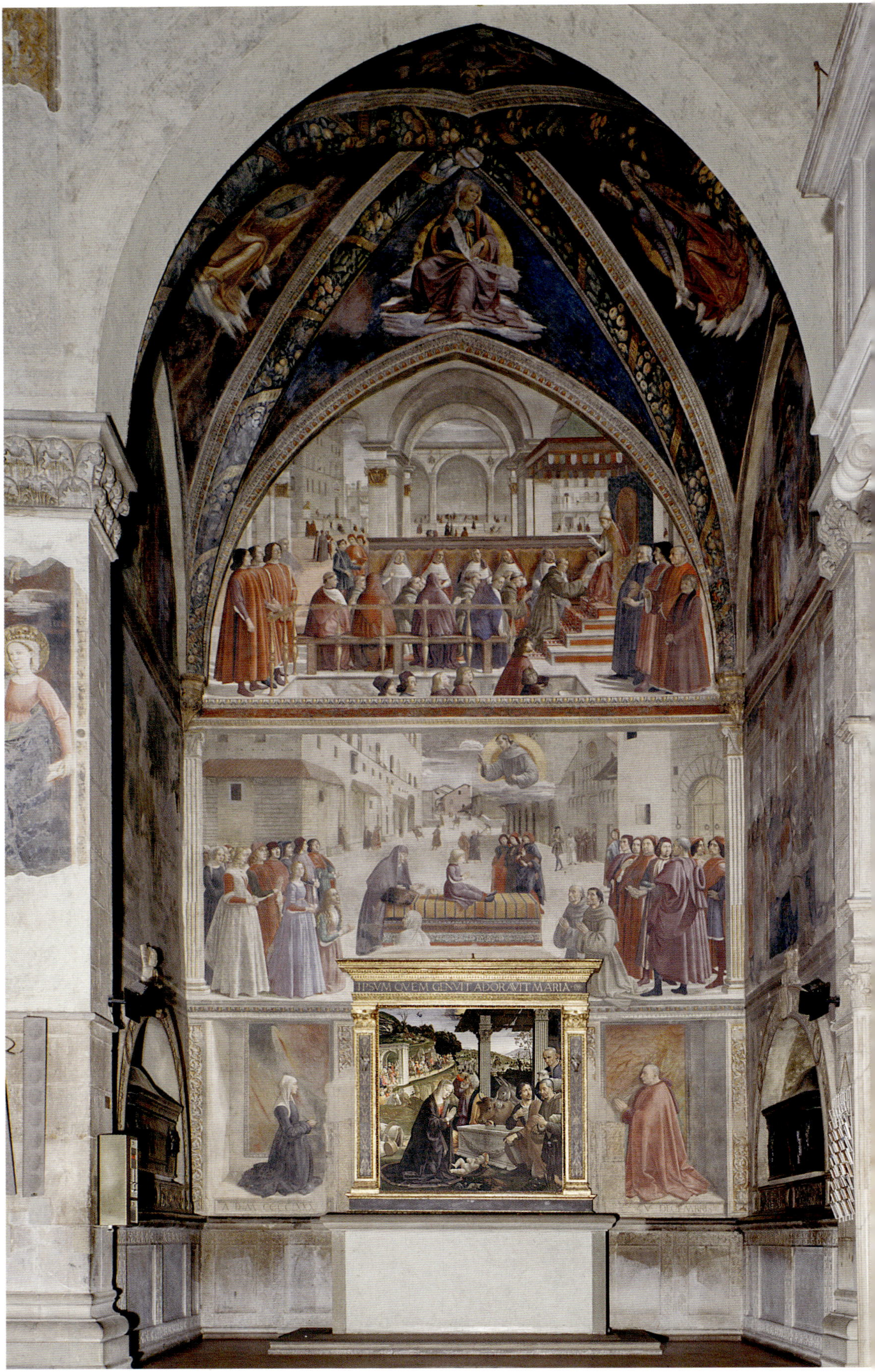
IPSUM QUEM GENUIT ADORAVIT MARIA

5

Patronage Networks

Looking at the Palazzo Strozzi, begun in about 1489, it is easy to imagine that it testifies to the wealth and power of a single man, Filippo di Matteo Strozzi (1428–1491), the individual who built it (FIG. 46). Yet, according to Filippo's son, his father sought to bring renown to 'himself and all his kin in Italy and beyond' with the new palace. It was constructed in close proximity to the homes of other members of his extended family, a family so large that it took the genealogist Pompeo Litta 22 plates to chart their family tree in the early nineteenth century. The Strozzi had lived in this area of Florence for many generations, close to their relatives, neighbours and friends (*parenti, vicini e amici*). Did the new building reflect Filippo's aspirations, or those of his entire clan and friendship network?

This question is fundamental to our understanding of Florentine social structures, and it has occupied social historians for several decades. It is closely aligned to another, which can again be exemplified through the Palazzo Strozzi: why does it look so similar to the Palazzo Medici (FIG. 47)? They share a basic format of three rusticated storeys, divided by string courses, that are ornamented with biforate windows and surmounted by an *all'antica* cornice. Could it be that Filippo sought to curry favour with the Medici with a building

Fig. 45
Domenico Ghirlandaio
Sassetti chapel

1483–5, fresco. Santa Trinita, Florence.

Fig. 46
Benedetto da Maiano and **Simone del Pollaiuolo,** known as **Il Cronaca**
Palazzo Strozzi

Begun 1489. Florence.

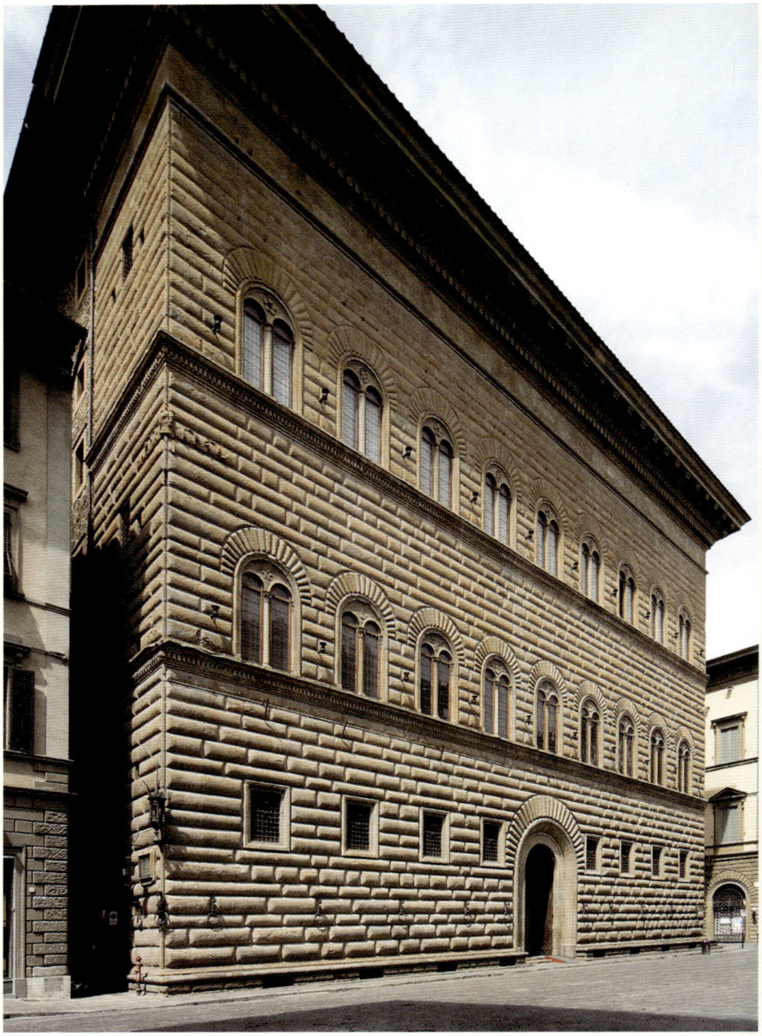

that mimicked their own? Or was he competing with them, outdoing them by building a palace that was even bigger than theirs? The position of the Strozzi was not assured in the late fifteenth century, even if they had once been extremely powerful. Two of the most important branches of the family had been exiled from Florence in the 1430s, as Cosimo de' Medici eliminated his political rivals. Filippo was the son of one of them, and had consequently lived much of his life in Naples. Now returned to the city of his ancestors, he knew he needed the support (the social patronage or clientship) of Lorenzo de' Medici to secure his position, but was not necessarily pleased by the idea. Maybe the visual similarity of these two buildings made the point to Filippo's friends, family and neighbours that the Strozzi were now allied to the Medici, despite their old enmity. Or perhaps it demonstrated to them that the Strozzi might once again triumph over their old rivals. Yet again, it may have been a cunning ploy

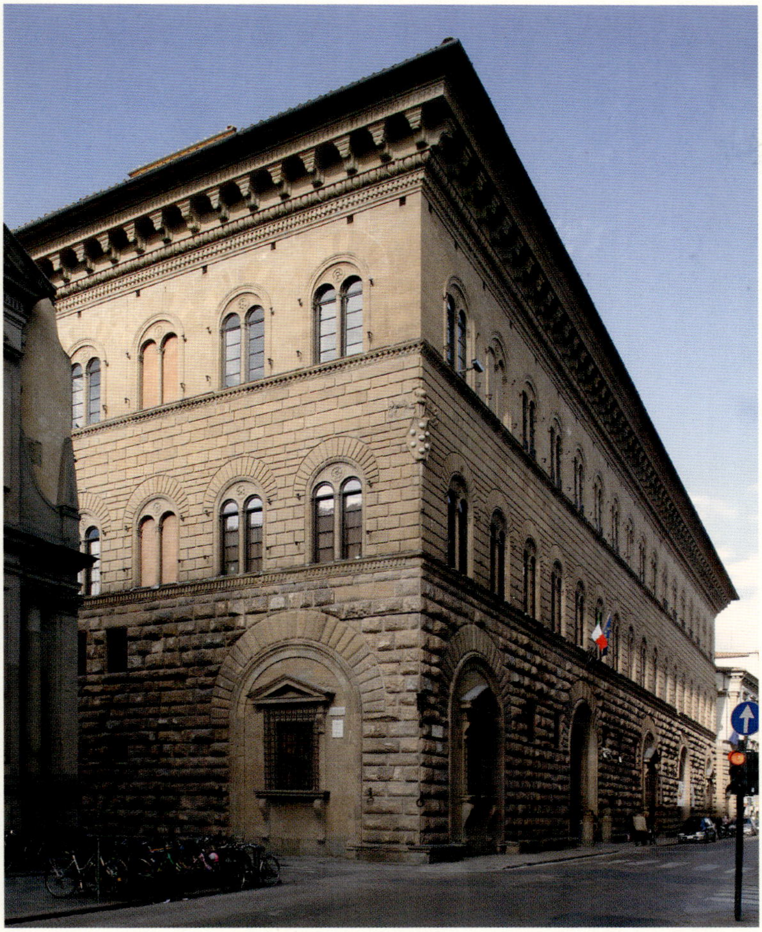

Fig. 47
Michelozzo di Bartolomeo Michelozzi
Palazzo Medici

ca. 1445–60. Florence.

to suggest one alliance visually, while doing the opposite politically. Whatever the case, architecture was being used to make visible a social relationship.

The distinctive nature of the Florentine Republic before the rise of the Grand Dukes in the sixteenth century engendered particular forms of patronage that were perhaps less prevalent in a duchy or principality. Some of these patronage relationships can be thought of as vertical, and others horizontal. Filippo's relationship to the de facto ruler of Florence was top-down (vertical) and somewhat different from the horizontal bond with his *parenti, vicini e amici*, even if they all manifest power dynamics that were, by their very nature, unequal.

Neighbourhood was an equally important factor in both types of patronage. For fiscal purposes, Florence was divided into four quarters, each focused on an important (often mendicant) church:

Santa Maria Novella (Dominican), Santa Croce (Franciscan), San Giovanni (the Baptistery) and, south of the river, Santo Spirito (Augustinian) (*see* map, page 6). These quarters were each subdivided into four smaller units, called *gonfaloni*, numbering sixteen in total. Although these divisions might seem purely administrative, they had a defining impact on family relationships and friendship patterns. The location of a family's palace was often determined by ties of marriage, and it could influence the friends and business contacts that its inhabitants made. It would certainly decide where a patrician chose to have a chapel, or be buried, and might even presuppose the artist he chose to decorate it. Neighbourhood affected patronage, both social and artistic, the dynamics of which can be charted in the decoration of chapels for private individuals and their families, whether in single altarpieces or entire fresco cycles.

Private Individuals

The choice of saints in an altarpiece, or in any sacred painting, was never arbitrary. It had little to do with the painter, but was rather the decision of the patron, often in consultation with the religious order in whose church the work was to be housed. As such, they are important visual documents, revealing something of the patron's devotional priorities and social world, with the result that seemingly minor paintings become as significant as those now judged to be important works of art when considered in social terms. The panel painted by Ghirlandaio for Stefano di Piero di Jacopo Boni's chapel in the church of Santa Maria Maddalena di Cestello, for example, shows the patron's name saint, Stephen, in the centre, between those of his father, Peter, and grandfather James (FIG. 48). James was also the name saint of Stefano's son, while Stephen was that of Stephen Harding, one of the founders of the Cistercians, the order resident at the church of Cestello.

Chapels, such as that of the Boni at Cestello, were tied not only to the individuals that founded them, but also to the entire family who might hear mass, or be buried, there. They were a source of pride for the family and said much about their social standing. They were also a significant site for dynastic memory. They reminded the family of their ancestors and the need to pray for their souls in Purgatory. The particular reason for a saint's inclusion in an altarpiece could be remembered down many generations. In the eighteenth century, for example, the Salviati family was sufficiently interested in their forebears for a genealogist (who was probably called Giovanni

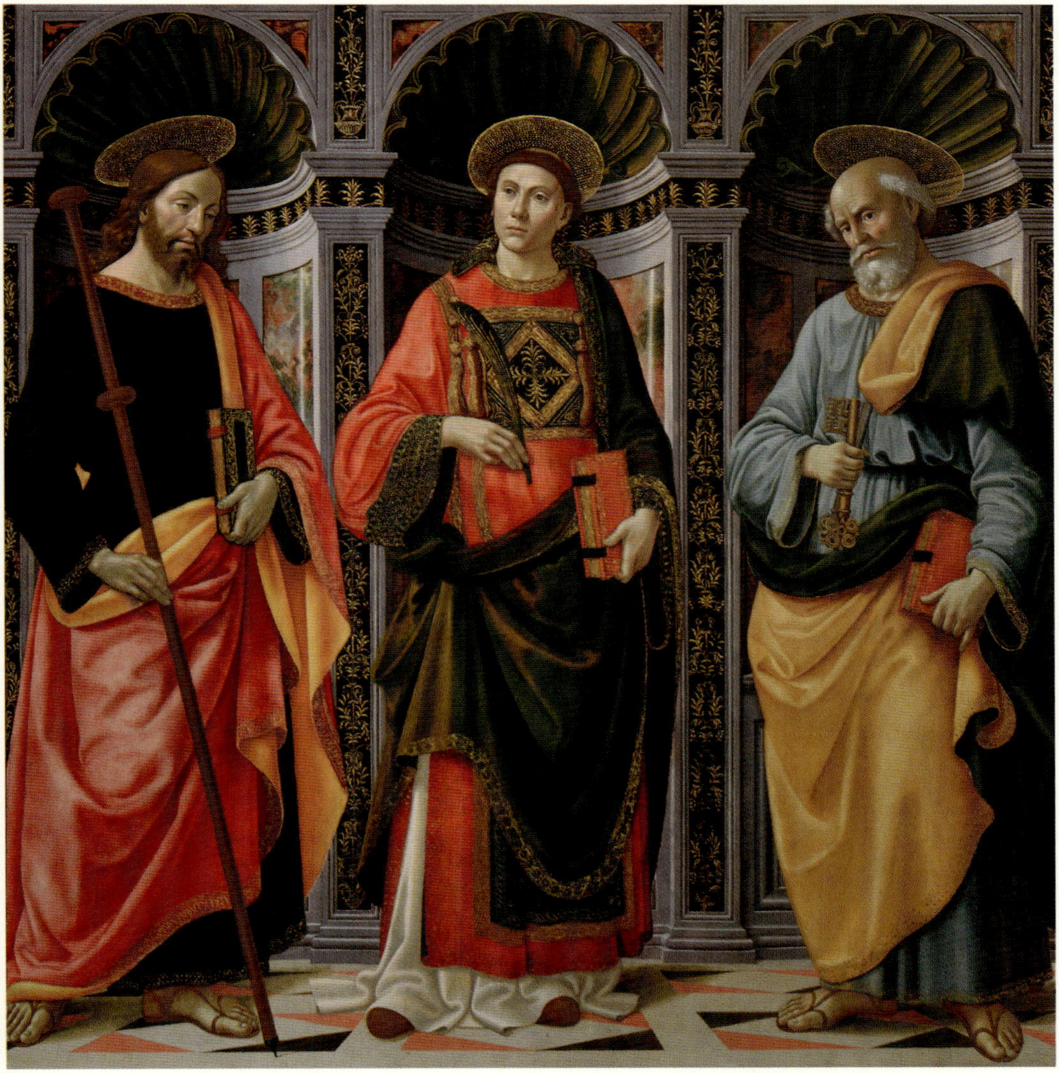

Battista Dei) to write an account of their chapel and its altarpiece, which was also at Cestello (diagonally across the nave from that of the Boni). It had been established with money left in the last will and testament of Jacopo d'Alamanno Salviati, whose three nephews – Alamanno d'Averardo, Giuliano di Francesco and Jacopo di Giovanni Salviati – commissioned the artist Cosimo Rosselli to paint its altarpiece. He delivered it on 30 October 1492 (FIG. 49). Almost 300 years later Dei was keen to account for the saints, and, quoting from fifteenth-century documents, he wrote that 'the painting … was paid for from money … for the tomb of the Cavaliere Jacopo … [who] had a special devotion to the Prince of the Apostles [i.e. St Peter]'. He

Fig. 48
Domenico Ghirlandaio
Saints James, Stephen and Peter (Boni Altarpiece)

1493, tempera on panel, 175 × 174cm ($68\frac{1}{2} \times 68\frac{7}{8}$in). Galleria dell'Accademia, Florence.

Fig. 49
Cosimo Rosselli
Virgin and Child with the Infant St John the Baptist and Saints James and Peter (Salviati Altarpiece)

1492, tempera on wood panel, 205.5 × 190cm (81 × 74¾in). Museo del Cenacolo di San Salvi, Florence.

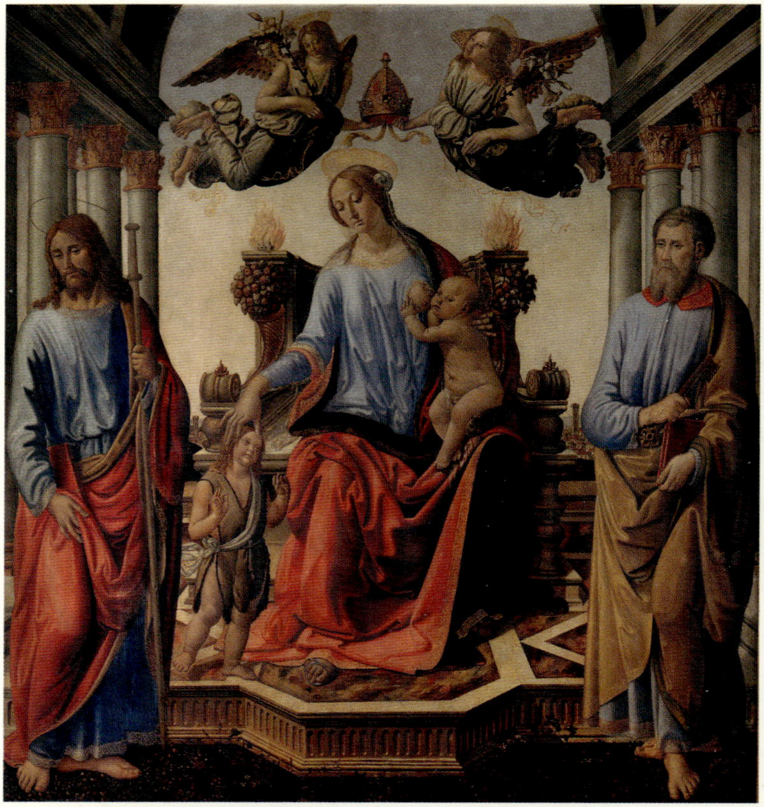

Fig. 50
Cosimo Rosselli
Salviati Altarpiece

Detail of Fig. 49.

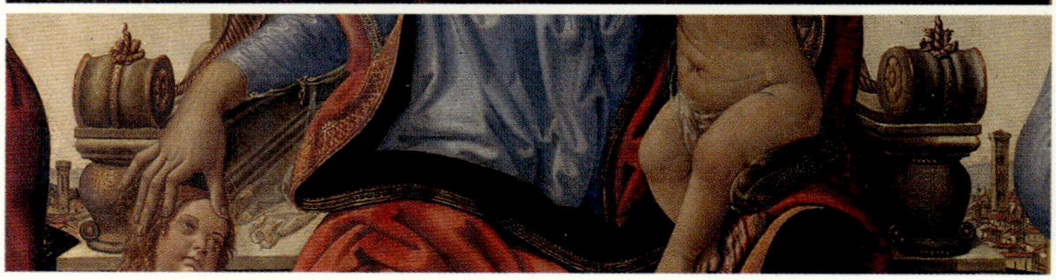

was able to explain the presence of Saints James (Jacopo in Italian) and Peter to the left and right of the Virgin. Dei continued by observing that 'in the two spaces between the seat of the Madonna and the Saints, [Rosselli] painted in the distance between certain houses, the bell tower of the Duomo [seen] from the side towards S. Pietro, and the bell tower of the Bargello [seen] from that of S. Jacopo, that were close to the Salviati houses' (FIG. 50). According to Dei, then, James was included because he was the name saint of Jacopo d'Alamanno Salviati, whose legacy had established the chapel, and Peter because Jacopo had had a special devotion to him. Yet the altarpiece not only reflected his particular devotional interests, but also depicted the neighbourhood in which he and his family lived. It was about him, his family and their neighbours.

Neighbourhood

The Nerli Altarpiece, painted by Filippino Lippi for a chapel in the newly rebuilt church of Santo Spirito, also depicts a neighbourhood in Florence (FIG. 51). In the background between the Virgin and St Catherine, he depicted a large patrician palace, before an imposing city gate, which is surrounded by buildings of more modest scale and ambition (FIG. 52). The area is identified with San Frediano, a relatively poor area to the west of Santo Spirito, even if it is not a 'portrait' of that district. Before the palace entrance, a man embraces a child, who stands beside a woman, presumably her mother and his wife. Together, they seem the very embodiment of the nuclear family – mother, father and daughter – even if, as we shall see, they stand in for

Fig. 51
Filippino Lippi
Madonna and Child with the Infant St John, Saints Martin of Tours and Catherine of Alexandria with donors (Nerli Altarpiece)

ca. 1490, oil on wood panel, 160 × 180cm (63 × 70⅞in). Santo Spirito, Florence.

The frame is original and, like the painted panel, carries the Nerli coat of arms, a shield with six vertical bands alternating in red and black.

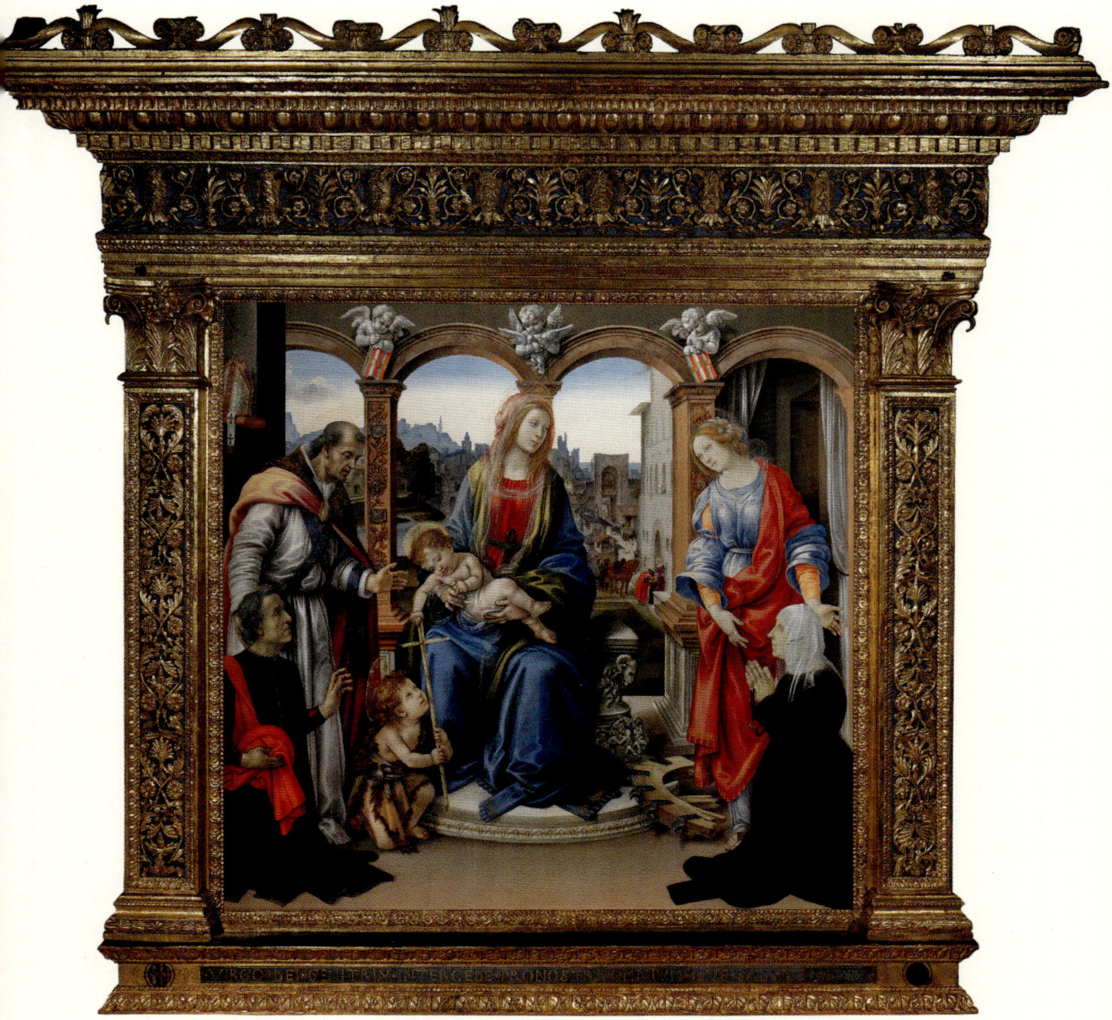

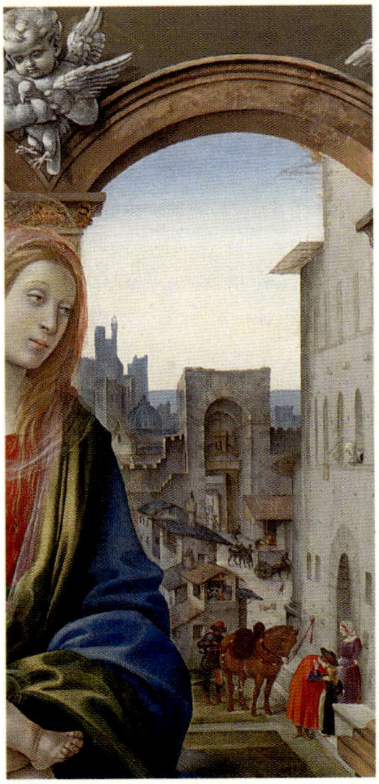

Fig. 52
Filippino Lippi
Nerli Altarpiece

Detail of Fig. 51.

the entire extended family. From their ages, it is clear that the mother and father are not the two donors who kneel in the foreground of the altarpiece, who are identified as Tanai di Francesco de' Nerli (1427–1498) and Nanna di Neri di Gino Capponi. They make humble pleas to the Virgin to intervene with her son on their behalf and secure them a place in Paradise. In this quest, they are assisted by two saints, who flank the Virgin, Christ and the infant St John. St Martin of Tours cups one hand behind Tanai's head and with the other points to the Virgin as if to propel Tanai towards her. St Catherine, by contrast, indicates away from the Virgin and towards Nanna, who kneels in pious adoration, having already caught the Virgin's attention.

Apart from the fact that the two figures in the background do not resemble Tanai and Nanna, we also know from Tanai's tax records that they did not live in this part of this street, but rather much further up it on Borgo San Jacopo. This might seem a minor point, but the road crosses two administrative sub-districts, or *gonfaloni*: Nicchio and Drago Verde. However, the vignette in the background does show the area of Florence that is traditionally associated with Tanai's family. The area shown in the background might not be the district in which Tanai and Nanna lived, but it is where Tanai's kin had resided historically.

In Renaissance Florence, kinship ties structured both artistic and sociopolitical patronage, at the heart of which was the family. Florentines distinguished between the *casa*, the household, which might include the immediate family with their domestic servants, and the *consorteria*, or clan in a dynastic sense. Neither was more important than the other. They were intimately connected, socially, politically and economically. In his treatise *On Civic Life* (*Della vita civile*, 1465), Matteo Palmieri wrote about how it was necessary to love not only your sons, grandsons and those of your blood (in other words, those of your *casa*), but also 'the stocks, *consortorie* and huge families, which must develop as its numbers overflow'. He made the point that small families will with time grow into large ones, reminding his reader that all parts of the extended family were important. The imagery of the altarpiece marks a distinction, then, between the *casa* and the *consorteria*.

Tanai acquired patronage rights to the chapel in Santo Spirito in 1493. However, it was not his only chapel, and it is telling that he was not buried there. He had two others, both on the Oltrarno (the south side of the river), in the administrative quarter of Santo Spirito. In his local parish church of Santa Felicita, which was just around the corner from his palace on Borgo San Jacopo and not far from Santo Spirito, he had another chapel decorated with an altar-

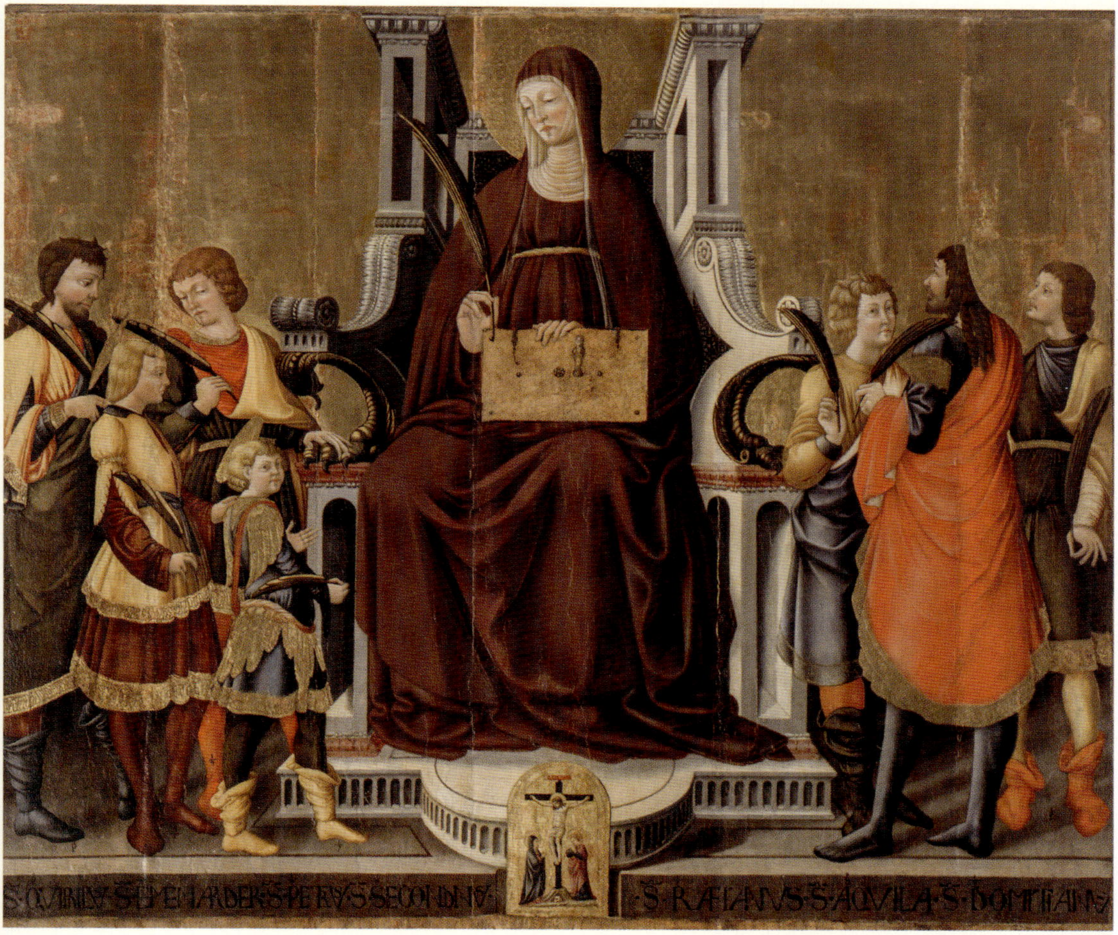

piece painted by Neri di Bicci (1418–1492; FIG. 53). In the observant Franciscan church of San Salvatore al Monte, which was also on the south side of the river, he established burial chapels for himself and his descendants, as can still be read on a tomb slab in the church: 'S[EPULCRUM] DESCEN[DENTIUM] TANAIS FRAN[CISCI] PHI[LIPPI] DE NERLIS.' What unites these various spaces is their location in a single administrative quarter, in which the Nerli family lived, centred on the church of Santo Spirito.

But if he already had a chapel in his local parish church, and a burial chapel for his family and his heirs in San Salvatore al Monte, why did Tanai need a third chapel in Santo Spirito? The reason was probably related to his wife. Nanna was a member of the Capponi family, one of the wealthiest, and oldest, families in the neighbourhood. She married Tanai in 1445, sealing an alliance between the Capponi and the Nerli that was of considerable importance to the

Fig. 53
Neri di Bicci
St Felicity and her Seven Sons (Nerli Altarpiece)

1464, oil on wood panel, 190.5 × 158.5cm (75 × 62⅜in). Santa Felicita, Florence.

Nerli. Being an old magnate family, they were excluded from public life until their fortunes began to change in the late 1430s. (Magnates were members of an old aristocracy that were barred from public office by the Ordinances of Justice in 1293–5, as part of a process that established a guild-based government.) Tanai's well-chosen marriage to Nanna was an important factor in effecting this change.

The Capponi dominated the right transept of Santo Spirito. They had had a burial chapel in the old church – we know, for instance, that Piero di Bartolomeo Capponi was buried in Santo Spirito on 13 June 1417 – but this seems to have been a space for the whole, extended clan: the *consorteria*. When the church came to be rebuilt after a fire of 1471, different branches of the family seemed to have wanted separate spaces within it. By 1500, anyone standing in the crossing of the church and looking east would have been confronted with three Capponi chapels flanking that of the Nerli (FIG. 54). They represented the three main lines of that family. One branch of the family, who were all frustratingly called either Gino or Neri, had a chapel in the northeast corner of the transept, which was decorated with an altarpiece by Piero di Cosimo (1462–1522) in about 1489–90 (FIG. 55). Nanna was the sister of Gino di Neri Capponi, who had rights over this chapel by the 1490s. This branch of the Capponi was the largest and wealthiest, and they lived nearby on via Santo Spirito. The tomb of their founder, Neri di Gino Capponi (1388–1457), was even immured within the wall behind a grille for everyone to see (FIG. 56), as though he were the founder of a dynasty.

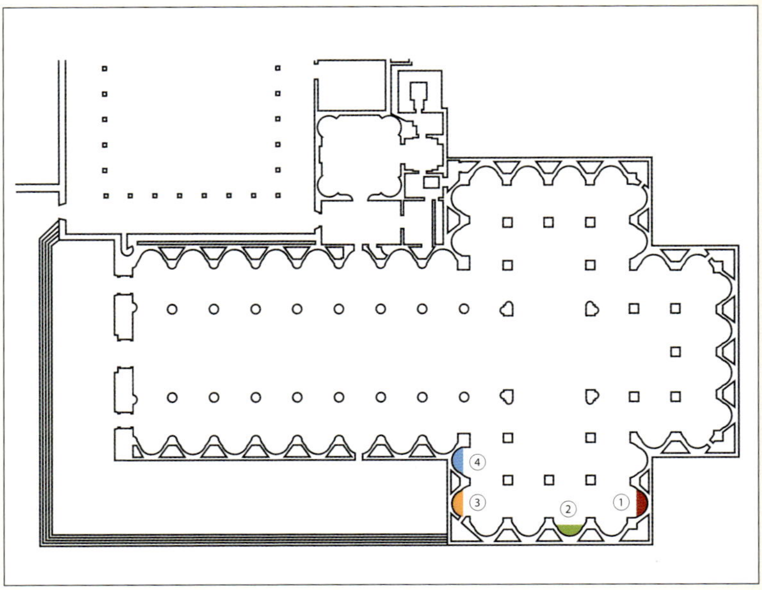

Fig. 54
Plan of Santo Spirito, showing the south transept

1. Capponi, rights acquired by Gino di Neri Capponi in 1459
2. Nerli
3. Capponi, rights acquired by the 'Altopascio' Capponi in the late fifteenth century
4. Capponi, rights acquired by Niccolò di Giovanni ('il Grasso') Capponi in 1485

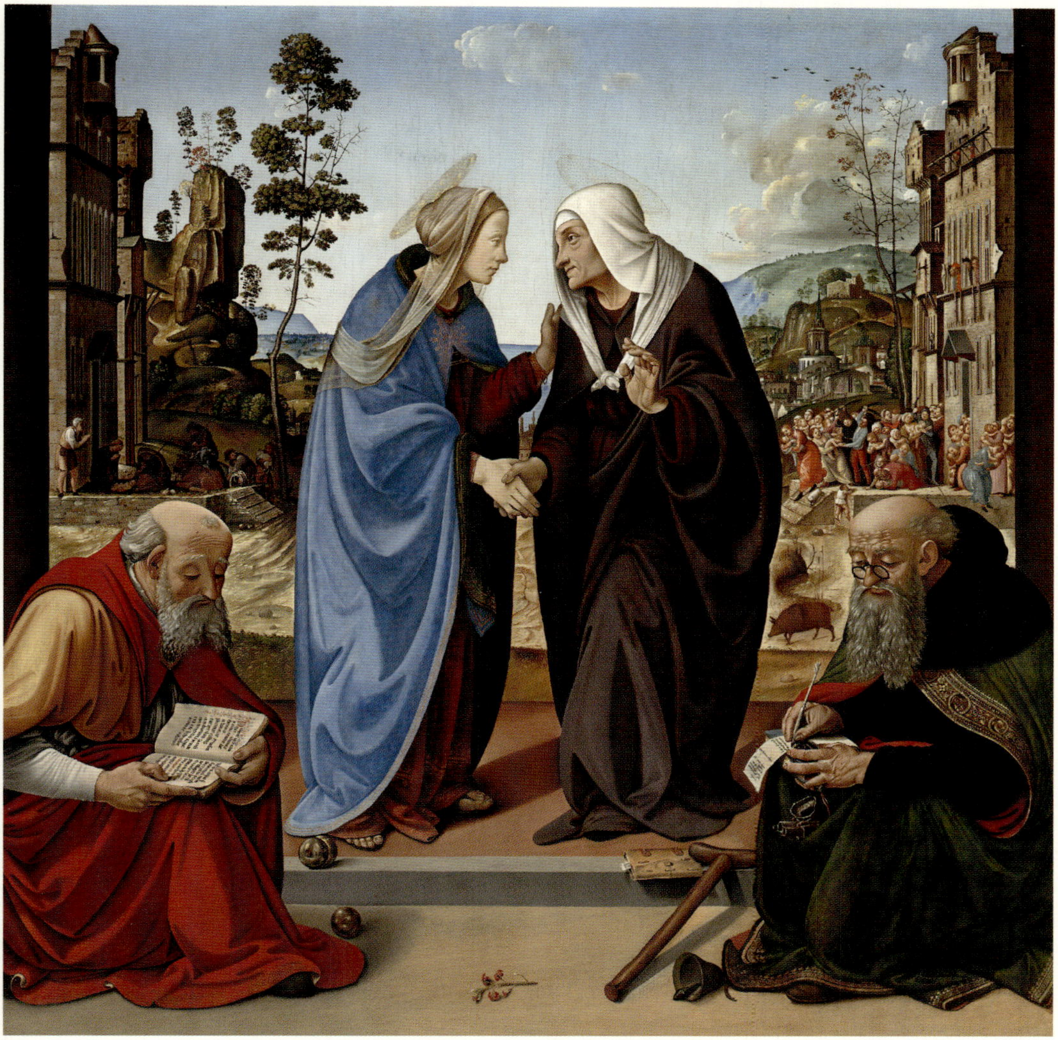

On the opposite side of the same transept, another branch of the Capponi acquired rights to a chapel in 1485. Their chapel was dedicated to St Augustine and was established by Niccolò di Giovanni 'il Grasso' Capponi (1416–1491). The chapel beside it was acquired by one Guglielmo di Nicola Capponi (b. 1449), from yet another branch of the family, in the last decade of the century. A brief glance at their family tree (FIG. 57) reveals that, although the founders of all these chapels – Gino, Niccolò and Guglielmo – were ultimately descended from the same Recco di Compagno Capponi (d. ca. 1331), they were only vaguely related. Gino was Niccolò's second cousin once removed. Distant though they might seem to us, to fifteenth-century understandings of the family, these different mem-

Fig. 55
Piero di Cosimo
The Visitation with Saints Nicholas and Anthony Abbot

ca. 1489/90, oil on panel, 184.2 × 188.6cm (72½ × 74¼in). National Gallery of Art, Washington DC. Samuel H. Kress Collection (1939.1.361).

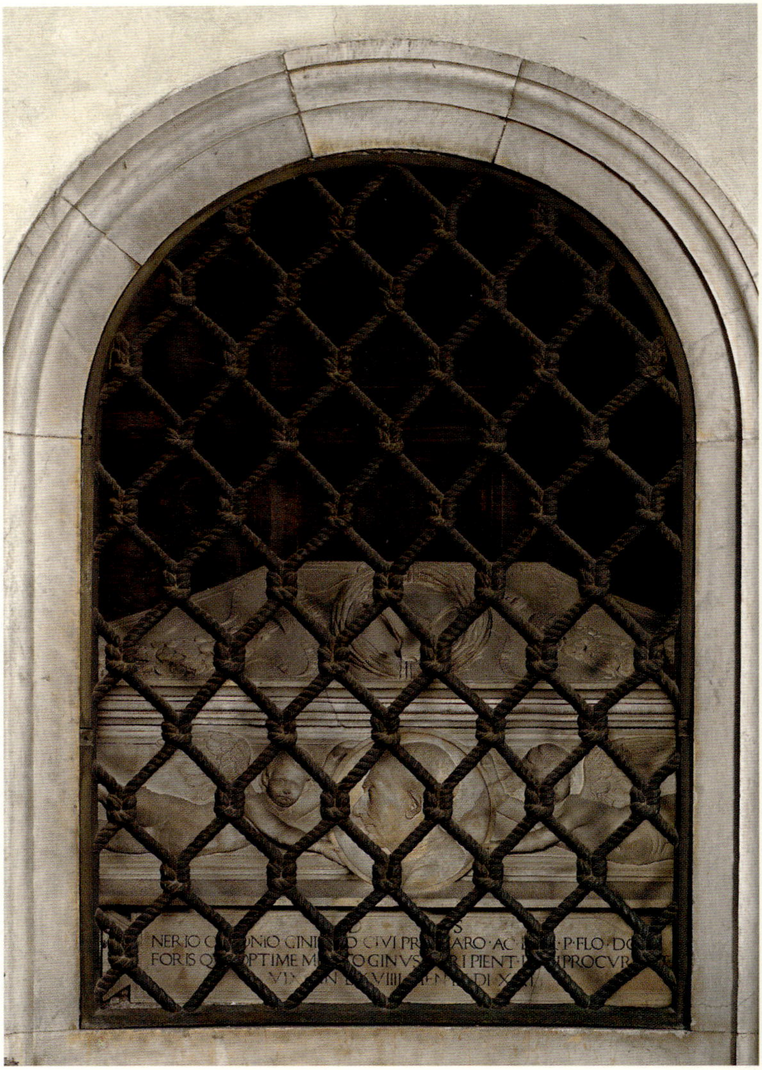

Fig. 56
Attributed to Bernardo Rossellino
Tomb of Neri di Gino Capponi

ca. 1458, marble. Santo Spirito, Florence.

bers of a single clan were bound by ties of kinship and shared paternal lineage. They certainly knew one another and supported one another in business and in life.

Given the misogyny of the fifteenth century (which we shall examine in the next chapter), and the importance of the paternal line to kinship networks, it might seem surprising that Tanai sought a chapel in Santo Spirito because of his wife, but he owed her family much. The visual emphasis of the altarpiece is towards Nanna, who, unlike her husband, catches the Virgin's attention. Surrounded by the chapels of her maiden family, the Capponi, the so-called Nerli chapel reminded viewers of the alliance brokered between the Nerli

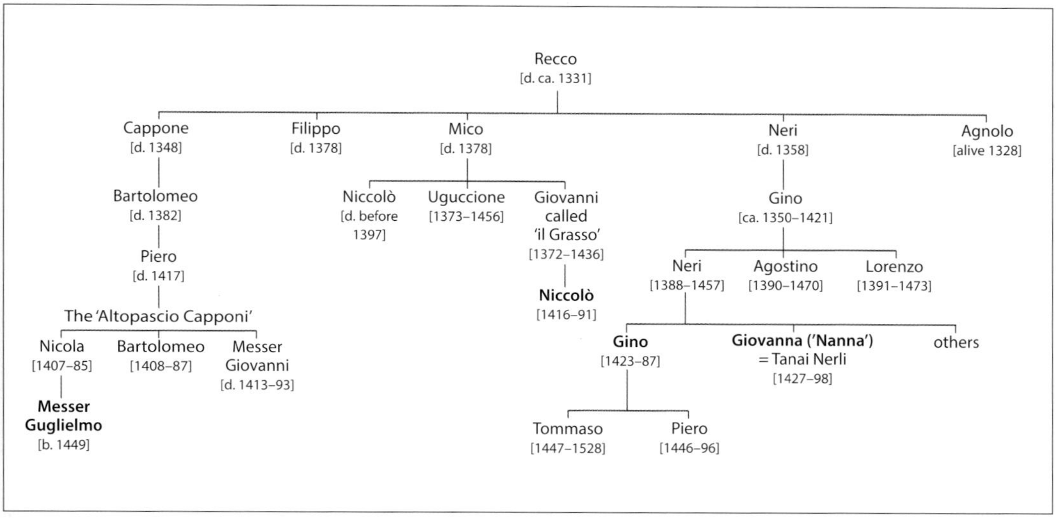

Fig. 57
Abbreviated Capponi family tree

and the Capponi when Tanai married Nanna. The Capponi and Nerli were part of the same clan, or *consorteria*. On his deathbed, Nanna's grandfather Gino di Neri Capponi (ca. 1350–1421) advised his sons that they should 'Stick together above all else with your neighbours and your kinsmen, and serve your friends within and without the city.' The Nerli chapel and its place in Santo Spirito is the visible trace of that desire to 'stick together'.

Old Families and New Men

These patterns were repeated again and again across the city. Prominent families vied for chapels in the major mendicant church in their quarter and, failing that, opted for a parish church in their *gonfalone*. In each case, they made visible the relationships among family, friends and neighbours. The Medici were no exception. They lived north of the Baptistery in the quarter of San Giovanni, and they focused their patronage on churches and institutions nearby: the observant Dominicans at San Marco, or the Servites at Santissima Annunziata. Their ancient parish church of San Lorenzo was slowly transformed into a family mausoleum, manifesting the most invisible of attributes: power. Cosimo ('the Elder') was buried before the high altar, in what appears to be one of the buttresses holding up the floor. He literally became part of its foundations (FIG. 58).

The reach of the Medici extended beyond their immediate quarter of the city. Lorenzo the Magnificent was especially good at

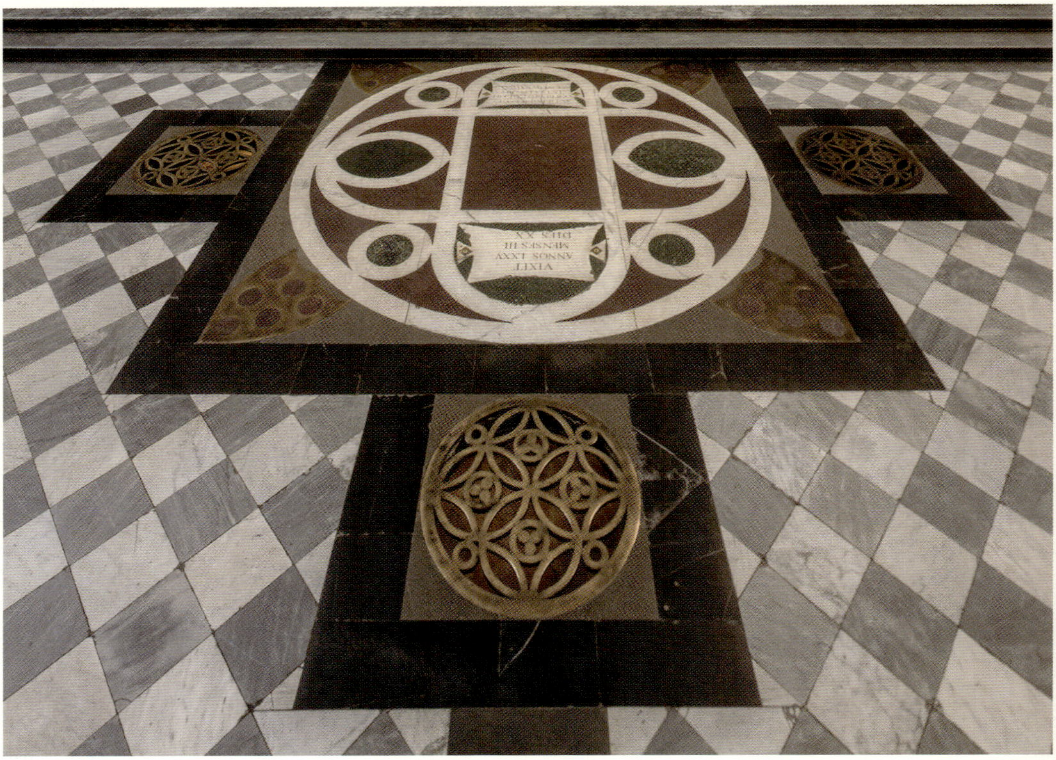

Fig. 58 (above)
Andrea del Verrocchio
Tomb of Cosimo de' Medici

1465–67, marble and bronze, 335cm (132in) square. San Lorenzo, Florence.

Fig. 59
Domenico Ghirlandaio
Tornabuoni chapel

1485–90, fresco. Santa Maria Novella, Florence.

influencing decisions through committees. By massaging the mechanisms of the bureaucracy, and by pressing on individuals who owed their position to his social patronage, he could have a bearing on artistic matters too. As we have seen, he had a deciding impact on the Sala dei Gigli, but you will not find his name anywhere in the documents (see Chapter 1), and he was never Ghirlandaio's 'direct' patron. It is well to remember that the Medici were never absolute rulers in the fifteenth century. Only after the fall of the Republic in 1530 did they become dukes. Their position as 'first among equals' was established by manipulating the institutions of government and drawing on personal ties. In other words, they adopted a similar approach to both social and artistic patronage. Unlike the relationship between the Capponi and the Nerli, which might be thought of in horizontal terms, as if between social equals, the political relationship exercised by the Medici was top-down, even if their fragile position in a republic meant that it had to be disguised.

We can witness the effect of Medici dominance from the other side, from the perspective of their partisans, those over whom they wielded power. It is best seen in the comparison of two famous fresco cycles: the Sassetti chapel in Santa Trinita, painted

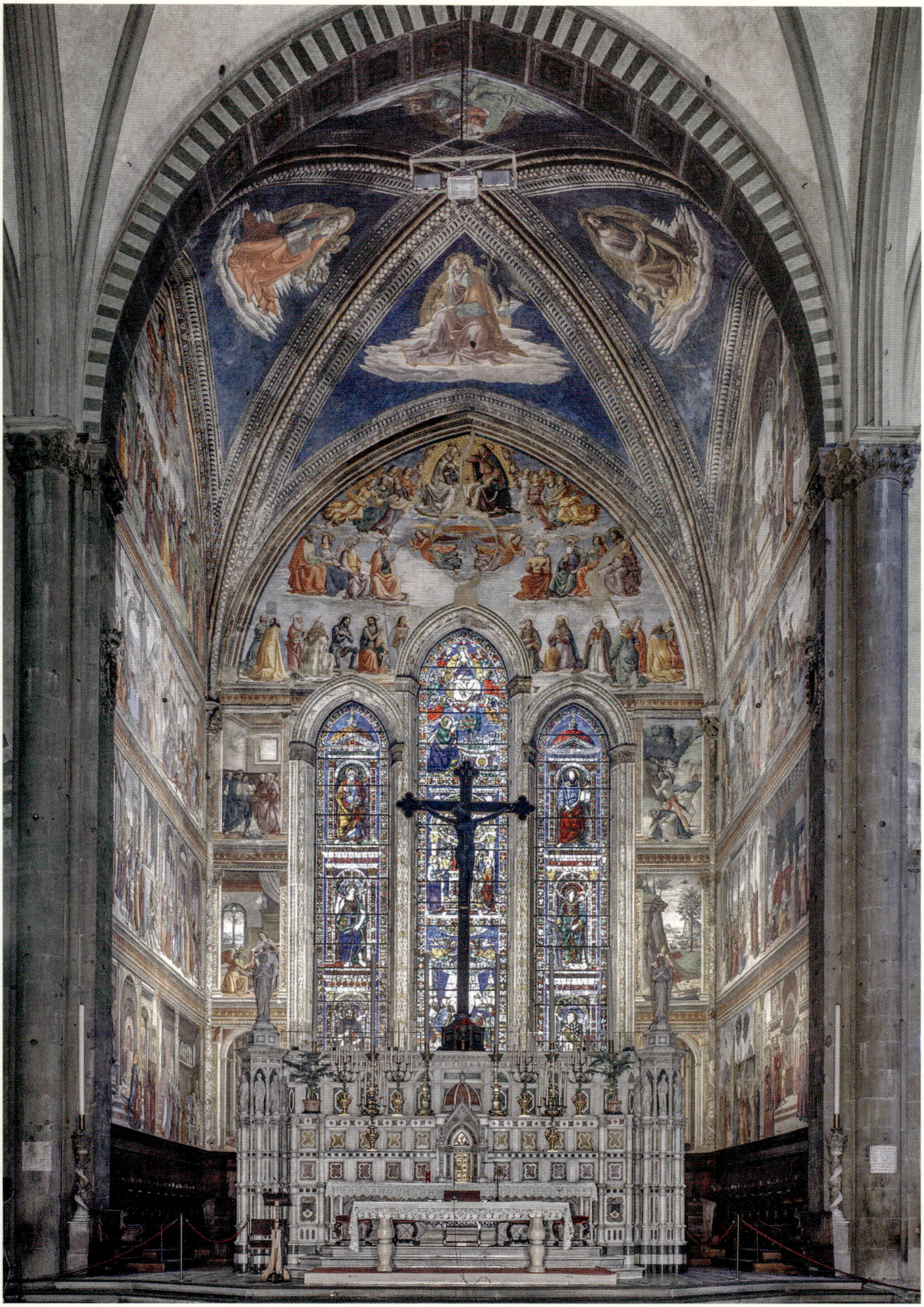

by Ghirlandaio and his workshop between 1483 and 1485; and the Tornabuoni chapel in Santa Maria Novella, executed by the same workshop a few years later, between 1485 and 1490 (FIGS. 45, 59). Neither was a new church, and their patrons appear to have had greater freedom in decorating the entire space, unlike at Santo Spirito or Cestello, where there was a clear attempt to stamp uniformity on the chapels from the outset. Both patrons opted for fresco cycles, as was traditional in these two churches. On the face of it, the two cycles are very similar: both were painted by Ghirlandaio in the 1480s; both are in churches in the same quarter of the city, not far from the homes of their respective patrons – Francesco Sassetti (1421–1490) and Giovanni Tornabuoni (1428–1497); and both Sassetti and Tornabuoni worked for the Medici bank. But the similarities stop there.

The two fresco cycles contain famous cityscapes (FIGS. 60, 61), as if their patrons wish to emphasize their loyalty to Florence. In this sense, they reflect a common sentiment, expressed by Giovanni di Paolo Rucellai, who wrote in his diary that his building programme and other generous acts were justified 'because they rebound in part to the honour of God and the city and to the memory of me'. However, Sassetti's and Tornabuoni's positions in that city were not the same. The former was a 'new man', who first achieved success under Cosimo and rose to be general manager of the Medici bank under Lorenzo. Tornabuoni, by contrast, was the head of one branch (the Tornabuoni) of an ancient magnate *consorteria*, the Tornaquinci. To achieve political office, the Tornabuoni might have had to shed their magnate status, but they had not forgotten their original lineage.

These differences in social position are reflected in their chapels. Tornabuoni's was in the more prestigious church, Santa Maria Novella, and in the most desirable position, directly behind the high altar. In fact, Sassetti had tried to secure rights to this space but had been unsuccessful. Yet the most striking difference between the two chapels is the way their patrons present themselves to the viewer. Both fresco cycles include scenes from the life of their name saints, John the Baptist for Giovanni Tornabuoni and Francis for Francesco Sassetti. The Tornabuoni chapel also narrates the life of the Virgin, for whom the Dominicans had a special devotion. Both chapels are also full of portraits, which, like the Nerli Altarpiece, are divided by gender. The names of all the individuals depicted in these chapels need not concern us; it is their relationship to the patron that matters.

In the *Confirmation of the Rule* in the Sassetti chapel, the main action takes place in the middle ground. Pope Honorius III confirms the rule of St Francis by which his followers were to live

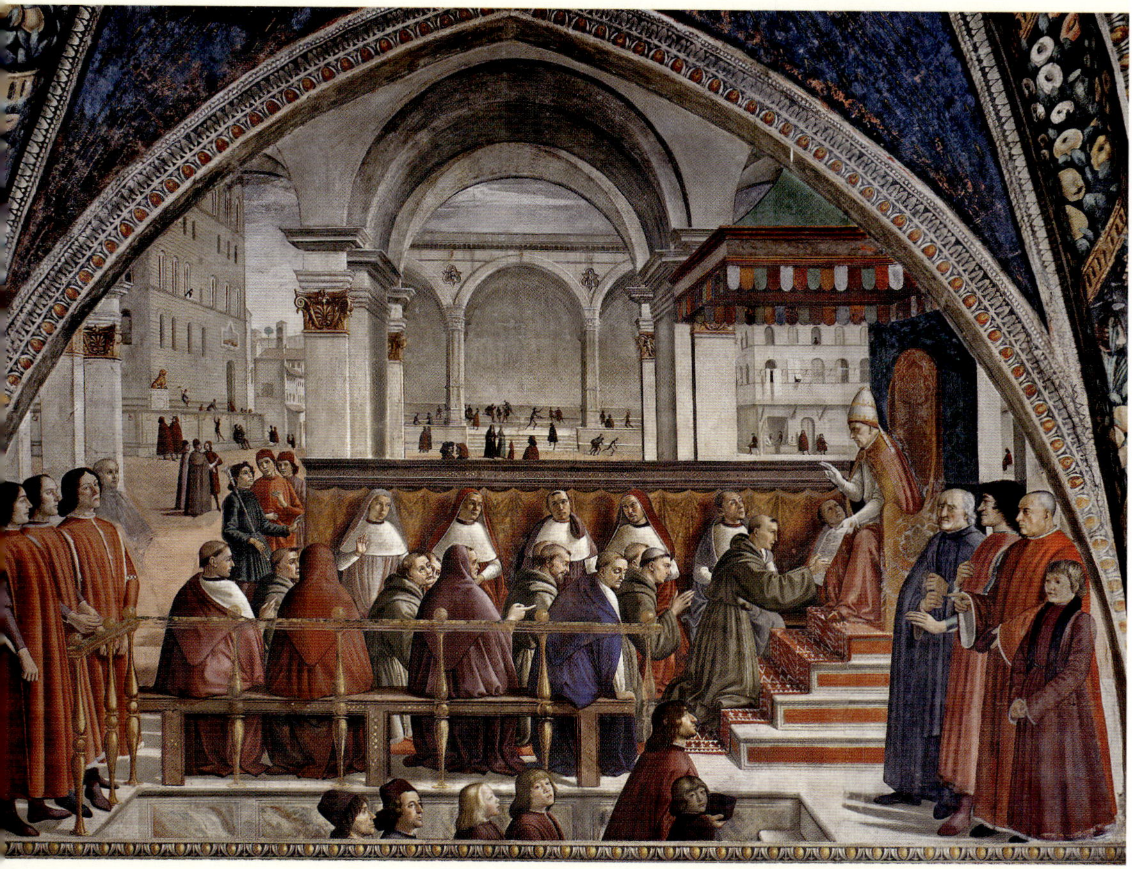

their lives (*see* FIG. 60). The event took place in 1223, but is witnessed by contemporary Florentines including Sassetti, who stands on the right-hand side between his son Teodoro and Lorenzo de' Medici. Beside Lorenzo is another Medici partisan, Antonio di Puccio Pucci (1418–1484), who, like Sassetti, owed his fortune and position to the Medici. Opposite them, in red, are Sassetti's three sons: Galeazzo, Cosimo and Teodoro (the last of whom died in 1478 and was, therefore, already dead when Ghirlandaio began painting in the chapel). Between these two groups, climbing a flight of stairs, are more children. But these boys were not related to Sassetti; instead they are the elder sons and nephew of Lorenzo, led by their tutor, Angelo Poliziano, a scholar and intimate of the Medici household. As patron of this fresco cycle, Sassetti has decided to have himself and his male heirs depicted with their social patron, Lorenzo, and his family. Whether we view Sassetti's decision as evidence of toadying, or as a shrewd political manoeuvre, it was nonetheless calculated to make visible a series of social relationships.

Fig. 60
Domenico Ghirlandaio
Confirmation of the Rule from the Sassetti chapel

1483–5, fresco. Santa Trinita, Florence.

A similar strategy was adopted in the Tornabuoni chapel, except that the relationship its patron chose to visualize was different. Lorenzo's mother, Lucrezia, was a Tornabuoni (see Chapter 6); in fact, she was Giovanni Tornabuoni's sister, making him Lorenzo's uncle. One might, therefore, expect to find Lorenzo depicted here, rather than in the Sassetti chapel, but he is nowhere to be found. Instead, Tornabuoni had himself depicted surrounded by his friends and kin, both male and female. As in the Sassetti chapel, it is the figures who stand in his immediate proximity that are most revealing. In the *Annunciation to Zacharias*, the Angel Gabriel tells Zacharias that his wife will bear him a son, the future John the Baptist (*see* FIG. 61). The miraculous conversation occurs in the centre of the composition, before an altar and beneath a triumphal arch. Once again, identifiable Florentines of Tornabuoni's time populate the scene, but only four are privileged enough to stand on the same elevated platform as the sacred protagonists. From left to right, they are Giuliano, Gian

Fig.61
Domenico Ghirlandaio
Annunciation to Zacharias
from the Tornabuoni chapel

1485–90, fresco. Santa Maria Novella, Florence.

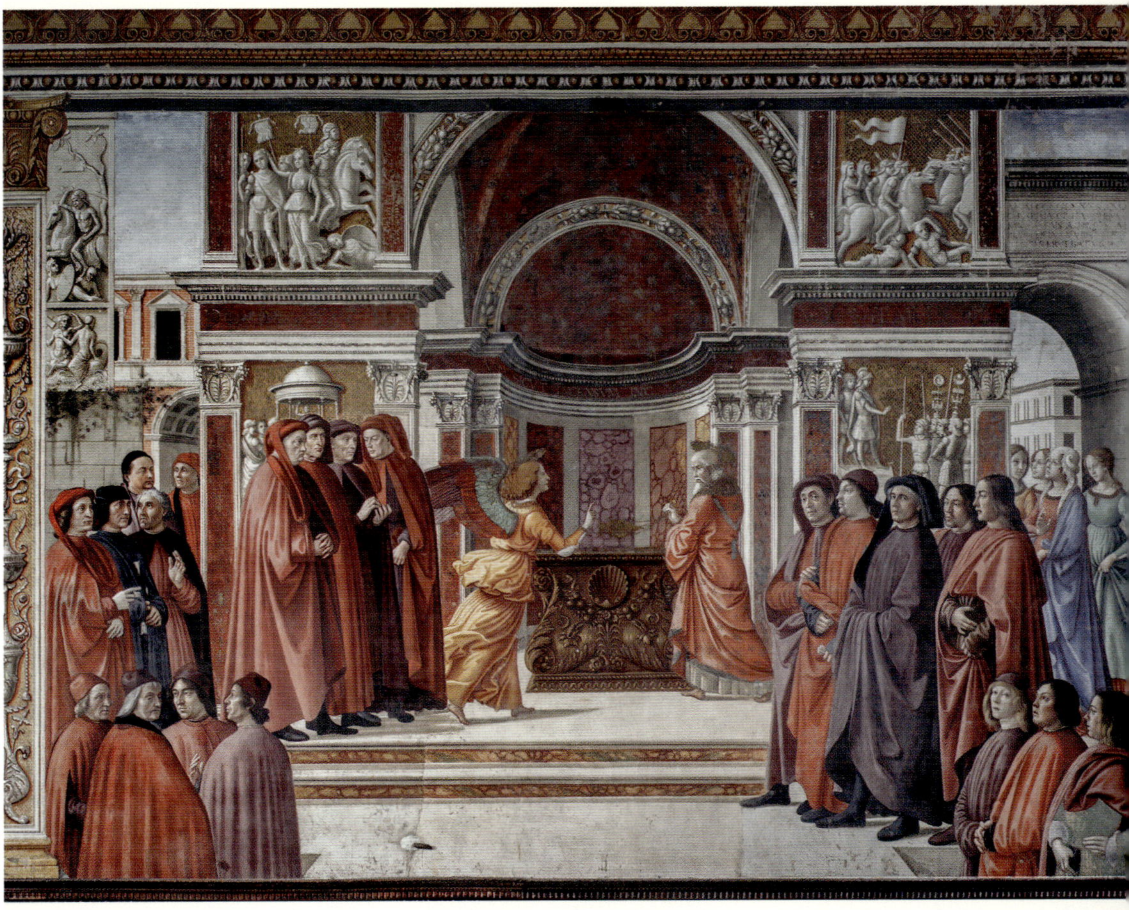

Francesco and Giovanni Battista Tornabuoni (the patron), together with Giovanni Tornaquinci. They represent the four main branches of the Tornaquinci *consorteria*, of which Giovanni Tornabuoni's line was but one. Although Giovanni is often discussed as the patron of this chapel, and he signed the contract with Ghirlandaio in 1485, the following year the friars of Santa Maria Novella granted patronage rights to the entire ancient *consorteria*. Far from being one of Lorenzo's new men, or even his uncle, Giovanni Tornabuoni presents himself as a proud member of an ancient magnate family.

The case studies we have examined in this chapter all date from the period of Medicean hegemony (1434–94). Relatives, neighbours and friends were equally important under the oligarchy, in the opening decades of the fifteenth century, and the renewed Republic of 1494–1512, which in many ways looked back to the era of guild patronage in the early fifteenth century. Without the '*gran maestro*', or '*maestro della bottega* [master of the shop]', as Lorenzo was described in about 1470 by Benedetto Dei, the dynamics were slightly different. Nowhere is the shift more apparent than in the sequestration of works of art from the Palazzo Medici, including the overtly republican *David* by Donatello (*see* FIG. 13) and the Hercules canvases by Antonio del Pollaiuolo, and their relocation to the Palazzo della Signoria. It is no surprise, then, that the opening decade of the sixteenth century brought a slew of new corporate commissions, whether from the government for the Sala del Gran Consiglio (*see* FIGS. 16, 17) or from the Calimala, once again keen to decorate the portals of the Baptistery with monumental sculpture.

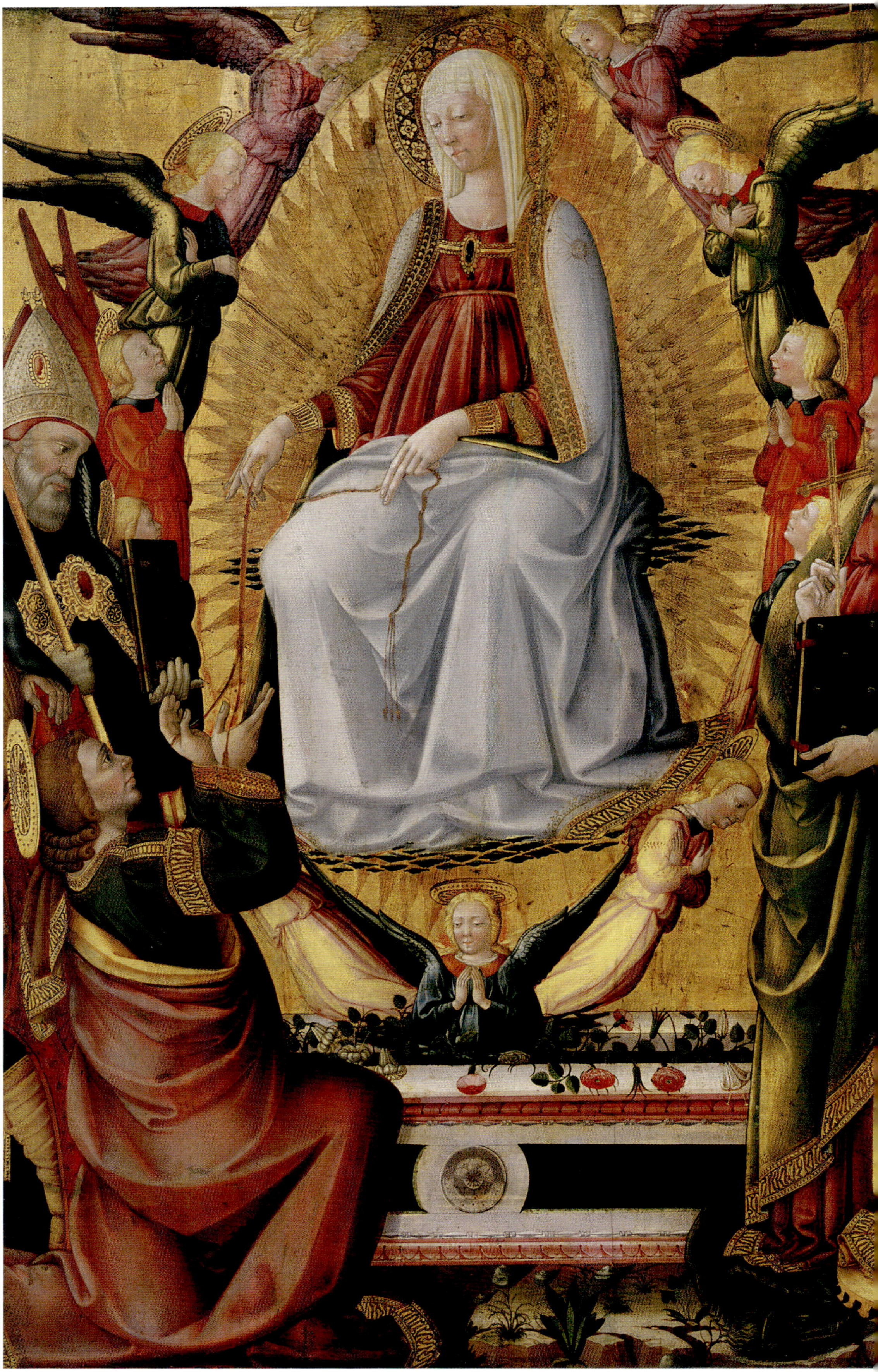

6

The Patronage of Women

Ghirlandaio's altarpiece showing the *Visitation with Mary Jacobi and Mary Salome* is exceptional in the degree to which it pictures women, commemorates an individual woman and addresses themes of particular relevance to women (FIG. 63). Completed in 1491, it adorned the Tornabuoni chapel in the church of Santa Maria Maddalena di Cestello, as part of the same rebuilding campaign that involved the decoration of the Boni and Salviati chapels, discussed in the previous chapter. The painting shows the pregnant Virgin as she visits Elizabeth, a relative and soon-to-be mother of John the Baptist. Elizabeth falls to her knees before Mary, having just recognized her as the mother of God.

Ghirlandaio reused a composition that had been employed almost 50 years earlier by Luca della Robbia at San Giovanni Fuorcivitas in Pistoia, but he made some significant changes (FIG. 64). The first was to have Elizabeth touch the Virgin's belly, a subtle shift that underscores her pregnancy. The second was to introduce two additional figures, who are identified by inscription as Mary Jacobi and Mary Salome. These two Marys were thought to have been the Virgin's half-sisters and the mothers of several of Christ's future disciples: James the Less, James the Greater and John the Evangelist.

Fig.62
Neri di Bicci
San Michele Altarpiece

Detail of Fig.69.

Fig.63
Domenico Ghirlandaio
Visitation with Mary Jacobi and Mary Salome

1491, oil on panel, 171 × 165cm ($67\frac{3}{8}$ × 65in). Musée du Louvre, Paris.

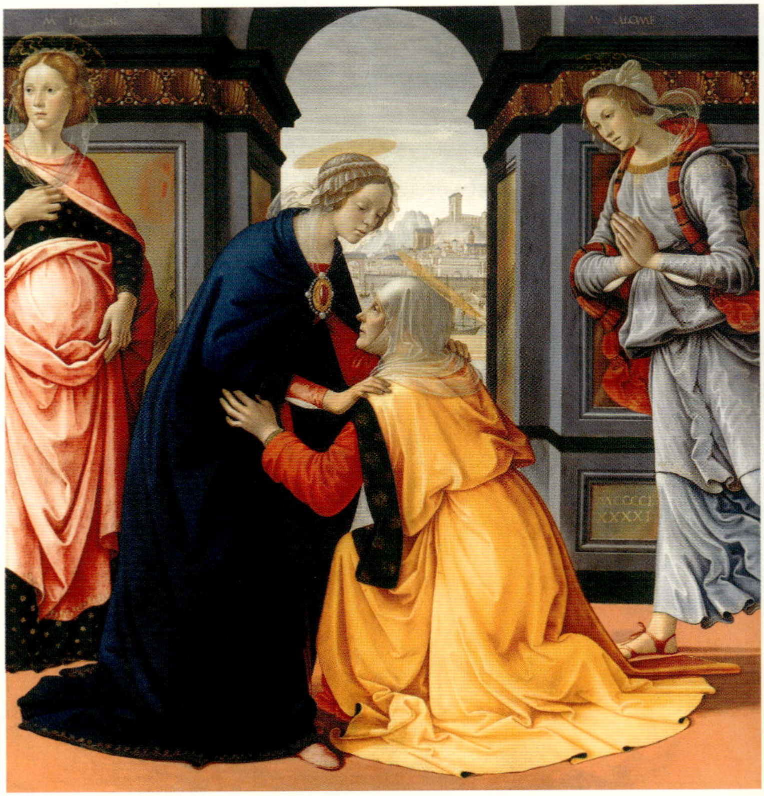

Mary Jacobi's stomach appears distended. Ghirlandaio draws attention to her womb through lighting and the maternal manner in which she cups it with her left hand. The third Mary of tradition, Mary Magdalene, was not included in Ghirlandaio's altarpiece, presumably because she was not related to the Virgin. In short, the altarpiece shows a series of mothers, all of them relatives of the Virgin.

The altarpiece was commissioned by Lorenzo Tornabuoni (1465–1497), the son of Giovanni Tornabuoni, whom we have already met. However, Lorenzo's reasons for acquiring *jus patronatus* (the right of patronage) over this chapel at Cestello were different from those of his father at Santa Maria Novella. Through it, he sought to commemorate his first wife, Giovanna di Maso degli Albizzi, whose maiden family – the Albizzi – lived in this part of Florence. Lorenzo and Giovanna had married on 15 June 1486, but she died only two years later, while giving birth to their second son. Lorenzo's mother, Francesca di Luca Pitti, had also died during childbirth, and was likewise remembered through a chapel painted by Ghirlandaio (now lost, but originally in Santa Maria sopra Minerva, Rome). Lorenzo would remarry Ginevra Gianfigliazzi in October 1491, while making preparations for Giovanna's chapel, but he would nonetheless die with a portrait of Giovanna still in his room (FIG. 65).

Giovanna was not buried at Cestello, but rather at Santa Maria Novella, surrounded by her husband's family. There, she was portrayed posthumously in a fresco, again showing the *Visitation* (FIG. 66). The chapel at Cestello, instead, was about individual commemoration. In 1492 the general chapter of the Congregazione di San Bernado (the provincial congregation of the Cistercian monasteries in Lombardy and Tuscany) agreed to celebrate an annual mass for her soul in the chapel, a practice that was supposed to continue for an entire century. Similarly, the abbot of Settimo, who led the provincial congregation, ordered the monks at Cestello to pray daily for her soul in the chapel, with an additional oration at the weekly mass. There is no sense that Lorenzo sought to honour himself or any other member of his family at Cestello, just Giovanna.

Ghirlandaio's altarpiece clearly engages with themes of motherhood and pregnancy, but – for all that it is concerned with subjects relevant to women, and commemorates an individual woman – it was commissioned by a man. Most of the works of art that have been the subject of this book were commissioned by men of the patrician class, acting individually or as members of an institution. They were Florentine citizens, emancipated adults who belonged to the major guilds and had generally reached the age of

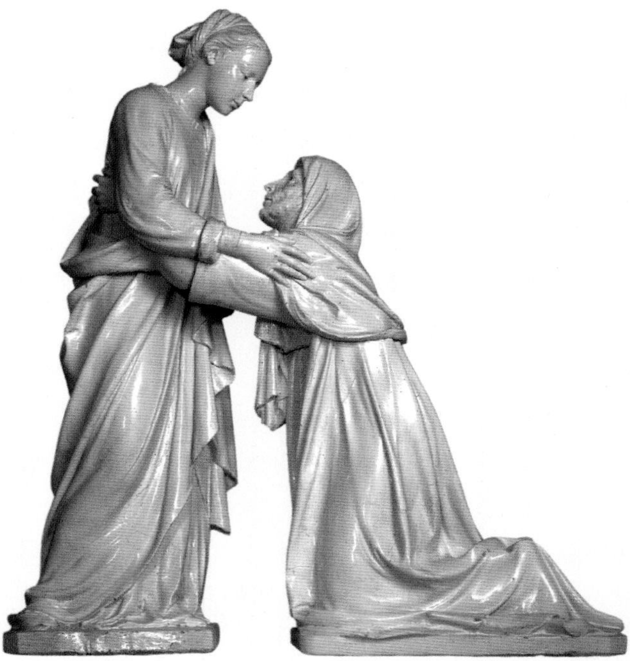

Fig. 64
Luca della Robbia
Visitation

ca. 1445, tin-glazed terracotta, 184 × 153 cm ($72\frac{3}{8} \times 60\frac{1}{4}$ in). San Giovanni Fuorcivitas, Pistoia.

30. They could be elected for government office and were, on the whole, rich. A few belonged to the magnate class. In contrast to these privileged few, there is relatively little evidence of works of art owned by Florentines further down the social scale, and what we can glean from occasional documents, such as inventories taken by the magistracy of the *pupilli et adulti* (which took care of widows and orphans in cases where the head of the family had died intestate), are almost impossible to correlate with surviving objects. Likewise, the evidence for women acting as artistic patrons in their own right is scanty. The dearth is particularly pronounced in Florence in the fifteenth century, unlike other centres in the Italian peninsula. However, their patronage was by no means non-existent, and it is to these few, but important, instances that we now turn our attention.

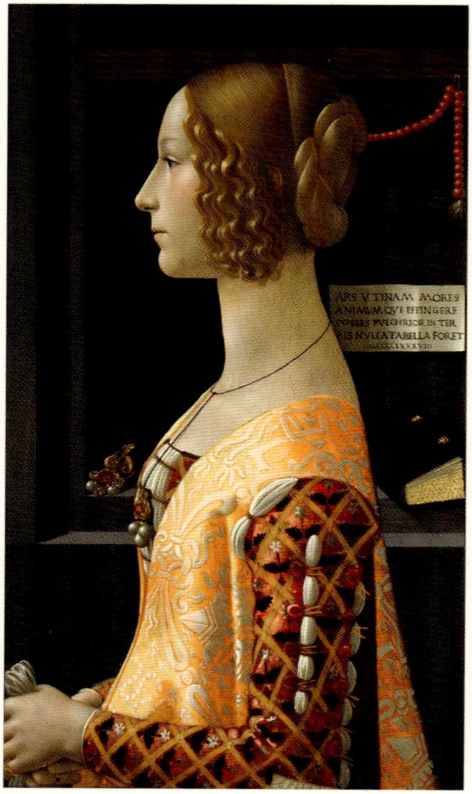

Fig. 65
Domenico Ghirlandai
Giovanna degli Albizzi

1489–90, tempera on panel, 77 × 49cm (30¼ × 19¼in). Museo Thyssen-Bornemisza, Madrid.

During the period, however absurd it might sound now, women were popularly understood as imperfect versions of men, less subject to reason than their male counterparts and prone to emotional whim. They were always controlled by men in some form or other. Not even in the courts were women independent, for the Florentine statutes ruled that 'no woman may act for or defend herself in civil cases, although she may respond to questions if these are put to her as necessary by adversaries'. Giannozzo Alberti, an interlocutor in Leon Battista Alberti's book *On the Family* (*Della famiglia*), written in the 1430s and 1440s, provides a sense of female subjugation when he instructs his new wife in her duties and notes her response: 'She replied by saying that her father and mother had taught her to obey them and had ordered her always to obey me [her husband], and so she was prepared to do anything I told her to.' The good wife was obedient to her husband, whose legal right over her required obedience (*obsequia*) and service (*servitia*). She should be modest and hardworking. Her value to her husband was in running the house and in her ability to bear children. Upon marriage, a woman, like her property, transferred from her natal to her marital family, although to some extent she still remained subject to her father's control (*patria potestas*). Even widows, or those women who were legally emancipated, required a male guardian – a *mundualdus* – to perform ordinary transactions.

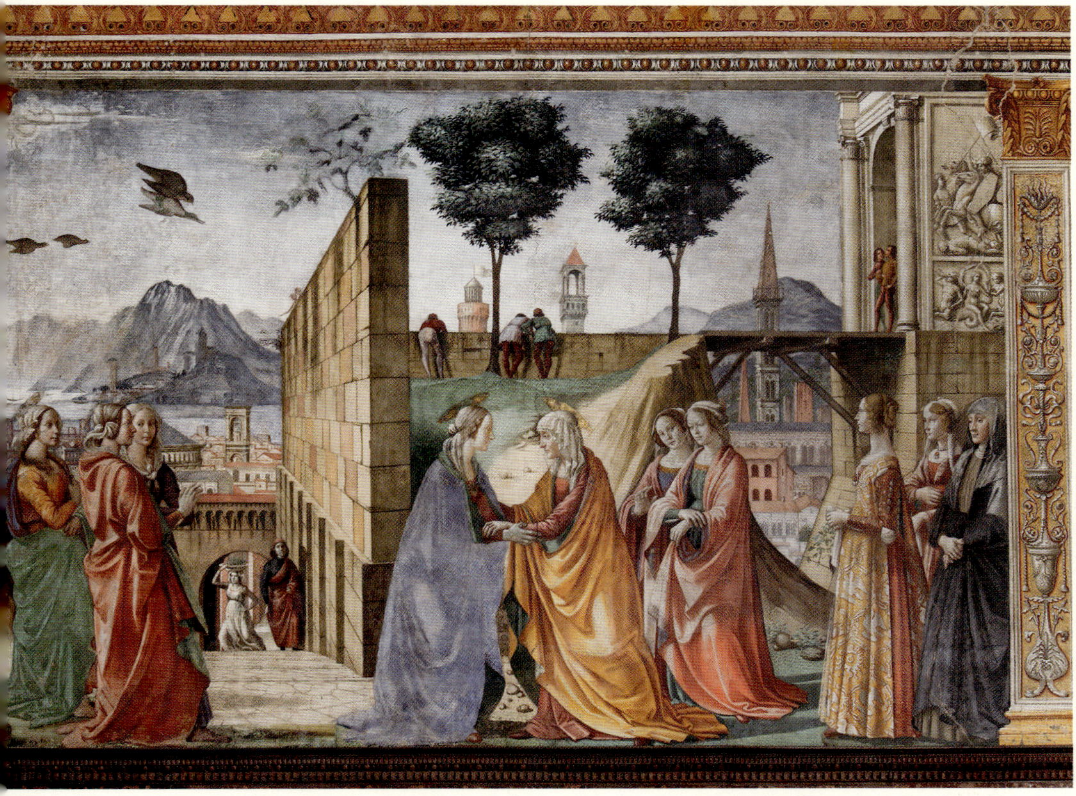

As a consequence of their legal status, women are rarely documented as patrons of works of art. Even had they been involved in the commissioning process, the nature of the documents that we use to determine patronage – contracts, inventories and occasionally the workshop or account books of artists – invariably record the men involved as signatories to any agreement. In other words, the nature of the evidence is such that the participation of women has been lost to history. In the few known instances of women contracting works of art directly from an artist, they were invariably commissioned with the help of a *mundualdus*. A good barometer is provided by the *ricordanze* (book of memories or *ricordi*) kept by the painter Neri di Bicci. Between 1453 and 1475 he received 142 commissions from laymen (men who were not in holy orders), but only 24 from women, nearly all with the assistance of a *mundualdus*. These commissions were invariably for religious settings. Only 7 percent of Neri's secular commissions came from women. Famous patrons and collectors such as Isabella d'Este in Mantua or Eleanor of Toledo in mid sixteenth-century Florence, who have become the subject of mythmaking and popular history, were the exception, not the norm.

Fig. 66
Domenico Ghirlandaio
Visitation from the Tornabuoni chapel

1485–90, fresco. Santa Maria Novella, Florence.

Giovanna degli Albizzi is identified as the woman in profile on the right-hand side of the fresco.

Fig. 67
Apollonio di Giovanni
The Triumph of Love

ca. 1460–70, tempera on poplar panel, 72 cm (28⅜ in) diameter. Victoria and Albert Museum, London.

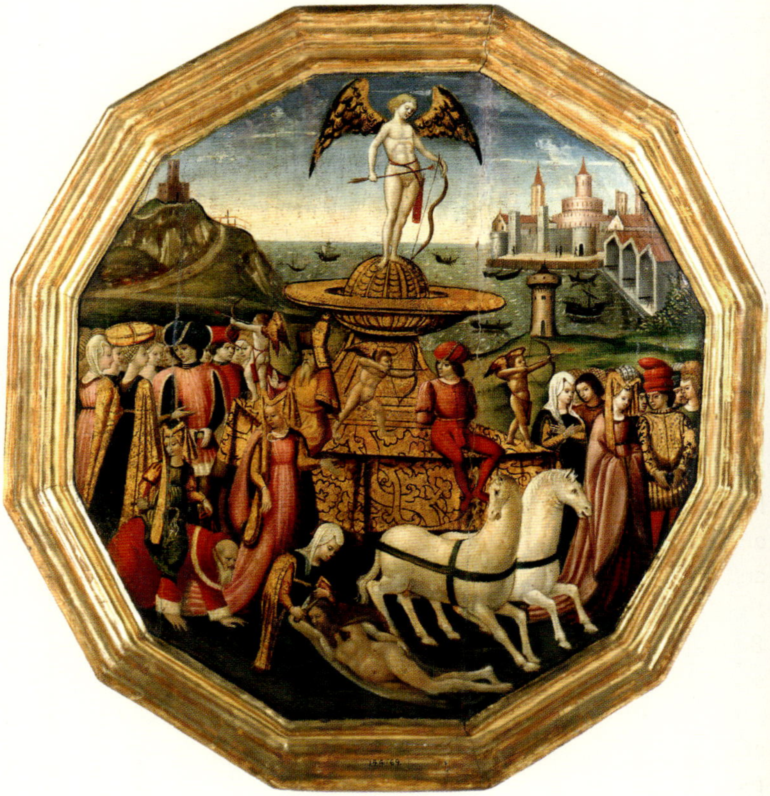

It would be untrue to suggest that women never commissioned works of art, however. Certain women were in a position to order objects because they were partially liberated from male control, at least compared with their peers. Perhaps their husbands had died or been exiled, or they were living in female religious communities. The exiled men of the Strozzi family had to rely on their spouses and female relatives, who were still resident in Florence, to administer their business affairs, while raising and educating their children. A vivid picture of their manoeuvrings survives in the letters of Alessandra Macinghi Strozzi, including a few discerning comments on pictures. But these women, who are the subject of this chapter, are not the only evidence of female agency in Florentine art. Certain object types were created for an explicitly female viewer. *Deschi da parto*, for example, were trays presented to wealthy women after they gave birth. They frequently include humorous scenes of women triumphing over men: Phyllis riding Aristotle or Delilah cutting Samson's hair (FIG. 67). They were clearly intended to be enjoyed by women. The images themselves provide evidence that they were designed and crafted with a female spectator in mind.

Widows and Nuns

Neri's records provide a glimpse of those women who were most likely to order works of art. Fourteen of his commissions were from nuns or *pinzochere* (religious women who lived a chaste life in poverty, often collectively, but had not taken vows), while five were from widows. Of the remaining five women who commissioned pieces from him, only one is known to have been married, while the status of the remainder is unknown. Fascinatingly, their social position was diverse, ranging from wealthy patricians, such as India Salviati (who, with her brother, commissioned an altarpiece showing the Assumption of the Virgin), to those in the lowest classes, among them Andrea di Barberino, the wife of a tailor, who ordered a painted cloth ('*una chortina*') showing Tobias and the Angel in January 1457. It is sadly lost. These women, notwithstanding their social standing, spent large amounts of money. Checa di Spigliato, a widow and the daughter of an armourer, commissioned an altarpiece showing the *Coronation of the Virgin with Saints* for Santa Maria dei Candeli (currently at San Bartolo a Cintoia); it cost her 105 florins, paid in instalments – the second highest price for a painting recorded in Neri's accounts.

As Neri's records suggest, widows were commonly patrons, and Florence had more than its fair share of them. In 1427, for example, about a quarter of all women were widowed (compared to only 4 per cent of men), and 14 per cent of all households were headed by widows (a figure that drops drastically to only 2 per cent if we consider only the wealthiest 472 households). Florentine men generally married on or around their thirtieth birthday, to women who were often still teenagers (they were on average 18 or younger, although the average age did rise to 20 or 21 in the second half of the fifteenth century), and so they died long before their wives. Widows had some independence, in that they might control their dowry and any income they received from their husband's estate, provided they were not forced back into marriage. Still, many young widows were returned to the care of their fathers, especially if they were childless.

As patrons, widows were often charged with the commemoration of their late husbands. Their children, both male and female, had an equal right to their dowries, so that they often spent it on works that would benefit the entire family, such as a chapel. Tita di Roberto Salviati, for instance, conceived and planned a marble altarpiece in memory of her husband, a Venetian called Girolamo Martini (d.1492), who had become a Florentine citizen. In his will, Martini expressed a wish to be buried in San Girolamo in Fiesole, in the hills above Florence, and provided 25 florins for his tomb. Tita saw to it,

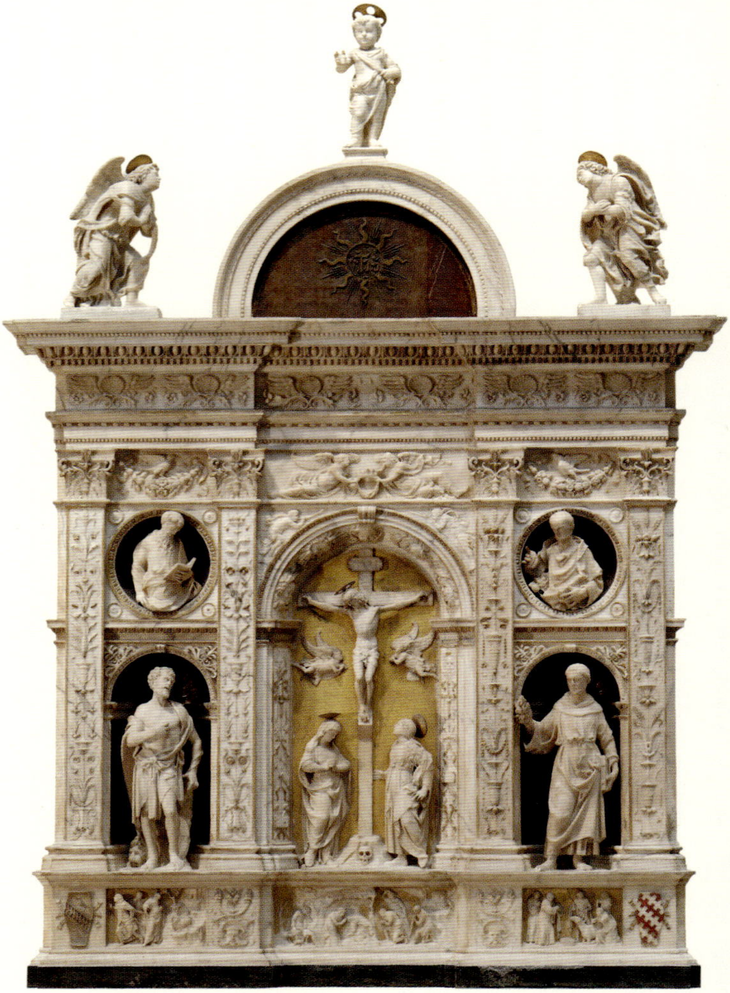

Fig. 68
Andrea di Piero Ferrucci
Salviati-Martini Altarpiece

ca. 1493, white and red marble, 365.8 × 274.3 cm (144 × 108 in). Victoria and Albert Museum, London.

overseeing the commission, making changes to the original brief and adding further money that Martini had left to her: 125 florins for a chapel and 180 florins for the altarpiece, which she commissioned from Andrea di Piero Ferrucci (1465–1526) in about 1493 (FIG. 68).

In the centre of the main panel, the Virgin and Mary Magdalene contemplate the Crucifixion, between Saints Jerome and John the Evangelist. St Jerome clearly relates to the dedication of the church and to the order (the Hieronymites) that occupied it. Of course, he was also Girolamo's name saint. The Magdalene, on the other hand, seems to reflect Tita's interests: not only was she the name saint of Tita's mother, Lena, but also she was an important model of female devotion to Christ. Despite Tita's extensive involvement, to which the surviving documentation attests, the altarpiece commemorates both husband and wife, and their respective family coats of arms decorate each end of the predella.

Women in holy orders were also patrons. Nuns became increasingly numerous during the period: between 1378 and 1552 the number of nunneries in the city increased from 18 to 47, and the average number of nuns in each house rose from 14 to 73. Neri recorded that on 4 September 1467 he consigned an altarpiece that had been commissioned by 'madonna Francesca', abbess of San Michele of Prato, a monastery of Benedictine nuns in a satellite town that formed part of the Florentine territory or *contado*. The abbess was to pay him in instalments according to an agreement drawn up by a notary, Ser Guaspare, who appears to have been her brother. The altarpiece and its predella still survive, although they have been separated (FIG. 69). The saints in the main tier, as much as the corresponding scenes from their lives in the predella, clearly relate to the lives of

Fig. 69
Neri di Bicci
San Michele Altarpiece

1467, gold and silver on panel, main panel 155.6 × 154.6cm (61¼ × 60⅞in), predella 28.5 × 201.2cm (11¼ × 79⅕in). Philadelphia Museum of Art, John G. Johnson Collection; predella (below), Museu Nacional d'Art de Catalunya, Barcelona. Francesc Cambó Bequest, 1949 (064972-000).

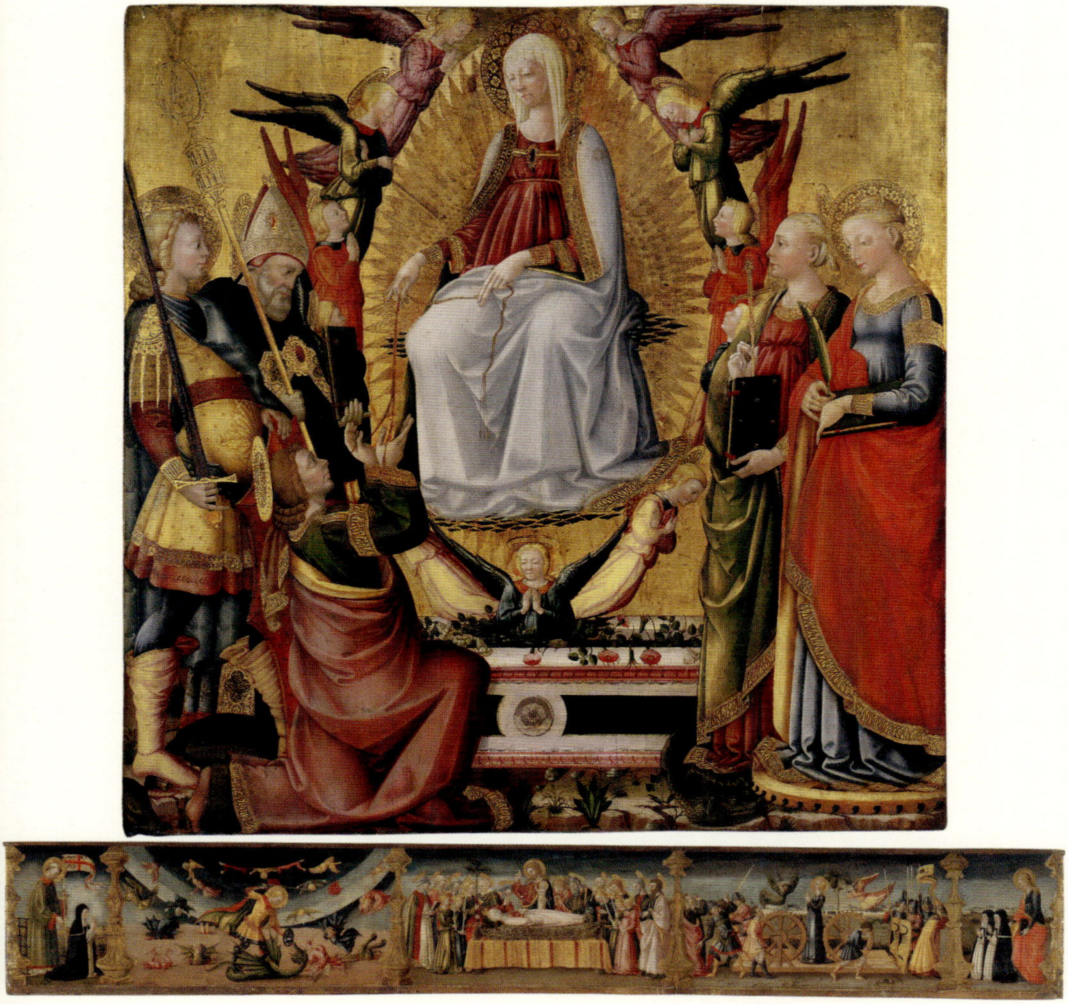

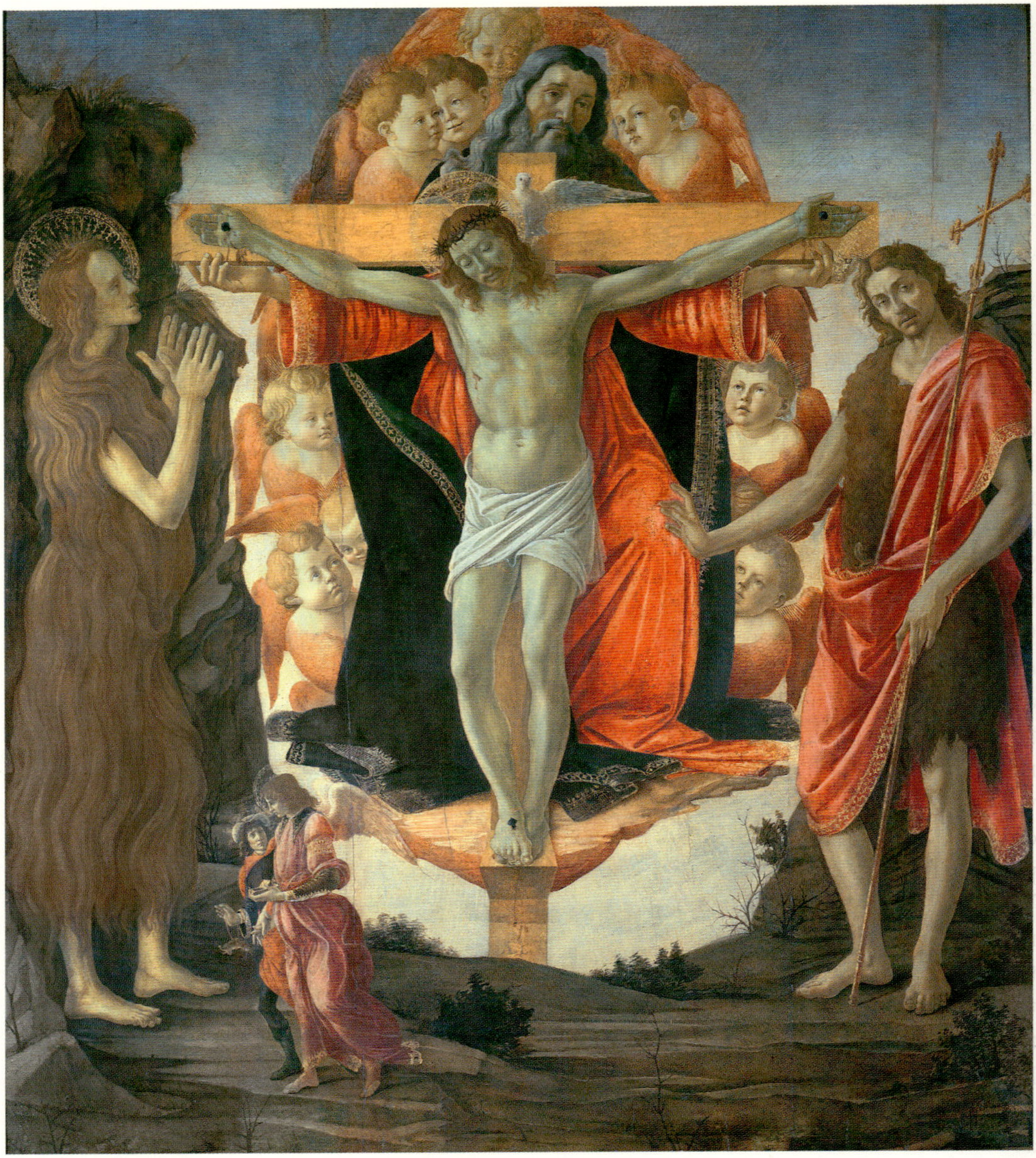

Fig. 70
Sandro Botticelli
Trinity with Saints Mary Magdalene, John the Baptist, Archangel Raphael and Tobias

ca. 1491–4, tempera and oil (?) on panel, 214 × 192.4cm ($84\frac{1}{2} \times 75\frac{3}{4}$in). The Courtauld Gallery, London.

the Benedictine nuns. The two male saints on the left (Archangel Michael and St Augustine) relate to the dedication of their church (San Michele) and the fact that they lived according to the rule of St Augustine. In the centre, St Thomas receives the Virgin's girdle, which was preserved as a relic in Prato (FIG. 62). The two saints on the right, Margaret of Antioch and Catherine of Alexandria, are less easy to explain in these terms. Instead, they seem to have served as models for the female monastic community, who were to follow their example in their own lives. Catherine was evidently especially venerated, since the scene of her martyrdom on a wheel was also chosen for the predella. Furthermore, Neri included members of the community at either end of the predella, where one might expect to find a coat of arms in a family commission. Both sides include nuns, one of whom is being presented by St Lawrence (and is presumably Francesca), while the other two are recommended by a female saint, who resists identification. Not only is this an altarpiece that was commissioned by a woman, but also it responded to the devotional needs of a female community.

It is rare to be able to trace through original documentation the patronage of a woman and then see how the finished work of art engaged female spectators. More often than not, we are left speculating on the role of women in the commissioning process (because their names do not appear in the documents) or trying to deduce which elements in an image might have held particular meaning for them. Such is the case with Botticelli's Trinity Altarpiece, which almost certainly decorated the high altar of the church of Sant'Elisabetta della Convertite on the Oltrarno (FIG. 70). The original contract has yet to emerge from the archive, but we know that Sant'Elisabetta housed a community of impoverished nuns, who had previously worked as prostitutes before repenting of their sins and taking the veil. It might not be possible to say who paid for the altarpiece, nor even through which male intermediary it was commissioned, but surely we can be confident that the presence of Mary Magdalene, both in the main panel and in the predella, spoke to the experience of these women. Who but a reformed prostitute herself could provide them with a model of exemplary piety? Similar cases can be made for three altarpieces commissioned from Fra Filippo Lippi (ca. 1406–1469) for the Benedictine communities at Sant'Ambrogio and Le Murate, and the Dominican tertiaries at SS Vincenzo e Stefano (the 'Annalena'). In each case, but to a differing degree, it seems likely that Lippi responded to the requirements of an abbess or took into consideration a female audience, even if, from their documented history, the voices of these women and their particular visual priorities are lost to time.

Lucrezia Tornabuoni

In addition to nuns and widows, scholars have tried to find evidence of one-off, exceptional female patrons. As with male patrons, the search has focused on those of the patrician class. Lucrezia di Francesco Tornabuoni (1425–1482), the aunt of Lorenzo Tornabuoni

Fig. 71
Fra Filippo Lippi
Adoration of the Child with Saints John the Baptist and Bernard of Clairvaux (Medici Altarpiece)

ca. 1459, oil on panel, 129.5 × 118.5cm (51 × 46⅝ in). Gëmaldegalerie, Staatliche Museen zu Berlin.

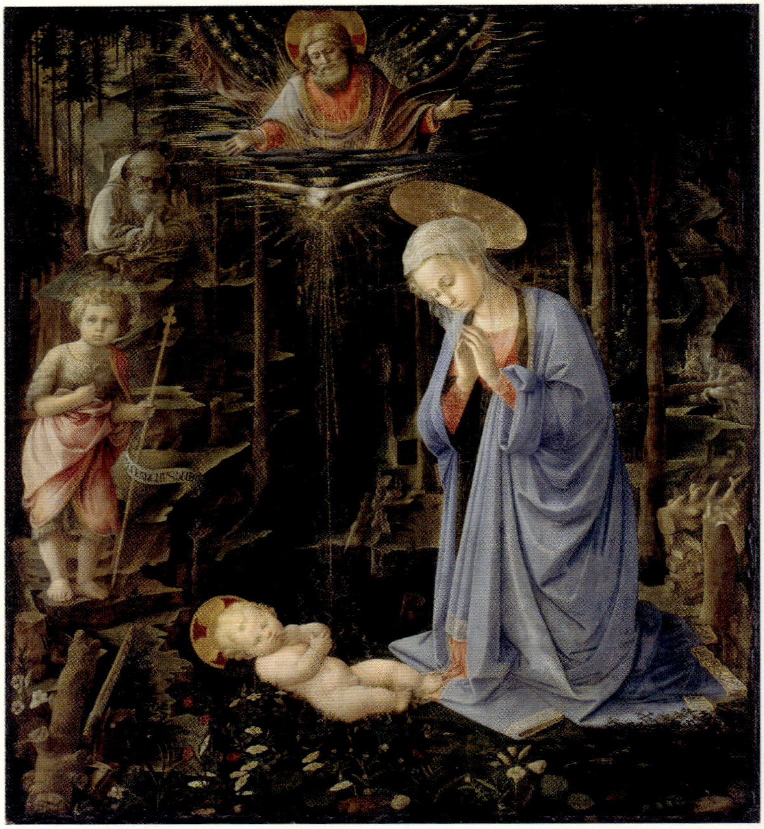

mentioned above, is sometimes singled out for special attention. She married Piero de' Medici in 1444 and they had six children, of whom two died in infancy. Educated and intelligent, she corresponded with the intellectuals and writers who frequented the Medici household, among them Gentile Becchi, Luigi Pulci and Agnolo Poliziano, and was an accomplished poet herself, writing in the vernacular. Lucrezia probably dispensed some degree of autonomous social and political patronage, especially after the death of her husband in 1469, but it is equally true that she exercised 'soft' power as an intermediary who brokered relationships with her son Lorenzo the Magnificent.

Five poems on sacred themes, eight lauds and a *canzone* have survived by Lucrezia's hand. Her poems reveal a deep piety, and a profound dedication to the young Baptist. Her spiritual life seems to have been modelled on his youthful withdrawal into the wilderness, evident in the *Life of St John the Baptist* (*Vita di San Giovanni Batista*) that she wrote. For this reason, she is often associated with the commission to Filippo Lippi for an altarpiece in the Medici chapel, which shows the Virgin adoring the Christ Child, together with the

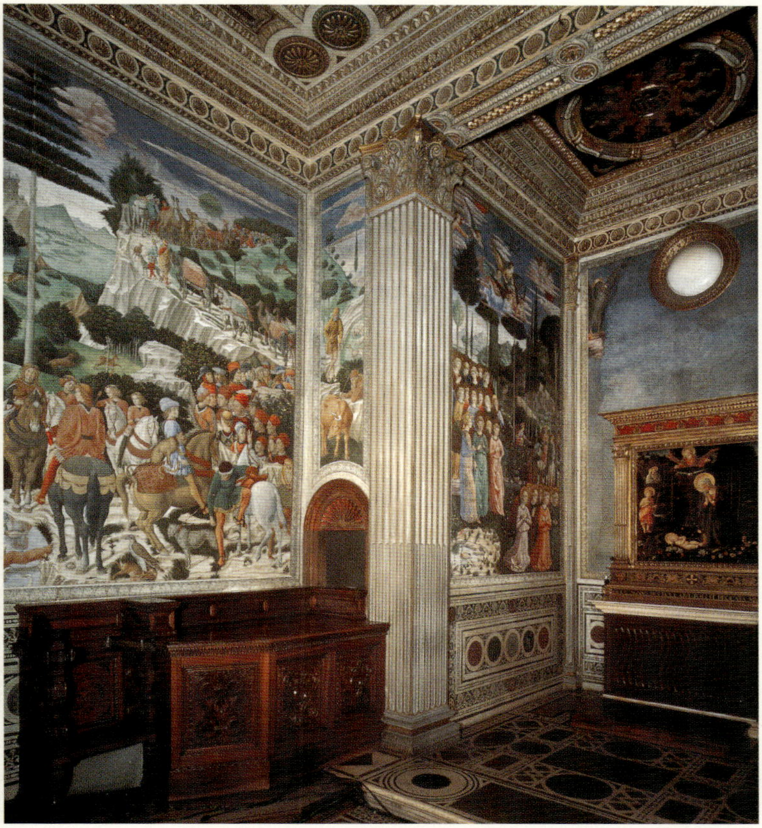

Fig. 72
The Medici chapel, including **Benozzo Gozzoli** *The Journey of the Magi*

1459–60, fresco. Palazzo Medici-Riccardi, Florence.

Gozzoli's frescoes show the procession of the Magi, proceeding towards Christ in Lippi's altarpiece. The altarpiece currently in the chapel is a fifteenth-century copy of the original, which is now in Berlin (Fig. 71).

young St John, an unexpected interloper (FIG. 71). It is a dark, ascetic space, somewhat akin to the 'shadowy paths' she mentions in her poetry as a metaphor for her own creative process. The altarpiece decorated the chapel in the Palazzo Medici, which was frescoed by Benozzo Gozzoli with the Journey of the Magi in the late 1450s for either Cosimo de' Medici or his son Piero (FIG. 72). Since the commission for the altarpiece is not documented, scholars continue to debate whether it proceeded from Cosimo, Piero or Lucrezia. And, as we have seen, even if Lucrezia was the motiving force, it is unlikely that her name would appear on the documents, were they to exist. In the end, all that is certain is that she was particularly devoted to the Baptist and that the altarpiece in her home showed, somewhat unusually for this date, the young St John.

Lucrezia was, however, a patron of manuscripts. Letters survive between her and Benedetto da Cepparello, her agent in Venice, for an illuminated missal that she was commissioning. She was clearly involved in the process, providing the scribe with parchment and paying the illuminator. Equally, her correspondents were keen to please her, and sought her advice. It has been suggested recently that she was also the patron of a manuscript containing an anonymous text of the *Life of St John the Baptist*, which was probably illuminated by the celebrated miniaturist Francesco d'Antonio del Chierico in the mid 1450s, when Lucrezia's husband was still alive (FIG. 73). The frontispiece contains both the Medici and Tornabuoni coats of arms.

There is another instance, too, in which we can be confident of Lucrezia's patronage (even if it may not have included works of art). She founded a chaplaincy dedicated to the Visitation, attached to the first chapel on the right of the Medici parish church of San Lorenzo, the Cappella della Vergine Nostra. She did not acquire patronage rights over the space, which remained with the canons of San Lorenzo, but she does seem to have expressed an interest that the chapel be associated with the Visitation, donating wax to be burned on the feast of the Visitation from the 1470s onwards. She might even have provided for a new altarpiece in the chapel, which can no longer be identified, but was certainly Marian and probably depicted the Visitation. Indeed, the feast of the Visitation continued to be associated with Lucrezia long after her death, when it was celebrated each year in the chapel in her memory (in addition to a mass on the first Wednesday after the Virgin's birth, 8 September). Lucrezia was the first Medici woman to have an impact on the decoration of San Lorenzo, a building that was slowly becoming a mausoleum to the men of her marital family (*see* FIG. 58).

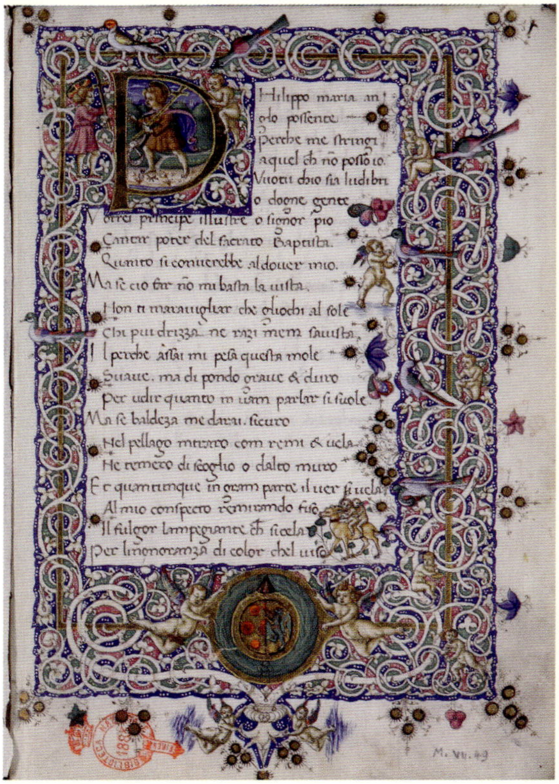

Fig. 73
Francesco d'Antonio del Chierico
Frontispiece to the *Life of St John the Baptist*

ca. 1455, parchment, 20 × 14.3cm (8 × 5½in). Biblioteca Nazionale Centrale, Florence (MS Magliabechiano VII, 49, fol. 1r).

Venus and Mars

In this chapter, we have concentrated on works of art commissioned directly by women, many of them widows, nuns or figures of unusual social standing. Such women were often allowed some freedom within a patriarchal system that, on the whole, denied women the means to patronize artists. Unearthing individuals forgotten by history is something of an old-fashioned quest in gender studies, and recent feminist scholars have instead focused their attention on the female viewer, frequently considering objects created for the home, the space to which many women were confined and over which they held most sway. They have also concentrated on certain moments in a woman's life, such as marriage, when *forzieri* (or wedding chests, now generally called *cassoni*) were produced for the nuptial chamber (FIG. 74). In conclusion, and in this spirit, I would like to consider an object made for the home, Botticelli's *Venus and Mars* (FIG. 75), an object assuredly commissioned by a man, but whose intended spectator is less obvious.

In truth, we know nothing about this painting before the mid nineteenth century. It was certainly commissioned around the time of a wedding, perhaps even for a member of the Vespucci family, since there are wasps (*vespe* in Italian) in the upper right-hand corner. From its style, we deduce that it dates from the 1480s, when it was probably inserted into the wainscot of a room or placed above an item of furniture at about shoulder height (hence *spalliera*, from *spalle*, the Italian word for shoulders). It shows the goddess of love, Venus, alert and awake, lying beside Mars, god of war, who is limp, asleep and almost entirely unclothed. Whether dressed or

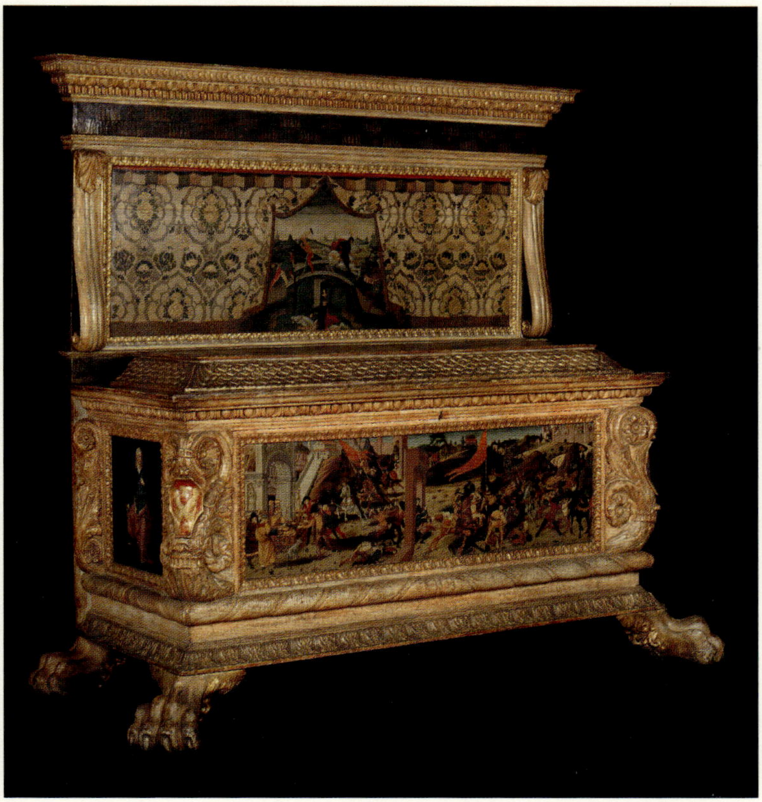

Fig. 74
Biagio d'Antonio and Zanobi di Domenico
Cassone and Spalliera with the Coat of Arms of Lorenzo Morelli and Vaggia Nerli
(Morelli Chest)

1472, tempera on wood, *cassone*: 190.2 × 193 × 76.2 cm (74¾ × 76 × 29⅞ in). The Courtauld Gallery, London.

This is one of a pair of *cassoni* commissioned on the marriage of Lorenzo Morelli to Vaggia Nerli, the daughter of Tanai Nerli and Nanna Capponi, the donors portrayed in Fig. 51. The *spalliera*, or back board, was not originally attached to the chest.

undressed, they are both beautiful. Between them cavort satyrs, or more accurately *panisci* (followers of Pan), who sport with Mars's sallet (helmet) and breastplate, while thrusting his phallic lance towards a conch shell.

The subject is Venus's adulterous coupling with Mars. It was known from Lucretius's *De rerum natura* and from Ovid, although the latter was probably not the source in this case. Botticelli, most probably on the advice of Poliziano, also refers to a lost painting by Aëtion, described by the ancient writer Lucian, that depicted the marriage of Alexander the Great to Roxana. There is no doubt that the scene is erotic – the penetrating lance and conch shell are hardly subtle – but it remains unclear whether Mars slumbers in a state of post-coital bliss, dreaming of amorous congruence, or if he is tormented by nightmares of sexual obsession. In either case, he is possessed by the viewer's eyes. Venus looks towards him, much as the spectator does. He is subjected to our gaze; his beautiful body is objectified for the gratification of the beholder.

The roles performed by Venus and Mars – respectively active and passive – invert normal gender paradigms for the Renaissance. Their engagement (or lack of engagement) with the viewer does so too. If we compare them with portraits from the period, female sitters are often subjected to a male gaze. Turned in profile, they cannot look back (FIG. 76). Here, instead, Venus is in three-quarter view, and awake. She can turn to look at us. What, then, are we to make of Botticelli's world turned upside down? The range of interpretations that have been advanced for the painting, from bawdy joke to erudite commentary on 'panic' and its Greek etymology, assume a male viewer at once learned and smutty; someone who identified with Mars, but did not wish to possess him lustfully. But does this painting not also provide evidence of another viewer, of a forgotten

Fig. 75
Sandro Botticelli
Venus and Mars

ca. 1485, tempera and oil on panel, 69.2 × 173.4cm (27¼ × 68¼in). National Gallery, London.

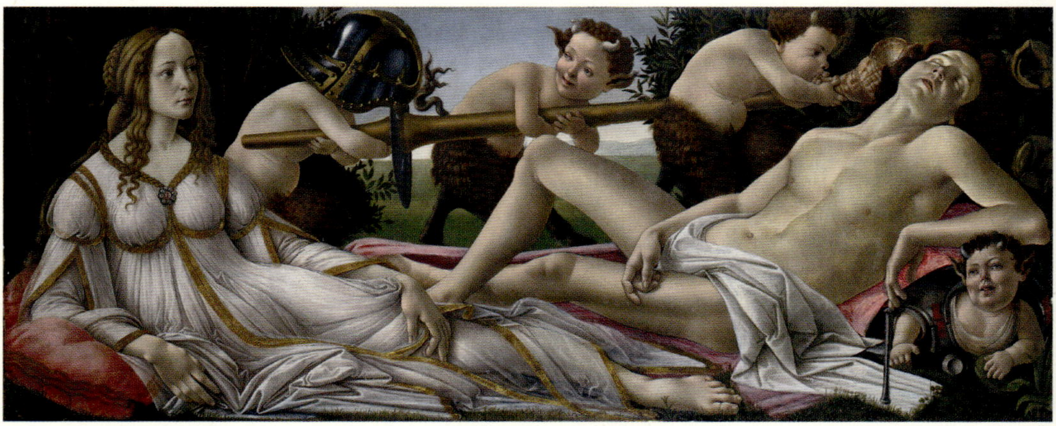

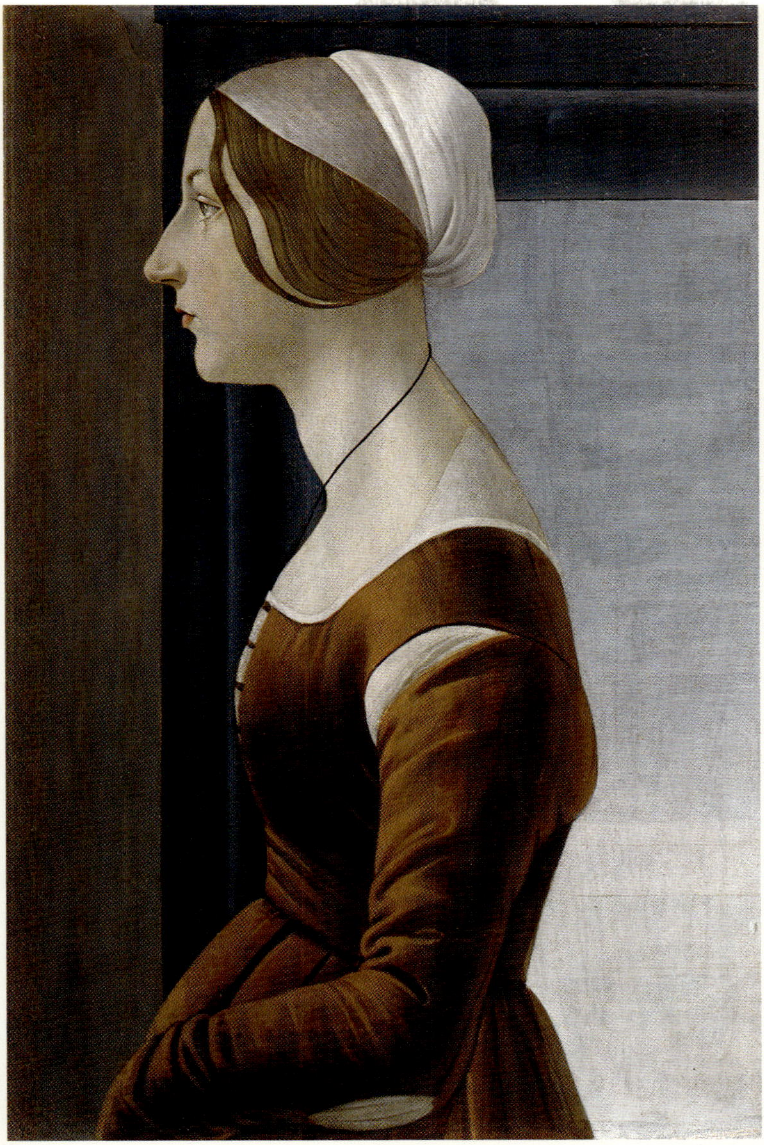

Fig. 76
Sandro Botticelli
Portrait of a Woman

ca. 1475, tempera on panel, 61 × 40cm (24 × 15¾in). Galleria Palatina, Florence.

Women were often portrayed in profile, subject to the viewer's gaze, while men frequently look out at the observer. However, the gendered distinction between profile and frontal is not universal. In Fig. 2, Ginevra de' Benci meets the spectator's gaze full on.

female spectator of the Renaissance? Would she not also take pleasure in it? If so, she would have inverted the conventions of humanist discourse, while still enjoying Botticelli's painting with intelligence, humour and perhaps some erotic titillation, too.

Having considered patrons over the last three chapters, we now turn our attention to the images they commissioned. The next two chapters are dedicated to questions of style, specifically to issues of space, nature and antiquity. They ask how and why Florentine images came to look as they did.

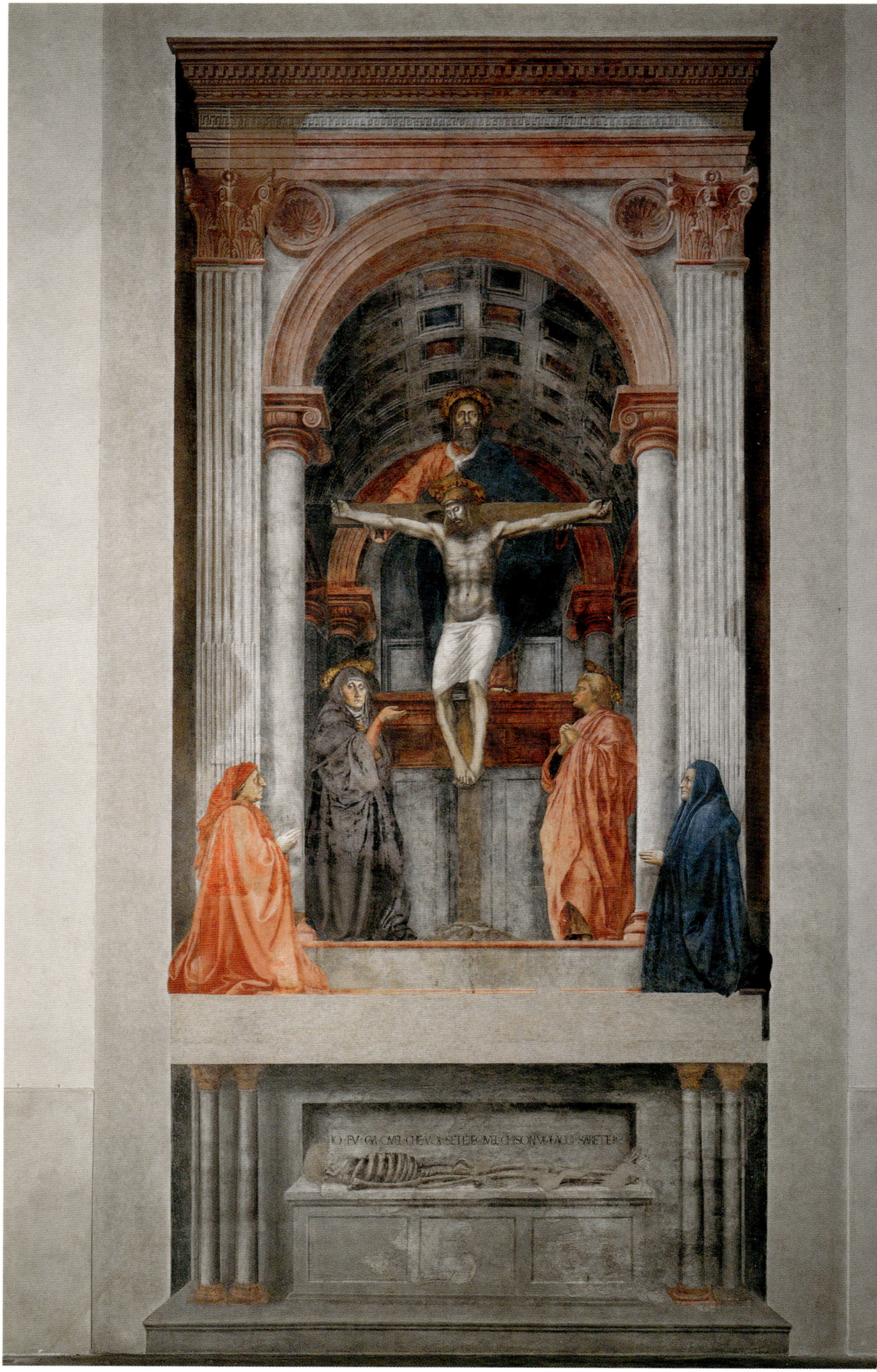

7

Style I: Perspectives on Space

A new question became urgent in the early decades of the fifteenth century that has had a lasting impact on Western art: how far should two-dimensional representation reflect the world we see around us? If we know a figure on the horizon to be the same size as someone standing beside us, should she be represented proportionally smaller, much as we see her, or at the scale that we know her to be? Should the colour of her clothing be as vibrant as we remember it, or less saturated, as we actually see it? In the West, we are so accustomed to a form of 'naturalistic' depiction that these questions seem nonsensical: obviously, she should be shown smaller and her clothes be less colourful. But what if she were the Virgin, the mother of God? How, then, should she be represented? Would it not diminish her sacred status to depict her tiny and faint? Answers to these questions are more complex than they initially seem, because they bring knowledge and sight into conflict. For artists, they presented a sizeable problem: should they follow their eyes or their mind?

The use of linear perspective was one solution to this thorny problem, even if it clearly privileged the eye over the mind in the construction of space. As a tool for artists, it was developed in Florence

Fig.77
Masaccio
Trinity

ca. 1426, fresco. Santa Maria Novella, Florence

The orthogonals can be traced along abaci (uppermost divisions of a capital) and through the coffering of the ceiling. They converge in a vanishing point that is the centre of the bottom step between the donors.

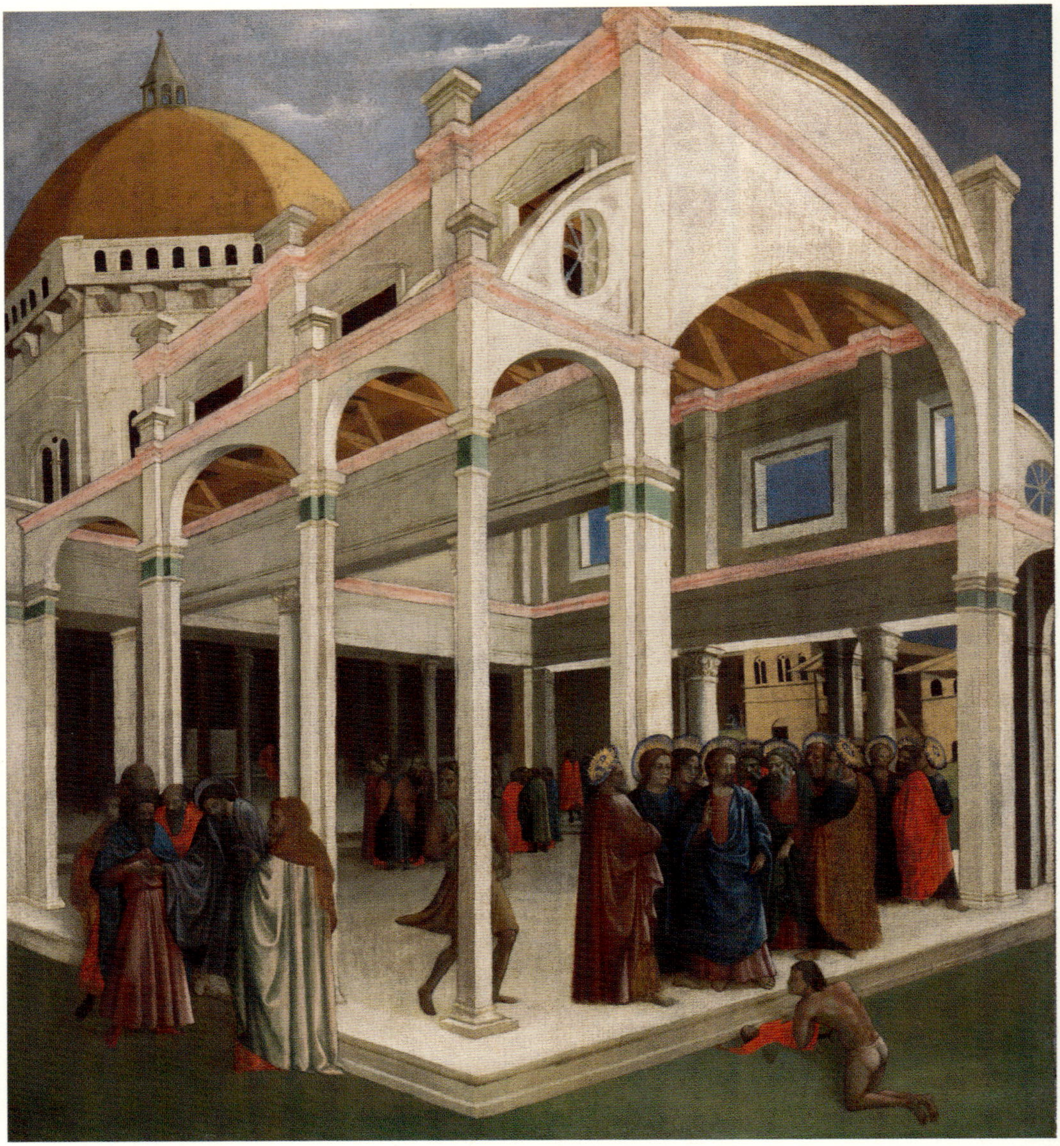

in the early fifteenth century, but as an understanding of sight, it had a much longer history in the study of optics. Its 'invention' was attributed to Brunelleschi by Manetti in two painted panels (now lost) that showed views of the Piazza della Signoria and the Baptistery (from the viewpoints shown in FIGS. 4 and 9). Whether or not he actually did invent it is less important than the fact that he was believed to have done so by the 1480s. Manetti was careful to call the technique 'what painters today call perspective [*prospettiva*]', clarifying that it derived from a branch of knowledge that 'consists of setting down properly and rationally the reductions and enlargements of near and distant objects as perceived by the eye of man'. We now use the word 'perspective' to indicate this form of construction, somewhat as Manetti's painters did, but in large part *prospettiva* was understood at the time in relation to optics, which has its roots in Greek antiquity and Arab science. In the mid 1430s instructions for the mathematical organization of space were committed to paper by Alberti in *De pictura*. It is a moot point whether Alberti followed and codified what was already well known to painters and sculptors, or if he was setting out rules that were entirely new. Works by Donatello and Masaccio from the 1410s and 1420s suggest that it had already been put into effect by sculptors and painters.

Perspective creates the illusion of three-dimensional space on a two-dimensional plane by calculating the relative scale of things mathematically. In general terms, the surface of the picture is aligned with the intersection of a visual pyramid with its apex in the eye of the viewer, whose existence it presupposes. Or, to use a metaphor employed by Alberti, the picture plane is likened to a window or veil through which the artist sees natural objects, which diminish in scale as they recede into space. The technique requires the artist to choose a vanishing point on the horizon line, where all parallel lines converge. These orthogonals (literally, 'at right angles') are then aligned with architecture or paving perpendicular to the picture plane in a system called one-point perspective, exemplified by Masaccio's *Trinity* in Santa Maria Novella (FIG. 77). Two-point perspective, in which there are two vanishing points on the horizon line, was also known, even if it was not theorized until the sixteenth century (unlike one-point perspective, which was described by Alberti). It was probably used by Brunelleschi in his experiments. Francesco d'Antonio (1393–1433) employed it, too, with uneven success, in a painting that relocates the scenes of Christ healing a madman and Judas receiving 30 pieces of silver to a temple modelled on the cathedral. The orthogonals project backwards from the corner of the building, following its two sides to separate vanishing points at left and right (FIG. 78)

The so-called discovery of linear perspective is held up as one of the most significant artistic developments of the Florentine Renaissance, and so it was. But it does not follow from the attention we give to linear perspective that previous generations were not able to portray space convincingly, nor that, once invented, it was eagerly embraced by all artists. Indeed, other cultures, whether in Europe or further afield, managed perfectly well without it and developed equally sophisticated systems for the representation of space. Given

Fig. 78
Francesco d'Antonio
Christ Healing a Lunatic and Judas Receiving Thirty Pieces of Silver

1425–26, tempera and gold on linen, 115.3 × 106 cm (45⅜ × 41¾ in). Philadelphia Museum of Art. John G. Johnson Collection, 1917 (Cat. 17).

The canvas has been cut, which obscures the right vanishing point. Tellingly, Vasari thought this painting was by Masaccio.

the universal claims sometimes made for linear perspective, Brunelleschi's discovery must be contextualized within a broader field.

Perspective in Practice and in Theory

A comparison of two panels of the *Virgin and Child*, by Giotto and Masaccio, reveals what makes perspective distinctive. Giotto's *Maestà* was painted in about 1310 and was probably intended for display on the choir screen at Ognissanti (FIG. 79). By contrast, Masaccio's *Virgin and Child* was once the central panel of a polyptych that was executed in 1426 for the Degli Scarsi chapel in Santa Maria del Carmine, Pisa (FIG. 80). Although they now seem similar in type and form, they would have appeared very different when Masaccio's panel was part of a much larger altarpiece. All the same, it is possible to contrast their treatment of the Virgin's throne. There has been a change in architectural vocabulary, for Giotto's has pointed 'gothic' arches while Masaccio's is decorated with miniature *all'antica* columns and strigulated flutes, derived from ancient sarcophagi. More importantly, there has also been a change in the way form is described in space. In both cases, the throne creates a convincing illusion of the space it occupies: the sides come inwards and the bases rise up to provide a sense of recession. However, the orthogonals in Masaccio's throne all converge on one point in the Virgin's womb, directing attention to this site of obvious symbolic meaning. In Giotto's throne there is no vanishing point; if you extend lines from the two mouldings at the height of the Virgin's shoulder, they converge between her breasts; those from the seat of the throne around her stomach; and those from the step, on which she has placed her feet, somewhere between her knees. Giotto constructed space empirically, by looking at the world around him, and then invented a throne by trial and error. Masaccio employed geometrical rules, derived from the study of mathematics and optics (whether by him or, more likely, his friends and advisors), to chart three-dimensional spatial

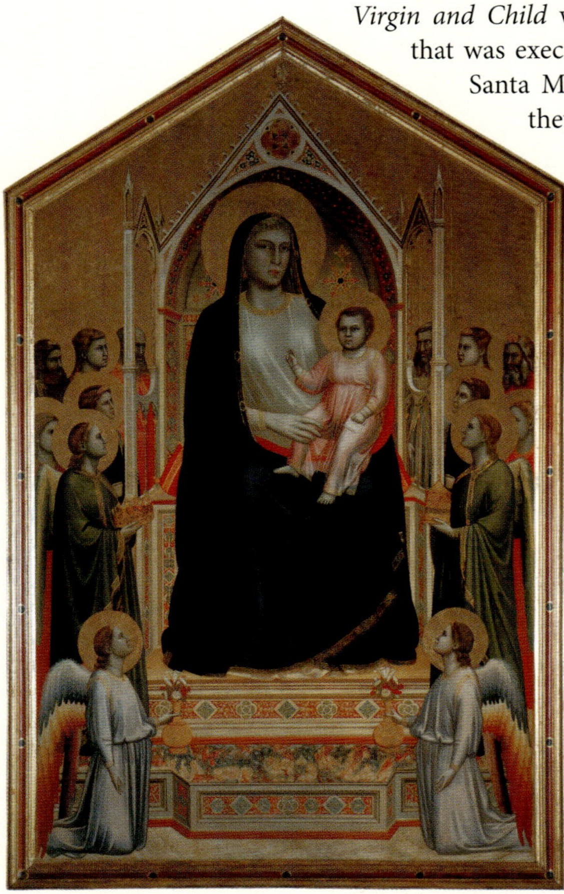

Fig.79
Giotto
Maestà

ca. 1310, tempera on panel, 325 × 204cm (128 × 80⅜in). Galleria degli Uffizi, Florence.

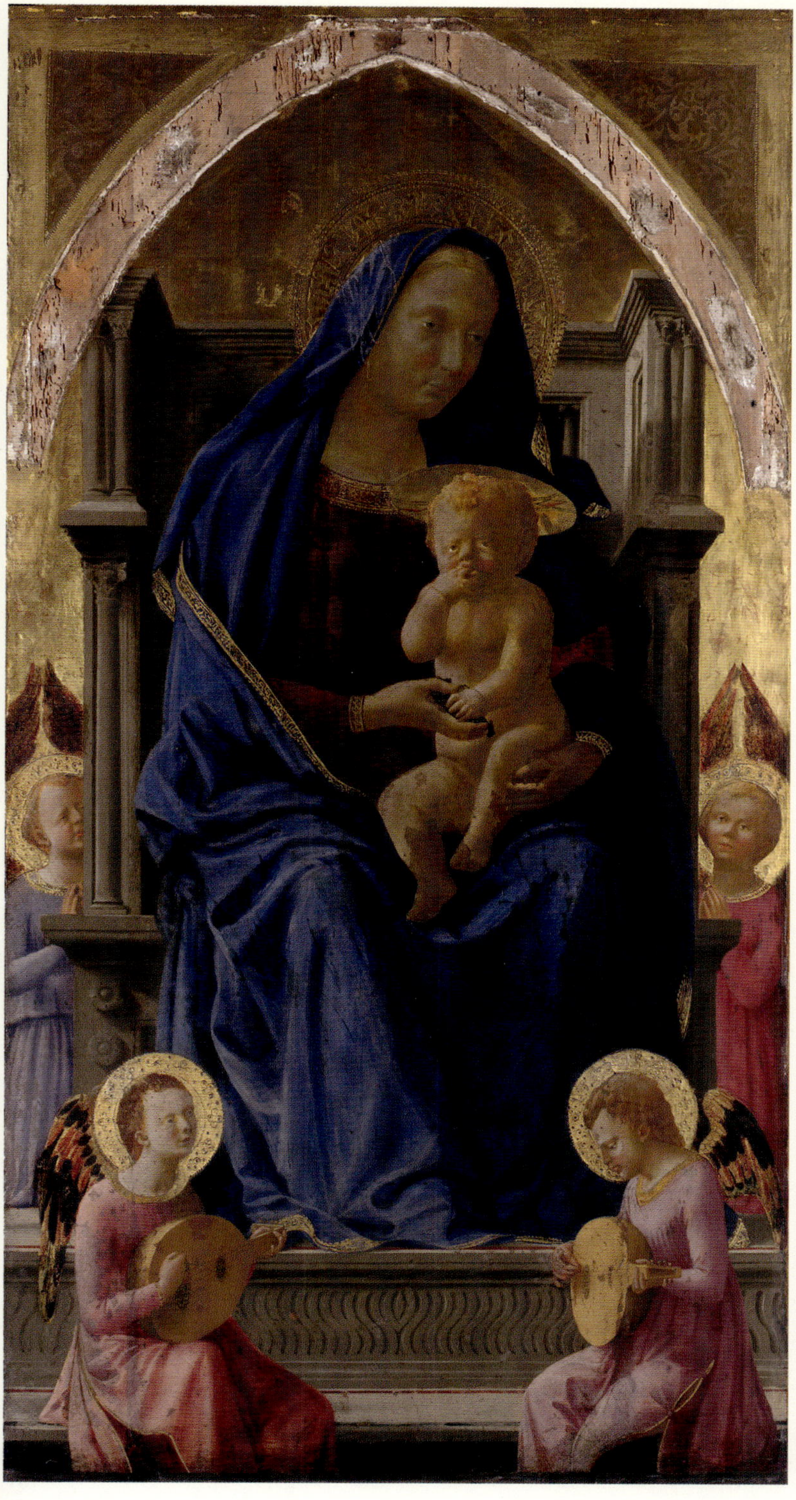

Fig. 80
Masaccio
Virgin and Child from the Pisa Altarpiece

1426, egg tempera on panel, 134.8 × 73.5cm (53 × 29in). National Gallery, London.

relationships on a two-dimensional support. Both created a convincing spatial illusion – neither one is *better* than the other – but their means were different.

Fourteenth-century artists were well aware that in the depiction of a room, say, the ceiling must come down and the walls inwards to suggest recession (FIG. 81). So, too, was Jan van Eyck (ca. 1390–1441), working in Bruges. The orthogonals of his *Arnolfini Portrait* cluster in a variety of different vanishing points, or 'vanishing areas', as one scholar has called them (FIG. 82). Were the orthogonals of the window on the left to have projected back to the same vanishing point as the floorboards (which are themselves inconsistent), the window would have plunged in a foreshortening that could only have looked disharmonious. Instead, van Eyck painted the room as he perceived it and knew it to be, rather than as it might have been projected on to the retina. He and Giotto were equally concerned with optical effects, but they did not plot them mathematically. So, when we talk of the 'invention' of linear perspective in Florence in the early fifteenth century, we are suggesting not that previous artists had not been interested in spatial recession or in the relationship between objects depicted in space, but rather that they had not calculated those relationships geometrically in relation to a fixed point outside the painting: the eye of the viewer.

Fig. 81
Giotto
Acceptance of the Rule from the Bardi chapel

1325–8, fresco. Santa Croce, Florence.

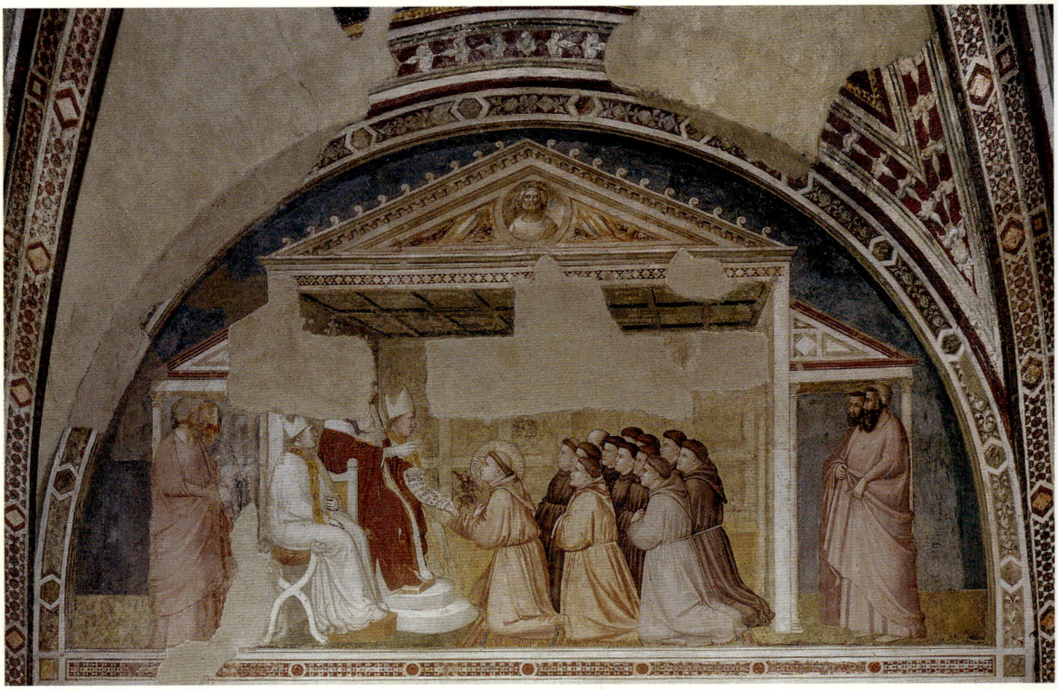

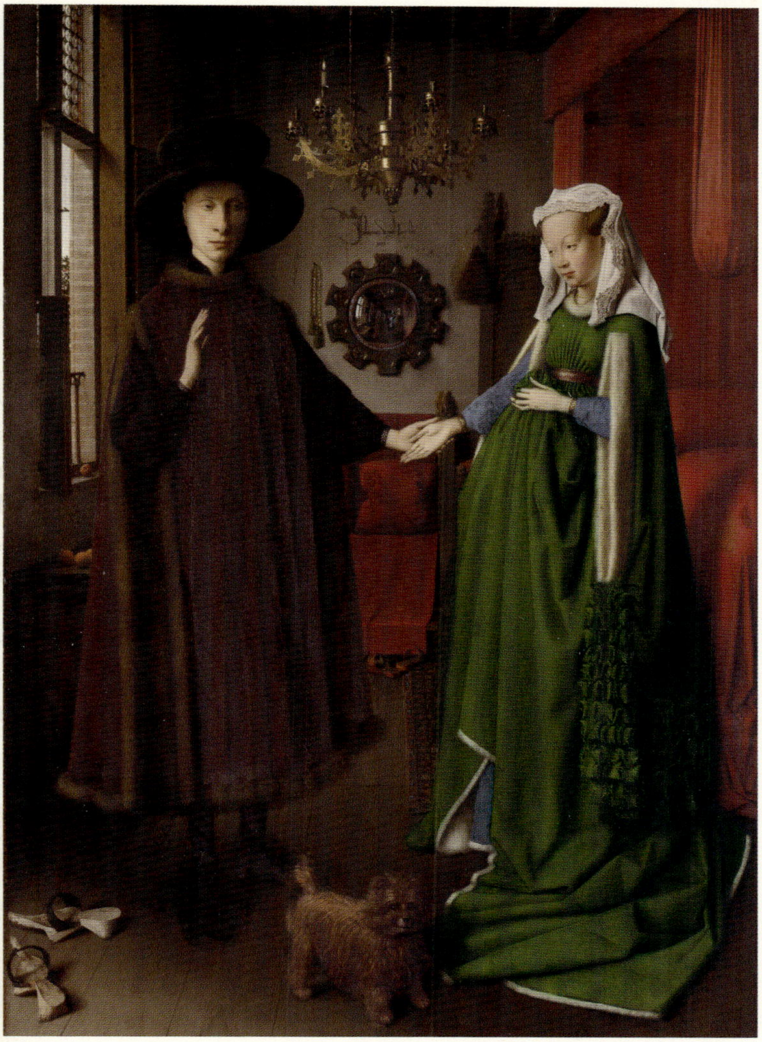

Fig. 82
Jan van Eyck
Arnolfini Portrait

1434, oil on oak, 82.2 × 60cm (32¼ × 23⅝in). National Gallery, London.

If we return to Giotto's and Masaccio's panels in this light, another important difference becomes apparent. Their treatment of space imagines the position of the viewer differently. In Giotto's case, we look down on the steps that lead up to the throne, and down on the Virgin's seat, but up at the underside of her canopy. The eye of the viewer is imagined to be somewhere around the Virgin's womb, even though such a viewer would have had to hover in the air, high above the nave of the church, to be in such a position. In Masaccio's image, the viewer's eye is level with the seat of the Virgin's throne, so that we look down on the steps and up at the architrave supported by the colonnettes. Masaccio's panel was once on an altar, and although it still seems higher than the viewer's actual position, it is much closer

Fig. 83
Diagram of perspectival construction

Alberti's principle is based on the idea that a pyramid is made up of triangles and that triangles are proportionally related to one another when they are 'similar', that is 'when their sides and angles stand in the same relationship to each other'. If you extend two sides of a triangle without changing the angle with which it meets the base, then the two triangles will be similar (as in the relationship between triangle ABC and triangle ADE). Imagine the base BC of the original triangle as a painting (or the intersection of the visual pyramid) and the new base DE as the surface in the world to be represented, then the spatial relationship between objects or figures in the world will be reproduced proportionally in the painting.

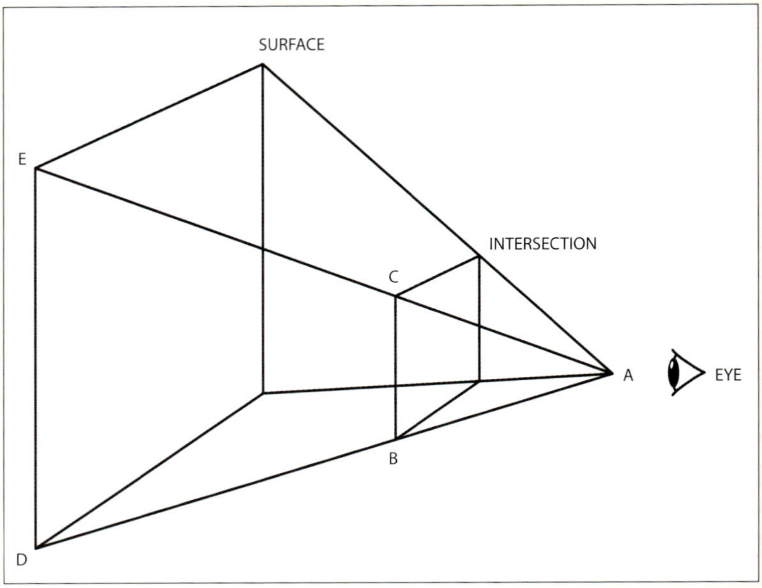

than in Giotto's work. We might say that Masaccio's spatial construction was tied to the actual position of the viewer in a way that Giotto's was not.

We do not know how Masaccio went about designing his throne, but we do know that within a decade of its completion, Alberti had written down instructions for designing objects in perspective. Most of the first book of *De pictura* is given over to an explanation of 'the power of sight and the understanding of the intersection'. He begins with a demonstration of Euclidean geometry, showing how a point joins to form a line, and a line to form a surface, before moving on to discuss how 'rays' transmit information about a surface to the eye: 'Let us imagine these rays,' he wrote, 'like extended very fine threads gathered tightly in a bunch at one end, going back together inside the eye where lies the sense of sight.' Essentially, these rays form a visual pyramid with its apex in the eye and its base on the surface being observed. The most important of them is the centric ray, which runs through the middle of the pyramid and will have consequences for the position of the vanishing point, as we shall see. Here, the reader becomes aware of the problem Alberti is trying to solve. For a painting to show figures and objects in space, proportionally relative to one another as if seen by the eye, a painting must represent an intersection of the visual pyramid. In his words:

> But as [a painting] is only a single surface of a panel or a wall [i.e. it is two-dimensional], on which a painter strives to represent many

surfaces continued with a single pyramid [where they are seen in three dimensions], it will be necessary for this visual pyramid to be cut at some point, so that the painter by drawing and colouring can express whatever outlines and colours that intersection presents. Consequently the viewers of a painted surface appear to be looking at a particular intersection of the pyramid. Therefore, a painting will be the intersection of a visual pyramid at a given distance, with a fixed centre and certain position of lights, represented by art with lines and colours on a given surface.

The principle is best understood diagrammatically (FIG. 83). If it is confusing, never mind. The important realization is that Alberti equates painting with what the eye sees. Inversely, painting itself is predicated on the presence of an embodied viewer before it. We are a long way from the idea that stained glass, for example, high above the viewer in a church, might be made for the eye of God alone.

Having articulated the theoretical principles, of which this precis is only the crudest of estimations, Alberti explained perspective in more practical terms, or, to put it in his words, he described 'the art of expressing the intersection in painting'. Here, he draws the famous comparison between a painting and a window: 'I draw a rectangle of whatever size I want, which I regard as an open window through which the subject to be painted is seen.' It is a practical method to be employed by an artist. More important than this observation, however, is the following one: 'I decide how large I wish the human figure in the painting to be.' It suggests that any composition is calibrated in relation to the human figure, which by implication comes to define painting; it is its most basic component and the

Fig.84
Diagram of perspectival construction

To establish the horizontal divisions of the pavement, Alberti imagined the pavement swung through 90 degrees. The equal divisions of the pavement are then projected to this point and to the 'centric point', both of which are at the height of the eye. The designer must draw the intersection of this triangle, as Alberti had earlier theorized, and measure the distances between the horizontal divisions.

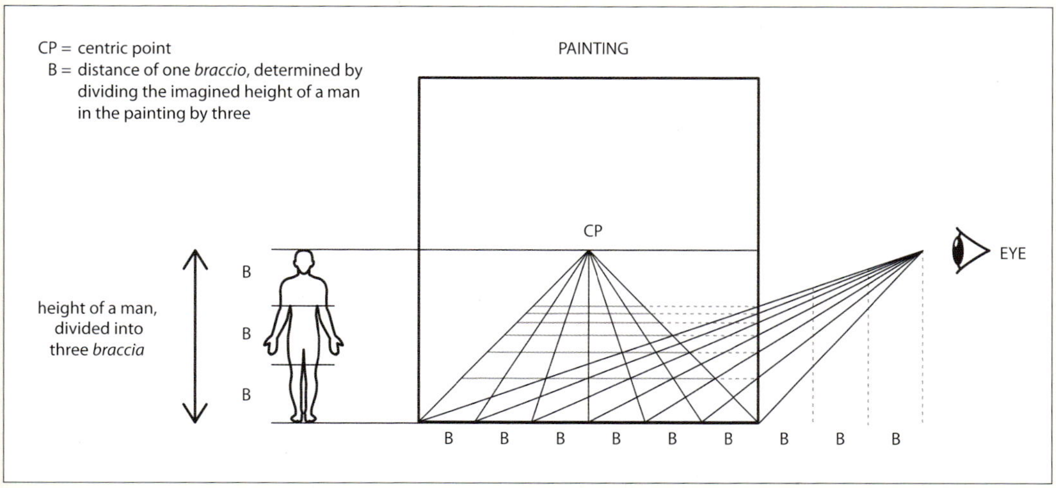

central element of the *storia*, as we have seen. Alberti goes on to say that he divides this figure into three, since a third of a man is roughly equivalent to the Florentine *braccio* (a unit of measurement equal to an arm's length, or about 58 centimetres [23 inches]), and divides the baseline of his painting into these divisions. He then establishes the 'centric point', or vanishing point, which cannot be further from the baseline than the height of a man. The centric point can then be linked to the divisions of the base by orthogonals. To complete the pavement, horizontals must be drawn across these orthogonals, giving rise to the problem of how to space them proportionally.

Alberti warns against a method adopted by some painters in which each successive space is divided in the ratio of 3:5 (which, incidentally, suggests that certain methods were already being practised by artists). His reasons are telling. These painters are mistaken, in his opinion, because 'even though the other equidistant lines follow with some system and reason, none the less they do not know where the fixed position of the vertex of the pyramid is for correct viewing'. The vertex is the eye of the viewer, revealing that the system is dependent on a fixed viewing position. There is only one point from which the painting can be seen for the illusion to be successful. Alberti solves the problem by suggesting a method for establishing the horizontal divisions. Again, his method is best understood through a diagram (FIG. 84), even if the details need not concern us. Far more important is the idea that Alberti's method, and one-point perspective more generally, depends on holding the eye in a fixed position. Brunelleschi had already come to the same conclusion.

Brunelleschi's 'Invention'

Manetti described Brunelleschi's discovery, hesitating over whether it was a new invention, unknown to the ancients, or the rediscovery of a rule known in antiquity and subsequently forgotten. Brunelleschi apparently demonstrated his new system with two painted panels. The first was square and only about half a *braccio* in height and width, small enough to be held in the hand. It showed the Baptistery as seen from just inside the door of the cathedral (*see* FIG. 9). Manetti described in some detail the extent of the view, which was painted with a miniaturist's precision. The second panel was larger and depicted the Piazza della Signoria from the corner of present-day via dei Calzaiuoli, including both the north and the west facades of the Palazzo della Signoria (*see* FIG. 4). It was evidently an exercise in two-point perspective, and was impressive enough for Manetti to marvel at it. Implicit in Brunelleschi's decision to paint these two famous sites in Florence is the fact that the use of perspective to render space is tied to the representation of urban scenes. Landscapes, or less ordered spaces in which there are no parallel lines, cannot be rendered perspectivally, as is evident in Uccello's *Battle of San Romano* (FIG. 85).

When he came to render the sky on both panels, Brunelleschi adopted a novel approach. In the view of the Baptistery, he covered the area with silver leaf, which he then burnished so that it become reflective, while on the panel showing the Piazza della Signoria, he cut away the timber along the line of the buildings where they met the sky. Manetti explained this idiosyncratic approach in terms of what might now called naturalism: 'And he placed burnished silver where the sky had to be represented, that is to say where the buildings of the painting were free in the air, so that the natural air and atmosphere [*aria e cieli naturali*] were reflected in it, and thus the clouds seen in the silver are carried along by the wind as it blows.' In other words, the sky with the clouds moving across it was reflected in the representation. The line between the painted world and the actual world was blurred. A similar motivation lay behind Brunelleschi's decision to remove the sky in the second painting. As Manetti reasoned, 'he cut away the panel in the area above the buildings represented, and took it to a spot in which he could observe

Fig. 85
Paolo Uccello
Battle of San Romano

ca. 1438–40, egg tempera with walnut oil and linseed oil on poplar, 182 × 320 cm (71⅝ × 26 in). National Gallery, London.

Uccello has littered his battlefield with lances to mark the orthogonals, as would a pavement in an urban view. In the landscape background, however, he has abandoned perspective and adopted a spatial system that is more often found in tapestries.

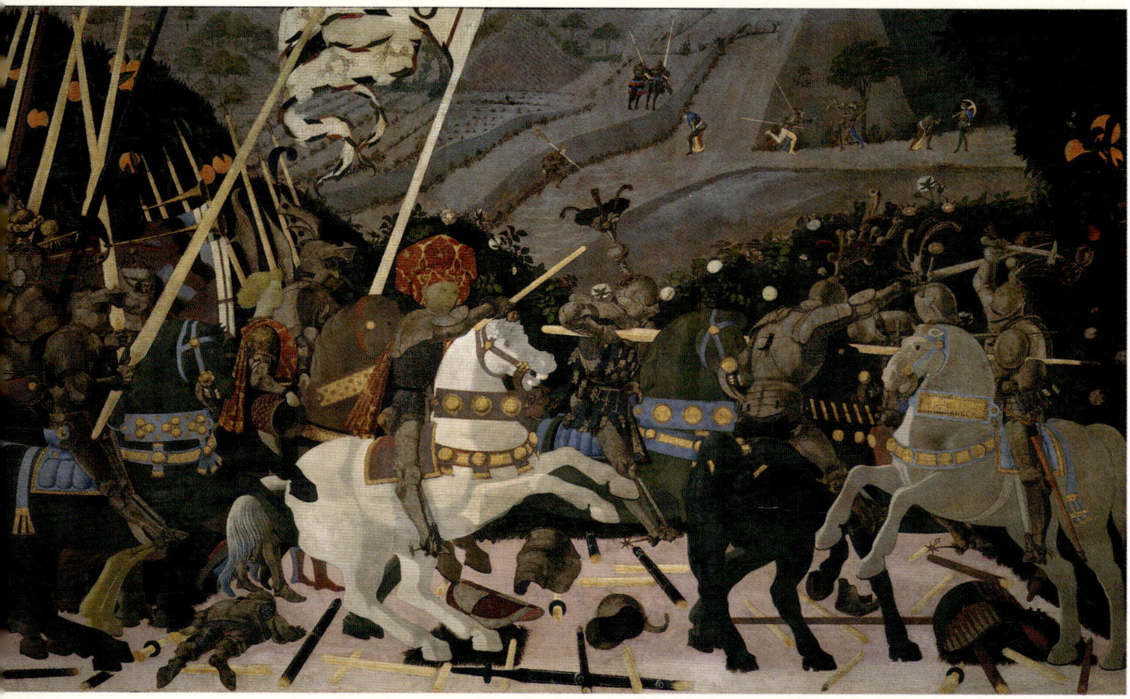

it with the natural atmosphere [*aria naturale*] above the buildings.' Here, then, the actual sky took the place of represented sky and, once again, real and depicted, nature and representation, were conflated. In both cases, the adjective Manetti used to describe the real air or atmosphere was '*naturale*', a word etymologically linked to nature, the implications of which will be discussed in the next chapter.

Finally, and most importantly, Manetti recorded how Brunelleschi intended his viewers to behold his two paintings. In the view of the Baptistery, he made a conical hole in the painting, about the size of a lentil on the painted side but widening to about the diameter of a ducat coin on the reverse. He required the viewer to look through the hole from the back, while holding a mirror in front of the image in such a way that the painting would be reflected in it. Such a peculiar practice is justified by Manetti, who explained that 'since in such a painting it is necessary that the painter postulate beforehand a single point from which the painting must be viewed … in order that no error would be made in looking at it (since any point outside that single point would change the shapes to the eye), he made a hole in the painted panel.' Manetti also revealed the consequence, for as a result 'the spectator felt he saw the actual scene [*el proprio vero*] when he looked at the painting'. The word used in this instance for actuality – '*vero*' – means truth and ties together the quest to depict nature (or the world 'out there') with truthfulness, as if the employment of perspective – and perspective alone – was necessary if an artist were to be true to nature.

Scenes represented using single-point perspective can be viewed only from a single point; from any other position, the representation of space is distorted. Brunelleschi appears to have realized this flaw in the system from the outset, and tried to ameliorate its effect by holding the viewer firm, establishing the position of the eye and setting the distance of the reflected image from it. The artist exercised direct control over the spectator, who necessarily had to forego their freedom to move around in front of the painting. As such, the introduction of a procedure for the representation of space comes to be embroiled in the dynamics of power. Perspective at once creates the illusion of a rational, knowable world before the viewer and holds him or her in a single position before it. It is, therefore, a powerful tool of illusionism and an equally potent instrument of power.

The fact that perspectival renderings of space are often tied to the urban environment takes on a new dimension when considered in relation to power. We like to think that the development of cities such as Florence – the clearing of squares, the building of sacred and civic structures – was a process of rendering space beautiful, much like Brunelleschi's representation of them on two panels. But it was also about control, about establishing authority through imposing edifices and providing structures for surveillance.

Brunelleschi appears to have come to this realization, at least as his discoveries were described by Manetti. When it came to his second panel, the one that showed the Piazza della Signoria, Manetti asked why Brunelleschi had not drilled a hole in it once again, given the problems associated with single-point perspective. He concluded, somewhat prosaically, that the panel was too large to be held up in one hand, and the distance required for the mirror too great for it to be grasped by someone extending their arm. As a consequence, Brunelleschi 'left it up to the spectator's judgement, as is done in paintings by other artists, even though at times they who look are not discerning'. Reluctantly, Brunelleschi had to accept the viewer's freedom, as other, less skilful painters were forced to do.

The Problems of Perspective

The discovery of linear perspective, and the establishment of rules for its practice, was nothing short of revolutionary. Its impact on Western art cannot be underestimated. Both Brunelleschi and Alberti tried to mimic in paint what was seen by the eye, and that was no small achievement. But their success has given rise to an assumption that good art is that which most closely approximates the world as it is revealed to the eye, not the mind, as if our perception of the world were determined solely by the optical functioning of the eye, unmediated by the brain. These ideas have led to various problems, both for artists at the time and for the telling of art history. In Florentine art of the period, linear perspective proved problematic for painters of sacred scenes: after all, how do you paint a vision or a miracle within a rational, supposedly knowable space? We shall return to this question in Chapter 9, but it is important to note here just how few painters of Alberti's generation actually put his precepts into practice. It is very rare to find a fifteenth-century Florentine painting that is entirely, and accurately, constructed according to one-point perspective. Beyond Florence, the idea that perspective is the 'right' way to depict space because it 'correctly' portrays what we see is dangerous on at least two accounts. The first is that any artist interested in the mimetic depiction of nature necessarily requires perspective. It would be absurd to suggest that Jan van Eyck was not interested in naturalistic depiction, yet he painted interiors

Fig. 86
Kamal al-Din Bihzad
Seduction of Yusuf

Dated 1488, watercolour and ink on paper, 30.5 × 21.5cm (12 × 8½in). National Library and Archive of Egypt, Cairo. MS Arab Farsi 908.

Jami's text, in Persian, is in blue and white panels around the white arch in the centre, while Sa'di's text, in Arabic script, is on a beige ground.

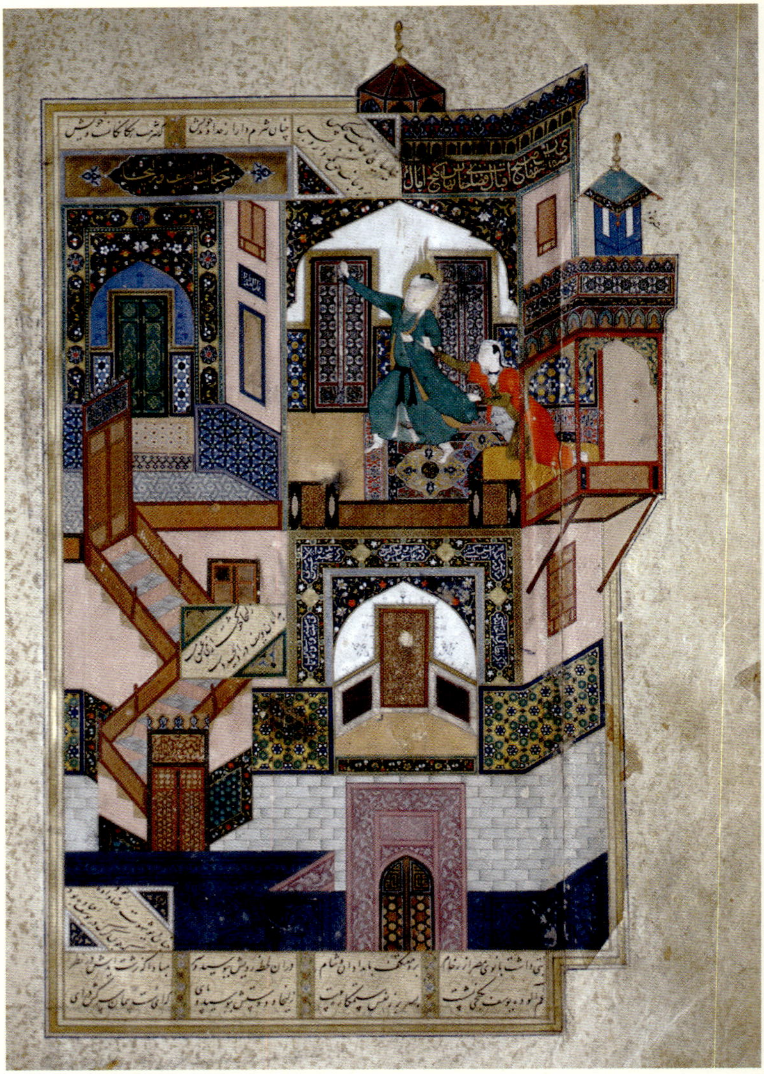

without consistent vanishing points and with orthogonals that never meet. The second is more worrying, because it judges those paintings that employ perspective as 'better' than those that do not. It is often manifest in seemingly innocent remarks: 'Look, the artist has got the room all wrong!' When the comparison is cross-cultural, it reveals a Western bias in art history. The *Seduction of Yusuf*, dated June 1488, by Kamal al-Din Bihzad (ca. 1450–1535/6) makes the point (FIG. 86).

Bihzad was probably born just after Brunelleschi died, and worked – at least during the earlier part of his career, which we shall be considering, in Herat in present-day Afghanistan. The *Seduction of Yusuf* illustrates a manuscript of the *Būstān* (*Orchard*) by the thirteenth-century Persian poet Sa'di (completed in 1257). It was copied by the scribe Sultan-Ali al-Katib for the Timurid sultan Musayn Mayqara (r. 1470–1506). The story is well known and has been told many times, from Genesis (where it is known as the tale of Joseph and Potiphar's wife) to the Quran. In the Jewish and Islamic traditions, Potiphar's wife is identified as Zulaykha. She makes advances on her husband's slave Yusuf, until, furious at his refusal, she accuses him of attempting to rape her. The story was recounted in verse by the poet Jami (1414–1492) in his *Haft Awrany* (*Seven Thrones*), the Persian text of which also appears in Bihzad's painting.

The composition allows the viewer to move around the spaces of a palace, and is therefore particularly germane in our discussion of spatial construction. The palace gate is represented at the bottom, closed, but the viewer nonetheless sees a courtyard behind it. A flight of stairs climbs upwards from behind another closed door. The eye moves across image and text together, before coming to a series of closed rooms, each decorated with tiles, their patterning strongly reminiscent of contemporary architecture in Herat. The viewer's ascent through the composition culminates in the innermost space, indicated by the balcony that opens over the courtyard. Here, Zulaykha throws herself at the beautiful, veiled Yusuf, whose virtuous restraint (in contrast to her lustful desire) is revealed through pose and gesture.

Bihzad's composition is designed to lead the eye around the palace, opening spaces to the viewer, but closing them to the protagonists. Jami described how Zulaykha drew Yusuf into the palace, leading him successively through seven rooms and locking each door behind them, which miraculously opened when Yusuf escaped her advances. This sense of opening and closing is captured for the spectator, whose eye moves freely from space to space. The rooms are encountered as they might have been *known* to a visitor, or its inhabitants, rather than *seen* by someone inside the palace. On occasion, the space is described through foreshortening (walls come inwards, for instance); on others, it is through its surface decoration. The equal prominence given to the entire picture surface, as much in its colour values as in its detail, is particularly striking, especially in the depiction of the tiles, which emphasizes their material presence, what might be called their 'reality'. The viewer does not see these rooms from a single point outside the palace, nor are they depicted using one-point perspective, but our comprehension of the space is in no way impaired. In fact, the very opposite is true: our experience is augmented by the ability to move between open and closed, flatness and depth, text and image. If anything, our sense of the 'reality'

Fig. 87
Lorenzo Ghiberti
Stories of Joseph from the *Gates of Paradise*

1425–52, gilded bronze, 79 × 79cm (31⅛ × 31⅛in). Museo dell'Opera del Duomo, Florence.

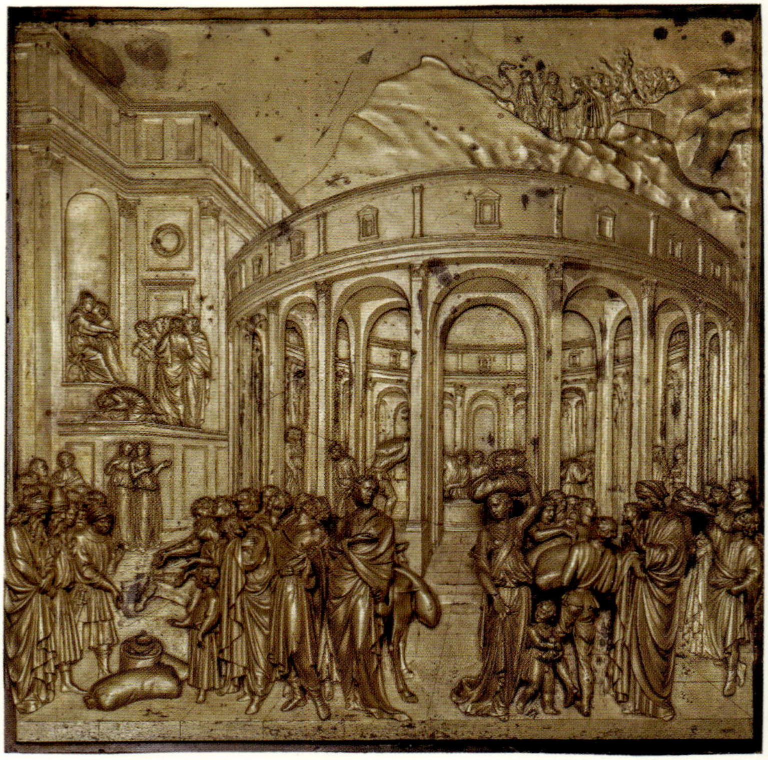

of the image is heightened. To judge Bihzad's painting in terms of Florentine perspective is to fail to see it on its own terms, and thus to recognize the achievement of an extremely sophisticated artist. But the comparison with Florentine aesthetic norms is not without value. If we turn the tables and look from Herat to Florence, the image constructed using linear perspective becomes strange again, and we can assess it for the idiosyncratic development it was. One final example should make the point.

One of Ghiberti's panels on the *Gates of Paradise* also tells the story of Joseph, although it omits the tale of Potiphar's wife (FIG. 87). A story of entrapment, revenge and forgiveness is played out across a composition organized strictly in line with the principles of linear perspective. High in the distant landscape, Joseph's jealous brothers sell him into slavery, having cast him down a well. The narrative then jumps forward both in time and in space. Several decades later Joseph, now vizier of Egypt, recognizes his brothers, who have come to buy grain during famine, even if they do not recognize him. In the middle ground, within a circular arcaded market, the brothers pack up and carry the grain that Joseph has allowed them. In the right foreground, the brothers return to Egypt once again in the company of their youngest brother, Benjamin, who was born after Joseph's departure. The story draws to its climax on the left, where a silver bowl is discovered in Benjamin's bag; he is accused of stealing it, but it was in fact planted by Joseph. Finally, in the middle distance again, but on the left, Joseph reveals himself to his brothers and is reconciled with Benjamin. The illusion of a single urban space is a tour de force of perspectival construction, not to mention a demonstration of artistic skill in foreshortening highly complex, rounded forms. The scene is united by a receding pavement and flanking buildings, whose orthogonals all meet within the market. Yet the impression that the viewer encounters a single space works against the episodic narrative. The buildings and pavement were used by Ghiberti to separate moments in a story that were distinct in both time and space, even if we encounter them in a spatially unified composition. In Bihzad's painting, our knowledge of the rooms within a palace, and of the pattern and colour of tiles, heightens our perception of the space. By contrast, in Ghiberti's relief our knowledge of the story is called on to reject the visual impression that the scene shows a single moment in time and space.

The strict adherence to geometrical principles in Ghiberti's architecture has resulted in a building whose receding flank appears exaggerated, and a circular market that billows outwards hyperbolically. Van Eyck's room for the Arnolfini might be 'incorrect' mathematically, but his subtle adjustments, whether conscious or not, have resulted in a space that is visually credible. His process of spatial interpretation is akin to that performed by our brain when it receives visual information from our eyes. The 'invention' of linear perspective was a major development of European painting, but it was (and is) an artificial system for organizing space. It might mimic *how* we see, but not *what* we see in the mind's eye. That linear perspective takes its precepts from the way we see the world does not make it any better (or worse) at interpreting nature than other visual regimes, but it does tie visual representation to two external factors: the eye of the beholder and the realm that is its referent. The former has already been discussed; it is now time to attend to the latter, to nature.

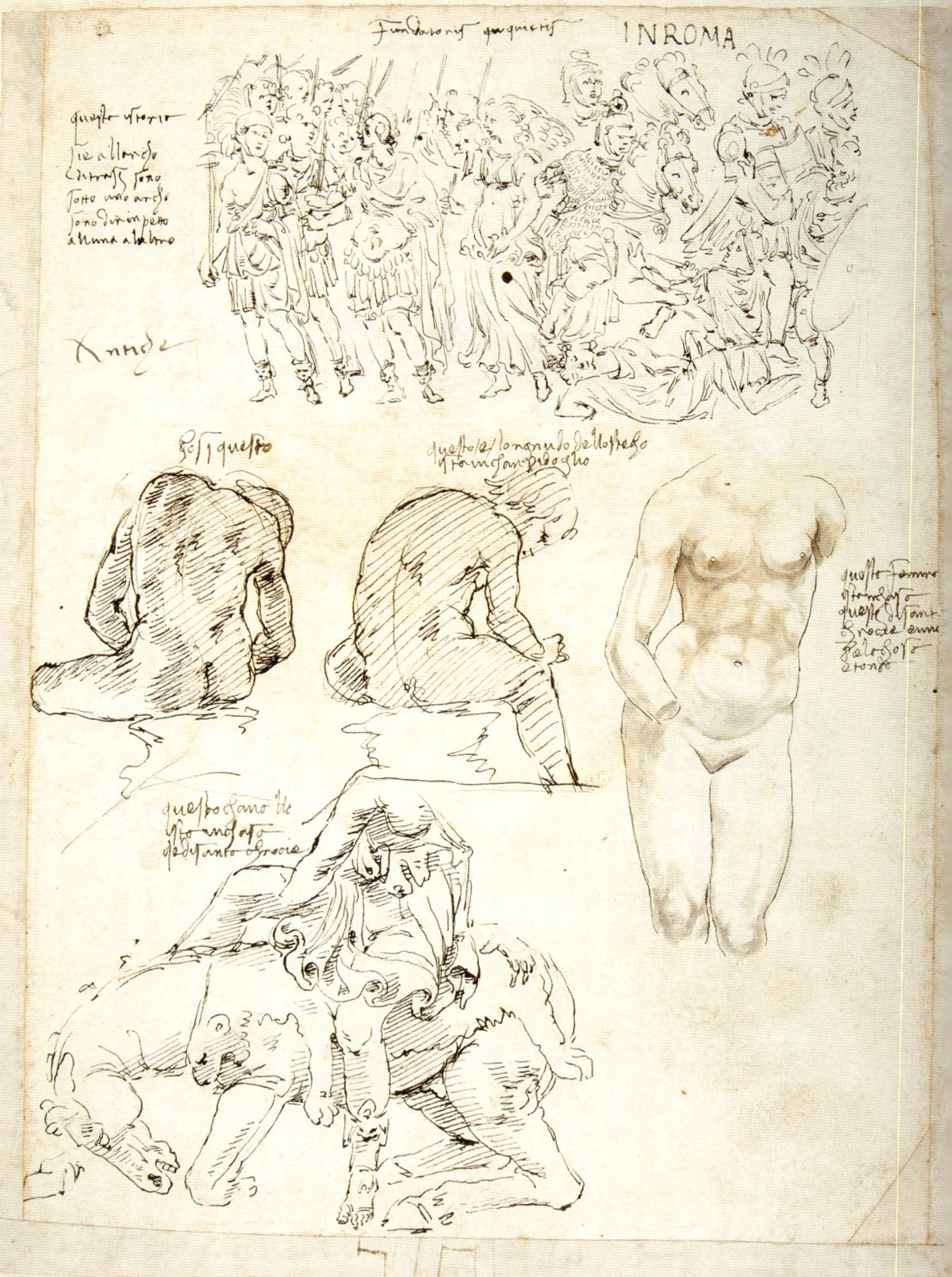
INROMA

8

Style II: A Turn to Nature or a Return to the Antique?

Brunelleschi's two demonstration panels included actual nature. In one case, clouds were reflected in the silvered surface; in the other, the panel was cut away to reveal the sky itself. Faced with an artistic practice that was mimetic, Brunelleschi seems to have asked how far artists should go in imitating nature, and – if Manetti is to be believed – he decided on an extreme position. The hand of the artist, he resolved, was to make no intervention between nature and its representation. The idea was not new. It was a trope of ancient art, at least as it was understood from Pliny's *Natural History*. Although that work had long been known, a relatively complete version arrived in Florence during the 1430s, procured from the Dominican convent in Lübeck by the humanist Niccolò Niccoli (1364–1437). Pliny recounts several episodes in which the relationship between art and nature was tested. The celebrated sculptor Lysippus was supposed to take no other model but nature. The most famous instance, and perhaps also the best-known in the Renaissance, was a competition between Zeuxis and Parrhasius. Zeuxis is supposed to have painted a backdrop for the theatre in which a still-life of grapes was so convincing that birds tried to peck at it. Parrhasius upped the ante by painting a curtain over the backdrop that fooled not only

Fig. 88
Drawings after Sculpture in Rome, Including a View of the Spinario from the Back (Holkham MS 701, fol. 34v)

Late 15th century, pen and ink on paper, 23.5 × 29.8cm (9¼ × 11¾in). Holkham Hall, Norfolk (MS 701 fol. 34v).

This drawing of the *Spinario* (Boy with Thorn) probably dates from the late fifteenth century and cannot therefore have been seen by Brunelleschi, but it is of a type that might have been in circulation earlier in the century.

nature (birds), but also his fellow artist, Zeuxis, who asked Parrhasius to pull it back, believing it to be real. Both Ghiberti and Filarete repeated the anecdote.

The illusionism that such episodes promoted seldom resulted in such a direct relationship to nature as that sought by Brunelleschi. What is style, at least in representational art, if not the manner in which forms in nature are mediated by the hand of the artist? As much as fifteenth-century artists interrogated the space of their images, they questioned the relationship between their representations of the world and the world itself. An art based on nature seems opposed to one founded in the idealizing styles of antiquity. Yet these two factors characterized the art of Renaissance Florence, and they would dominate Italian art for centuries to come. In the fifteenth century, taking inspiration from nature was not the same as it would be for the landscape painters of the nineteenth century; nature was not considered by the earlier artists to be idiosyncratic or individual.

Revival of the Antique

The Renaissance is defined as a rebirth of interest in the antique past. That is, after all, what 'Renaissance' means. The most forward-looking artists looked backwards for inspiration. The rebirth took many forms. Artists studied antique sculpture that had remained visible across the centuries, while humanists, wealthy individuals and artists began to collect antiquities. Ghiberti had a collection of antique sculpture, from which he drew inspiration (FIG. 89), while Donatello was said to have an expert knowledge of ancient works of art. In a letter to Niccoli, written from Rome on 23 September 1430, the scholar Poggio Bracciolini described how he had acquired certain ancient Greek heads from another correspondent, Francesco of Pistoia, then in Chios. They were a Juno, a Minerva and a Bacchus, and were attributed to Polykleitos and Praxiteles, although Bracciolini was rightly sceptical about their authorship. Collectors, like Bracciolini, were a new type in the fifteenth century, and they were distinguished by their desire to possess old objects rather than commission new ones, even if many of the most famous collectors of the period were also patrons. Since antiquities were often found in fragments, sculptors found work restoring them, reinstating limbs or long-lost noses (*see* FIG. 20). Collectors found new ways to display their prized objects. Bracciolini mentioned that his busts would ornament his *studiolo*, but courtyards and gardens proved equally

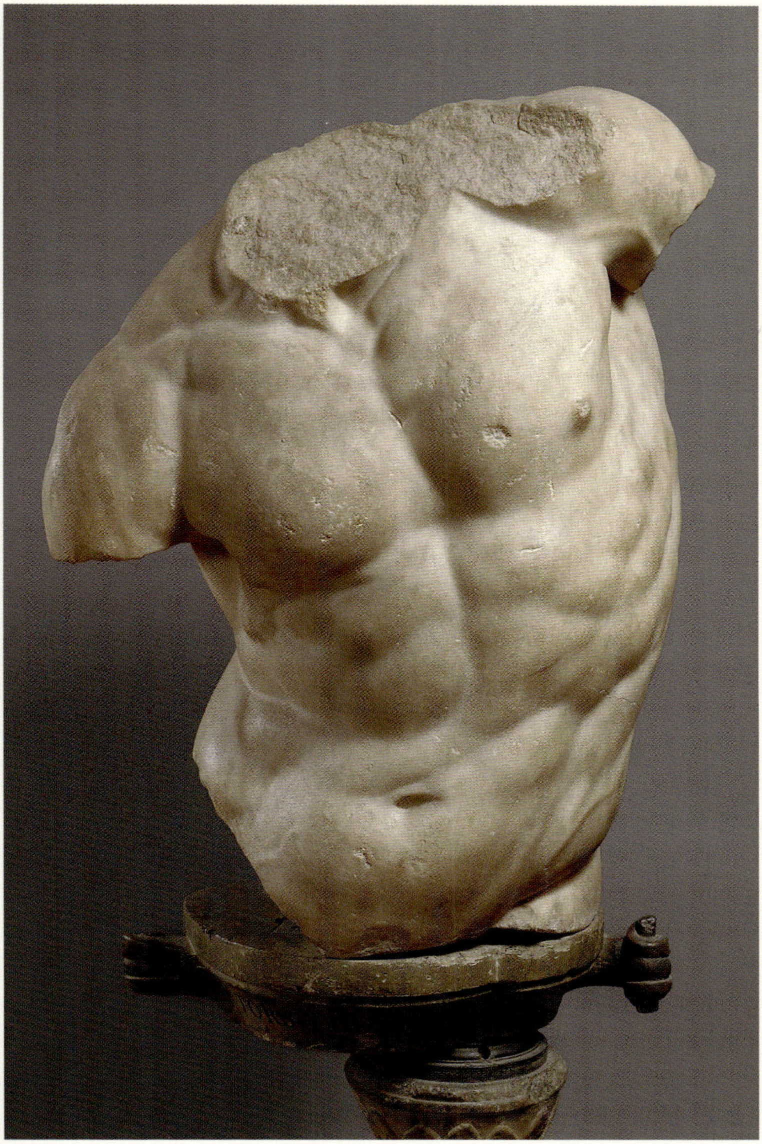

Fig. 89
Gaddi Torso

2nd century BCE, marble, 84.4cm ($33\frac{1}{4}$in) high. Galleria degli Uffizi, Florence.

Ghiberti probably owned this fragmentary torso, which is sometimes thought to have been the inspiration for the figure of Isaac in his competition panel.

appropriate. The Medici installed some of their ancient sculpture in a garden near San Marco, where artists – including the young Michelangelo – came to study them.

In Florence, relatively few large-scale works of antique sculpture survived from antiquity. A few sarcophagi were placed around the cathedral and Baptistery, and were sufficiently impressive to warrant mention by Boccaccio in the *Decameron*, but almost no free-standing sculpture was on public display. When a figure of what was thought to be a 'consul' (FIG. 90) was unearthed during excavations

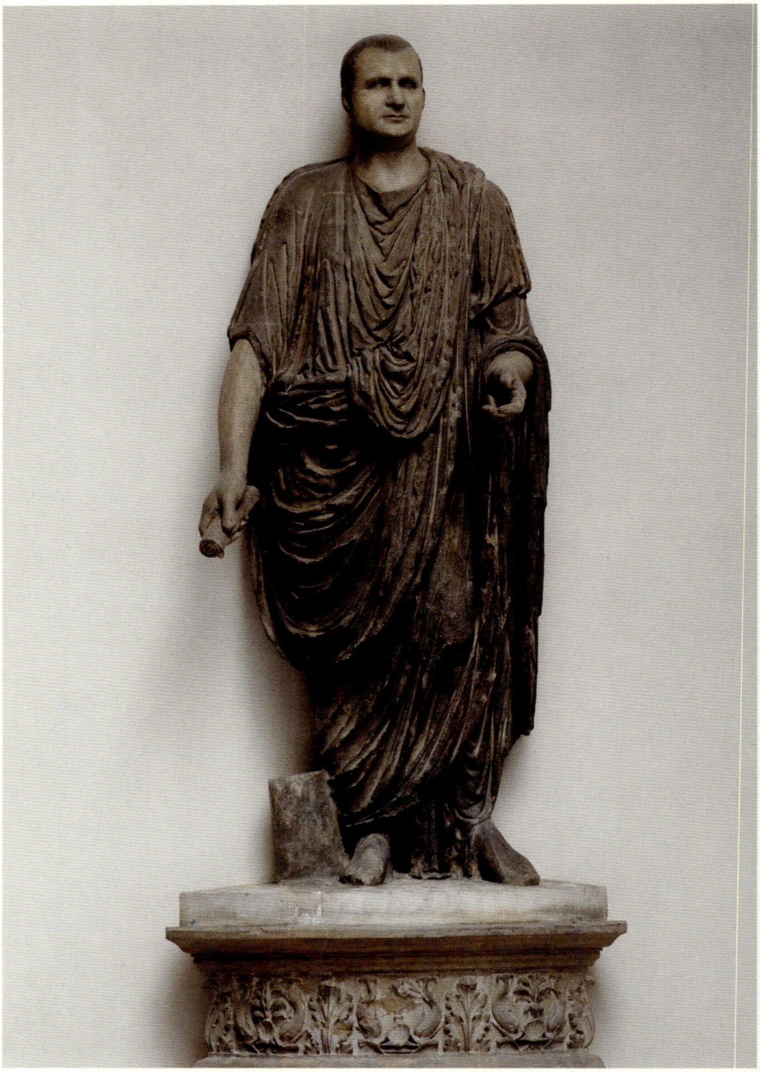

Fig. 90
Senator Marcino, Roman general

2nd century CE, marble, 210cm (82$\frac{5}{8}$in) high. Palazzo Gondi, Florence.

of a building for the Parte Guelfa, it caused enough of a stir for the sculptor Francesco da Sangallo to remember the occasion many years later, in 1567. It was subsequently moved to the Palazzo Gondi, where it remains in the courtyard. Much more was visible in Rome, freely available for artists to draw and study (FIG. 91). Although it can often be difficult to document the fact that a painter or sculptor visited the Eternal City, their works leave little room for doubt. Brunelleschi had surely seen the *Spinario* by the time he came to cast his competition relief and included a figure pulling a thorn from his foot (*see* FIG. 35), unless he knew the pose from drawings by other artists (FIG. 88).

Antique sculpture was thus a source of inspiration. It provided artists with a repertoire of motifs and formal solutions, as well as a set of types. The enormous bronze equestrian monument to Marcus Aurelius was the impetus for several monuments to *condottieri*, produced by Florentine sculptors far from their home town (FIG. 92). It provided them with a challenge – to cast a horse and rider on a monumental scale – but it also suggested the form for the first dated small-scale bronze of the Renaissance (FIG. 93), itself the revival of a type known in antiquity (even if antique *bronzetti* were generally single figures rather than reduced equestrian monuments).

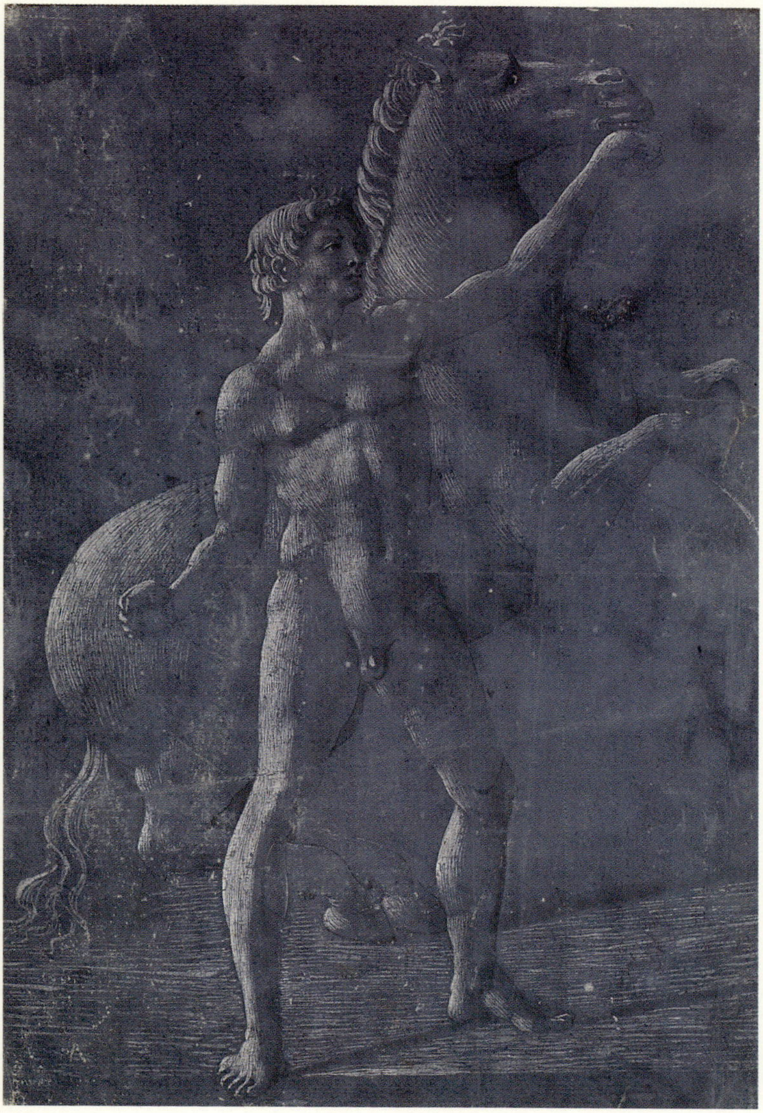

Fig. 91
Attributed to Benozzo Gozzoli
A Horse Tamer

ca. 1447–9, silverpoint, grey-black wash, heightened with white, on blue prepared paper, 35.9 × 24.6cm (14⅛ × 9⅝in). The British Museum, London.

This drawing is loosely based on one of the so-called *Horse Tamers*, a pair of colossal antique equestrian sculptures on the Quirinal Hill in Rome that probably show Castor and Pollux. Gozzoli, or someone close to him in style, has animated the sculpture, either working from his imagination or by re-posing a model in the workshop.

Fig. 92
Marcus Aurelius

ca. 175 CE, bronze, 424cm (167in) high. Capitoline Museums, Rome.

This sculpture inspired several monuments to mercenary captains, including Donatello's *Gattamelata* in Padua and Verrocchio's *Bartolomeo Colleoni* in Venice.

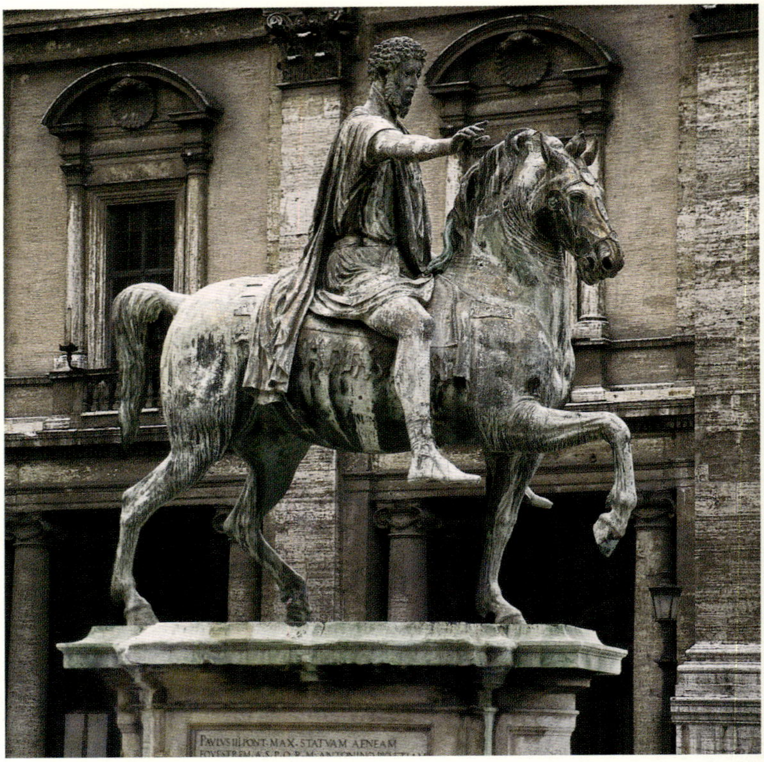

The plinth of Filarete's *Marcus Aurelius* carries the date 1465 and a long dedicatory inscription to Piero de' Medici, to whom Filarete had presented the sculpture as a gift. Filarete (Antonio Averlino; ca. 1400–ca. 1469) was in Rome creating bronze doors for Old St Peter's in the early 1440s, when he presumably saw the original, which had remained visible throughout the Middle Ages. It was then on the Lateran, where it is documented as early as the twelfth century; it was moved to the Capitol in 1538 by Pope Paul III. Medieval sources attest to the fact that the rider was routinely identified as Constantine, who converted Rome to Christianity.

Filarete's version is not only radically reduced in scale, but also a free interpretation of the ancient sculpture. True, he copied certain details faithfully, such as the distinctive patterning of the ephippium (the emperor's saddle blanket), and he restored lost elements, such as the fragmentary breaststrap, but in spite of these antiquarian interests he altered the original form. Most obviously, he added an oversized helmet, complete with a depiction of the abduction of Deianira, Hercules' wife. His real contribution, however, was a change of effect. Filarete's horse springs forward; it does not walk majestically. His emperor gestures in salutation; he does not command imperially. A

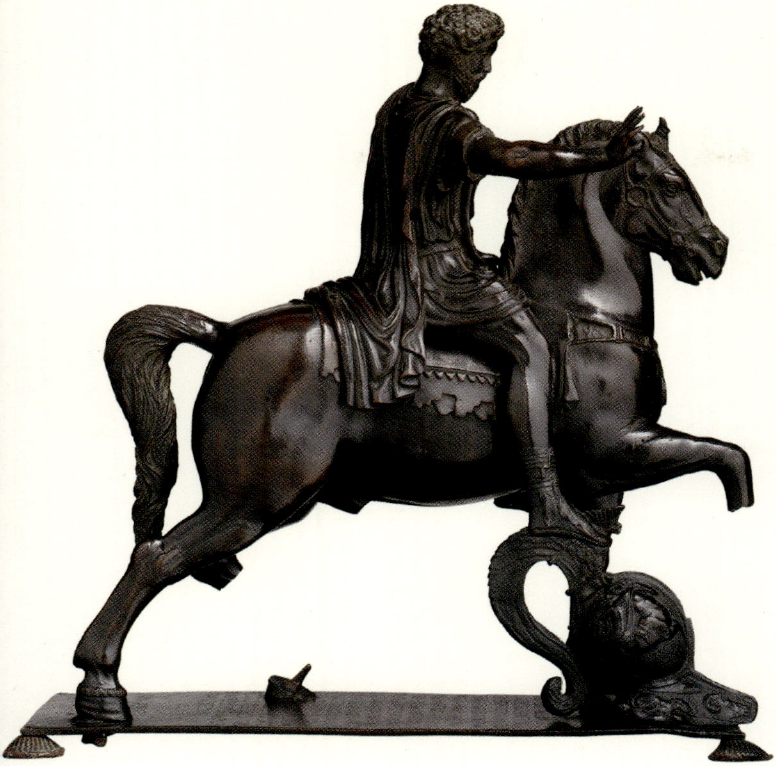

Fig. 93
Antonio Averlino,
known as **Filarete**
Marcus Aurelius

Dated 1465, bronze with some gilding and enamel, 38.2cm (15in) high. Staatliche Kunstsammlungen, Dresden (Inv. H4 155/37).

Medieval writers described the rider as Constantine, not Marcus Aurelius, even if they acknowledged that the identification was wrong. Filarete identified the horseman as Commodus.

monumental equestrian sculpture has become an object for display in the *studiolo*, one to be handled as a precious object, a status that is reinforced by the treatment of the horse's trappings, which were gilded and inlaid with enamel. Filarete was not simply imitating antiquity, he was emulating it. He was seeking to improve on his model.

Painters, too, took inspiration from ancient sculpture, not least because antique painting was unknown before the discovery of Nero's Domus Aurea in the late 1480s, and even then it was a long way off, in Rome. Both Masaccio and Botticelli turned to the *Venus pudica*, appropriating the same sculptural source to very different ends. The original was by Praxiteles and dates from the fourth century BCE. It has long been lost and is known only through Roman copies, of which the *Medici Venus* (FIG. 94) and the *Capitoline Venus* are the best known. In the late fourteenth century, a commentator on Dante, Benvenuto da Imola, must have known a version of the sculpture, for he recorded having seen a Venus in a private Florentine house, 'holding her left hand over her genitals and her right hand across her breasts'.

Masaccio turned to a similar source for his depiction of Eve in the *Expulsion from the Garden of Eden* in the Brancacci chapel

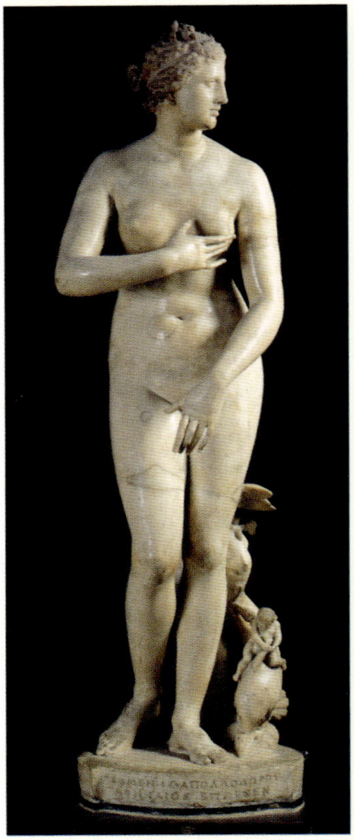

Fig. 94
After **Praxiteles**
Medici Venus

1st century BCE, marble, 155cm (61in) high. Galleria degli Uffizi, Florence.

No version of this sculpture can be documented before the sixteenth century. However, one was certainly known to artists from an early date, since it was copied by Giovanni Pisano on a pulpit in the early fourteenth century.

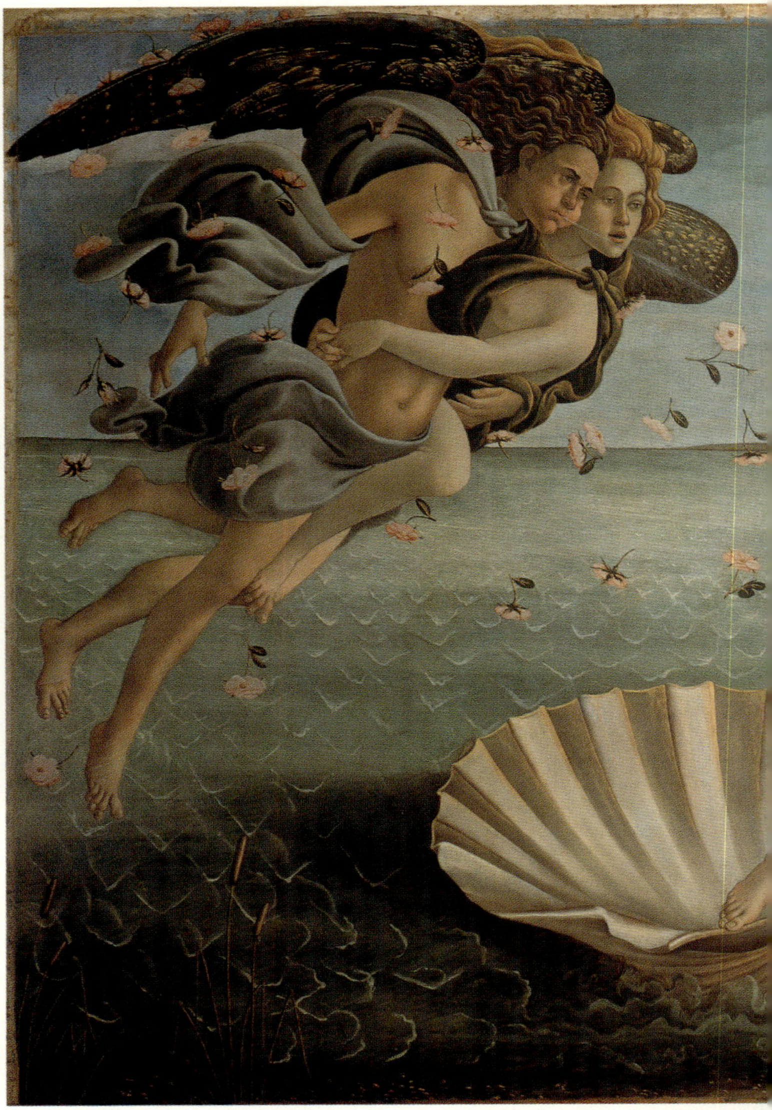

(FIG. 95). Venus had suddenly been Christianized. Masaccio appropriates the general form, but nothing else: the *contrapposto* stance of the original, dynamic yet fixed in a single position, has changed into a walk; the calm beauty of the face has mutated into an image of despair. Venus's gesture of covering her breasts and sex has been transformed from one of modesty to one of shame, as the full horror of being cast out of Paradise becomes apparent to Eve. Masaccio exploited Venus's action to emphasize Eve's nakedness. She might not be the goddess of love any more, but the implications of the pose could not be more appropriate to the narrative.

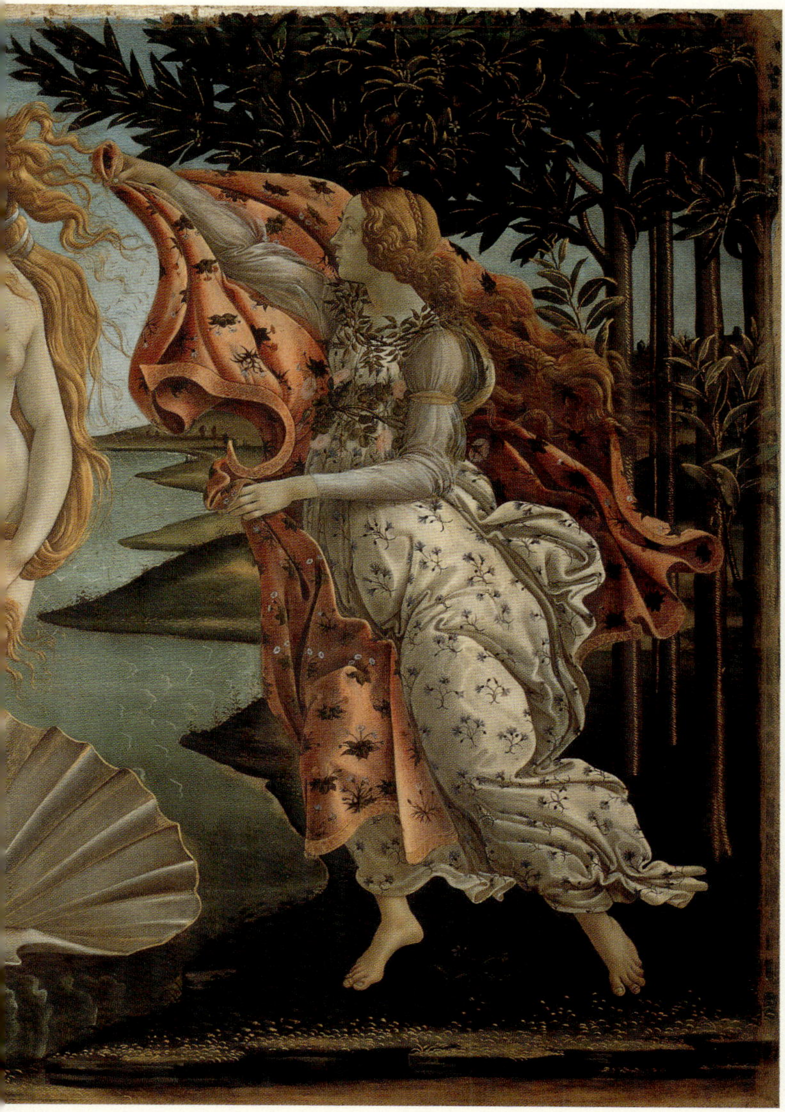

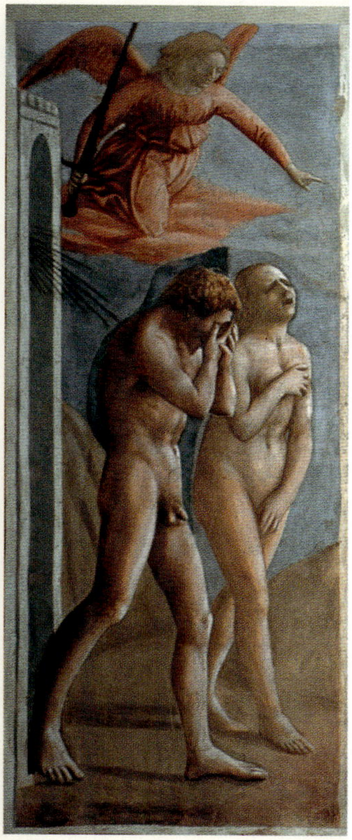

Fig. 95 (above)
Masaccio
Expulsion of Adam and Eve
from the Brancacci chapel

ca. 1426–7, fresco. Santa Maria del Carmine, Florence.

Fig. 96 (left)
Sandro Botticelli
The Birth of Venus

1480s, tempera on canvas, 172.5 × 278.5cm (68 × 109⅝in). Galleria degli Uffizi, Florence.

Botticelli recycled the pose for his mythological canvas showing *The Birth of Venus* (FIG. 96). Here, the ancient source was clearly related to the modern subject matter – Venus remains Venus – even if, once again, Botticelli has effected significant changes. She has grown long blonde hair, gleaming with real gold, and the proportions of her body are attenuated, with high, apple-like breasts. Her eyes glisten beneath dark, arched eyebrows. These characteristics are typical of the traits that poets celebrated in their ideal ladies, expressed in a vernacular lyric tradition that stretches back to Petrarch and the description of his beloved Laura. As such, Botticelli's Venus

Fig. 97
Michelangelo Buonarroti
Battle of the Lapiths and Centaurs

ca. 1490–2, marble, 84.5 × 90.5cm (33³⁄₈ × 35⁵⁄₈ in). Casa Buonarroti, Florence.

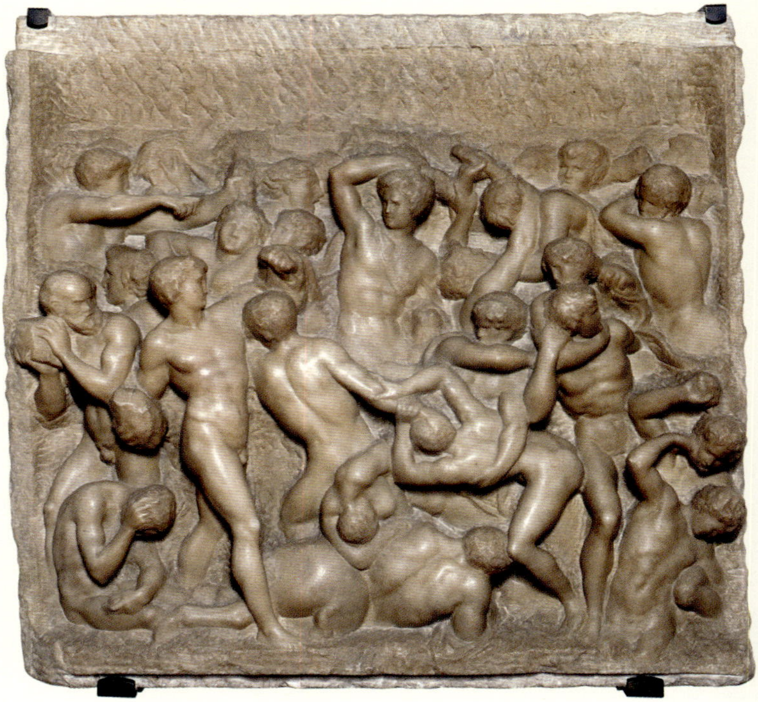

conflates an ancient type with a more recent poetic tradition, combining a Latin form with a vernacular – a Florentine – canon of beauty. She might have the pose of the *Venus pudica*, but the style of her depiction is much more recent and local.

This relationship with the art of classical antiquity was described using the words '*all'antica*' in the fifteenth century. The phrase means 'in the antique manner', not 'after the antique' nor 'as in the antique'. It implies a degree of interpretation and adaption, of emulation in short. Neri di Bicci could describe an altarpiece frame – a quintessentially Christian object – as *all'antica*, because it employed motifs derived from ancient architecture, not because it was a type that existed in antiquity. We might think of Michelangelo's *Battle of the Lapiths and Centaurs* (FIG. 97) as *all'antica*, for although it has no direct source in any ancient relief, its thrashing figures, intertwined and fighting, were nonetheless inspired by ancient sarcophagi. However, Michelangelo was not merely working in the antique manner; he was seeking to surpass it. Botticelli might have updated the style of his ancient counterparts, by making their forms distinctly modern and Florentine, but Michelangelo was trying to better them in a more self-consciously antique visual language.

Nature and Idealization

The ideal to which Florentine artists increasingly aspired during the fifteenth century was one born in the ancient world. Yet when we read texts from the period, some of which were discussed in Chapter 3, they make as many references to nature as they do to the ideal forms of antiquity. As we saw, Manetti described Brunelleschi's bust in the cathedral as '*al naturale*' (*see* FIG. 29). Alberti began *De pictura* with an instruction to learn the principles of mathematics, after which, he tells us, 'We will go on, to the best of our ability, to explain the art of painting from the basic principles of nature.' Tellingly, Alberti refers to the 'principles of nature', rather than nature itself, as if he were indicating its underlying structures, rather than its surface appearance. And, lest we think Alberti's theoretical text was intended only for an elite audience, Savonarola expressed similar opinions in a treatise *On the Simplicity of the Christian Life*, which appeared in Latin in 1496 and was quickly translated into the vernacular for wide consumption: 'We find that the more things please us the more they imitate nature so that those who praise a painting say, "Look, these animals seem alive, and these flowers seem natural [*naturali*]."'

When it came to figure studies, working from nature involved looking at living figures, perhaps by posing assistants in the workshop and studying them in drawings. In Verrocchio's *Sleeping Youth* (FIG. 98), whose function and subject remain mysterious, the

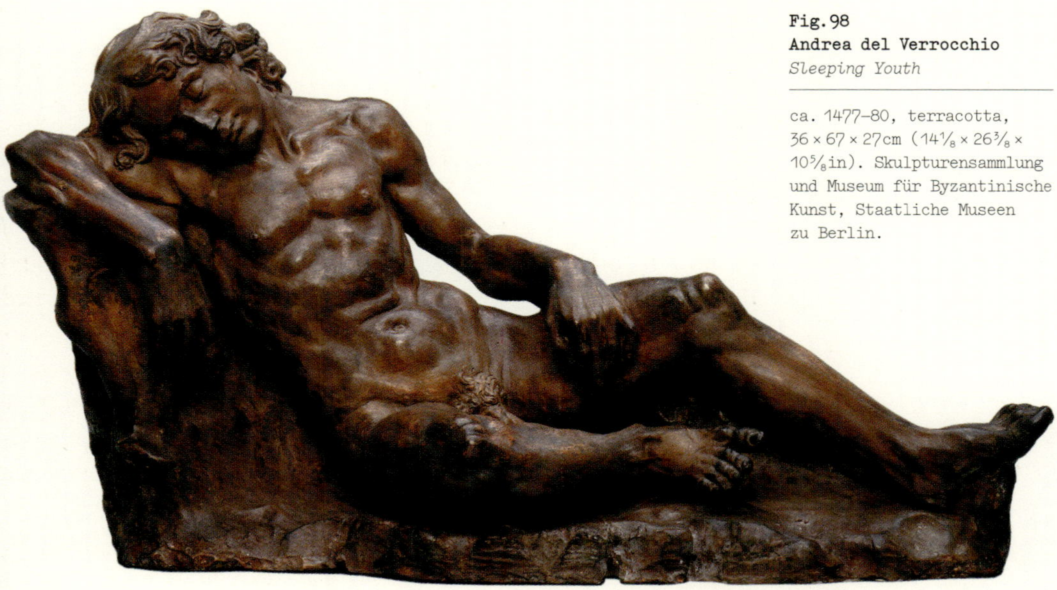

Fig. 98
Andrea del Verrocchio
Sleeping Youth

ca. 1477–80, terracotta, 36 × 67 × 27cm (14⅛ × 26⅜ × 10⅝in). Skulpturensammlung und Museum für Byzantinische Kunst, Staatliche Museen zu Berlin.

Fig. 99
Michelangelo Buonarroti
A Study of a Seated Nude Man for the Battle of Cascina

1504–5, pen and brown ink, grey and brown wash, heightened with white over lead point and stylus, 41.9 × 28.6cm (16½ × 11¼in). The British Museum, London.

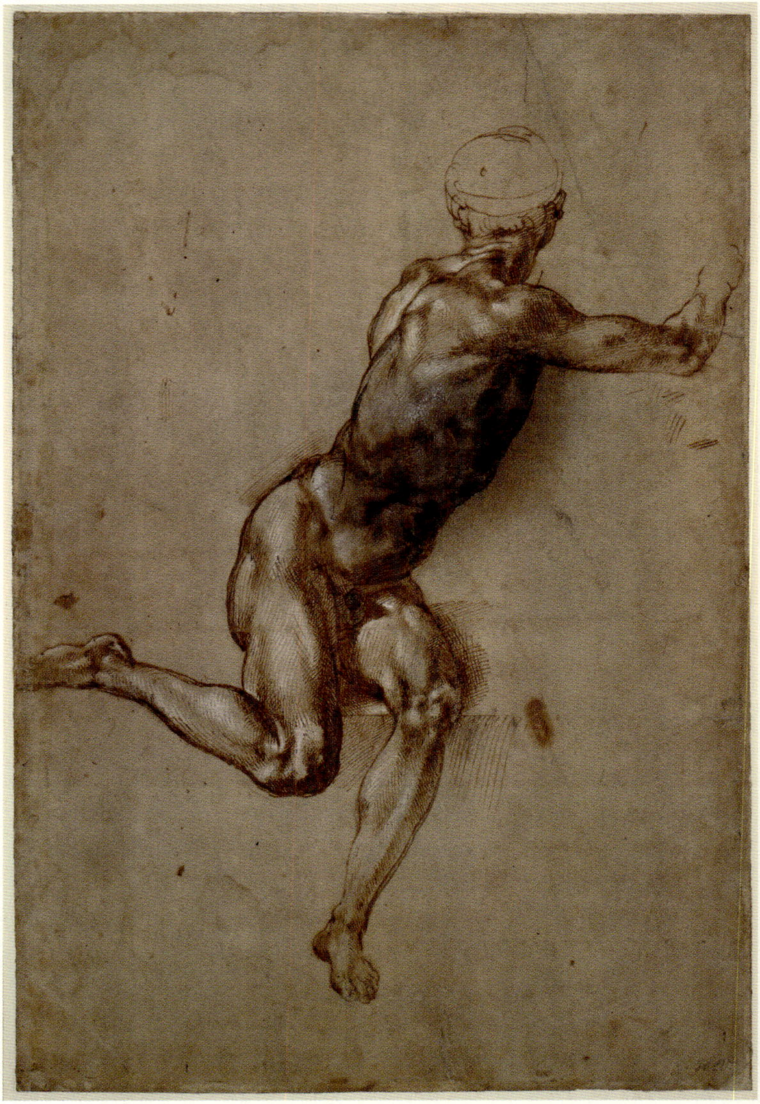

sculptor has not derived his figure from antique sculpture, but rather has examined a living body. The features of the head, and especially the hairstyle, are distinctly Florentine. Verrocchio's first step was most probably to draw from the live model. The manner in which the skin folds between the stomach and the chest suggests that the artist was trying to understand the effect of the pose on the musculature of the abdomen. The body is distinctive, almost individual. It is not idealized, at least not in a classical sense, even if it is particularly taut and well developed, revealing that an ideal does still lie behind it: Verrocchio did not choose to sculpt a fat old man.

Studying from nature also involved improving it, much like the rhetorician, described by Quintilian, who embellishes facts to persuade his audience. Michelangelo's drawing of a twisting nude man, made in about 1504–5 in preparation for his *Battle of Cascina*, is a case in point (FIG. 99). The pose is impossible, as anyone who tries to adopt it soon discovers, but it was necessary compositionally, for it is through the contorted position of this figure that the viewer's eye is led from the foreground into the melee of figures further back (*see* FIG. 17). Michelangelo probably posed the model in one attitude, drew his legs and groin, then turned him slightly in order to sketch his head, arms and shoulders. The proof is in the technique: the upper and lower sections of the body are hatched in pen and ink with some white heightening delicately applied, but the torso is a mess of different media, including wash, suggesting that Michelangelo worked and reworked it as he sought to invent a convincing musculature that would link the two bodies. The result is an idealized figure, distant from anything we can observe in nature, but nonetheless studied from it.

Alberti explained how nature and the ideal were reconciled. In *De pictura*, he described how the ancient painter Zeuxis went about preparing a panel for the temple of Lucina at Croton as an example to painters of his own time:

> Because he believed that all the things he desired to achieve beauty not only could not be found by his own intuition, but were not to be discovered even in Nature in one body alone, he chose from all the youth of the city five outstandingly beautiful girls, so that he might represent in his painting whatever feature of feminine beauty was most praiseworthy in each of them.

Alberti's anecdote, which he took from Cicero and Pliny, illustrates how nature was idealized by Renaissance artists. By looking to the natural world, they were seeking out not its idiosyncrasies, but rather its underlying (God-given) principles, combining elements from imperfect wholes to form new, perfect ones. In this sense, the artist mimicked the generative power of nature, its ability to create, rather than the superficial appearance of those creations, each imperfect in itself. The model allowed invention, the crucial factor in defining authorship, at least as it was emerging during the Renaissance. No contradiction existed, then, in styles that simultaneously looked to the idealizing forms of antiquity and to nature. Artists in antiquity, such as Zeuxis, had followed a similar course, discovering the principles that governed nature, combining her purest forms into ideal bodies. Ancient works of art provided an example of nature perfected.

A Different Understanding of Nature

In the second half of the fifteenth century another understanding of nature emerged. In Neoplatonic philosophy, nature ceased to be God's greatest creation; rather, it stood in opposition to the mind and therefore constituted a lower state of being. However, these ideas had less impact on artistic practice than did a new, detailed attention to the physical appearance of objects in nature. Such interest in the specific rather than the general was prompted by an appreciation for Netherlandish art that was already well established by the 1470s and received added impetus with the arrival of Hugo van der Goes's *Portinari Triptych* in Florence in 1483 (FIG. 100). This new attitude was also accompanied by a quasi-scientific

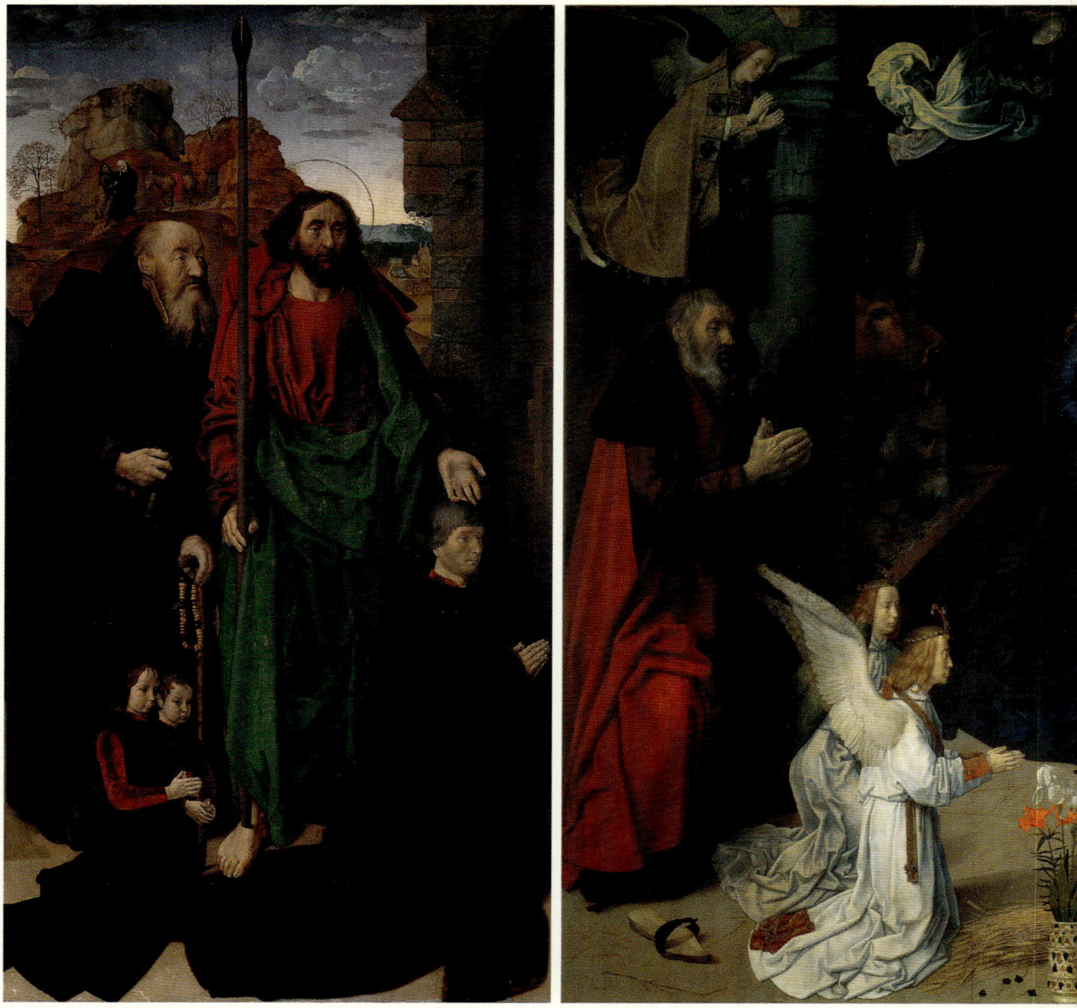

investigation into the structure of things based on empirical observation. The eye of the artist had become analytical, spurred on by an enquiring mind.

When it came to the depiction of the body – where the ancient ideal was most strongly felt – this trend would lead to the artist dissecting bodies, which (contrary to popular belief) had long been a regular practice in the universities. It was no longer enough for the artist to observe how the body appeared on the surface; he must now look beneath it to understand how it worked. Antonio del Pollaiuolo was said by Vasari to have performed dissections, even if the evidence of his works suggests otherwise. Michelangelo's biographer Ascanio Condivi maintained that at the hospital of Santo Spirito in the early 1490s, the teenage Michelangelo had access to corpses from

Fig. 100
Hugo van der Goes
The Adoration of the Shepherds with Donors and Saints (Portinari Triptych)

1476–9, oil on oak, 253 × 586 cm (99⅝ × 230¾ in). Galleria degli Uffizi, Florence.

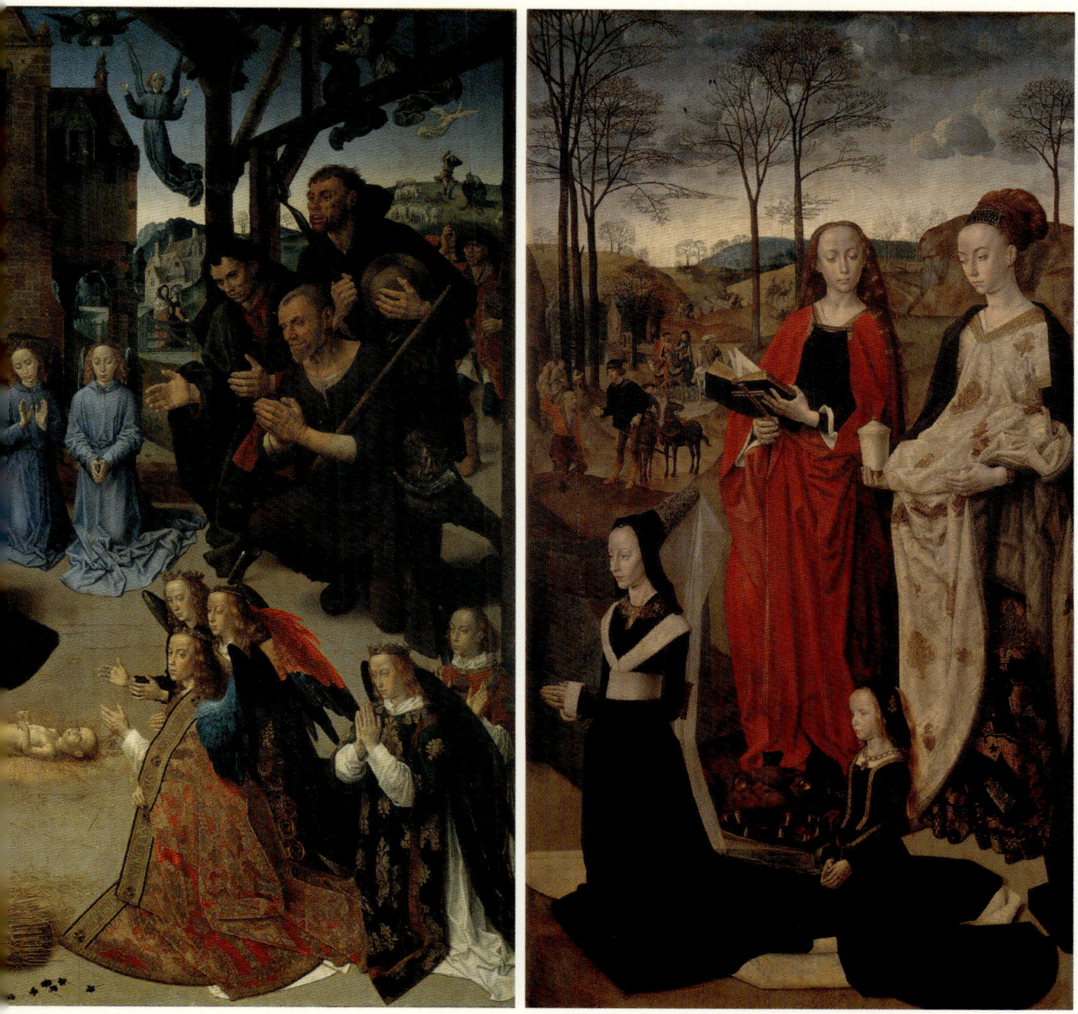

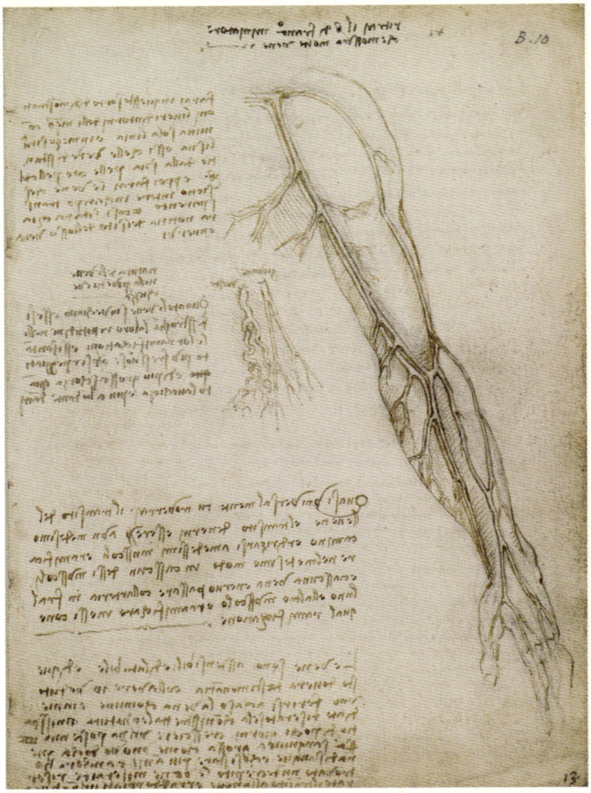

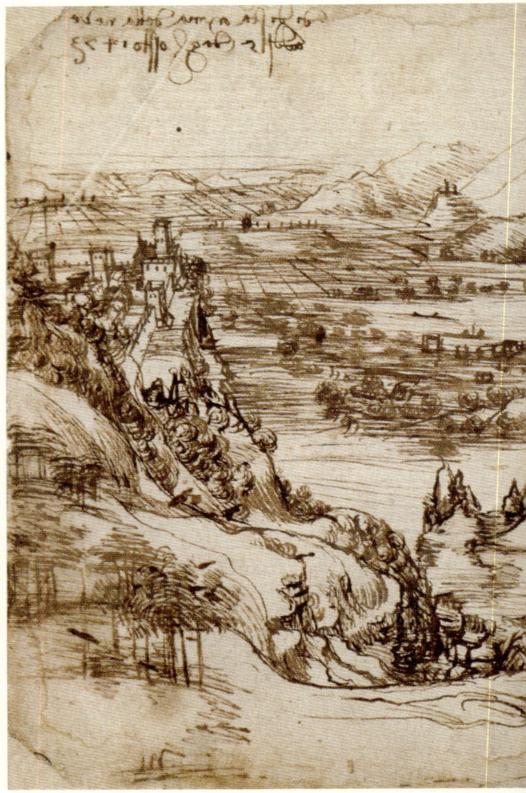

Fig. 101 (left)
Leonardo da Vinci
Veins of the Arm

ca. 1508, pen and ink over traces of chalk, 19.2 × 14.1cm (7½ × 5½in). Royal Library, Windsor (RL19027r).

This drawing shows the left arm together with a small sketch that contrasts the blood vessels of a child and an old man. Leonardo's description of how he dissected the centenarian is on the reverse of this sheet.

Fig. 102 (centre)
Leonardo da Vinci
Landscape

Dated 1473, pen and ink on paper, 19.6 × 28.7cm (7¾ × 11⅜in). Galleria degli Uffizi, Florence.

which to study anatomy. This fact is often used to explain the extraordinary anatomical accuracy of Christ's body in Michelangelo's *Crucifixion* for Santo Spirito, although why he should have given the 33-year-old man the body of an adolescent is less obvious.

Leonardo, of course, is remembered as the most famous anatomist-artist of the period. During the winter of 1507–8 he eagerly awaited the death of a centenarian at the hospital of Santa Maria Nuova, before cutting him open and drawing the results (FIG. 101). He left an account in his notes:

> And this old man, a few hours before his death, told me that he was over a hundred years old, and that he felt nothing wrong with his body other than weakness. And thus, while sitting on a bed in the hospital of Santa Maria Nuova in Florence, without any movement or sign of any mishap, he passed from this life.
>
> And I dissected him to see the cause of so sweet a death. This I found to be a fainting away through lack of blood to the artery which nourishes the heart and the other parts below, which I found very dry, thin and withered. I performed this dissection

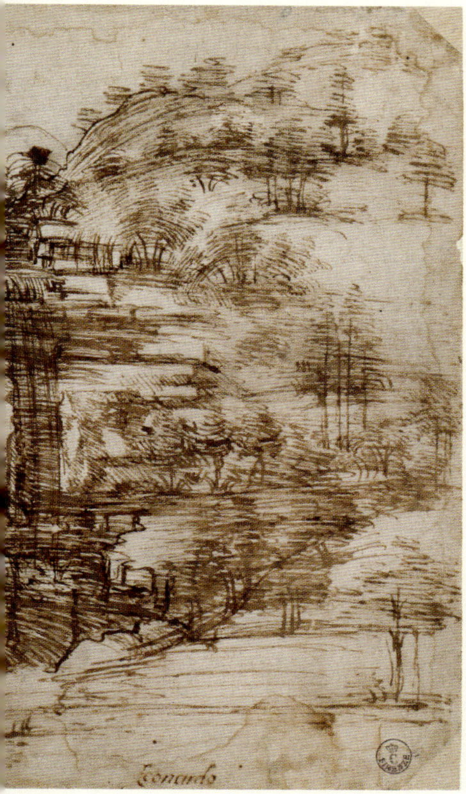

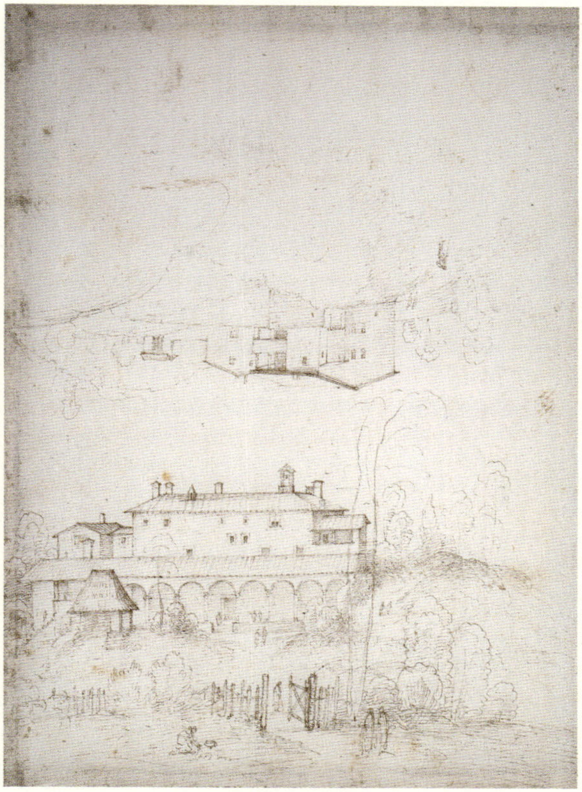

with great ease because of the absence of fat and humours which greatly hinder the recognition of the parts. The other dissection was of a child of two years, in which I found everything contrary to that of the old man.

Fig. 103
Fra Bartolomeo
View of the Ospizio di Santa Maria Maddalena at Caldine

ca. 1508, pen and brown ink on paper, sheet 27.9 × 21.4 cm (11 × 8⅜ in). Smith College Museum of Art, Northampton, MA. Purchased (SC 1957:59).

This drawing comes from an album that once contained 41 sheets by Fra Bartolomeo. Many show landscapes that can be identified, such as the present drawing, which shows the Dominican convent of Santa Maria Maddalena at Pian di Mugnone, near Caldine.

Leonardo's early interest in the natural world is evident from a landscape drawing (FIG. 102), the first of its kind, which he dated in his characteristic mirror script to the 'day of Holy Mary of the Snows on the 5 August 1473'. Leonardo's precision suggests that the drawing records an actual landscape that he observed on that day, even though scholars have never been able to pinpoint it exactly, beyond the vague suggestion that it shows the Arno valley. The inscription has the force and veracity of a dated contract: at this time, in this place. A few decades later Fra Bartolomeo would fill an album with landscape drawings, many of which can be identified (FIG. 103). Representation had become specific enough to identify a location.

Evocations of the Arno valley appear in Florentine art in the early 1460s, initially in the work of Alesso Baldovinetti for the

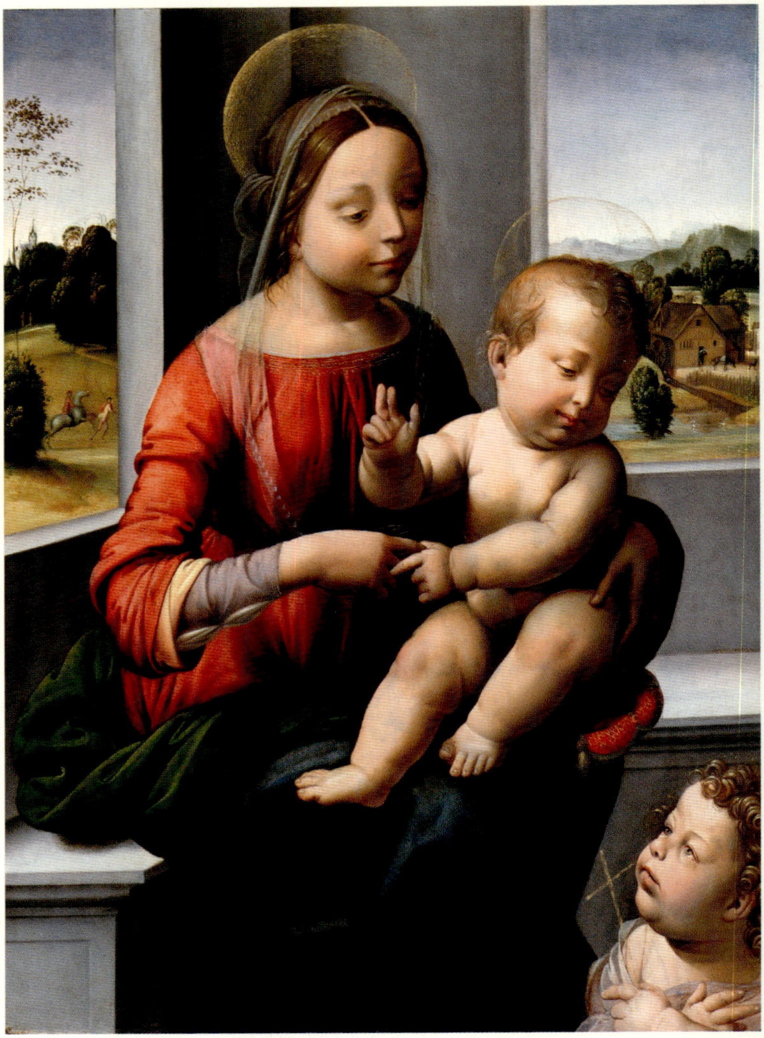

Fig. 104
Fra Bartolomeo
Virgin and Child with the Young St John the Baptist

ca. 1497, oil and gold on panel, 58.4 × 43.8cm (23 × 17¼in). Metropolitan Museum of Art, New York. Rogers Fund, 1906 (06.171).

The watermill in the background of this painting is copied from Fig. 105.

courtyard of Santissima Annunziata and in altarpieces painted by the Pollaiuolo brothers (*see* FIG. 139). They were accompanied by a change in viewpoint. Rather than the landscape rising behind the protagonists in the foreground, the viewer now looks down on it, as sometimes occurs in Netherlandish and Sienese painting, such as in the backgrounds of Jan van Eyck's *Madonna of Chancellor Rolin* or Giovanni di Paolo's *Madonna of Humility*. In the courtyard of Santissima Annunziata, Baldovinetti might have been copying the viewpoint adopted by Netherlandish artists in their paintings, but in other instances, we can trace motifs appropriated directly from Netherlandish art. Such is the case with Fra Bartolomeo's *Virgin and Child with the Young Saint John the Baptist* (FIG. 104), in which a

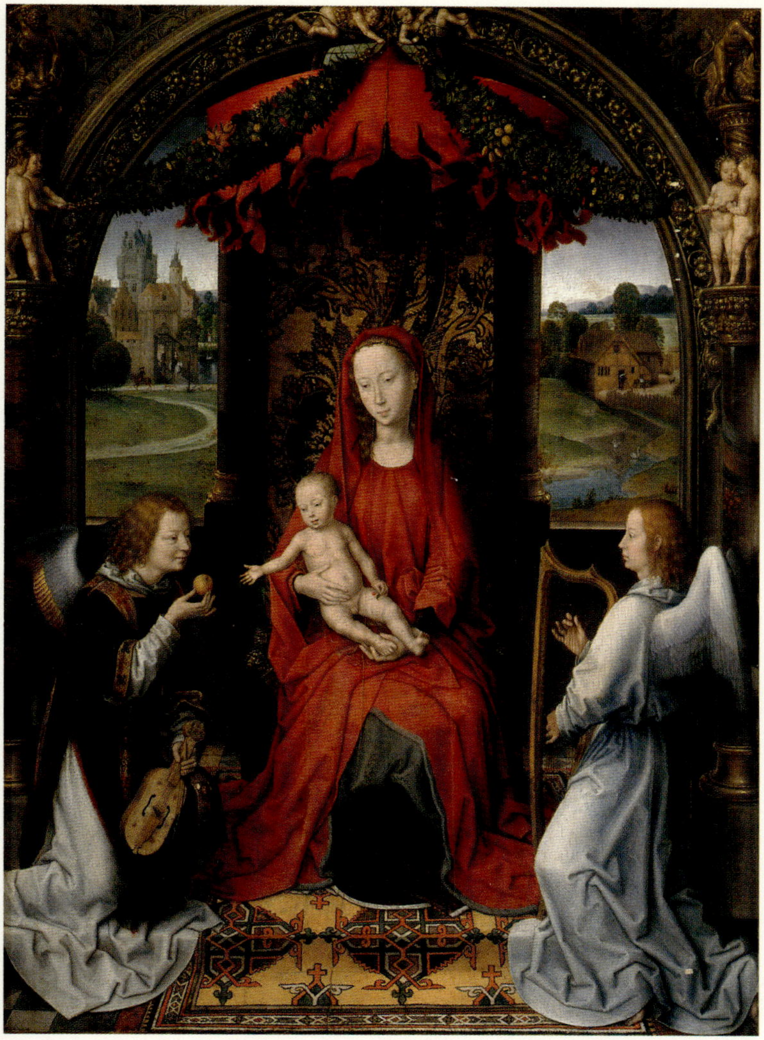

Fig. 105
Hans Memling
Virgin and Child with Angels (central panel of the *Pagagnotti Triptych*)

ca. 1480, oil on oak, 57 × 42 cm (22½ × 16½ in). Galleria degli Uffizi, Florence.

small watermill in the background was lifted directly from a triptych by Hans Memling painted for the Dominican Benedetto Pagagnotti (FIG. 105).

More often than not, however, the backgrounds of Florentine paintings evoke generic northern townscapes, with gothic spires and turrets, quite different from Florentine domestic architecture. We are a long way, however, from Fra Bartolomeo's recognizable landscapes, or Leonardo's view of the Arno valley. These landscapes are fantastical, even if they are naturalistic in their attempt to evoke the effects of nature, such as atmospheric recession or reflections on water. The example of Netherlandish art, then, provided an alternative to ancient art that was different in its aesthetic, but not in its relationship to nature. In both cases, the encounter with nature was mediated by art, whether through the idealizing tendencies of the ancient world or the naturalistic details and architectural vocabulary painted by artists in Bruges. Direct observation of the real world was something different, something entirely new, which through the so-called scientific revolution of Galileo and others in the next century would transform our relationship with the natural world.

Portrait Busts and the Impression of Nature

One genre bucks the trends outlined above: portrait sculpture. Few image types can claim a closer relationship with nature than portraiture. Portraits, by definition, make reference to a sitter in the real world, and must therefore suggest enough of their physical appearance to be believable. The mythical origins of portraiture always stress that connection, whether in Narcissus's reflection in a pool of water (Alberti) or the trace of a lover's profile on the wall (Pliny). The independent portrait was new to fifteenth-century

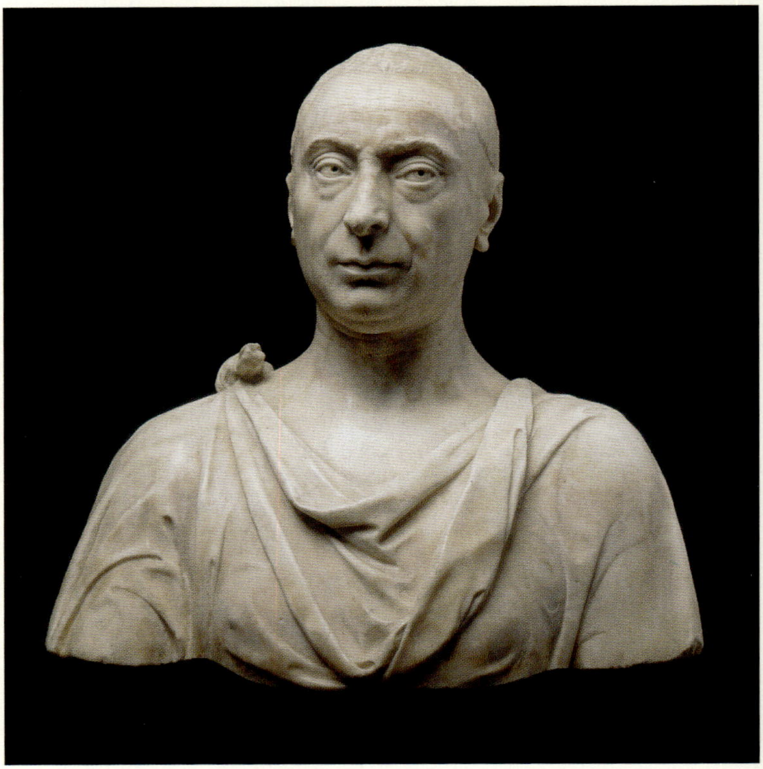

Fig. 106
Antonio Rossellino
Bust of Francesco Sassetti

ca. 1464, marble, 52cm (20½in). Museo Nazionale del Bargello, Florence.

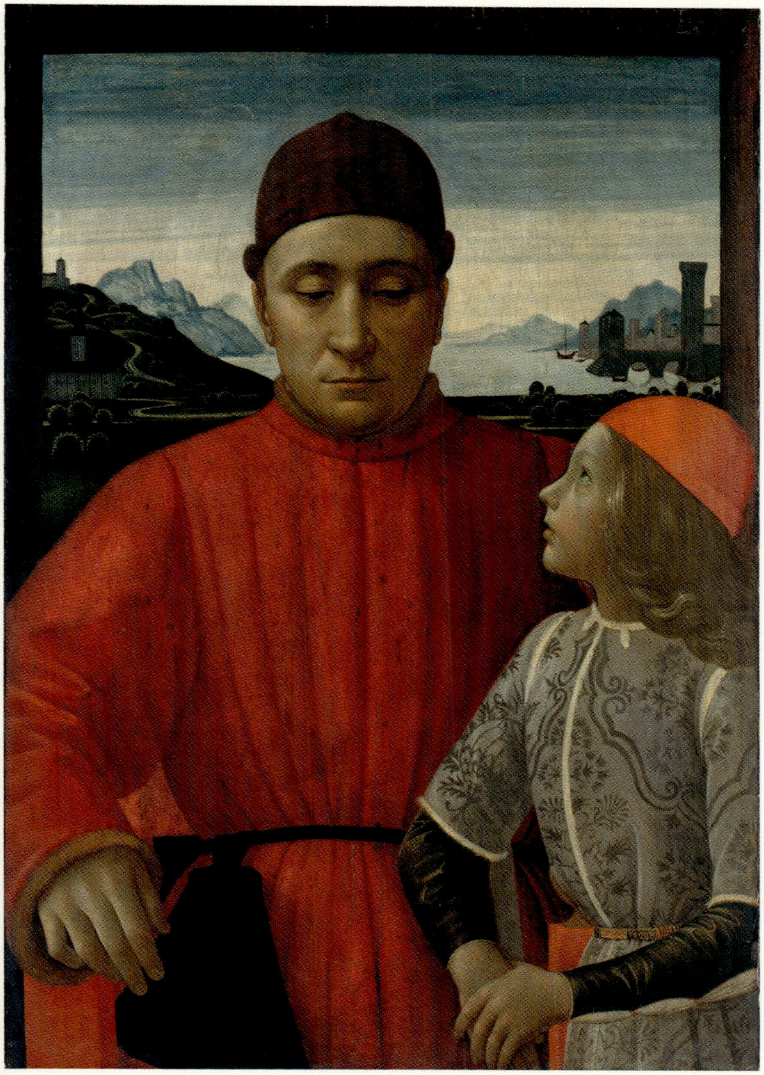

Fig. 107
Domenico Ghirlandaio
Francesco Sassetti and his Son Teodoro

ca. 1488, tempera on panel, 75.9 × 53cm (29⅞ × 20⅞ in.), Metropolitan Museum of Art, New York. The Jules Bache Collection, 1949 (49.7.7).

This painting and the sculpture opposite both show the same man, Francesco Sassetti, yet there is an entirely different attitude to nature and idealization in the two media.

Florence, inspired by antique busts on the one hand, and Netherlandish panel paintings on the other – twin sources that trapped it between questions of idealization and nature. The portrait bust also owed a debt to head reliquaries, which, for all their connection to the actual body they contained, represented an ideal of the saint that was far removed from their historical appearance. Nonetheless, it was the portrait bust, rather than the painted portrait, that most obviously crossed the line between perfected nature and truth to nature (FIGS. 106, 107). Sculpted busts of fifteenth-century Florentine men, more so than women (although there are some notable exceptions), look back at us from the past with a startling veracity: we see the

Fig. 108
Domenico Ghirlandaio
Old Man with a Young Boy

ca. 1490, oil on panel, 62 × 46cm ($24^{3}/_{8}$ × $18^{1}/_{8}$in). Musée du Louvre, Paris.

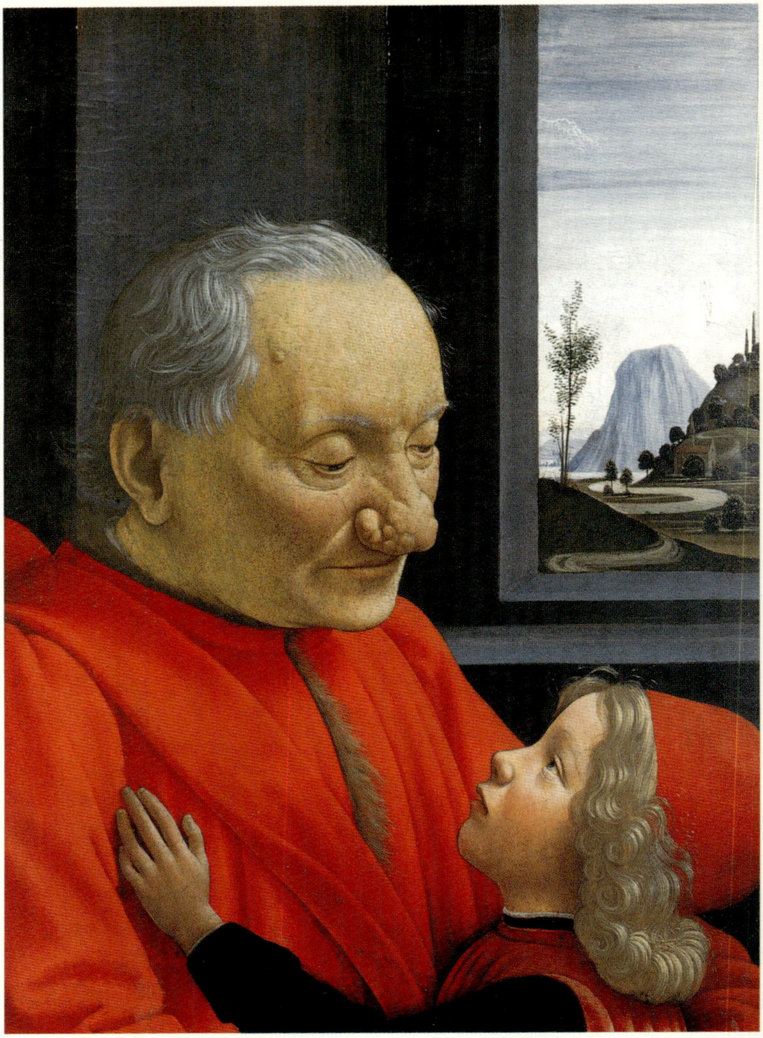

blemishes on their skin, their stubble and receding hair, their sunken cheeks. They could not be further from the idealized beauty of the figures in the sculpture and paintings they owned.

I am not suggesting that portraits were neither idealized nor changed from observable nature. Despite the obligation to depict sitters '*al naturale*', artists were expected to flatter their patrons, whose representation was governed by fashion and convention, both artistic and poetic (*see* FIG. 65). After all, the ultimate portrait was an unattainable ideal: Simone Martini's image of Petrarch's Laura, known only from his sonnets (1327–68), is much like the poetic image of the beloved portrayed on the heart of the lover. And even those painted portraits that purport to show the sitter 'warts and all', such as Ghirlandaio's touching double portrait of an old man with a child (FIG. 108), reveal themselves to be the outcome of adjustment and alteration when compared to the preparatory drawing, executed directly from the sitter, whether dead or alive (FIG. 109).

However, portrait busts are of a different order. Since they are life-size, their physical presence aids verisimilitude. Yet scale and substance were not all. Such busts were often carved from life- or death masks, taken directly from the sitter's face. Even now, their use is betrayed by a distorted ear, caused by the application of cloth to take the plaster mask. In the case of a terracotta bust of Niccolò da Uzzano, the bust itself was probably built up around a cast of a death mask (FIG. 110). The actual impression of nature remains incorporated in the work of art. Of course, this is not unmediated nature, either. The artist's hand is still evident in the build-up of terracotta around and over the mask; his invention in the choice of pose and costume; and his skill in the subtle colouring. But a line had been crossed.

It is difficult to find a word with which to describe this direct connection to nature. Some scholars opt for 'realism', but it remains problematic. It implies a completely unmediated representation of nature, as if untouched by the artist. It is also often used with respect to the social position of individuals in a work of art, whether the

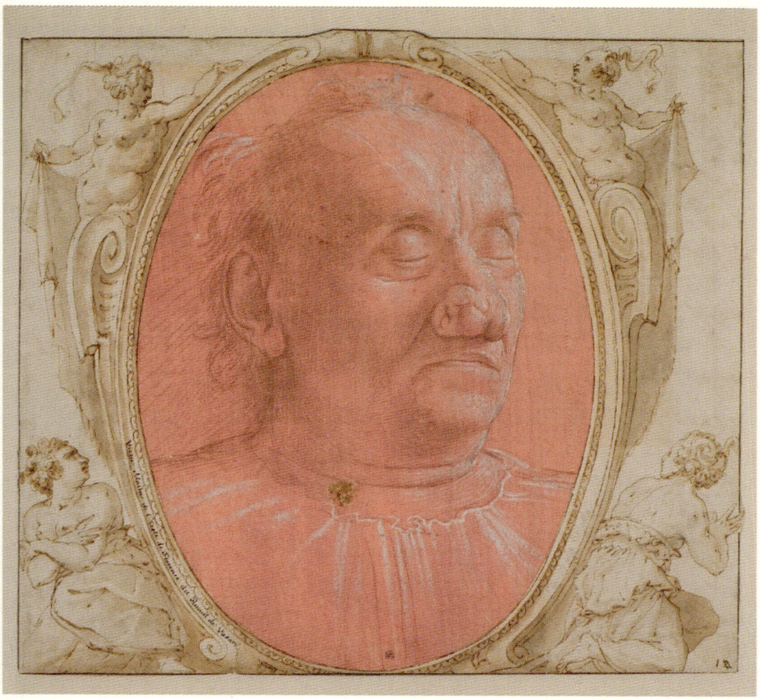

Fig. 109
Domenico Ghirlandaio
Head of an Old Man

ca. 1490, drawing, 28.8 × 21.4cm ($11\frac{3}{8} \times 8\frac{1}{2}$in). Nationalmuseum, Stockholm.

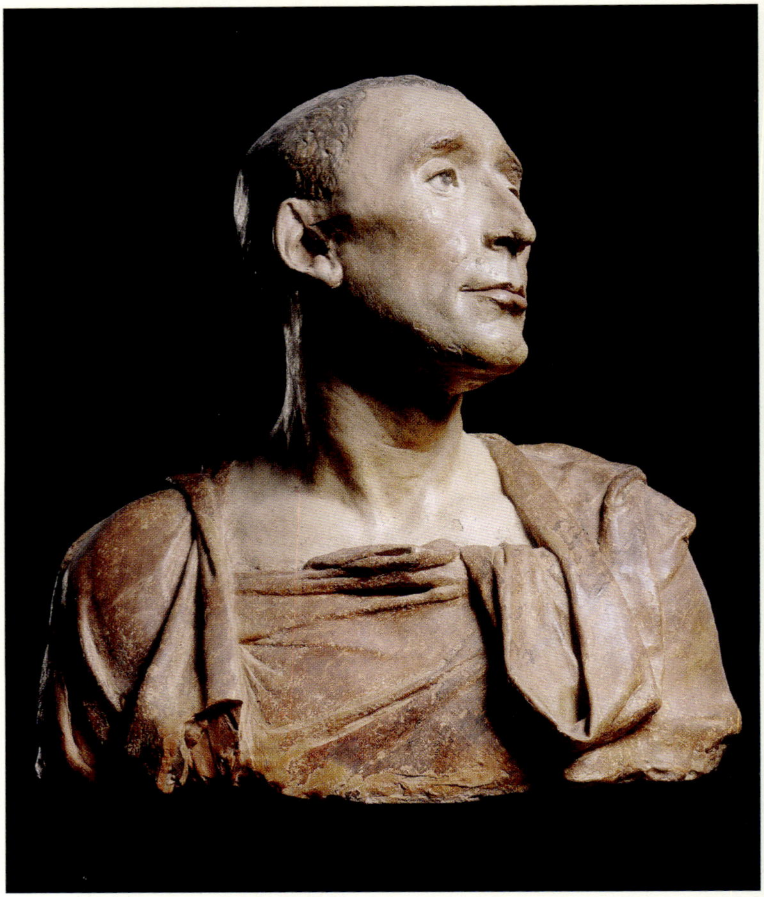

Fig. 110
Attributed to Desiderio da Settignano
Niccolò da Uzzano

1450–55, painted terracotta, 46 × 44cm (18⅛ × 17⅜in). Museo Nazionale del Bargello, Florence.

peasants depicted by Caravaggio a century or so later or by Gustave Courbet in the nineteenth century (so-called social realism). It will not suffice to describe the phenomenon we have been discussing. The words used in the fifteenth century are not much help, either. Landino, who included a brief homily to famous Florentine artists in the introduction to his commentary on Dante's *Comedy* in 1481, described Masaccio as an '*optimo imitatore di natura*', a great imitator of nature, because he attended to the imitation of truth ('*all'imitatione del vero*'). As we have seen, what was meant by 'nature' in the fifteenth century is not the same as our 'naturalism', and 'truth' as understood from the paintings of Masaccio seems a far cry from the direct contact with nature that I have just been describing. Perhaps what remains is the idea of nature pressed into the work of art, much like the memory of an image on a seal pressed into wax.

Style as Choice

We have seen how artists imitated nature, using the example of their predecessors in antiquity. They selected its finest forms and recombined them in a process that ultimately sought to improve on nature, through invention and skill. Nature was perceived through various filters, whether the art of Lysippus and his kin, or that of Netherlandish painters of more recent times. It was also just beginning to be examined empirically. The discussion so far has assumed that style acted independently from subject matter; that somehow these various influences came into play in any and every work of art. And yet, when we look at some of the most exceptional objects that have come down to us from the Renaissance – such as Donatello's *Mary Magdalene* (FIG. 111) – they seem to break these rules. Where is classical antiquity; where are nature's finest forms?

The obvious point to make here is that the precepts were not hard-and-fast rules. Artists adapted the appearance of their works to meet various pressures: the needs of patrons, the context of a work of art, the exigencies of the material, or the requirements of its subject matter. Mary Magdalene had been a prostitute, who repented of her sins and retreated to the desert to atone for her former life. The *Venus pudica* would have been entirely inappropriate as a formal source, as much as a stylistic one, being more evocative of her previous life than of her new one. Donatello's brilliance was to find a style – a mode of depiction – that realized in physical form her mental and moral state. In this case, subject matter determined form and style. Elsewhere, other factors come into play. Filippino Lippi's additions to the Brancacci chapel in the early 1480s might be obvious to us today from his distinctive facial types, or the Netherlandish backgrounds he included, but they appear very different from his other works of about the same date, at least stylistically. The difference can best be explained by an attempt to blend his style with that of Masaccio and Masolino, whose frescoes were painted half a century earlier.

Style, in other words, was a choice, whether for Donatello or Filippino, and that choice was determined, in part, by the expectations the viewer brought to the work of art. It remains for us to consider, then, different forms of spectatorship in Renaissance Florence, the subject of the next chapter.

Fig. 111
Donatello
Mary Magdalene

Probably 1450s, gilded and polychromed wood, 188cm (74in) high. Museo dell'Opera del Duomo, Florence.

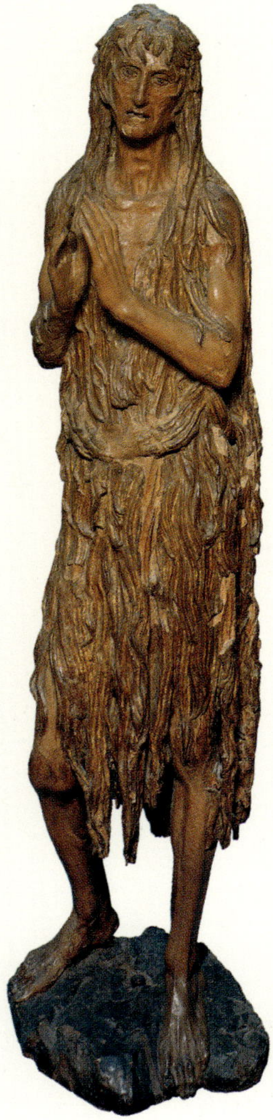

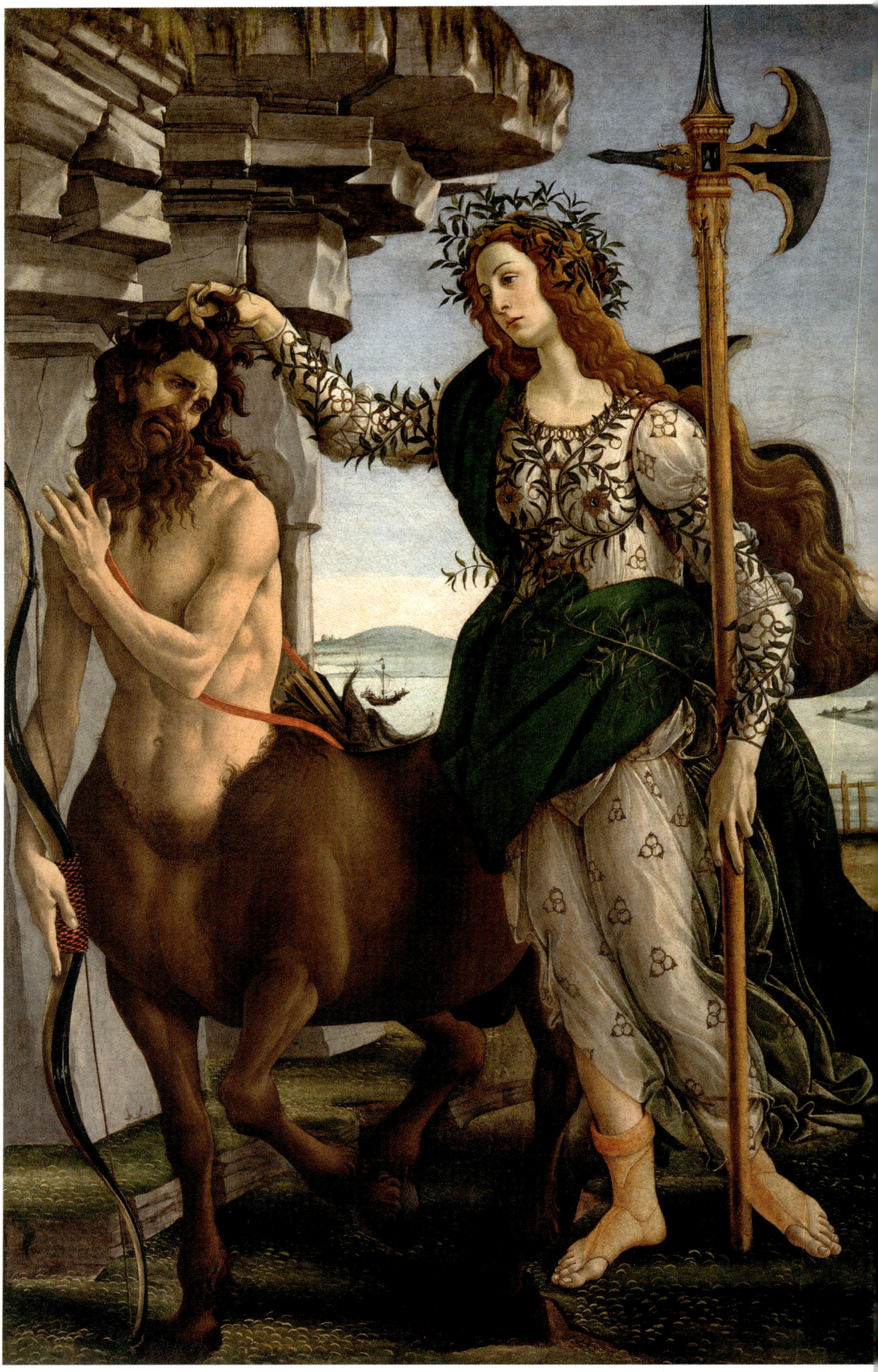

9

Modes of Viewing: Sacred and Secular Art

Changes in style brought with them new problems. Perspective transformed the description of space, and the example of nature and the antique vivified the relationship between what viewers saw in the world around them and what they beheld in art. Did the changed appearance of traditional subject matter alter what people thought about it? Previous generations had been interested in mimetic art, but Florentine artists of the fifteenth and sixteenth centuries took illusionism to new levels. We have examined these broad stylistic developments; now we shall consider their implications for sacred and secular art, in which they played out differently. In sacred art, viewers were long accustomed to certain object types – altarpieces, for example, or small devotional panels – and they had expectations about how to approach them, whether through the structure of the liturgy or through their own, more private prayers and meditation. What happened, then, when these expectations were at odds with their style? With secular art the situation was different, for there was the question not only of new styles, but also of new subject matter. As the fifteenth century progressed, recondite mythological subjects became increasingly common in patrician homes, and with them new expectations about

Fig. 112
Sandro Botticelli
Pallas and the Centaur

ca. 1482, tempera on canvas, 204 × 147.5cm (80⅜ × 58in). Galleria degli Uffizi, Florence.

In 1498/9 this painting was in the possession of a cadet branch of the Medici family (Lorenzo the Magnificent's cousins), where it was displayed over a door.

how these open-ended, discursive images were to be viewed. Stylistic change brought with it a change in the perception of what could be represented in art.

Idolatry and the Perils of Illusionism

The Old Testament explicitly outlaws the worship of images: 'Thou shalt not make unto thee any graven images … Thou shalt not bow down thyself to them, nor serve them' (Exodus 20:4–5). The prohibition was against the worship of images or idols as if they were gods themselves, a practice known as idolatry. The relationship of the Abrahamic religions with images has always been complex, especially since the Western Church largely condoned them before the Reformation. In Renaissance Florence, sacred images were still justified in much that same way as they had been defended by Pope Gregory the Great at the beginning of the seventh century. In a letter written to Serenus, Bishop of Marseilles, whom he reproached for having destroyed a work of art, Gregory pointed out that 'What Scripture is to the educated, images are to the ignorant, who see through them what they must accept; they read in them what they cannot read in books.' His insights were codified at the Council of Nicaea in 787. Centuries later they were developed into a complex theology of images by Thomas Aquinas (ca. 1225–1274), and repeated by his fellow Dominican and Archbishop of Florence, Antoninus Pierozzi, in the mid fifteenth century. For both Thomas and Antoninus, images must instruct, for they were to be the books of the illiterate. They should also recall sacred history, bringing the examples of Christ, the Virgin and the saints into the minds of the faithful. And, if used properly, they should direct emotion to the proper contemplation of God. Sacred images must therefore be didactic and memorable, and inspire devotion.

These tenets for sacred imagery were not new in the fifteenth century. Instead, innovation came in format and style. The most significant change in altarpiece design, for instance, was the development of an altarpiece that was not divided into separate panels (as was the polyptych), but instead unified into a single field within a rectangular, *all'antica* frame: the *tavola quadrata* or *pala* (the former term was in use in the fifteenth century; the latter has been adapted more recently by English-speaking scholars to describe an altarpiece of this type). The form, which would slowly become standard across the Italian peninsula, was a Florentine invention of about 1440. It eventually superseded the polyptych, a change in taste that

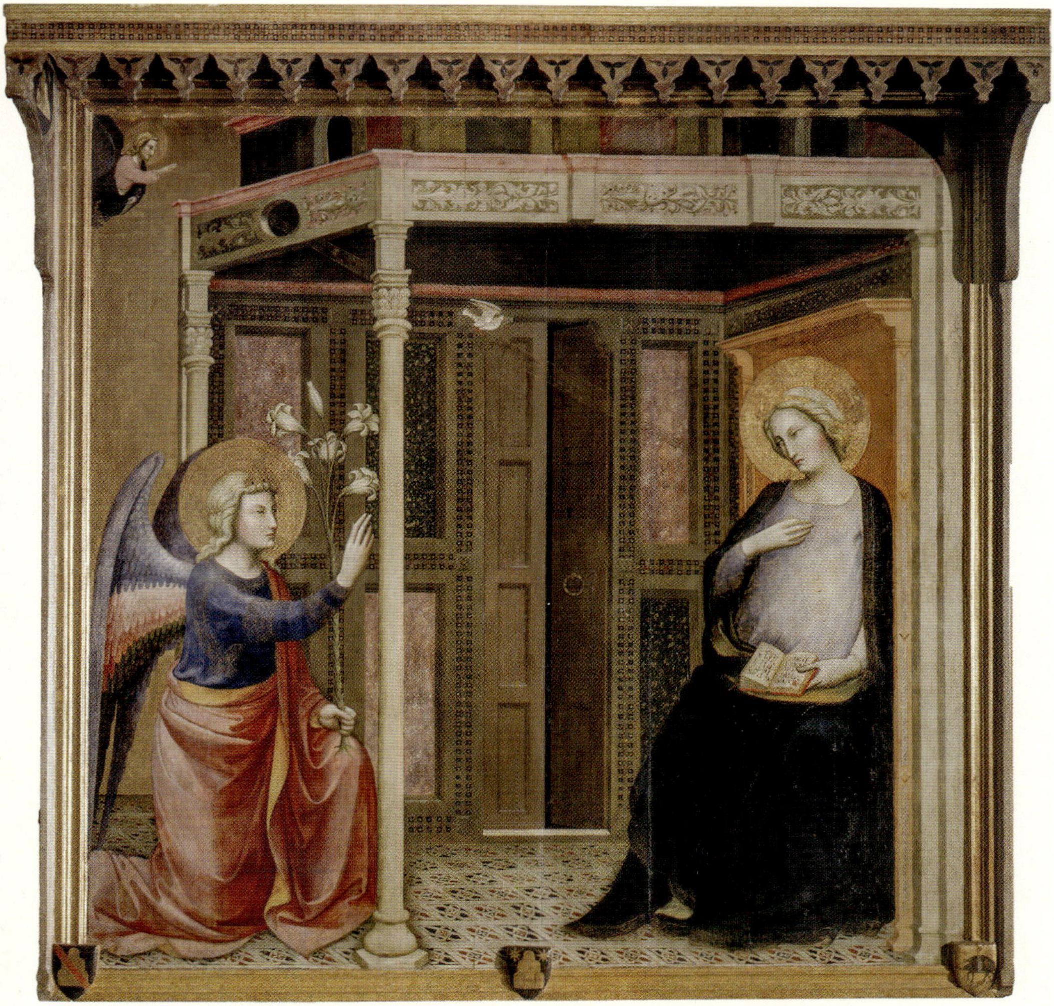

was quicker in Florence than elsewhere. The earliest examples were painted by Fra Filippo Lippi (*see* FIG. 116) and Fra Angelico, both *frati dipintori*, or painter-friars. The *tavola quadrata* combined a Christian type – the altarpiece, whether narrative or iconic – with ornament derived from pagan antiquity. The latter is important, since precedents exist in which the field is entirely unified, but the decorative vocabulary remains essentially gothic, whether in Florence or further afield (FIG. 113).

Fig. 113
Master of the Straus Madonna
Annunciation

ca. 1395–1405, tempera on panel, 190 × 200 cm (74¾ × 78¾ in). Galleria dell'Accademia, Florence.

The development of this new type was associated with Brunelleschi's newly built churches (and perhaps also with Michelozzo's additions to the friary of San Marco), and especially with a decree by the prior and chapter of San Lorenzo in 1434 that required chapels to be decorated with 'a rectangular panel without gables or finials

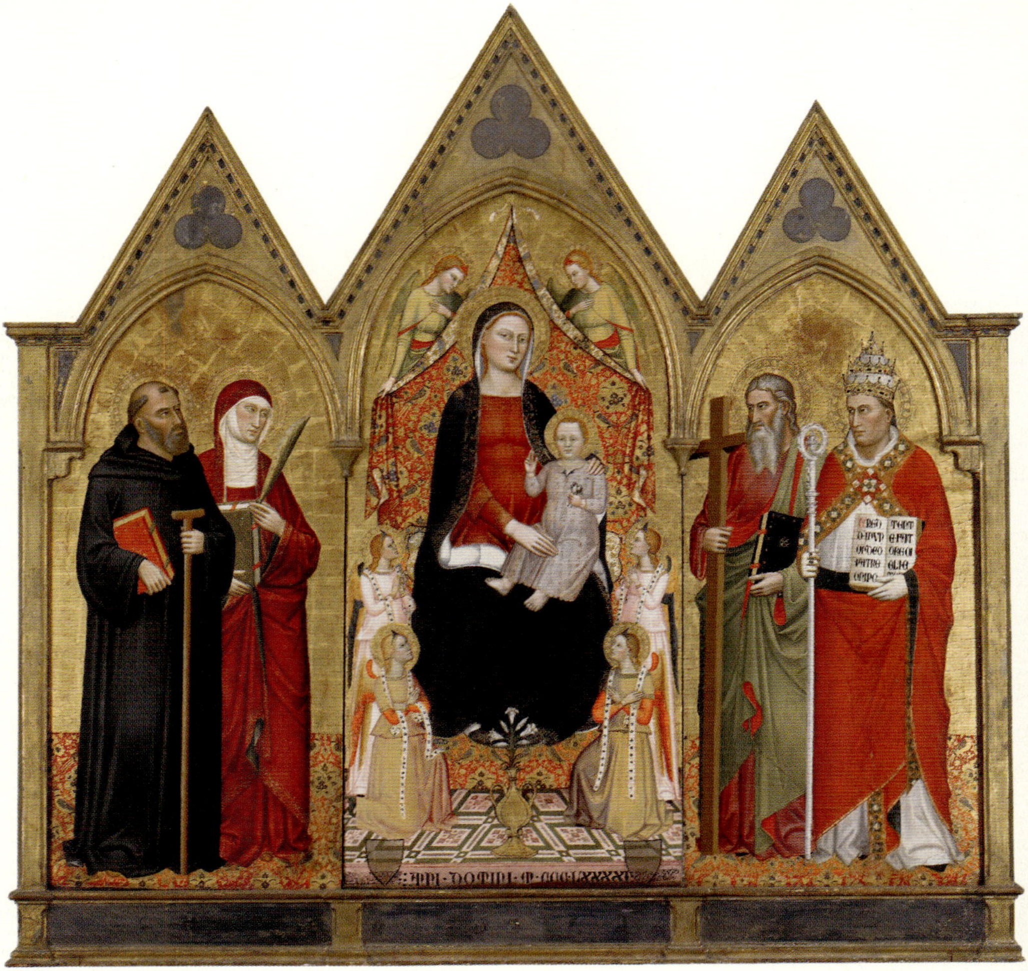

Fig. 114
Jacopo di Cione
The Virgin and Child with Saints Amatus Abbot, Concordia, Andrew and Pope Mark

1391, tempera on panel, 194.3 × 205.7 × 12.1 cm (76⅜ × 81 × 4¾ in). Academy of Arts, Honolulu. Gift of Anna Rice Cooke, 1928 (2834).

This altarpiece was in old San Lorenzo and was transferred by the Rondinelli family from their old chapel to the new family altar in the reconstructed church, just to the left of the main chapel.

[*tabula quadrata et sine civoriis, picta honorabiliter*]'. The decree established conditions for the furnishing of chapels in the new church of San Lorenzo, which would have united them formally. Although at San Lorenzo the vision was not entirely successful – since some families brought their old gold-ground polyptychs from the previous church (FIG. 114), which was being slowly replaced by Brunelleschi – it was realized to a much greater degree in the 1480s and 1490s in the transepts of Santo Spirito, where the effect can still be appreciated.

It is important to remember that while the look of altarpieces began to change, both in type and in style, their role and function remained essentially the same. Hierarchical divisions, which were so clearly defined by the internal frames of a polyptych, were still required to be manifest, even though Christ, the Virgin and various saints occupied the same, naturalistically rendered space. In one of the earliest manifestations of the *tavola quadrata*, the St Lucy Altarpiece by Domenico Veneziano (d. 1461), the artist used architecture to re-inscribe hierarchy (FIG. 115). All the figures occupy the same space, yet they are divided by an arcade and their relative status is signalled by the ornament on the back wall: a full shell for the Virgin and Child, a half-shell each for Saints John the Baptist and Zenobius, and half an arch for Francis and Lucy. The Virgin and Child might be further back illusionistically, but the viewer is in no doubt that they are more important than the flanking saints, nor that John and Zenobius (the two patron saints of Florence) trump Francis and Lucy, the titular saint of the church.

One of the contenders for the first Renaissance *pala* is Lippi's *Annunciation* in the Cappella degli Operai at San Lorenzo, which he probably painted in the late 1430s (FIG. 116). He made several

Fig. 115
Domenico Veneziano
Virgin and Child with Saints Francis, John the Baptist, Zenobius and Lucy (St Lucy Altarpiece)

Early 1440s, tempera on panel, 210 × 215cm (82⅝ × 84⅝in). Galleria degli Uffizi, Florence.

This altarpiece was originally on the high altar of Santa Lucia dei Magnoli.

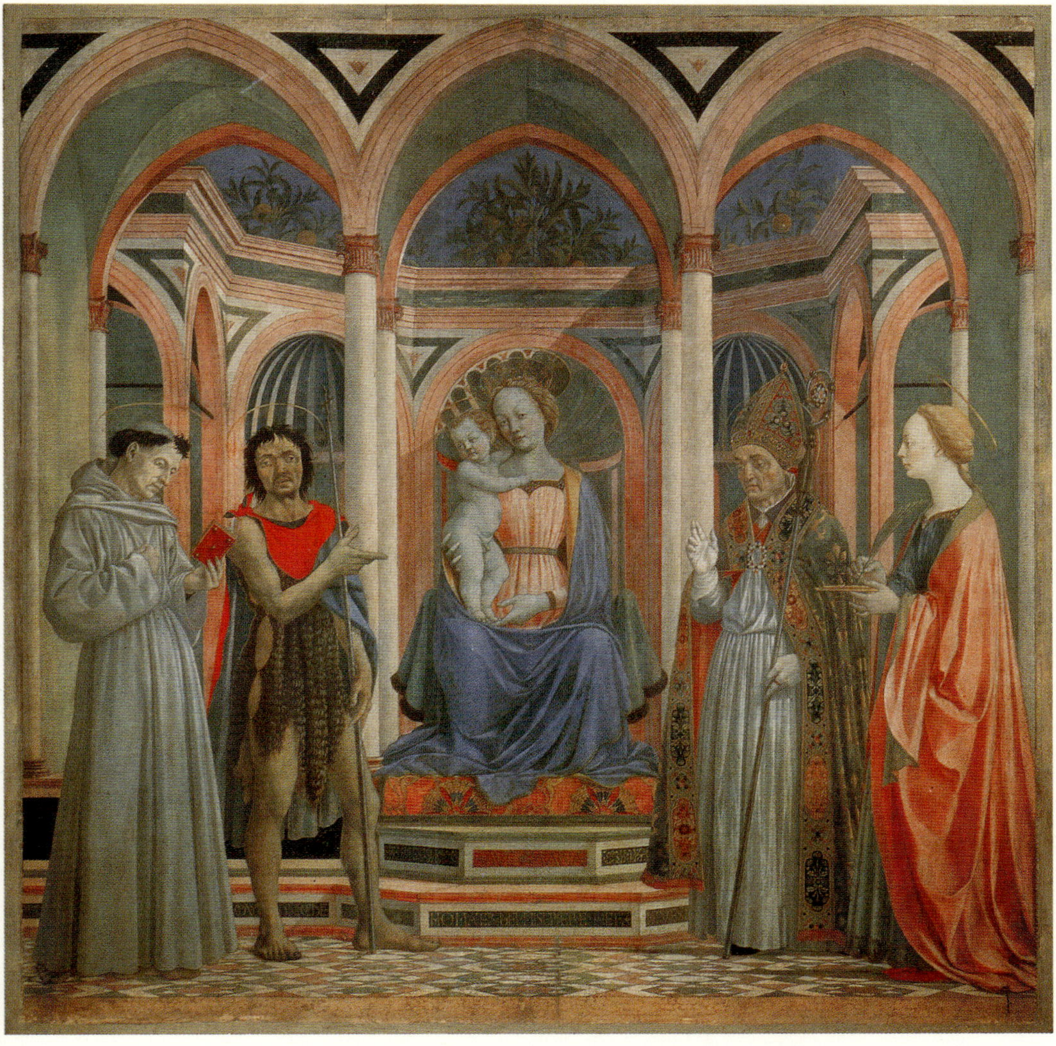

surprising decisions in arranging the illusionistic space occupied by the Virgin and her visitors. The first was to compress the Annunciation into the right-hand half of the altarpiece. When compared with the *Annunciation* painted by the Master of the Straus Madonna 40 years earlier, it is puzzling. Perhaps Lippi was seeking to correct for the fact that the viewer approaches the chapel from the left and sees the right half of the altarpiece first. The second decision was to render the background with a rigorously applied perspective, whose vanishing point is again just to the right of centre, around Gabriel's lily, but not to apply the same geometry to the foreground (especially the architecture in the upper left and right spaces), which is instead worked out empirically to avoid the distortion that would have been created if he had used the same vanishing point. The solution is significant, since this background is among the earliest 'correct' perspectives on a painted panel (rather than in fresco), and it therefore demonstrates that from the very outset artists were aware that perspective could not be applied rigorously if they were to create a harmonious space. Nonetheless, one of the consequences of constructing the background through linear perspective was to establish a fixed relationship between viewer and representation, as we saw in Chapter 7. So, whether he was making adjustments for the viewer arriving in the chapel from the crossing of the church, or thinking about the devotee directly in front of the altarpiece, Lippi was thinking hard about how the space of his image would relate to that of the spectator. Given that the altarpiece is the work of a Carmelite friar, well versed in the theology of images, we can be confident that he was sensitive to the effect that pictorial decisions would have on theological ones.

The space of the foreground is equally unusual. It is divided by status, much as Domenico's altarpiece was to be, such that the mystery of the Incarnation occurs on a different, lower floor from that occupied by the two watching angels. Into yet another subdivision of the foreground the painter introduced a water flask. It is a *trompe l'œil* device that appears to sit on the predella box in a half-niche between Gabriel and the Virgin. It is clearly symbolic (the clarity of the glass is a symbol of the Virgin's purity, while its form is a reminder that she was a vessel for the incarnate Christ), but it also prompts the viewer to think about whether it is a real water bottle sitting in the space of the chapel, or one painted within the illusion of the image. Whether initially mistaken for an actual vase, or appreciated immediately for Lippi's skill in inventing and painting it, the conceit draws attention to the fact that the altarpiece is a fabricated thing, that it is a representation.

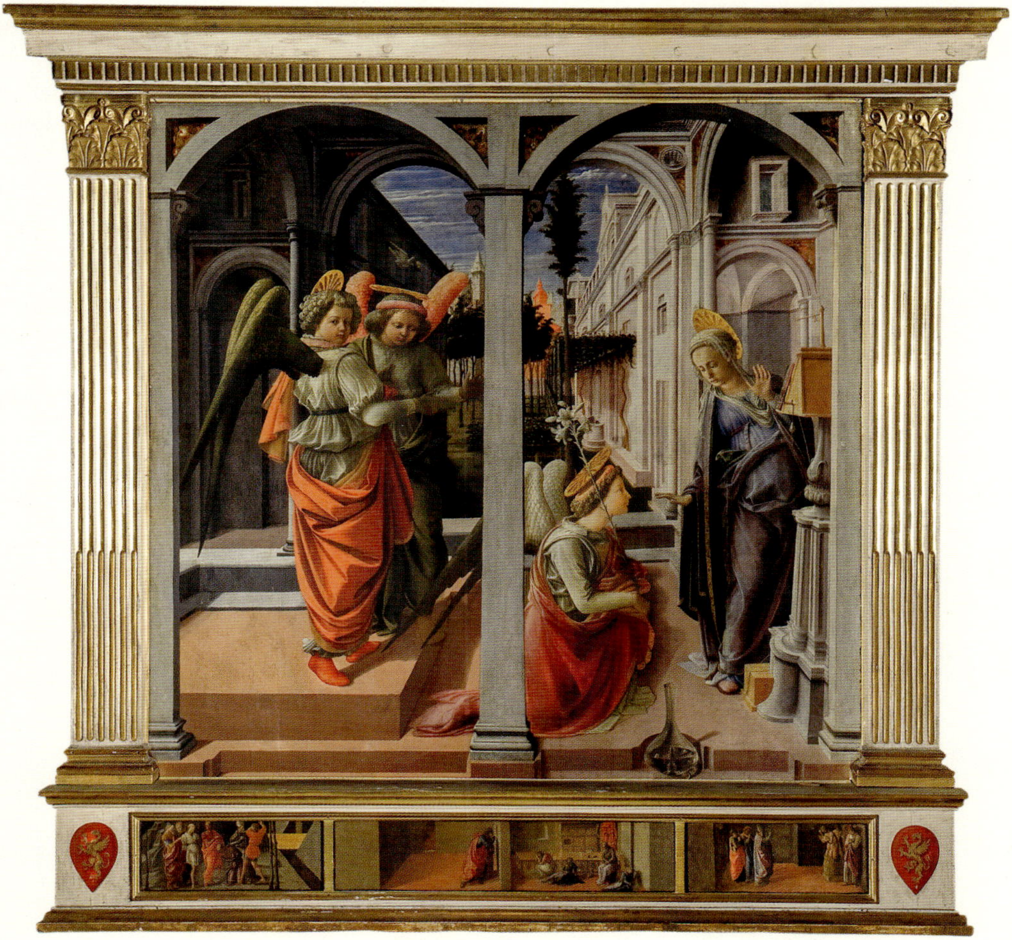

Fig. 116
Fra Filippo Lippi
Martelli Annunciation

ca. 1440, tempera on panel, 175 × 183 cm ($68\frac{7}{8}$ × 72 in). San Lorenzo, Florence.

Taken together, these various compositional decisions reveal the extent to which Lippi has pondered the relationship between the altarpiece and its spectator, and the divisions of space within the image itself. Space is symbolic, for it demarcates different levels of the sacred (the angels; the Annunciate Virgin), but it is also a representational tool that marks different levels of reality, from the space in which the mystery of the Incarnation takes place to that occupied by the water flask. The intent is not to deceive, but rather to draw attention to the fact that the altarpiece is a made object, as if to proclaim that it was invented by a masterful artist. The result is to destabilize the very illusion that Lippi has worked so hard to achieve.

The strategy is common to many of Lippi's altarpieces. He frequently introduced an element – at San Lorenzo it was a water flask, but elsewhere it might be an axe (*see* FIG. 71), a balustrade or even a patron – that alerts the viewer to his invention. He would seem to be reminding the spectator that they are not actually witnessing the angelic salutation to the Virgin, much less the moment of the Incarnation of Christ, but rather a panel with paint on it that depicts these events. This prompt is important because it speaks to an anxiety over the much-heralded naturalism of Florentine painting; a fear that the devotee might mistake a painting for reality and thus commit the sin of idolatry.

The devout were supposed to worship the prototype behind the material image or icon. Aquinas explained that 'the honour given to an image reaches to the prototype', that is, 'to the exemplar', by which he meant Christ. He was repeating a long-held belief and was in fact quoting St John of Damascus, who was himself quoting Saint Basil the Great. Honour done to the material object was not idolatry, then, provided it was directed to the exemplar behind and beyond it. In other words, a picture or sculpture must be recognized as a *representation* of something else. When images still presented Christ or the Virgin as an icon, stylized through centuries of formulaic repetition, the style of the depiction helped viewers to recognize it as a representation, even if they sometimes failed to take up the prompt. But what happened when the goal of the artist was to give his image the illusion of nature? Would he not be tempting the pious beholder to confuse it for the prototype? If so, he would be encouraging sin. The challenge Lippi faced was to paint a convincing image of the Annunciation, with all the immediacy of naturalistic depiction, while finding a means to remind his viewers that they saw not the Virgin herself, but only her image. His destabilizing incursions into the pictorial field – his water flasks and balustrades – achieve this end masterfully. Yet such ambition still fell short of what was expected of a sacred image, for, while it must not coax the viewer into worshipping it as an idol its own right, it should direct the mind of the viewer to the prototype beyond it, in this case to the Virgin herself.

Prayer and Meditation

In considering this second aspect, we have moved from the challenges faced by the artist to the demands placed on the beholder, even if the former (the artist) designed his images with the expectations of the latter (the viewer) in mind. An educated friar such as Fra Angelico, familiar with the theology of Aquinas or St Augustine, would have known that sight was not only corporeal, it was also spiritual and intellectual. Prayer and meditation helped the pious to move beyond what they could see with the physical eye to what they

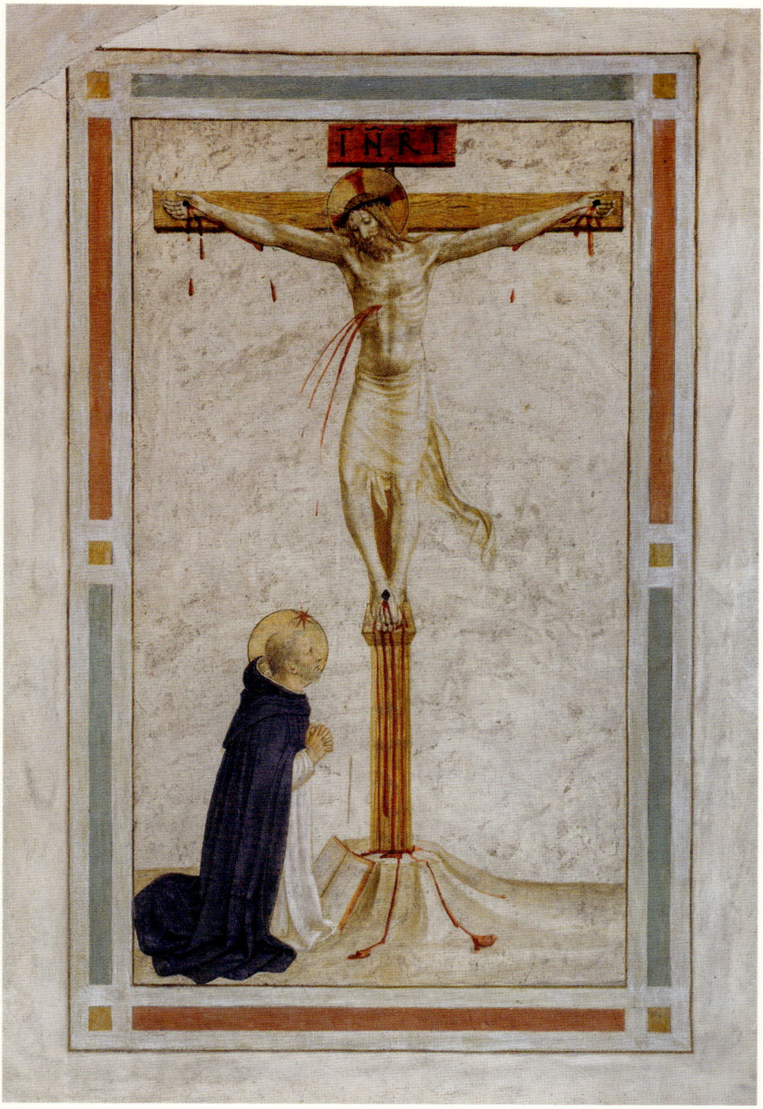

Fig. 117
Fra Angelico
Crucifixion with St Dominic

ca. 1442, fresco. Convento di San Marco, Florence.

The gestures of St Dominic in the frescoes of the novitiate reflect the nine ways in which he prayed, which were recounted in a thirteenth-century treatise on prayer, *De modo orandi*.

imagined with the spiritual eye, in the hope of eventually engaging with the divine on an entirely intellectual level. In this way, devotees moved beyond the physical image in front of them. This three-step process of 'seeing' (corporeal, spiritual, intellectual) was a commonplace of fifteenth-century devotion; not only could the literate read about it in any number of popular devotional tracts, but anyone could hear about it from charismatic preachers. However, the movement from external vision to internal visualization and abstract intellectualization must have been troubling to artists. Was a painter such as Fra Angelico not a professional visualizer of sacred figures and histories, someone whose work was to bring images before the corporeal eye? His role was to create images; to turn pigments and plaster into credible representations of the saints and Christ. How, then, did he create visible images that lifted the eye and the mind to the invisible?

This problem is common to all Christian imagery, but we can observe it most acutely in the rarefied circumstances of the friars' dormitory at the convent (or friary) of San Marco. The dormitory runs around three sides of a cloister, on the first floor, where it is divided into cells, each of which was frescoed by Fra Angelico and his workshop in the second quarter of the fifteenth century. Their function was closely related to the knowledge and status of their incumbents. Novices (young boys training to be clerics) occupied the south wing of the dormitory and were provided with images that were suitably didactic, instructing them visually in the ways of their founder, St Dominic (FIG. 117). Lay brothers, or *conversi*, were probably accommodated on the north side of the dormitory. Unlike clerics, they had not taken holy vows, but instead attended to the

Fig. 118
Fra Angelico
Communion of the Apostles

1438, fresco. Convento di San Marco, Florence.

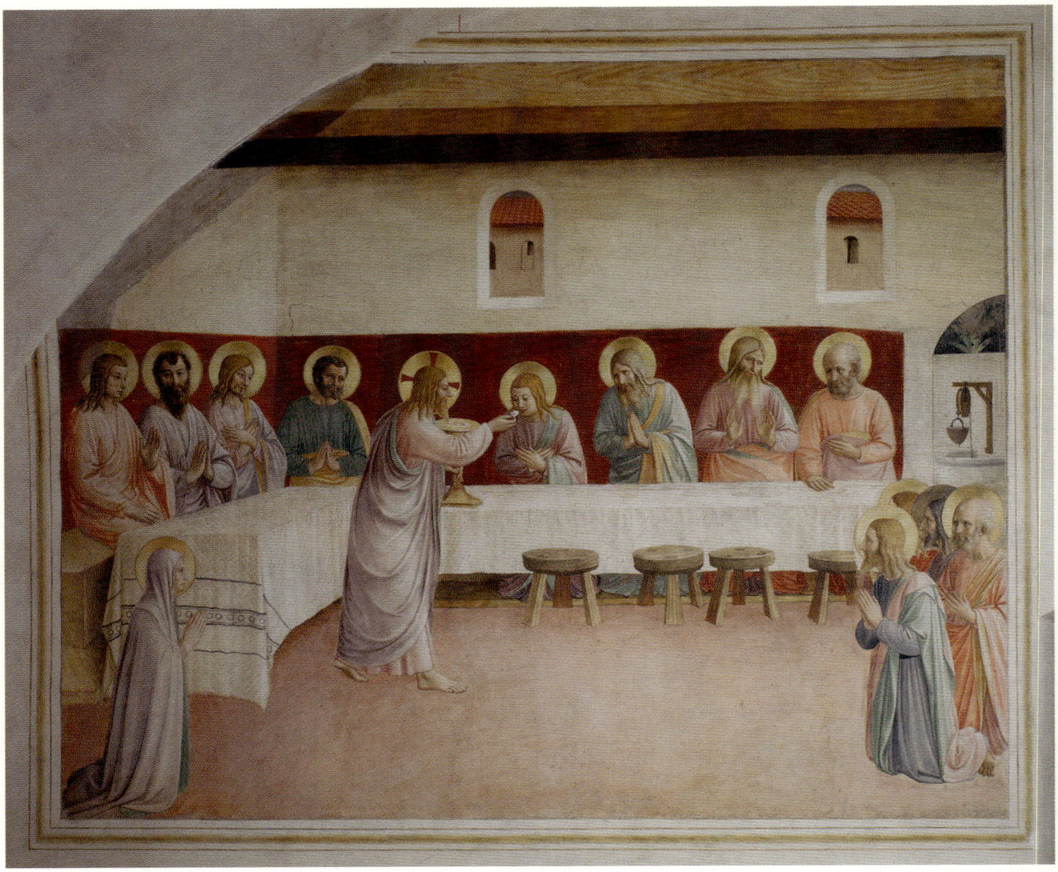

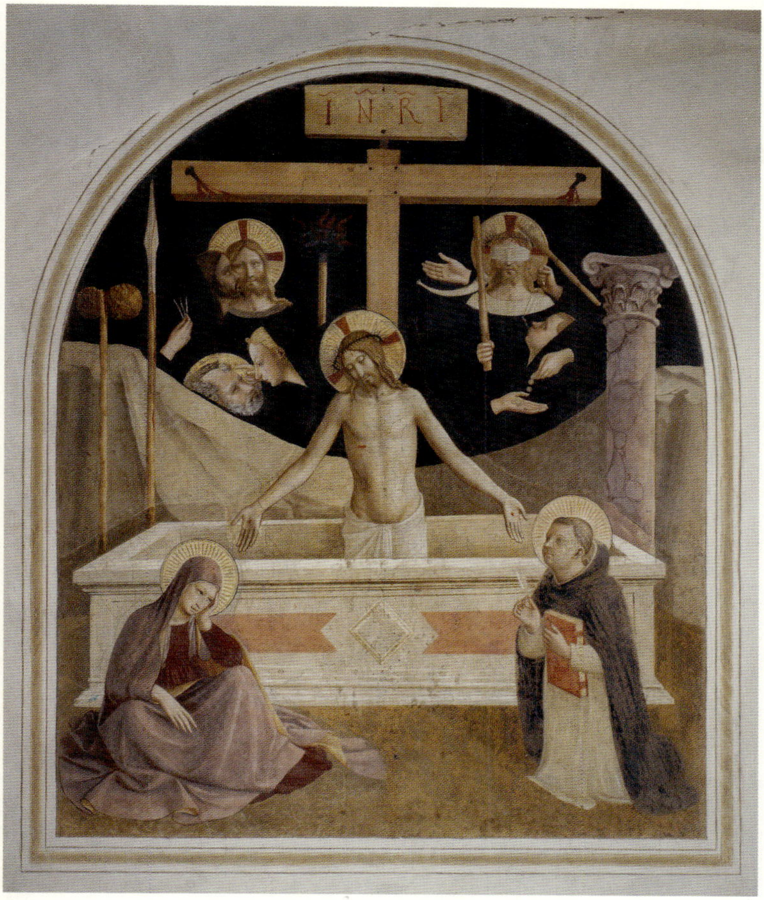

Fig. 119
Fra Angelico and assistants (Benozzo Gozzoli?)
Homo Pietatis

ca. 1438–45, fresco. Convento di San Marco, Florence.

domestic needs of the community: cooking, cleaning and practising trades that earned them an income. Often uneducated and from the lower social orders, they were valued for their manual skill rather than their intellectual ability. The images in this area of the dormitory have a strong narrative bias and are often relatively straightforward visualizations of the gospels (FIG. 118).

Between these two wings, to the east, are 20 cells where we assume the clerics were housed, individuals who had taken holy orders and completed their year-long probation as novices. They were literate and theologically conversant. Unsurprisingly, then, it is here that we find the most complex images, mystical and spiritually demanding works in which Fra Angelico has grappled with how to lift the mind to an intellectual contemplation of the divine. In general, the scenes in this wing of the dormitory relate to the Dominican liturgical calendar, especially the *temporale*, which marked the main events of Christ's life. The feast of Corpus Christi was especially important to the Dominicans and was therefore included in the *temporale*, which might explain the decision to paint a curious fresco in cell 27, since it focuses on Christ's body. The fresco shows the *homo pietatis*, a pitiful image of the half-length Christ as the Man of Sorrows, standing in his tomb, surrounded by symbols of the Passion (FIG. 119). In the foreground, the Virgin rests her head on her hand, facing away from her son in deep contemplation, while St Thomas Aquinas, kneeling, stares upwards and outwards. At first glance, the image seems disjointed and unfamiliar.

Both the symbols and the figures are abstracted from any particular context – sometimes they are reduced to nothing more than half a head or a bodiless hand – so that the viewer is required to imagine how they fit into a narrative and what their meaning might be. The fresco reworks an iconography known as the *arma Christi*, in which Christ is surrounded by the instruments with which he was tormented at the Passion. In Fra Angelico's fresco, from left to right, we see the sponge and lance that pierced his side, the kiss of Judas, the denial of Peter, the mocking of Christ, the 30 pieces of silver with which Judas betrayed Christ, and the column of the flagellation. We also see the cross of the Crucifixion, and the tomb. These vignettes and aides-memoires are not arranged in any obvious order. They have a visual symmetry, but not a chronology or narrative sequence. Rather than narrating an ordered story, the various symbols and disembodied figures prompt the memory to recall particular moments from the Passion, allowing the incumbent of the cell to meditate on each independently, drawing connections between them or imagining scenes and events not realized in paint. No text 'explains' this image; rather, the beholder must remember various texts and patch them together like a quilt. It is not a narrative scene, but an iconic one, even if it calls on the viewer to imagine stories.

The image in cell 27 is a non-narrative scene in another sense, too. The Virgin and Thomas are not here as protagonists, unlike the Virgin and St John in Lorenzo Monaco's depiction of the *arma Christi* (FIG. 120). Instead, they exemplify how the friar was to look at the fresco. Again and again, in meditative texts of the late Middle Ages and Renaissance, readers were told to imagine the Passion through the suffering of the Virgin. In cell 27, however, she does not wail with despair, but is rather contemplative. She presents a model of internal contemplation. By contrast, Thomas – the great scholastic theologian – suggests another form of internalized vision. He might stare with the fixed gaze of the corporeal eye, but he appears not to see externally. Certainly, he is not beholding the scene behind him. His vision is intellectual, a fully internalized understanding of God.

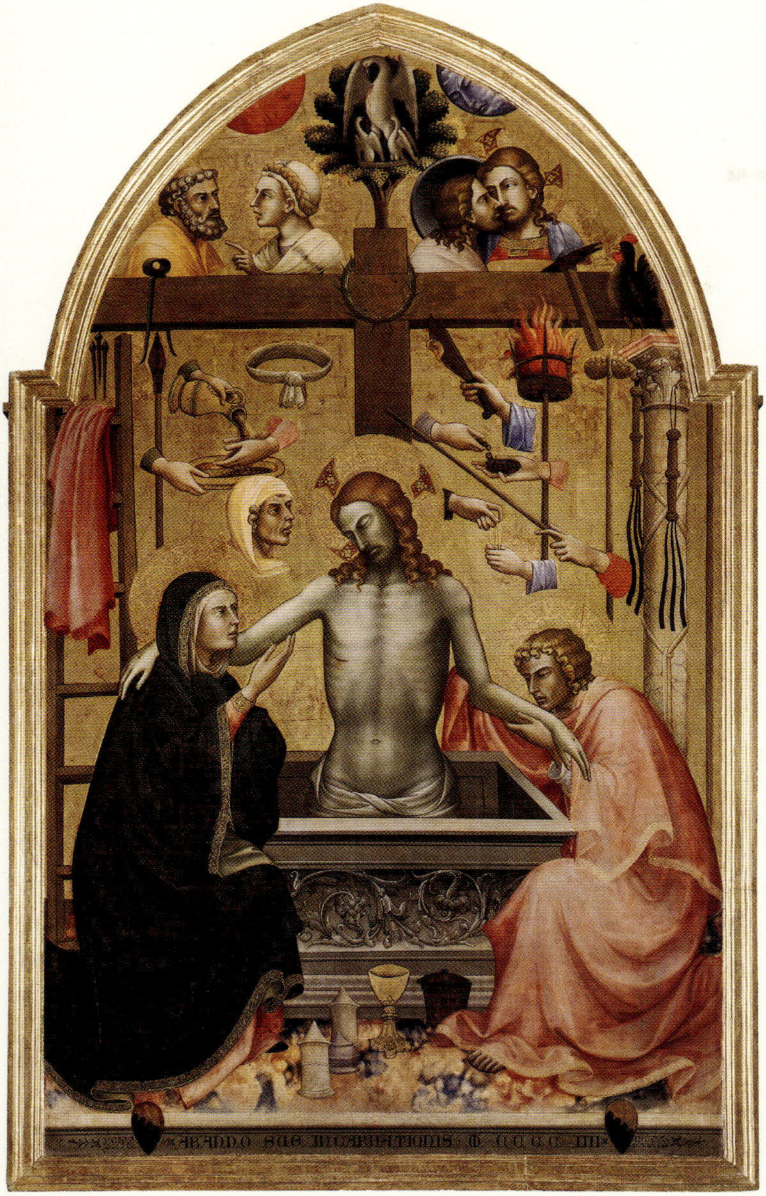

Fig. 120
Lorenzo Monaco
Homo Pietatis with the Arma Christi

1404, tempera on panel, 265 × 172 cm (104⅛ × 67¾ in). Galleria dell'Accademia, Florence.

The image in cell 27 calls upon its beholder to interpret it by following the example of the figures depicted within it. The friar was to pray before it and meditate on its meaning. A high degree of scriptural and theological knowledge was assumed on his part, and he was trusted to have a fully developed imagination. Fra Angelico's skill resided in his ability to design an image that stimulated the corporeal eye, while also catering to the needs of the spiritual and intellectual eyes.

The Discursive Image

The challenges facing artists of secular imagery, especially of mythological subjects, were of a different order, and so were the demands those images played on the spectator. The appearance of paintings and sculpture that showed scenes from ancient mythology or history is one of the crowning achievements of the Renaissance, and although important contributions were made elsewhere – especially in the courts of Ferrara and Mantua or in the Republic of Venice – Florence played a central role in the development of a secular art. While artists of sacred images tried to square new styles and formats with a traditional understanding of the role such art was supposed to perform, artists of mythological paintings, such as Botticelli and Filippino Lippi, had to contend with an entirely new genre altogether. Their secular art was designed for a wholly different context from

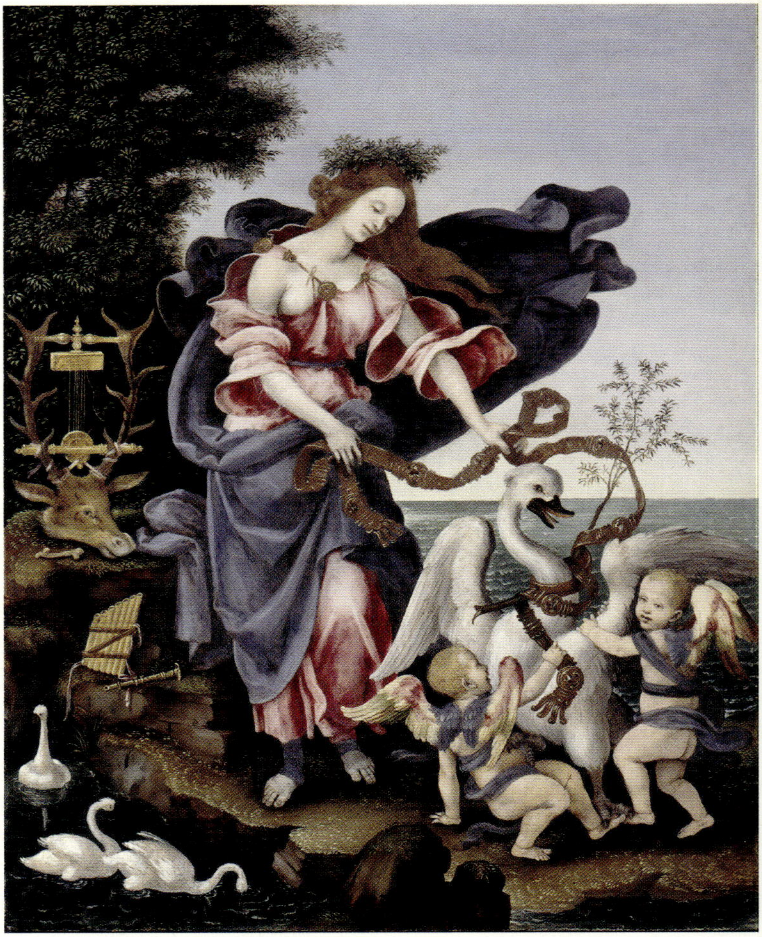

Fig. 121
Filippino Lippi
Erato

ca. 1500, oil on oak panel, 62.5 × 51.8 cm (24⅝ × 20½ in). Gemäldegalerie, Staatliche Museen zu Berlin.

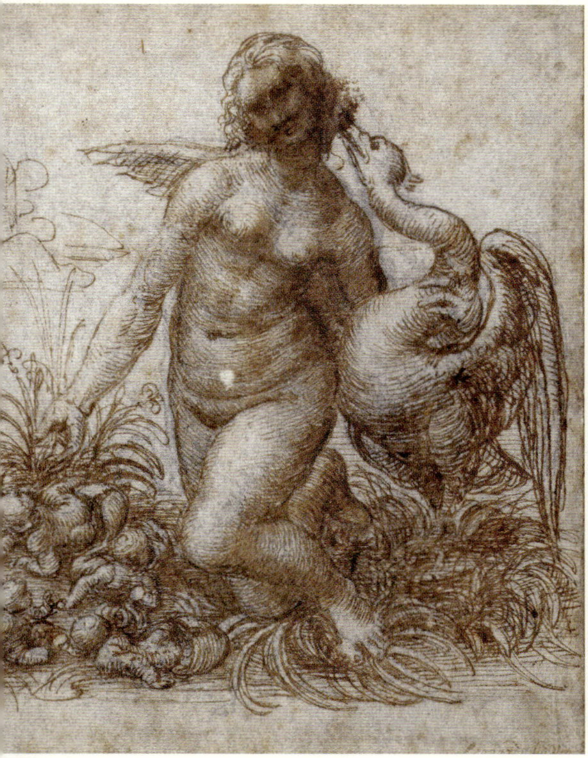

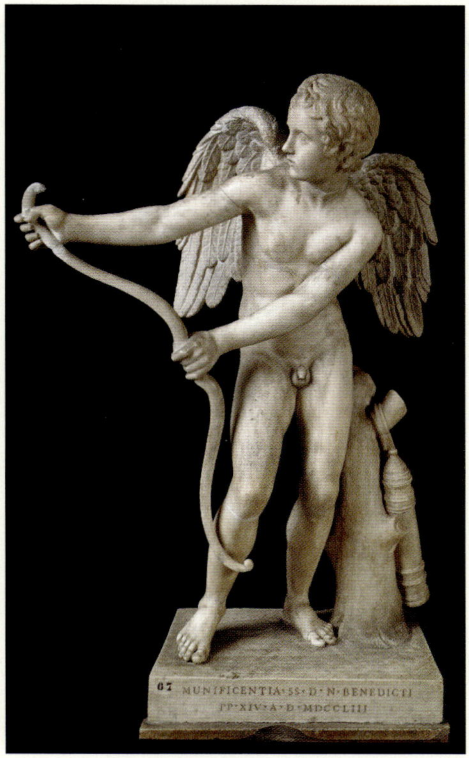

their sacred images. It was destined for the home, where it relied heavily on the stimulation of the embodied eye for its effect. These paintings offered an alternative paradigm for what art should be and how it should be beheld.

Filippino Lippi's *Erato* was intended for domestic display and was probably commissioned for a Florentine palace, although, with the passage of time, we no longer know which one (FIG. 121). Not only did it occupy a different space from Fra Angelico's *Homo Pietatis*, but also the *Erato* was viewed in fundamentally different ways from it. It gave rise to meaning by a different process. The painting shows one of the nine ancient muses, Erato, who binds a swan with a golden belt, together with two putti. Beside her are musical instruments: the kithara, pan pipes and a flute. Erato inspired lyric poetry and was often associated with love; her name has the same root as Eros. The action of tying up a swan, a bird that is a traditional symbol of Venus, would seem to refer to the virtue of chastity, or at least to the proper limitation of love within marriage. It is no surprise, then, that Lippi's painting belongs to a category of objects probably commissioned around the time of a wedding.

Fig. 122 (left)
Leonardo da Vinci
Leda and the Swan

ca. 1503, pen and ink with wash over black chalk on paper, 16 × 13.7cm (6 3/8 × 5 3/8 in). Collection of the Duke of Devonshire, Chatsworth House, Derbyshire.

Fig. 123 (right)
Eros Stringing his Bow

Roman copy after Greek original of the 4th century BCE, marble, 123cm (48 3/8 in) high. Capitoline Museums, Rome.

This sculpture is first documented in 1572 at the Villa d'Este, Tivoli.

The identification of the subject of the painting as Erato required a considerable degree of classical learning on the part of the viewer. Unlike an image of the Virgin or a scene from the Passion, this figure would not – we presume – have been instantly recognizable to most Florentines. Indeed, we recognize this representation today as Erato only because of its close similarity to a description published in Vicenza of the wedding celebration of Costanzo Sforza and Camilla d'Aragona in May 1475. The festivities occurred at some distance from Florence, in Pesaro. This source was not necessarily Lippi's, nor his patron's, but rather the means by which we now identify the iconography. It seems unlikely that visitors to a patrician home in the early sixteenth century stood before this painting with text in hand. How, then, did they know what they were looking at? The image was a new invention and did not repeat a familiar formula that the artist might reasonably expect his audience to know. The subject matter of similar *all'antica* paintings was sometimes confused: when Botticelli's painting of a centaur and an armoured woman was inventoried in 1498/9, the scribe thought the woman was Camilla and the hybrid mythological beast a satyr (FIG. 112). In

Fig. 124
Sarcophagus of the Muses (detail)

180–200 CE, marble, entire frieze 67 × 224cm (26⅜ × 88⅛in). Kunsthistorisches Museum, Vienna.

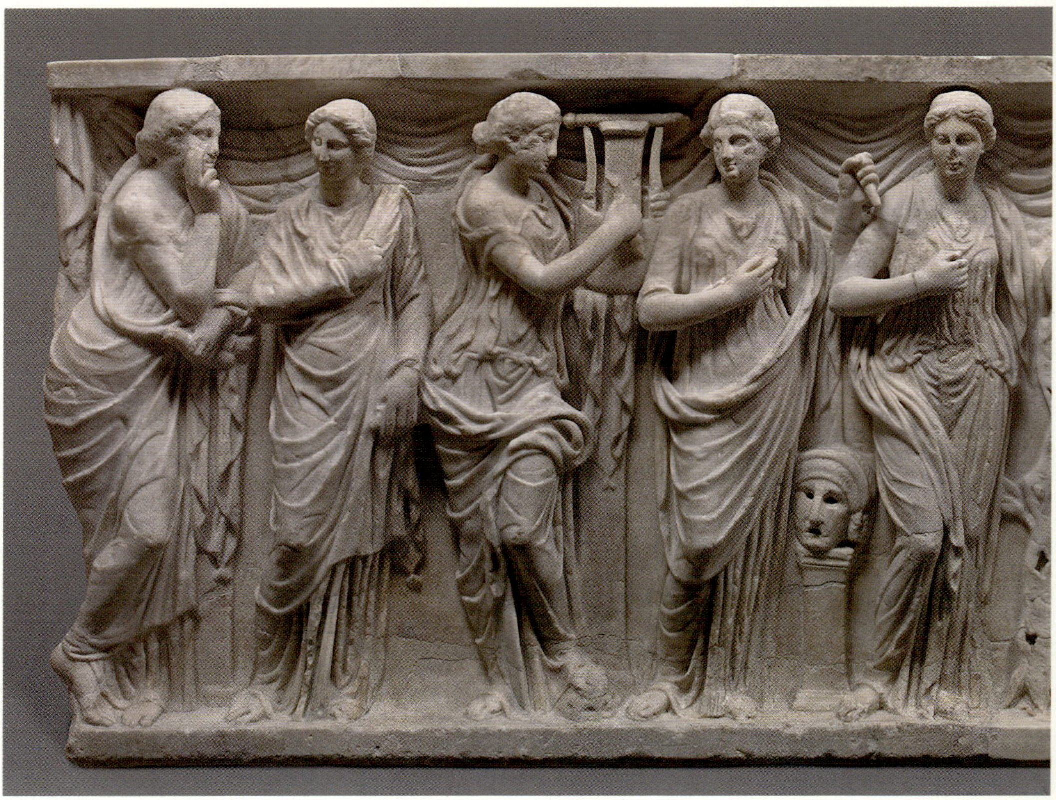

1516, when it was inventoried again, the female figure was recognized as Minerva (or Pallas in Greek mythology) and the creature correctly identified as a centaur.

In all likelihood, the first spectators of Lippi's *Erato* discussed the image with their host, who had probably commissioned it, and speculated on its meaning in a discursive manner. They might have discussed, as did the author of the text mentioned above, the 'pure Venus' and how she was distinguished from her lascivious counterpart ('*Venere sancta, et non quella lasciva*'), or they could have mused on why the swan might symbolize 'chastity and restraint' ('*cingulo de castità et continentia*'). They could even have observed similarities to other mythologies that involve swans, especially that of Leda, whom Leonardo was drawing at about the same time (FIG. 122).

The similarity of Lippi's invention to Leonardo's sketch prompts a question of whether paintings of this sort gave rise to meaning visually. Both works were meant to delight the eyes, for which Lippi's subject could not have been more appropriate, since the anonymous author of the ancient Orphic Hymn *To the Muses* wrote of Erato that she 'charms the sight'. Lippi's painting gave pleasure visually, but it also offered up significance through visual means. Perceptive viewers could appreciate visual concordances between the *Erato* and other works of art. Art historians have long approached artworks by asking what visual sources an artist had in mind when working out his composition. These same sources might well also have been known to their educated, humanist viewers, whose visual knowledge of antique artworks was put to the test before them. Lippi probably appropriated Erato's arms from an imperial Roman sculpture *Eros Stringing his Bow* (FIG. 123), while her legs derive from a figure on a second-century *Sarcophagus of the Muses* that was around Santa Maria Maggiore in Rome by the sixteenth century (FIG. 124). We know that Lippi saw it in the late fifteenth century, because he studied it in a drawing that has survived (FIG. 125). In both cases, form and subject come together: the first is a thematic relationship between Eros and a painting concerned with love; the second is more direct, because Lippi has based his figure of Erato

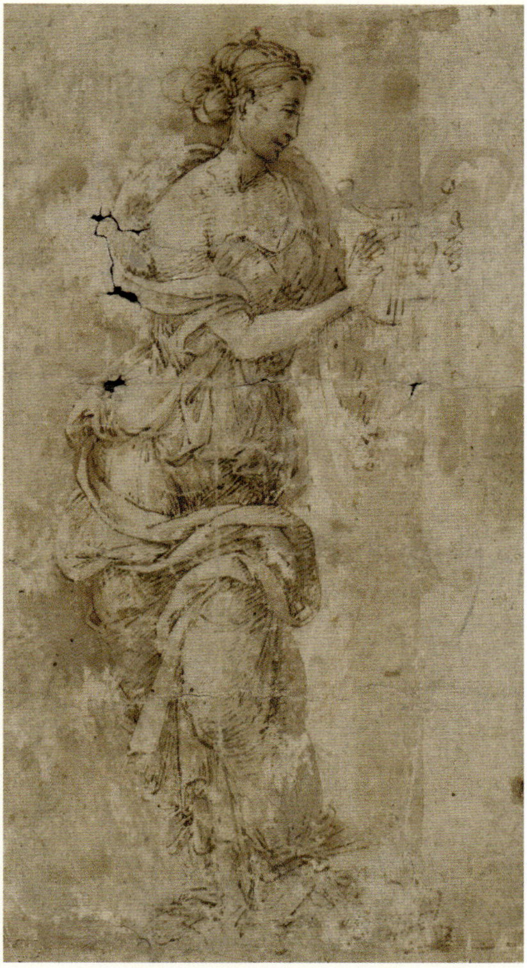

Fig. 125
Filippino Lippi, after the antique
Erato

Late 15th century, pen and ink on paper, 16.5 × 9cm ($6\frac{1}{2} \times 3\frac{1}{2}$in). The British Museum, London.

on an ancient figure of the same muse. Surely these significant visual rhymes would have been a source of pleasure to visually literate spectators, for whom they would have provided the same material for discussion as ancient texts.

The meaning of Lippi's *Erato* was neither fixed nor predetermined. Scholars, who place their faith in the study of iconography, are sometimes frustrated by images of this type because they cannot be explained by a single text. I am not suggesting that such fluid works of art were not mediated by texts or other images – quite the opposite, in fact – just that they are not, and were not, *explained* by a text. The painting depended on the viewer, perhaps in the company of several friends and learned acquaintances, to provide it with meaning from a series of prompts. It was discursive and open-ended. As a means of engaging with an image, the discursive mode was quite different from the meditative one described above for the contemplation of sacred art. It was also new and would have profound implications for Western art.

It is impossible to conclude a section on discursive works of art without mentioning Botticelli's *Primavera* (FIG. 126), a painting that by the end of the fifteenth century was above a *lettuccio* (day-bed) in the home of Lorenzo the Magnificent's cousins, Lorenzo and Giovanni di Pierfrancesco de' Medici. Its subject matter has eluded explanation, as least to those who seek a single text by which to explain what is going on. None has ever been found. It is better understood as a visual poem, pieced together from many texts – ancient and modern, Latin and vernacular – and a variety of visual sources, likewise old and new. To recognize the protagonists on the right-hand side, for instance, the viewer must know Lucretius's great poem *De rerum natura*: 'Spring comes, and Venus, and Venus's winged herald marching before, with Zephyr and mother Flora a pace behind, strewing the path in front with beautiful colours and filling it with scents.' On the right, Zephyr as god of the west wind sweeps down and clutches Chloris, a nymph who was transformed into Flora after her rape by Zephyr. Flora appears one step before Chloris, distributing flowers from her appliqué dress, which is bunched up at the hip. Chloris, however, was not mentioned by Lucretius. To interpret the visual passage between Zephyr and Flora, the viewer must instead be reminded of Ovid's *Fasti*, a poetical calendar of the Roman year, in which Flora explains how she came to be a goddess. Botticelli even translated Ovid's beautiful observation that Chloris's mouth 'breathed the roses of spring'. By a similar process, the left-hand side of the painting recalls one of Horace's odes, combined with a passage in Seneca's *De beneficiis* in which he spoke of the Graces in

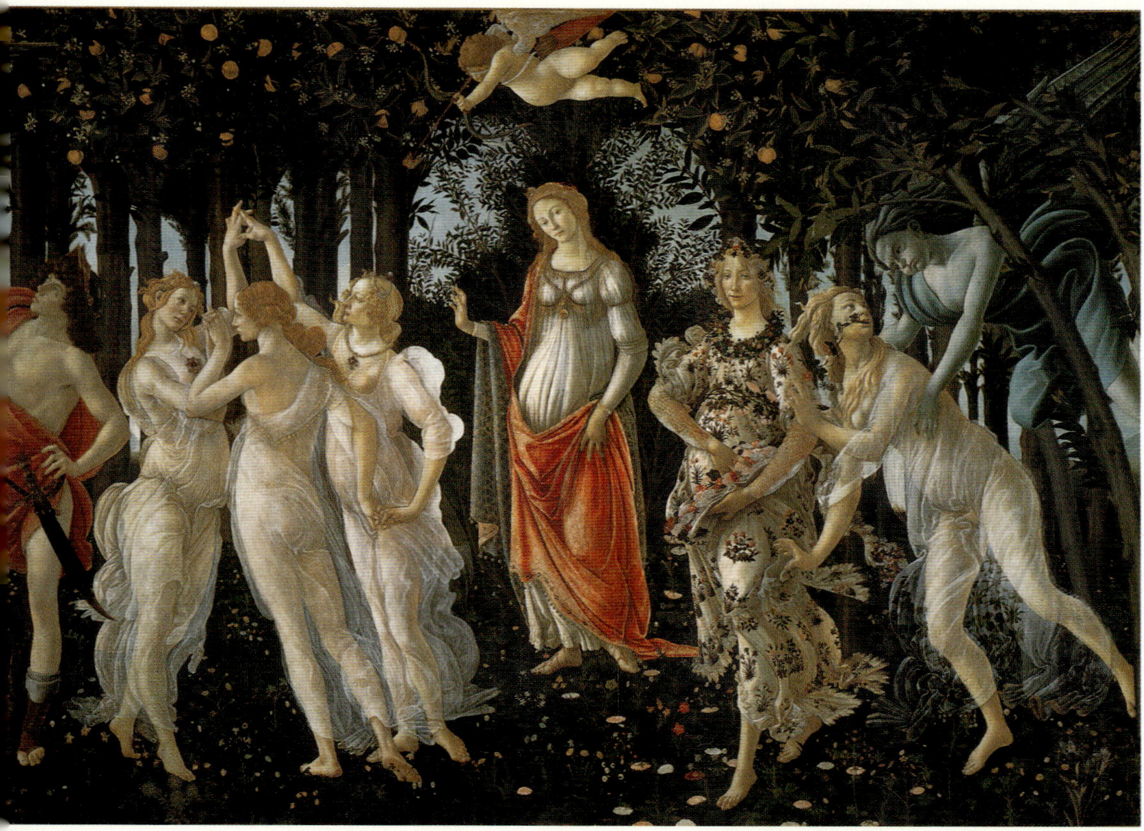

their flowing robes, and mentioned them in conjunction with Mercury. The well-read spectator might equally have learned of the three Graces from their mention by Alberti, or from their frequent appearance in ancient art.

The fact is that the *Primavera* is over-determined by textual and visual sources, yet none explain it. To realize it as a poem on the subject of Spring, viewers were required to invent the poem from the prompts before them, much like the artist, who had assembled it from similar sources, some perhaps known to him, others relayed to him by learned advisors. Its meaning was not fixed, but would be created – invented, even – but those beholding it in an endless unfolding of signification. In that it put the onus on the viewer to engender meaning, the *Primavera* shared something with Fra Angelico's *Homo Pietatis*, but the similarities stop there. Their modes of spectatorship were fundamentally different: one discursive, the other meditative. Between them they encompass the extremes of what it meant to behold images in Renaissance Florence.

Fig. 126
Sandro Botticelli
Primavera

Late 1470s, tempera on panel, 203 × 314 cm (80 × 123⅝ in). Galleria degli Uffizi, Florence.

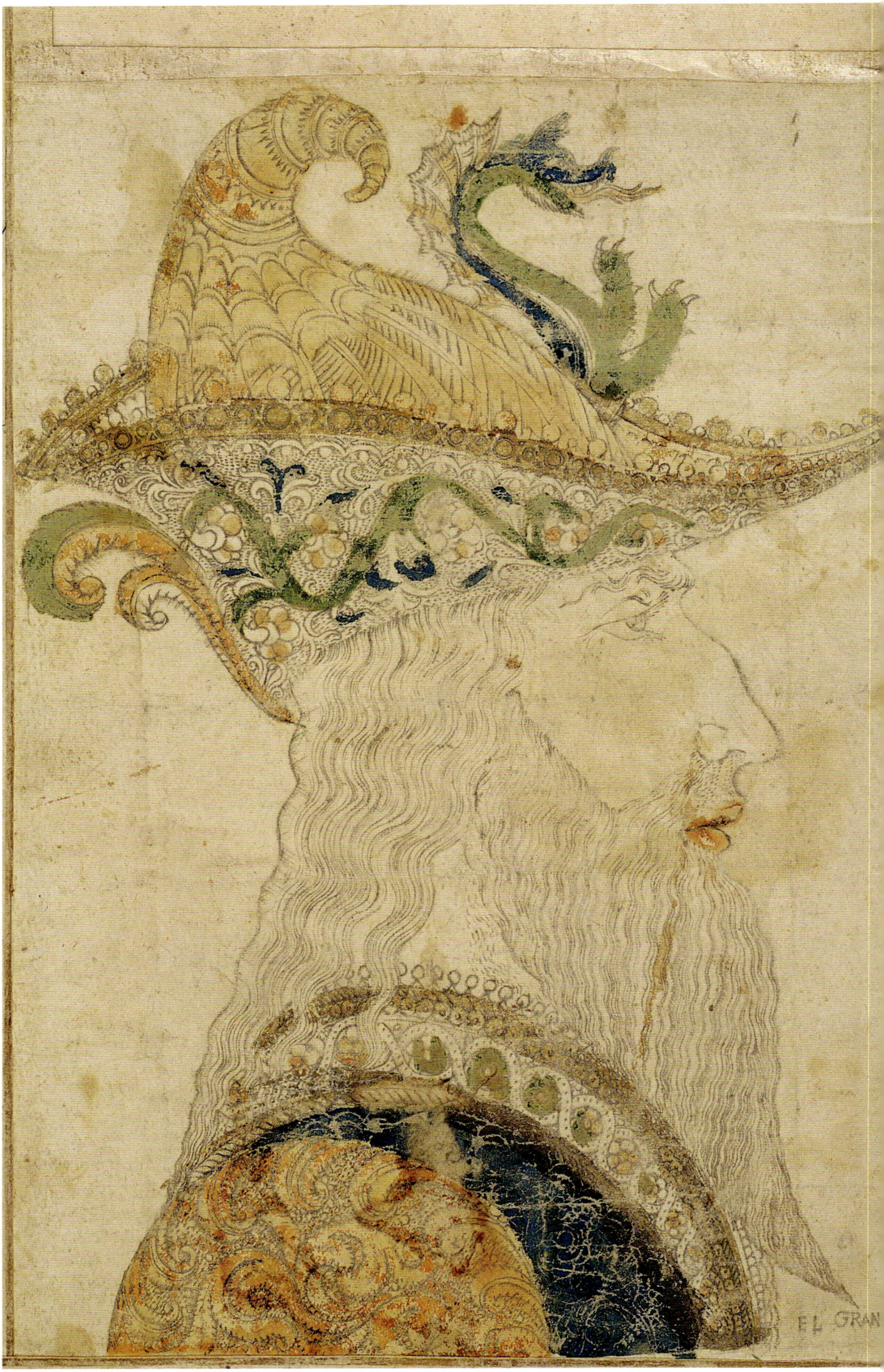
EL GRAN

10

Medium and Material

The spectators of Florentine works of art came to objects with certain expectations, not only about their proper function or their subject matter, but also about their medium and materials. This chapter is about innovation in medium, and an awareness of material that gave significance to works of art. Some media were traditional and had long been employed by Florentine craftsmen, while others, such as prints, were newly invented, facilitated by technological change. They brought with them new associations, new audiences and new subject matter. Central to our discussion will be a distinction between what we understand by the words 'medium' and 'material'. The former will be examined in relation to prints, especially copperplate engravings, and the latter through the example of the Cardinal of Portugal's chapel.

Fig. 127
'El Gran Turco'

ca. 1460–85, engraving with watercolour on paper, 24.9 × 18.7cm (9⅞ × 7⅜in). Topkapi Palace Library, Istanbul.

The printmaker imagined Mehmed's features through those of the Byzantine emperor, John VIII Palaiologos, whose likeness was well known in the Italian peninsula through medals, unlike that of Mehmed.

Engravings

The appearance of printing, whether of text or image, during the period was nothing short of revolutionary. The point is often made and cannot be emphasized enough. Not until the invention of television in the twentieth century, and the internet thereafter, would there again be such a transformation in our ability to communicate images and ideas to one another. Printing was not a Florentine invention. It was not even a European one. Moveable type was known in China and Korea long before Johannes Gutenberg, a goldsmith from Mainz, introduced a similar system that would transform the production of books in Europe. The first book to be printed in Florence, Servius's commentary on Virgil, was undertaken by Bernardo Cennini in 1471, only six years after the earliest press appeared in the Italian peninsula. The technology came from Northern Europe, and it is therefore little surprise to find that the Florentine printer Niccolò di Lorenzo (Niccolò della Magna) was originally from Breslau. Some booksellers, too, were from north of the Alps, such as Albertus Liebkinkt, who set up shop in Florence in the 1460s selling books imported from Strasbourg. By the end of the century there were about 18 presses in the city, including that of the Giunti family. The production of printed books and that of printed images were closely aligned.

The printing of images, especially on fabric, was also practised in Asia long before it was in the West. In Florence, once again, the production of single-leaf prints followed earlier developments in the areas of present-day Germany and the Netherlands, where the earliest dated engraving was produced in 1446. Despite the importance of printmaking, much of our knowledge of the invention and first development of prints is murky, especially in Italy. Many of the first, anonymous Italian engravings exist in only one or two impressions, and it is not clear whether they were only ever made in short print runs, or have simply been lost to the ravages of time. If they were made in such small numbers, what would that mean for our understanding of their function and status? Could they have been produced for a small circle of people? Some prints were commissioned, such as those that illustrate Landino's *Commentary on [Dante's] Comedy* printed in 1481, but others were surely produced speculatively, a rare occurrence in the fifteenth century, when most works of art were ordered bespoke. We have long been used to thinking of prints as a mass medium for popular consumption, but these assumptions should not be projected backwards on to the fifteenth century, when printmakers were still coming to realize their potential.

Among the earliest Florentine engravings to survive is a group in an album at Topkapi Palace Library in Istanbul. Many of them are unique impressions. The album includes a hand-coloured engraving of '*El Gran Turco*' (FIG. 127), a portrait of Sultan Mehmed

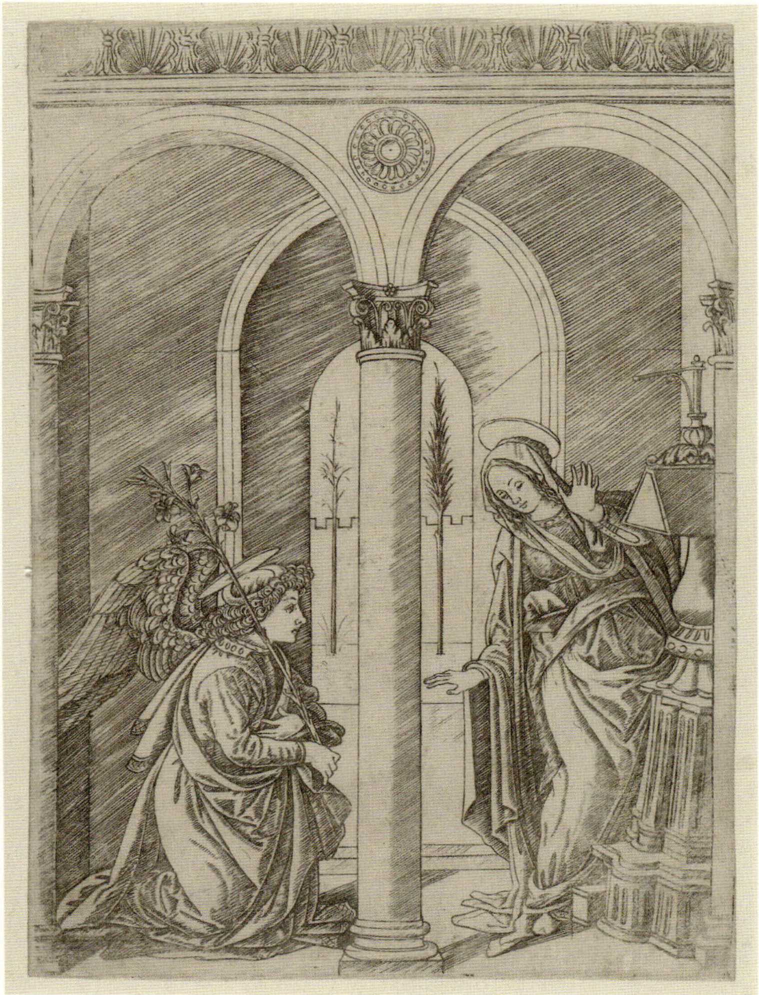

Fig. 128
Attributed to Francesco Rosselli
The Annunciation

ca. 1490–1500, engraving on paper, 22.5 × 16.4cm (8⅞ × 6½in). The British Museum, London.

This engraving, which is one of a series, is characteristic of the broad manner.

II (1431–1481), the leader of the Ottoman Turks who had conquered the Byzantine Empire in 1453. It is one of only two known impressions, of which the other is in Berlin. The Italian engravings in Istanbul are accompanied by other images of Chinese, Persian and Turkish origin that probably belonged to Mehmet's political rival, the Aq Qoyunlu Yaqub Beg, but circumstantial evidence suggests that this small collection of prints was once in the possession of Mehmet himself. They might even have been presented to him by a Florentine visitor to the Ottoman court, from which the Florentines were trying to negotiate trading concessions. If prints were really the popular, cheap mass medium that they would later become, it is hard to know how to explain these one-off images in the collection of such an illustrious individual.

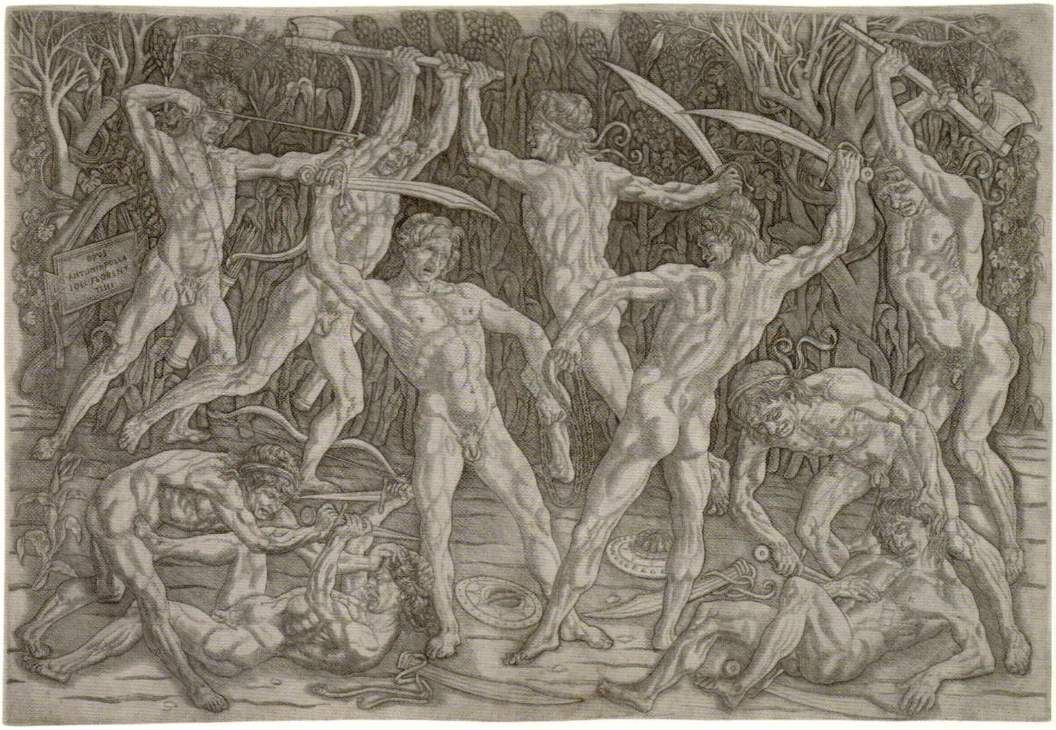

Fig. 129
Antonio del Pollaiuolo
Battle of Nude Men

Probably late 1470s, engraving, first state, 42.4 × 60.9cm (16¾ × 24in). Cleveland Museum of Art, Cleveland. Purchase from the J. H. Wade Fund (1967.127).

Around 40 impressions of this engraving survive, an extremely high number for any fifteenth-century engraving, although only a single first state is known.

Accompanying these questions about audience is the matter of function, and the role played by engravings in Florence before the sixteenth century. Some prints were obviously devotional, such as a series relating to the mysteries of the rosary, thought to be by Francesco Rosselli (ca. 1448–ca. 1513; FIG. 128). Rosselli's engravings showing the *Life of the Virgin* were, in one case, pasted on to a plank of wood to serve as a predella to an altarpiece, an extremely rare object that was sadly lost in Berlin during World War II. Prints were often pasted into books, demonstrating the close relationship between single-leaf prints and the culture of printed books. Artists, including Antonio del Pollaiuolo (and Andrea Mantegna outside Florence), quickly realized that prints were an effective means of spreading their inventions, and thus of establishing their fame. Whether they intended their prints to act as pattern books is less certain, even if other artists might have used them as such (FIG. 129).

While questions of audience and function must remain open, we are on safer ground when it comes to technique. Despite the importance of northern prints for the development of printmaking in Italy, intaglio engraving in Florence developed in close conjunction with gold- and *niello* work (*niello* is the name for a category of engraved silver object in which the incised lines were filled with a black alloy of silver, lead and sulphur to help them contrast against the background; FIG. 130). The Vatican Librarian, Giovanni Tortelli, listed *niello* as a new technological invention in his philological work *De orthographia* (1449), incorrectly deducing that it had been unknown in antiquity. The tools and techniques of the goldsmith were the same as those of the print engraver. A sense of the ease with which a goldsmith might move between these materials because of a single, shared technique is provided by Manetti when he describes the young Brunelleschi:

> Because of his foundation in drawing he quickly became very proficient in that profession in which he soon displayed himself most wonderfully. Within a brief period he became a complete master in *niello*, enamel, and ornamental architectural reliefs, as well as in cutting, mounting, and polishing all kinds of precious stones.

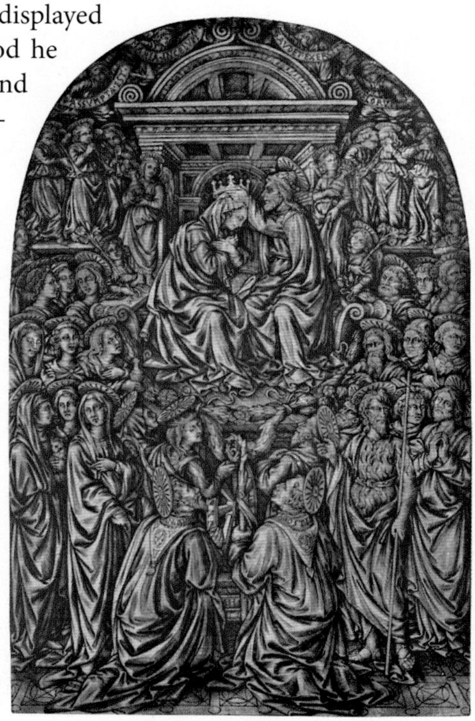

Fig. 130
Maso Finiguerra
Pax

1452, silver and *niello*, approx. 13 × 8.5cm (5⅛ × 3⅛in). Museo Nazionale del Bargello, Florence.

More than once in this book, we have noticed how many Florentine artists received their initial training as goldsmiths, a fact that goes some way to explaining not only the linear bias of much Florentine art, but also the fact that more engravings survive from Florence in the period before 1500 than from any other Italian centre.

The initial steps towards the production of engravings were probably taken in the 1450s by goldsmiths, among them Maso Finiguerra (1426–1464). In the introduction to his *Life of Marcantonio*, Vasari maintained that Finiguerra was the first to practise copperplate engraving, a claim that is now routinely dismissed. However, it is likely that Finiguerra did invent a technique for pulling sulphur casts from his engraved silver plaques before they were filled with *niello*, from which he pressed prints (as Vasari also suggested). Finiguerra might not have invented copperplate engraving, but he did begin the shift from one medium to another, a shift that was made possible by a common technique.

The earliest Florentine engravings are divided roughly between those in which the modelling is built up using fine, cross-hatched lines (*see* FIG. 131) and those in which it is composed of broader parallel lines, linked by a return stroke (*see* FIG. 128). Since the nineteenth century they have been called the ‘fine’ and the ‘broad’

Fig. 131
Mercury

ca. 1460–85, engraving on paper, 32.4 × 21.8cm (12¾ × 8½in). The British Museum, London.

This engraving is typical of the fine manner.

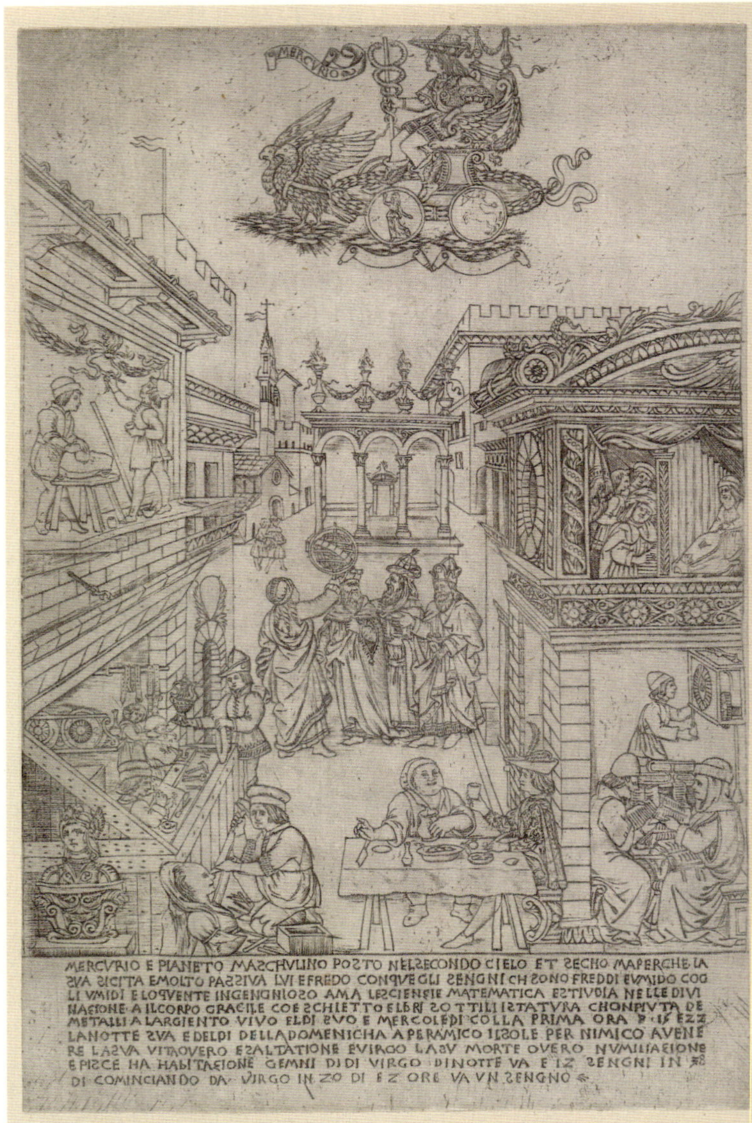

manners respectively, the former characteristic of the foremost prints executed in the third quarter of the fifteenth century, and the latter having developed subsequently. The names matter less than the fact that these two styles derive from a difference in tools. Fine manner prints were probably made using the *ciappola*, a tool with a round or flat blade, unlike the burin, which is lozenge-shaped in section and produces broader lines.

Scholars have attempted to discover the makers responsible for these different manners, but continue to be frustrated. From the

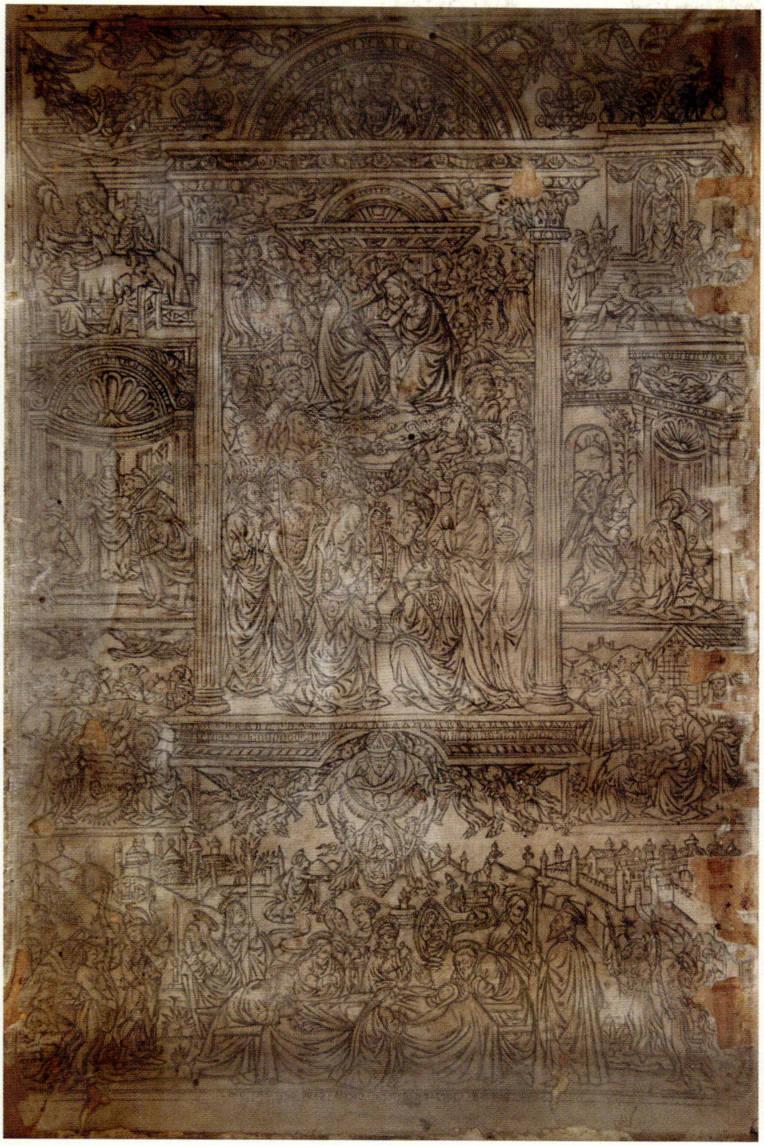

Fig. 132
Piero Baldini
Coronation of the Virgin and Scenes from her Life (Žatec Virgin Vita)

ca. 1460–80, engraving on paper, 30.5 × 20.5cm (12 × 8in). Inside the cover of Meffreth von Meissen, *Hortulus Reginae de Tempore*, with the engraved name of Pietro di Doffo Baldini. Regional Museum, K.A. Polánka, Žatec, Czech Republic (MS HK 902).

The importance of this print derives from its inscription across the bottom: 'MAESTRO PIERO DIDOFO DIDOFFO DIBALDINO BALDINI'. It and Antonio del Pollaiuolo's *Battle of Nude Men* (see Fig. 129) are the only 'signed' engravings from fifteenth-century Florence. Note the similarity of the composition to that of Fig. 130.

study of style, the use of certain letter forms and the recurrence of motifs, it is now fairly certain that there were at least two workshops in Florence (with any number of individuals working in them) that produced prints in the fine manner; one of those was responsible for the *Planet Series* (FIG. 131) and the other for the *Passion Series*, now in Vienna. The names of the engravers are not known, even if the maker of the *Planet Series* is often called Baccio Baldini. In spite of all scholarly activity to the contrary, Baldini has not emerged from the archive and we cannot be certain that he ever existed. Vasari called him a pupil of Finiguerra and a collaborator with Botticelli. Vasari also thought that Baldini had trained as a goldsmith, even though his name does not appear in the matriculation rolls of the Silk Guild, to which the goldsmiths belonged. A 'maestro Piero di Doffo Baldini' (ca. 1437–before 1480) engraved his name on a print that is now in the Czech Republic (FIG. 132), and it is possible that Vasari confused Piero Baldini for Baccio. Until more substantial evidence emerges, however, it is probably best to abandon Baccio Baldini as the author of early prints.

The next generation of copperplate engravers in Florence, those working in the later 1480s and 1490s in the broad manner, are better known, at least by name: Francesco Rosselli, brother of the painter Cosimo Rosselli; Cristofano Robetta (1462–ca. 1535); and Lucantonio degli Uberti. Antonio del Pollaiuolo produced his famous and extremely ambitious *Battle of Nude Men*, probably in the 1470s, the only securely attributed Florentine print of the century (*see* FIG. 129). Not unusually, these engravers also found work as illuminators or stationers, entered into partnership with book printers and undertook commissions as goldsmiths.

Perhaps because of the commonality of technique across media, or the similarity of aesthetic, early Florentine prints are often associated with either goldsmiths' work and *nielli*, or with drawings. Thus the blurriness, derived from the burr on the copperplate, that occurs in areas of cross-hatching in fine manner engravings looks very similar to the areas of dense hatching in *niello* engraving, where the engraver has sought particularly deep shadows (compare FIGS. 130, 132, for example). The same blurriness can also be compared to the wash on a pen-and-ink drawing. Our desire to relate prints to other media, while surely justifiable on the practical level of technique, has had the effect of diluting what must have been the initial impact of a new technology. We lose sight of a new medium searching for its purpose and utility. Their newness offered their viewers a novel way of visualizing the world around them, and they created fresh expectations of what subjects could be depicted. The sudden appearance of prints before the eyes of Florentines must, quite literally, have generated a new way of seeing: a new visuality.

Let me illustrate this point by examining a single example. Preserved in the Graphische Sammlung in Munich is the only known impression of the print *Fight for the Hose* (FIG. 133). Its maker is unknown, but it is certainly of Florentine origin because it contains several motifs that appear in other Florentine prints, such as the falcon descending to catch an ermine on the mantle of the woman on the right, and heraldic motifs that relate to Florentine families (the full-blown

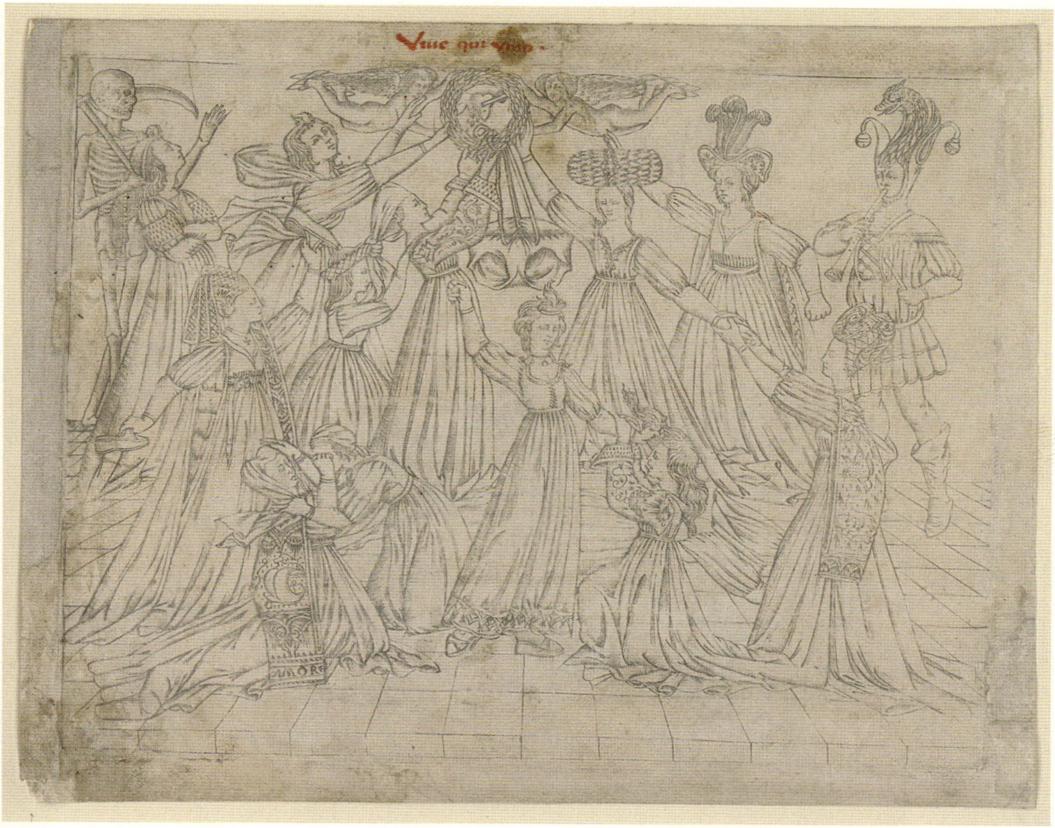

sail was a Rucellai device; the three feathers was employed by both the Rucellai and the Medici). The print is annotated above the wreath '*Vive qui vinci[s]*' (live who conquers) in the hand of the Nuremberg humanist, physician and early collector of prints Hartmann Schedel (1440–1514), who presumably acquired it in Italy, when studying at the university of Padua, and pasted it into one of his manuscripts.

Fig. 133
Fight for the Hose

ca. 1460–85, engraving on paper, 20.1 × 26.2 cm (8 × 10 3/8 in). Graphische Sammlung, Munich.

The engraving shows 12 women locked in combat for a pair of underclothes, suspended from a wreath and encircled by an arrow-pierced heart. The motif of fighting for hose is related to proverbial marital conflicts between husbands and wives, epitomized in the expression 'to wear the trousers'. The theme of love, suggested by the garlanded heart, is reinforced by the word 'AMORE' woven into a cloak worn by a woman at the bottom left. Above her, a skeleton enters carrying a scythe, presumably symbolizing Death, who is balanced (both compositionally and thematically) on the right by a jester playing a wind instrument. Despite the carefully delineated pavement that recedes according to the laws of perspective, the proportions of the figures are such that they belie these conventions: the women in the background are conspicuously larger than the combatants in the foreground.

The iconography was not Florentine, but of Northern European origin, where it is known from misericords in the cathedrals at Rouen and Villefranche-de-Rouergue. It also appears in literature. The thirteenth-century fable by Hués Piaucele, *De sire Hain et de dame Anieuse*, pitches a husband and wife against each other in a bloody conflict for his breeches and thus for dominance in the house. The subject matter was presumably adapted by a Florentine engraver from a German print, attributed to the Master of the Banderoles (FIG. 134). The Florentine print departs from its prototype in the introduction of the wreath, heart and putti, and more surprisingly in the substitution of Death for a costumed male figure. The print also deviates from the northern prototype in the representation of the flooring. The Master of the Banderoles represented horizontal floorboards with nailing that recedes unconvincingly. The Italian artist, however, has contrived to produce a convincing perspectival pavement. The deviation from its model suggests conscious intent, even though the apparent problem of scale in the size of the figures

Fig. 134
Master of the Banderoles
Fight for the Hose

ca. 1464, engraving on paper, 25.7 × 19.5cm (10 × 7¾in). Kupferstichkabinett, Staatliches Museen zu Berlin.

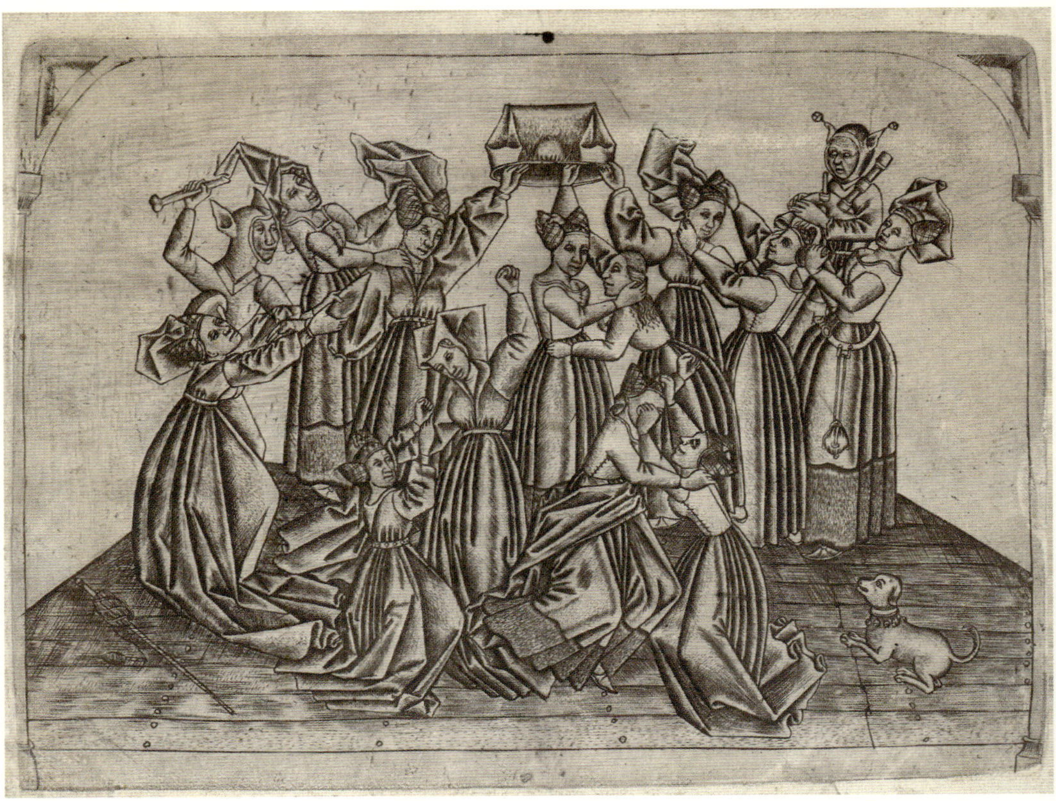

undermines it. Such disjunctions signal a world turned upside down, in which women take on roles traditionally associated with men, inverting fifteenth-century conceptions of social order. The idea is reinforced by the women's headdresses, some of which parody jousting equipment.

Not only was this subject matter unknown in Florentine art, but also its bawdiness was alien to painting and sculpture. In prints, Florentines found a medium for the expression and appreciation of the 'lower' forms of human existence. They even poked fun at it. In the previous chapter, we saw how the appearance of secular subject matter, inspired by the history and mythology of the ancient world, was accompanied by a new, discursive mode of viewing. These developments accompanied a shift in expectation about what could be represented in painting and sculpture. While their media were traditional – panel painting, for instance – their subject matter was not. Similarly, the invention of a completely new medium, such as copperplate engraving, prompted a change in the perception of what could be represented. Florentines had no preconceived expectation of what prints should show. It comes as no surprise, then, that some of the first Florentine prints embrace subject matter not found in any other medium.

Materials

Did the materials of the new medium play any part in their meaning? The materials themselves (paper and ink for the image, and copper for the matrix) were traditional, and, although the press itself was new, the technique for engraving the plate had been practised for centuries by goldsmiths. Paper must have carried certain connotations – an engraving would presumably have been judged differently according to whether it was printed on parchment or linen – but the real impact of printmaking came from the new medium.

Materials could also have meaning, however. They have their own history, which is closely aligned to the techniques and technology used to manipulate them out of the natural state and into works of art. The history of the way these materials have been employed does not always align with our histories of style or representation. Botticelli's *Primavera* (*see* FIG. 126) was highly innovative in its style, its subject matter and the mode of viewing that it presupposes, yet its materials – egg tempera on a poplar support – could not have been more traditional. Indeed, Botticelli remained essentially a tempera painter long after oil painting was known and commonly practised

Fig. 135
The Cardinal of Portugal's chapel, showing the tomb wall

San Miniato al Monte, Florence.

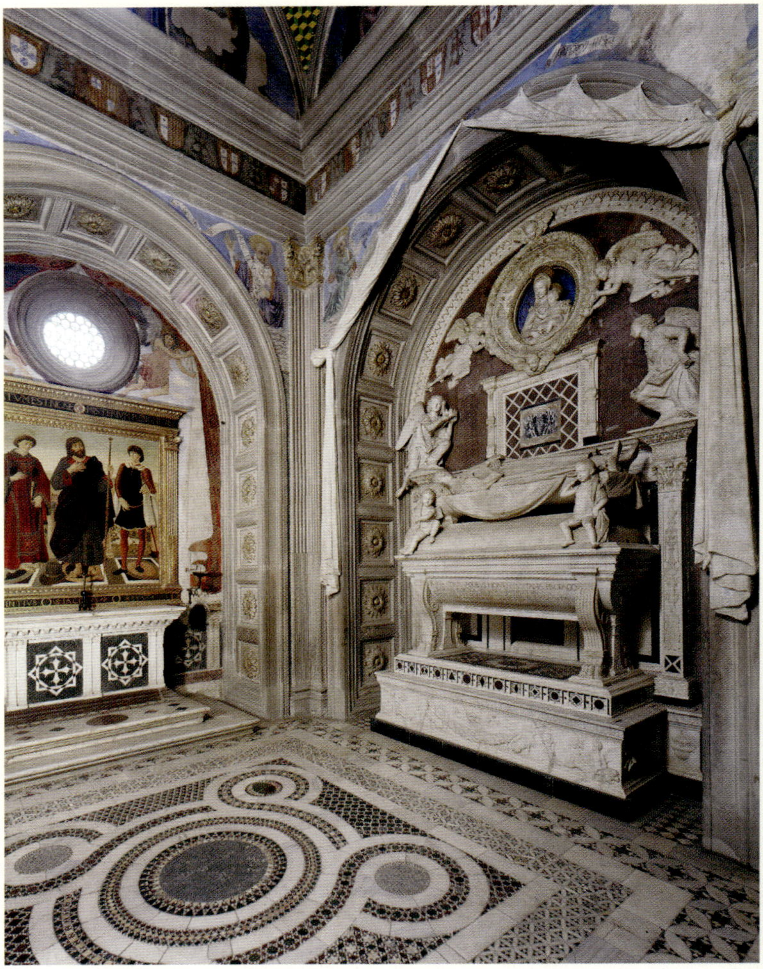

in Florence. The idea of Florence as a centre of innovation is sometimes called into question, then, when we approach the materials used in the traditional media of panel and fresco painting, or marble and wood sculpting. However, to question Florentines' originality in their use of materials is not to deny their acute awareness of materials. Not unusually, they exploited materials for their capacity to convey certain ideas. The non-figurative tombs of the Medici in San Lorenzo are one such case, where meaning is entirely bound up in the symbolic associations of certain costly materials (*see* FIG. 58). The chapel of the Cardinal of Portugal is another.

On 27 August 1459 Jaime of Lusitania died in Florence en route from Rome to Austria. A member of the Portuguese royal family known for his piety, he was only 25 years old and already a cardinal deacon of Sant' Eustachio in Rome. King Afonso V of Portugal was his first cousin and his brother-in-law; Philip the Good, duke of Burgundy, was married to his aunt; and Emperor Frederick III had wed his first cousin Leonor. The Florentine bookseller and biographer Vespasiano da Bisticci recorded that Jaime had expressed a wish to be buried at San Miniato al Monte in Florence. His chapel was built and decorated in little over a decade (1460–73) by a diverse team of craftsmen (an architect, four sculptors, three painters and various others) who worked together to achieve a harmonious and integrated interior. It is an all-embracing artwork, a *Gesamtkunstwerk*, in every sense: in the variety of artists involved, in the wealth and diversity of materials, and in the visual games it plays with the viewer. It is also extremely well documented. As such, it provides an ideal opportunity to discuss different materials and media, as they were showcased by a variety of different artists. Yet its sumptuousness made it atypical. After all, it was a royal funerary chapel in Republican Florence, replete with the coats of arms of every member of the Portuguese royal family.

The chapel is a free-standing structure that projects outwards from the aisle of San Miniato al Monte. It was inspired, in part, by Brunelleschi's earlier projects at San Lorenzo and Santa Croce, combined with early Christian models, such as the so-called mausoleum of Galla Placidia in Ravenna and São Fructuoso de Montelios near Braga in Portugal. However important these precedents, they do not account for the material richness of the space and the extent to which it acknowledges the presence of the spectator, which are among its most innovative aspects.

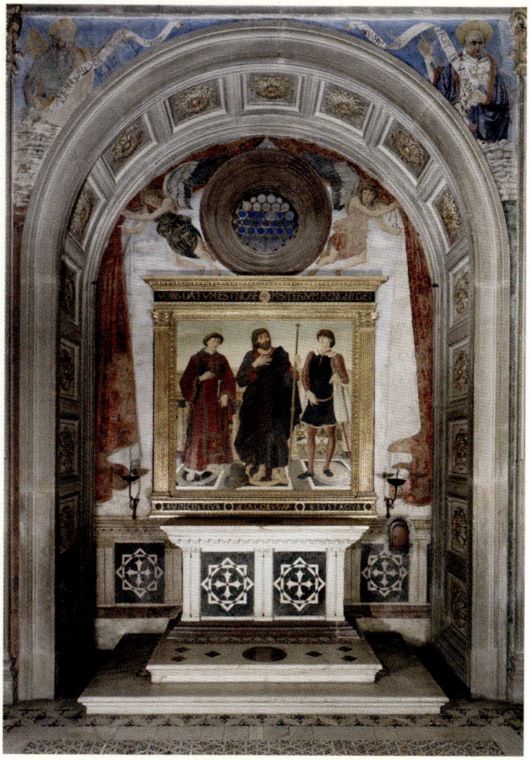

Fig. 136
The Cardinal of Portugal's chapel, showing the altar wall

San Miniato al Monte, Florence.

Approaching the chapel from across the nave, the viewer is stuck first by both the impressive entrance arch and the tomb on the right-hand wall (FIG. 135). We are immediately aware of the departed cardinal, not only through the effigy on his tomb, but also through his coat of arms, which emblazons the lunette over the entrance. In death, Jaime of Lusitania faces downwards towards the viewer at the threshold of his chapel, his closed eyes and marble visage modelled from a death mask taken by Desiderio da Settignano. Through his face, our gaze is directed up towards the Christ Child in the *tondo* above him, his hand raised in benediction. Our eyes then pass on to the Virgin, in whose arms he is held, and she directs our gaze across the space of the chapel to

Fig. 137
The Cardinal of Portugal's chapel, showing the bishop's throne

San Miniato al Monte, Florence.

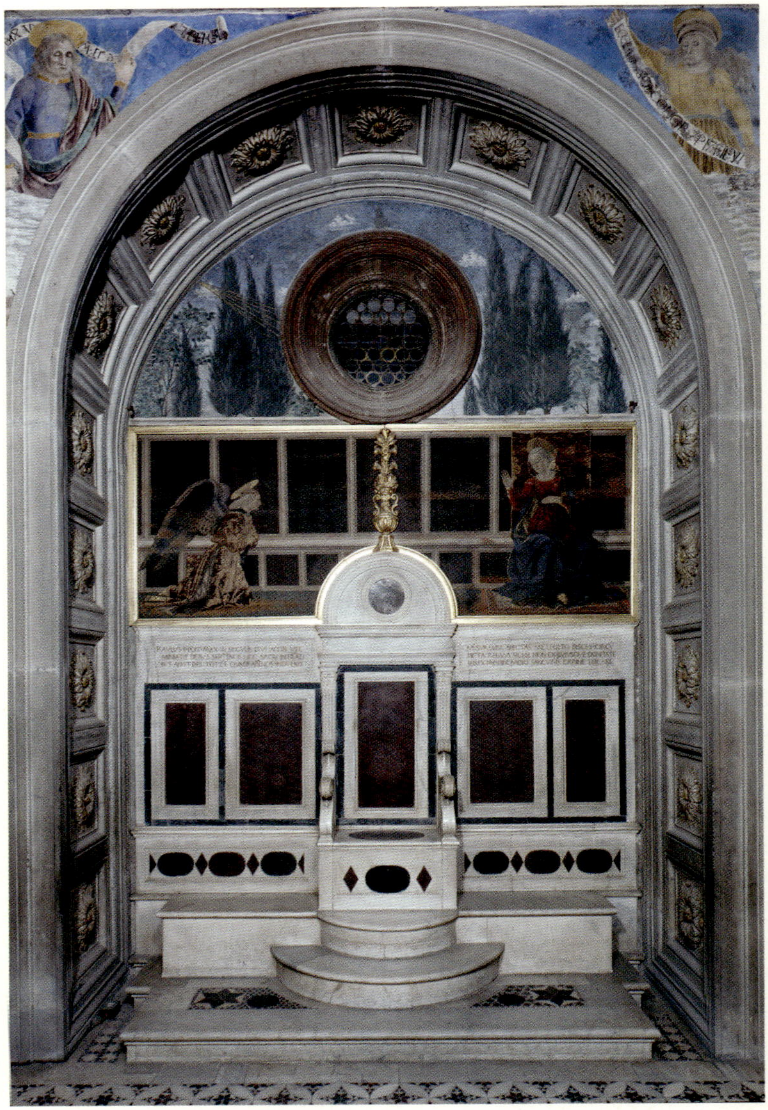

the altarpiece, where St James – the cardinal's name saint – looks back at her (FIG. 136). He is flanked by Saints Vincent and Eustace, respectively the patron of the Portuguese Royal house and the dedicatee of the cardinal's titular church in Rome. St Vincent looks out at the viewer, completing this circuit of glances and gestures. Or, if our attention continues to be drawn to the left, we become aware of a throne, perhaps intended for a bishop, that faces the tomb and redirects us back to it (FIG. 137). By the movement of the spectator among this holy congregation, the cardinal comes to be inserted into the company of Christ, who will judge him, the Virgin, who will intercede on his behalf, the various saints whose example he was to have followed, and the Church (symbolized in the episcopal throne) that has provided the means of his salvation. The space is activated and its meaning derives from the interaction among the various elements, rather than from any one of them individually.

Materials also engaged in sophisticated games in the chapel, analogous to the charged gazes and gestures that were used to move the eye around the space. On the left-hand wall, the actual marble revetments that flank the throne are mimicked in the faux marble panels painted by Alesso Baldovinetti to represent *verde di Prato* marble and porphyry (*see* FIG. 137). The forms of the ceiling (FIG. 138) are repeated in the floor. The original grille that stood in front of the chapel was probably reflected in the painted one that stands behind the saints in the altarpiece. On the altar wall, angels draw aside curtains painted in fresco to reveal the altarpiece (*see* FIG. 136), while the curtains that surround the tomb are of white marble, once picked out in gold to resemble damask (*see* FIG. 135). And, although they are long gone, we know that the chapel was originally hung with green damask *paramento* (hangings) supplied by a certain Francesco in October 1466, which were later replaced (or accompanied) by red

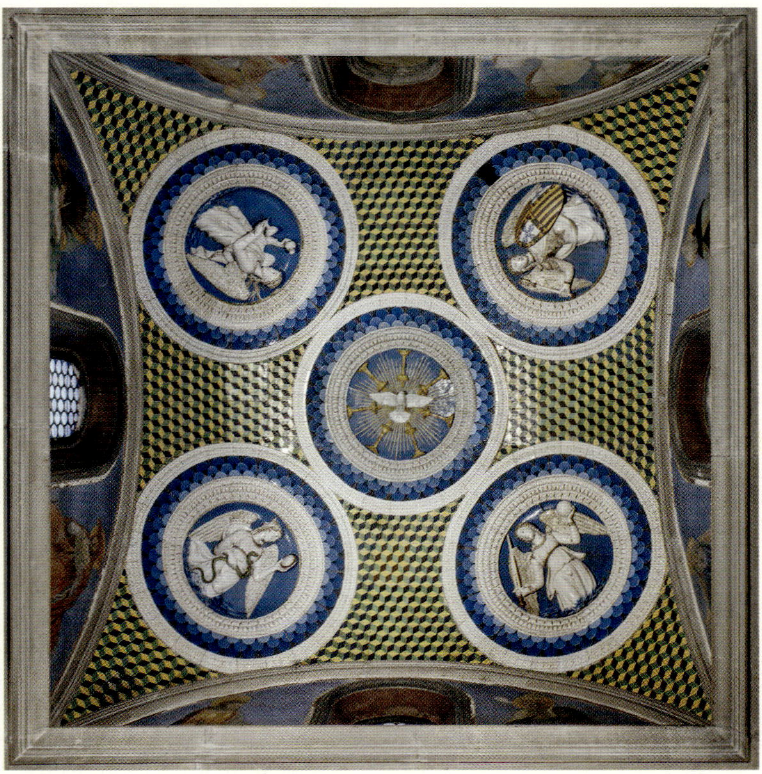

Fig. 138
The Cardinal of Portugal's chapel, showing the ceiling

San Miniato al Monte, Florence.

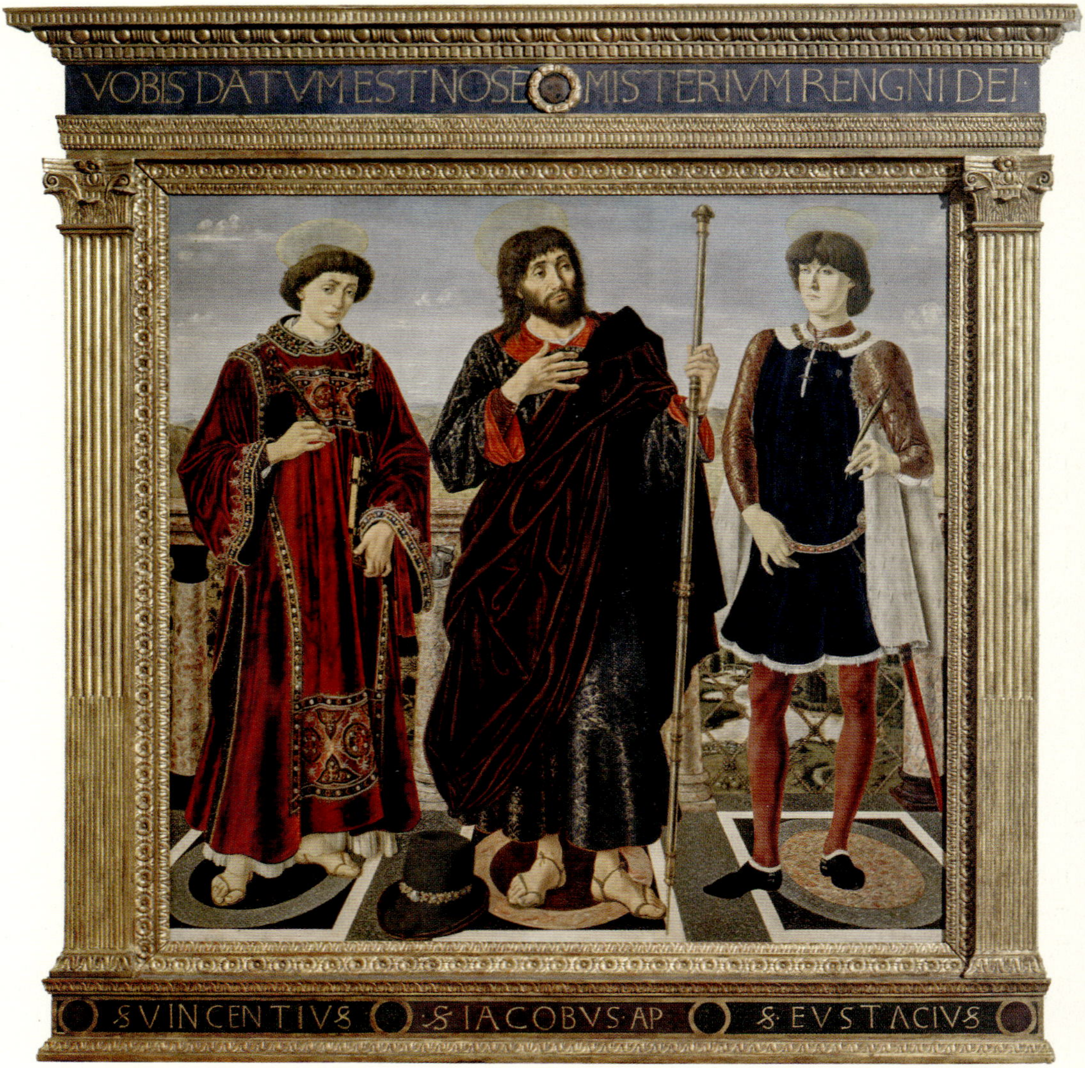

velvet ones. There were, in other words, actual curtains and curtains represented in both paint and marble. In this sense, the materials behaved like images in that their meaning derives partially from their substance and partially from what they represent.

Such careful and harmonious coordination among the different elements of this space, each worked by a different artisan, confirms that there was someone who conceived its design from the outset and oversaw its delivery. Ordinarily, we might expect it to have been the architect, Antonio di Manetto Ciaccheri (ca. 1404/5–1460), but he died shortly after submitting his complete design. The sculptor Antonio Rossellino could have taken over, or perhaps it was the cardinal's former tutor, Álvaro Afonso, Bishop of Silves in the Algarve, who was one of his executors and is named in the inscription over the entrance to the chapel: 'Álvaro, bishop of Silves, oversaw the erection of this structure which, the cardinal's body having been transferred and the altar of Saints James, Vincent and Eustace endowed, he consecrated on the 11th before the Kalends of October 1466 [i.e. 21 September 1466].'

The chapel is a riot of different materials, which necessitated a team of artisans with diverse skills, expert in working them and employing new technology. Giovanni di Matteo, the elder brother of Bernardo and Antonio Rossellino, carved all the architectural elements in 1460–1 (those on the outside are in brownish *pietra forte*, while the inside is articulated with grey *macingo* and *rosso scuro* for the oculi). Antonio and his workshop, which included Bernardo, carved the tomb between 1461 and 1466. It is predominantly in white marble, against a 'damasked' porphyry background that has lost its gilding, but includes a curious tablet of tan onyx that frames a black-and-white veined piece of petrified wood, in which the organic materials of the original timber have become quartz (*see* FIG. 135). The floor, too, is elaborately inlaid with various stones and marbles, modelled on Cosmatesque work of the thirteenth century, made by Stefano di Bartolomeo.

This list of materials is far from exhaustive. It does not include the various forms of painting, or the tin-glazed terracotta ceiling. Nor does it include the enamelled brass roundel set into the frame of the altarpiece (FIG. 139); the gilded lily in the *Annunciation* perhaps supplied by Giuliano da Maiano; or the carved and inlaid benches, the gold-and-enamel crucifix and the silver lamps (now lost). Many other materials have since disappeared: the stained glass, made by the glassmaker Francesco di Bonaventura; the two altar-cloths supplied by Giuliano and Arrigo di Giovanni; the missal by Benedetto di Giovanni or the bronze grille supplied by Pasquino di Matteo di Francesco da Prato. It is as if every conceivable material was deployed to create a sumptuous and regal chapel, fitting for a royal incumbent.

These different materials are significant in various ways. Porphyry, for instance, had imperial associations and was therefore appropriate for a royal chapel. The Medici appear to have used it in much the same way, both in their private chapel at the Palazzo Medici and around their tombs at San Lorenzo (*see* FIG. 58). It was rare and expensive, and carried a distinct set of connotations. Other materials had associations with particular sites, such as the piece of petrified (or silicified) wood, which, it has been speculated by one scholar, was brought back from the Holy Land and found its way

Fig. 139
Antonio and Piero del Pollaiuolo
Saints Vincent, James and Eustace

1467–68, oil and tempera on wood panel, 172 × 179cm (67¾ × 70½in). Galleria degli Uffizi, Florence.

This is the original altarpiece, now in the Uffizi. The altarpiece currently in the chapel is a modern copy.

Fig. 140
Nuno Gonçalves
Detail from the *St Vincent Polyptych*

ca. 1470, oil (?) and tempera on oak, this panel (the Infant panel): 206.4 × 128cm (81⅛ × 50⅜in). Museu Nacional de Arte Antiga, Lisbon.

into the chapel via the duchess of Burgundy, or perhaps, another suggests, was discovered while digging the foundations of the basilica. The meaning of both was symbolic; it related not to the qualities of the material itself, but rather to associations it had developed over time.

Other materials were meaningful as media. As these words are employed here, the essential difference between 'medium' and 'material' relates to technology and significance. For example, both a drawing and a print can be similar as materials – they might both be made of ink on paper – but they were produced by different processes, and the meanings imputed to them as a medium were likewise different. In the chapel, this distinction is most obviously observed in the ceiling (*see* FIG. 138). Executed by Luca della Robbia between March and October 1462, the shallow dome was made in tin-glazed terracotta, a resilient medium that was uniquely Florentine. Like printmaking, it was also new, having been developed by della Robbia himself in the early 1440s, using a calcium-rich clay and a tin-opacified lead-alkali glaze. Except in the proportion of minerals in the glaze and their application, the materials are the same as for maiolica, which had been invented in what is now Iraq sometime in the ninth century and came to Italy via Spain. It was practised in various places near Florence, including Montelupo to the west. Aesthetically, however, della Robbia-ware is very different, with brilliant white figures, typically on a blue ground. As a medium, then, its associations are distinct from those of a maiolica plate or *albarello* (pharmacy jar), even if its materials are essentially the same. Scholars still debate the meaning of della Robbia's ceiling, given that it is in the place typically occupied by mosaic work in early Christian architecture, but we can be certain that it looked specifically Florentine. At this date, no other city was producing tin-glazed terracotta of this type. In the context of a funerary chapel for a foreigner, the celebration of a new Florentine medium is significant. While the sumptuous marbles of his tomb conferred status on the royal cardinal, the striking Florentine ceiling acted as a reminder of the city that had honoured him with a funeral and burial chapel. It provided a sense of Florence as a centre of innovation and cultural exchange.

There is a final element to our discussion of medium and material in the chapel. It is in the use of new technology and supports for the paintings, which prompt the question of how they engendered meaning, and to whom. As elsewhere, the various painted elements showcase the full range of techniques – from panel painting to fresco – and several different practitioners: Alesso Baldovinetti and the Pollaiuolo brothers. Baldovinetti began frescoing the Evangelists

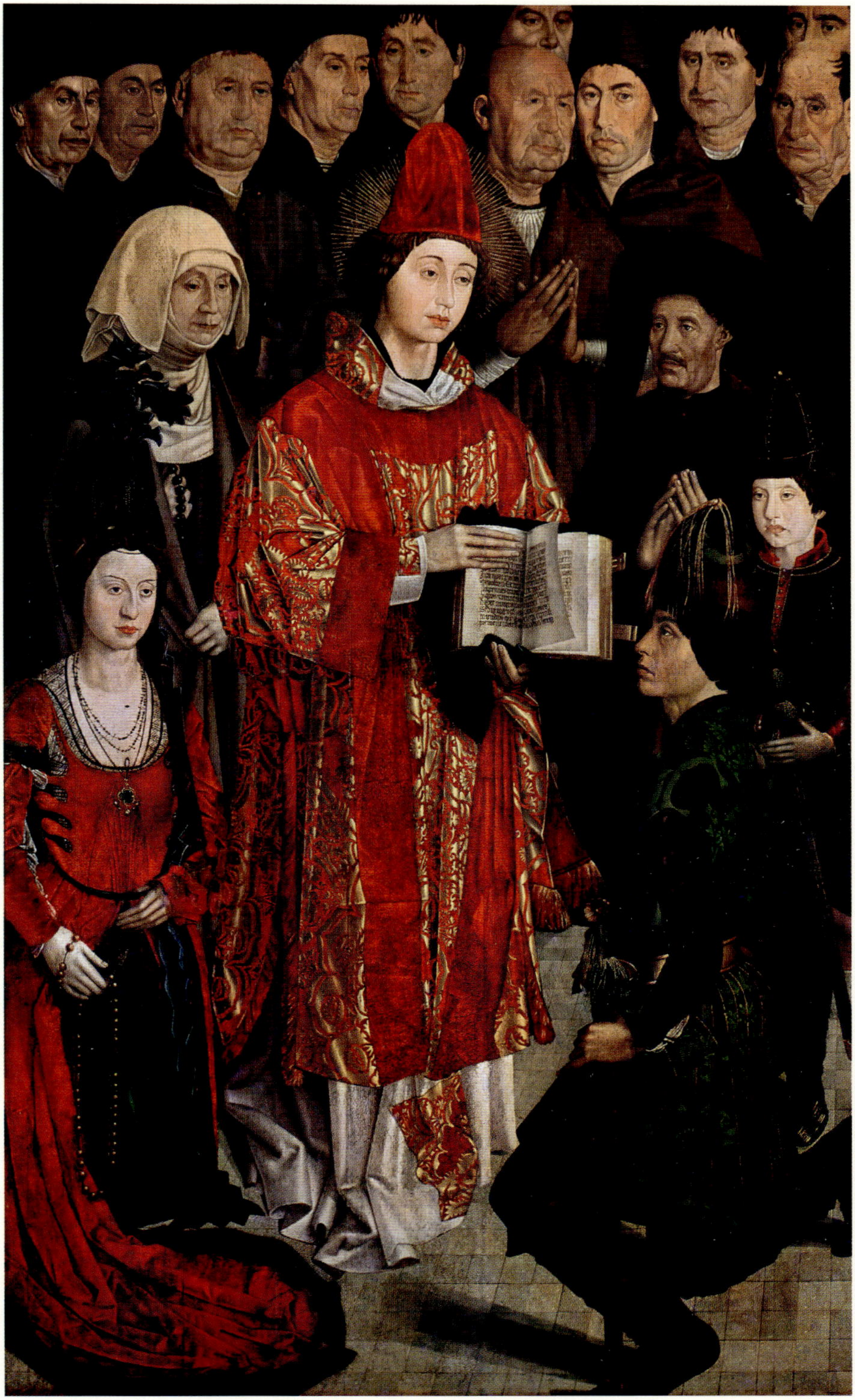

and Doctors of the Church in the lunettes in October 1466, shortly after the chapel was consecrated on 12 September 1466 (he had completed them by November the following year, together with the coats of arms in the frieze). He also worked the spandrels with Old Testament figures in the spring of 1468, also in fresco. When it came to the scene of the Annunciation on the wall above the throne, which he probably completed during the winter of 1467–8, he painted on panel rather than plaster, at least up to the height of the faux marble panelling. For the trees and sky, however, he returned to fresco (*see* FIG. 137). And, as if this decision was not curious enough, the panel itself is made of oak, which was customary as a support in Northern Europe but not in Florence, where panels tended to be made of poplar. The altarpiece on the adjacent wall was also painted on an oak support that was joined together by Giuliano da Maiano, who supplied the frame (*see* FIG. 139). It was painted by another workshop – the Pollaiuolos' – between May 1467 and March 1468, and they also executed the angels that hold back the curtains around it, as a mural rather than a painting on panel.

The employment of oak as a support is so unusual that it must be related to the patronage of the chapel, otherwise it is difficult to explain. Its arrival in Florence is recorded in a payment of 25 February 1466 as '16 planks brought from Flanders for the chapel [*16 pezzi d'asse venuti di Fiandra per la cappella*]'. Both panels are painted in a highly experimental technique, too. In the altarpiece, there is a very thin preparation of lead white, while in the *Annunciation* there is no preparation at all, gesso or otherwise. The altarpiece was executed in a mixed technique of oil and tempera, with differing amounts of oil to achieve varying degrees of impasto or liquidity. Painting in oil was a Northern European technique that was not widely known in Florence at this date, even if oil glazes over tempera had been used by Florentine artists for some time. Netherlandish painting was valued highly in the Iberian peninsula, such that an oil technique on an oak support, which we tend to think of as Netherlandish, might also have been understood in Florence as Portuguese. Scholars have noticed just how similar it is to that of Nuno Gonçalves, royal painter to Afonso V of Portugal, whose *St Vincent Polyptych* has an oak support with a very thin preparatory layer (FIG. 140). Could the choice of material and technique, then, reflect the taste of those who executed the cardinal's will, or those who paid for it? The chapel was financed, in large part, by Jaime's relatives – the duchess of Burgundy and other members of the Portuguese royal family – and its execution was supervised by Cardinal Álvaro, as we have seen. Effectively, the paintings are Florentine in style, but 'northern' in technique (in so far as that technique was understood in Florence in the late 1460s). However strange it might seem to us, a material support such as oak carried meaning, but for whom, given that it was entirely covered up in the process of painting? Who, other than the far-off patrons and the artists themselves, knew that these two Florentine panels, painted by Florentine artists, followed a Portuguese technique? We cannot know for sure, but we can examine how the chapel was received elsewhere. A decade or two after its completion, the entire chapel was emulated in Naples. Antonio Piccolomini Todeschini, Duke of Amalfi, commissioned a burial chapel for his wife, Maria of Aragon, at Sant'Anna dei Lombardi in Naples that carefully copied the space of the Florentine chapel, replicating the architectural details, the tomb and even the Cosmatesque floor. According to Vasari, the duke had seen the chapel in Florence and admired it greatly. However, Piccolomini had the painted altarpiece replaced with a marble one that was made by Antonio Rossellino and installed by him in 1477. Implicitly, Piccolomini acknowledged that the material of the panel was significant to its patrons. In Naples, marble mattered more than oak.

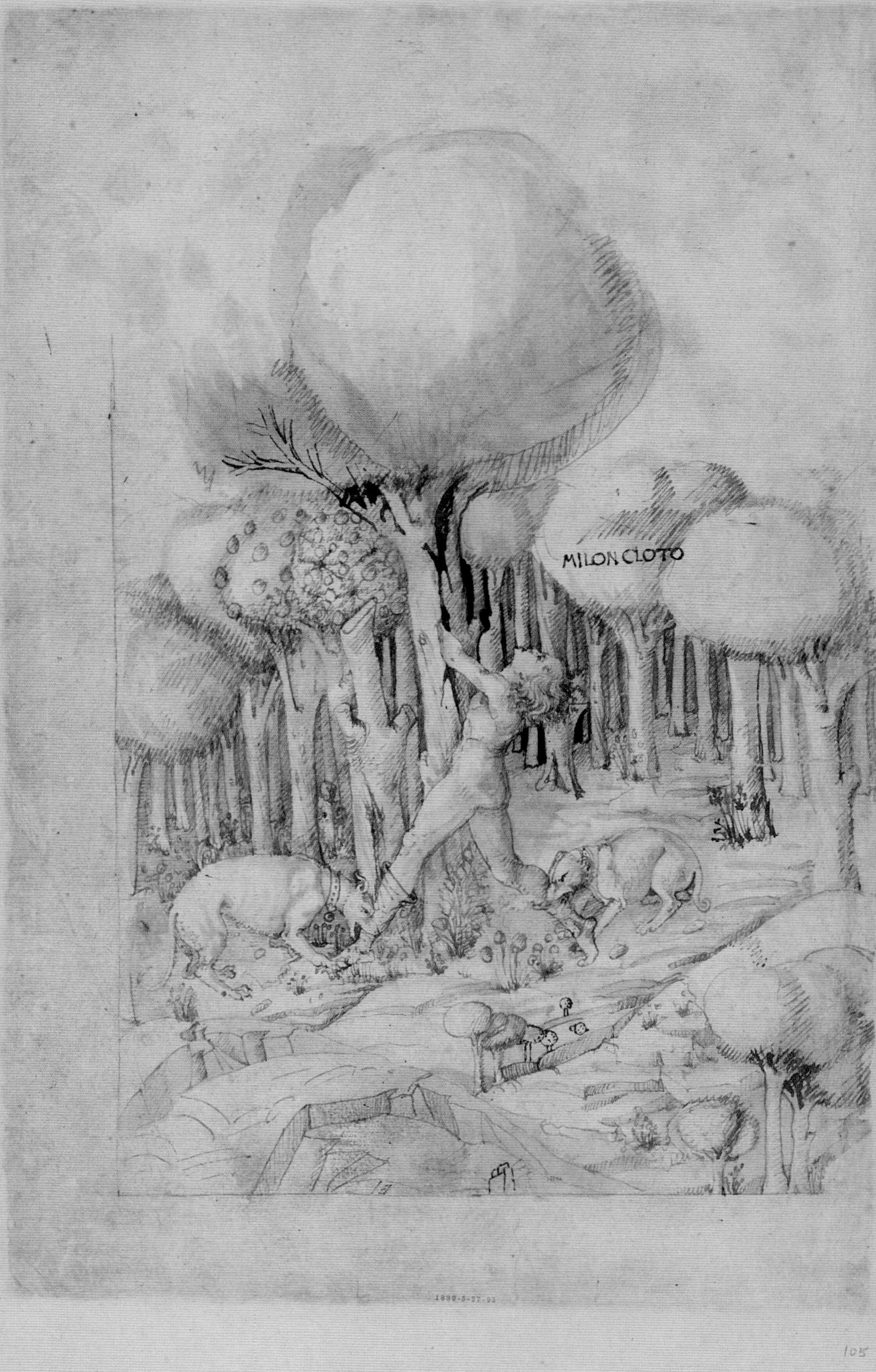
MILON CLOTO

Conclusion

A Self-Conscious Art

The impact of Florence on Western art has been profound. The imitation in distant Naples of the Cardinal of Portugal's chapel suggests that Florence played an artistic role far beyond its political borders. The products of the city's artisans might have only contributed to its internal economy (at least when compared to the foreign capital that flowed in from the wool and textile trade), but in terms of cultural capital, Florentine art has come to represent the city to the external world unlike anything else. In a guidebook published in 1510, Francesco Albertini (ca. 1469–after 1510) described how Florentine artists achieved fame in Rome, Venice, Naples, France, Spain and Hungary, a process that has continued unabated ever since, even if it has reversed: rather than sending artists outwards, Florence now draws people in. One needs only to observe the endless waves of tourists that wash over the city each year to realize how successful it has been in marketing its artistic heritage. Nothing could have been easier than to conclude by pointing to the numerous instances in which Florentine artistic developments were taken up beyond its borders as a justification for why the art of Renaissance Florence remains worthy of study today.

Fig. 141
Milo of Croton from *The Florentine Picture Chronicle*

ca. 1470–5, pen and brown ink with brown wash over black chalk, 32.6 × 22.6cm ($12\frac{7}{8} \times 8\frac{7}{8}$in). The British Museum, London.

The draughtsman choses the moment of Milo's death, rather than the moment of maximum drama that was selected by Pollaiuolo (*see* Figs. 142 and 143).

Yet to do so would contravene the spirit of this book. It would assert, once again, that anyone wanting to know about the history of art really should know something about Florence. Such is not my intention. My aim has been to attend to local conditions of production and to put them in the context of the patronal and institutional structures of Florentine society. It has been to suggest that there were sometimes forces at play that might not sit comfortably with our ideas of a civilized and tolerant society. Florence was not basking in the glow of a 'golden age' during the Renaissance (even if it was partially responsible for the creation of that myth in the first place). The problem has remained, however, of how to assess this local tradition in a book that aspires to provide an overview. How do we understand Florence's position in global art history without making imperialistic claims for its pre-eminence? I have, consequently, sought to place its stylistic innovations within a broader context, if only to make them strange again; I have attempted to expose how the process of writing about art in the city came to present its artistic achievements as exceptional; and I have tried to show the extent to which its art was indebted to developments elsewhere.

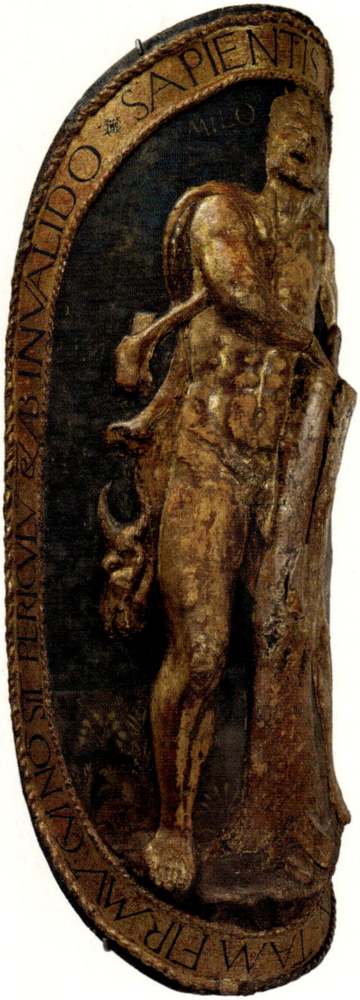

Fig. 142
Antonio del Pollaiuolo
Milo of Croton
(view from the left)

Third quarter of the 15th century, gilding, gesso and leather over wood, 118 × 46cm ($46\frac{1}{2} \times 18\frac{1}{8}$in). Musée du Louvre, Paris.

I began this book by saying that bold claims have been made for the art of Renaissance Florence and that they have provoked a backlash. I will end it by making some of my own, in the full knowledge that they are subjective and partial. I believe passionately that we still have much to learn from Florence. The fact that it gave rise to a literature on art, that stylistic innovations were accompanied by complex thinking about the nature of mimesis and representation, and that such a strong emphasis was placed on visual stimuli as the source of knowledge, must suggest that it remains worthy of study, at least to those engaged by art history. Add to this list the extraordinary wealth of documentation that survives in various Florentine archives – which continues to allow us to pose questions about works of art and find answers to them after more than half a millennium – and a compelling case emerges for writing books such as this one. The art of Renaissance Florence was not any better than that resulting from similar moments of outstanding artistic achievement elsewhere, nor are the structures for writing about Florentine art superior to those deployed in the study of art from other parts of the world. But to acknowledge these facts is not to deny that something exceptional did happen in the city on the Arno sometime between the early fifteenth century and the beginning of the sixteenth.

The Renaissance in Florence, as well as the Renaissance across a broader geographical reach, is often presented as the period that gave rise to a notion of 'art'. 'Art', as we understand it now, is imbued with nineteenth-century ideas of 'art for art's sake' that would have been alien to the men and women of fifteenth-century Florence. Art of more recent times has also broken a long-standing connection between skill and idea, hand and mind, and has opted instead to celebrate the concept within a work of art, a notion that would be equally unfamiliar to the Renaissance. During the period we have been considering, the word *arte* was most often used to designate a guild, or to indicate some manual skill, in which case its meaning was closer to 'craft' or 'skill' than 'art' as we currently understand it. All the same, an idea of 'art' was nascent. We get hints of it in Florentine writings on painting, sculpture and architecture, or in the high seriousness with which *artefici* (craftsmen) pursued their craft. How could a painting such as the *Primavera* have been created without an idea that it would constitute a form of knowledge, or would itself give rise to knowledge?

Many of these ideas are epitomized in a Florentine shield, now in the Louvre in Paris (FIGS. 142, 143), which we shall examine by way of conclusion. It is an item of parade armour, fashioned in relief by Antonio del Pollaiuolo, in which an image is built up from wood, overlaid with leather, gesso, paint, gilding and possibly rope. It depicts an athletic nude, his eyes tight shut, as he screams in pain, his hands trapped in the cleft of an oak tree. An inscription identifies him as Milo, a wrestler of legendary strength and skill who lived in Croton during the sixth century BCE. Pollaiuolo represented him as his life hangs in the balance. While walking in a forest, Milo came across a tree trunk split open with wedges, and he attempted to force it apart by placing his hands in the cleft. When the wedges fell out, he was caught and unable to defend himself against the wild beasts that came to devour him, a scene captured by the unknown draughtsmen of *The Florentine Picture Chronicle* (FIG. 141). Unlike the draughtsman of the *Picture Chronicle*, Pollaiuolo chose to depict the narrative at a point when Milo's fate has not yet been determined. He might still liberate himself if only he could muster the strength to break free from the ensnaring grasp of the tree. It is the moment of greatest drama.

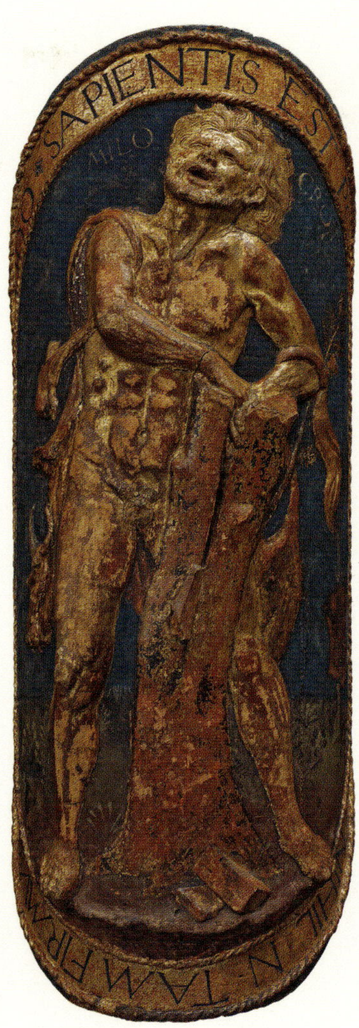

Fig. 143
Antonio del Pollaiuolo
Milo of Croton
(view from the front)

Third quarter of the 15th century, gilding, gesso and leather over wood, 118 × 46cm (46½ × 18⅛in). Musée du Louvre, Paris.

Milo's body is tense and strong. Pollaiuolo heeded Alberti's warning that 'it would be ridiculous … if we gave Milo, the strongest man of all, light and slender flanks'. Pollaiuolo composed the figure carefully to take full advantage of the shape of the support. As Milo tries to lever his hands free, his chest pushes forward as if propelled by the curve of the shield, his legs counteracting the forward thrust by buttressing the body on either side of both his body and the shield. The Renaissance is often characterized as the period in which value shifted from materials to artistic invention, yet Pollaiuolo's masterstroke was to use the materials themselves to supplement his invention. He captured the tension in the story with the body stretched across the shield ready to spring forth, much like the leather surface beneath it, tightened across its wooden support. He drew an analogy between the tree trunk from which Milo desperately tries to free himself, and the tree trunk that was made into a shield. The lateral pull of Milo's arms is not only against wood, as represented on the surface, but also against the actual wood of the support. The sense that the wooden shield, like the tree stump, is about to tear apart is hinted at by the rope border. The Greek traveller Pausanias recalled that Milo 'would tie a cord round his forehead as though it were a ribbon or a crown. Holding his breath and filling with blood the veins on his head, he would break the cord by the strength of these veins.' The reference to the cord in the rope border, which billows out to follow the form of the shield, only serves to heighten the tension, as if it too is ready to burst.

Pollaiuolo holds the entire scene in suspense, between life and death, illusion and material, representation and reality. The image is an illusion of nature and at the same time aware that it is only an illusion. It is, in other words, self-conscious. It calls on the viewer to recognize both Milo and Pollaiuolo; it demands that we acknowledge the artist's skill of hand and dexterity of thought. Yet Pollaiuolo's shield is not a triumph of invention over matter, nor of mind over hand. Rather, it depends on its materials, their substance and the manner in which they have been worked, to give shape and significance to Pollaiuolo's invention. To me, it embodies a bold fusion between hand and mind that makes Florentine art compelling and endlessly fascinating.

Primary Sources

This section lists the main primary sources discussed in each chapter above, and is intended to provide the reader with an idea of the evidence on which my assertions are based. Where sources are published and readily accessible, either in hard copy or online, only the reference is given. Archival material, or material that is not easily found, is transcribed below. The material appears in the order in which it appears in the chapter, not alphabetically, with the exception of several sources that recur throughout the book, which are listed and discussed first. Bibliographic references abbreviated here are provided in full in the bibliography.

Leon Battista Alberti's *On Painting*

For the Latin version, see Alberti, Leon Battista, *On Painting and On Sculpture: The Latin Texts of De pictura and De statua*, trans. Cecil Grayson (London: Phaidon, 1972). This edition includes an English translation which is also available, without the original text, in an edition published by Penguin.

For the vernacular version, see Alberti, Leon Battista, *De pictura (redazione volgare)*, ed. Lucia Bertolini (Florence: Edizioni Polistampa, 2011). The Spencer translation of Alberti is from the vernacular version: Alberti, Leon Battista, *On Painting*, trans. J. R. Spencer (New Haven: Yale University Press, 1966).

Lorenzo Ghiberti's *Commentaries*

Ghiberti, Lorenzo, *I commentarii*, ed. Lorenzo Bartoli (Florence: Giunti, 1998). There is no complete translation of Ghiberti's text, but partial translations are available in Gilbert, Creighton, *Italian Art 1400–1500: Sources and Documents* (Englewood Cliffs, NJ: Prentice-Hall, 1980), pp. 76–88; Richardson, Carol M., Kim Woods and Michael W. Franklin (eds), *Renaissance Art Reconsidered: An Anthology of Primary Sources* (Oxford: Blackwell/Open University, 2006), pp. 138–42; and an edition published for the students of the Courtauld Institute of Art in the late 1940s.

Antonio di Tuccio Manetti's *Life of Brunelleschi*

Manetti, Antonio, *The Life of Brunelleschi*, ed. Howard Saalman, trans. Catherine Enggass (University Park, PA, and London: Pennsylvania State University Press, 1970). This edition also includes an English translation.

Neri di Bicci's *Book of Memories*

Neri di Bicci, *Le ricordanze (10 marzo 1453–24 aprile 1475)*, ed. Bruno Santi (Pisa: Marlin, 1976). The *ricordanze* are not translated into English.

Giorgio Vasari's *Lives*

The critical edition of Bettarini and Barocchi combines the editions of 1550 and 1568 on each page: Vasari, Giorgio, *Le vite de' più eccellenti pittori scultori e architettori nelle redazioni del 1500 e 1568*, ed. Rosanna Bettarini and Paola Barocchi, 6 vols (Florence: Sansoni, 1966–87).

There are several English translations of Vasari's *Lives*. The translation by George Bull for Penguin has been used here, simply because it is readily available to students and translates the prefaces in their entirety, unlike other English translations: Vasari, Giorgio, *Lives of the Artists*, trans. George Bull (Harmondsworth, Middlesex: Penguin, 1965, and frequently reprinted). However, the translation is loose and I have changed it in several places. I have also provided the original Italian for stylistic terms that will reappear in subsequent chapters.

Introduction

Vauxcelles, Louis, 'Le Salon d'Automne', *Gil Blas*, 17 October 1905: 'La candeur de ces bustes surprend, au milieu de l'orgie des tons purs: Donatello chez les fauves.'

Chapter 1: Symbols, Saints and Heroes

For the Sala dei Gigli documents, see Gaye, Giovanni, *Carteggio inedito d'artisti dei secoli XIV, XV, XVI* (Florence, 1840), vol. 1, pp. 577–80, although they contain some errors. Hegarty, 1996, published an appendix to her article with further transcriptions, although it does not contain all the documentation.

Rinuccini, Alamanni, 'Dialogus de libertate', *Atti e memorie dell'accademia toscana di scienze e lettere La Colombaria*, vol. 8 (1957), pp. 265–303: 'Florentinam civitatem semper libertatis avidam, semper studiosam prae caeteris extitisse, adeo ut inter publica signa aureis, ut nosti, litteris inscriptum libertatis nomen ubique conspicatur', p. 274. There is an English translation by Renée Neu Watkins, *Humanism and Liberty: Writings on Freedom in Fifteenth-Century Florence* (Columbia, SC: University of South Carolina Press, 1978), p. 197.

The *titulus* under the figure of Brutus reads: 'BRVTVS EGO ASSERTOR PATRIAE REGVMQ[V]E FVGATOR'.

Lorenzo de' Medici referred to himself as a 'citizen with some authority' in a letter to Pierfilippo Pandolfini in November 1481; see Medici, Lorenzo de', *Lettere*, ed. Michael Mallett (Florence: Giunti, 1990), vol. 6, p. 100: 'Io non sono signore di Firenze, ma cittadino con qualche auctorita.'

The translation of the inscription on the Florentine seal is taken from Wright, 2005, p. 82.

For the inscription beneath Donatello's marble *David*, see Janson, 1957, and Caglioti, Francesco, *Donatello e i Medici: storia del David e della Giuditta*, 2 vols (Florence: Olschki, 2000).

For discussion of how the renovations in the Palazzo della Signoria were financed, including the Sala dei Gigli, see Rubinstein, 1995, pp. 31–2; Hegarty, 1996, p. 265 nn. 4, 6. For the request to tax foreign artisans made by the Signoria to the councils on 19–21 November 1477, see Rubinstein, 1995, p. 32 n. 239: 'considerando l'opera del palagio non essere finite … et non volendo tocchare per questo le borse de' nostri cittadini'; 'decta taxa è picchola rispecto al gran denaio' that foreigners 'cavano da questi paesi, ne' quali vivono'.

Chapter 3: Writing about Art

The critical editions of the main texts discussed in this chapter are listed above. All have useful introductions.

There is a transcription and English translation of Manetti's *Huomini singhularii in Firenze dal MCCCC. innanzi* in Murray, Peter, 'Art Historians and Art Critics IV, XIV Uomini singhularii in Firenze', *The Burlington Magazine*, 49 (1957), pp. 330–6.

For the *Fat Woodworker*, see Manetti, Antonio, *Vita di Filippo Brunelleschi: preceduta da La novella del Grasso*, ed. Domenico De Robertis, with Giuliano Tanturli (Milan: Il polifilo, 1976). There is an English translation by Valerie Martone and Robert L. Martone published in New York (Italica Press), 2008.

For Manetti as '*architectus et civis*', see Vasari, Giorgio, *Le vite de' più eccellenti pittori, scultori ed architettori*, ed. Gaetano Milanesi, 9 vols (Florence: Sansoni, 1906), vol. 4, p. 309.

For a critical edition of the *Libro dell'arte*, see *Cennino Cennini's* Il libro dell'arte: *A New English Translation and Commentary with Italian Transcription*, ed. and trans. Lara Broecke (London: Archetype, 2015).

Chapter 4: Guilds, Confraternities and Competition

For Ghiberti's matriculation records, see Krautheimer, 1956, docs 103, 104, 115, 115a, 116.

The various statutes for the Medici e Speziali have been published on various occasions (see, for example, Waźbiński, 1987, vol. 2, pp. 411–17). Those consulted here are transcribed in Ciasca, Raffaele (ed.), *Statuti dell'arte dei medici e speziali* (Florence: A. Vallecchi, 1922). From the statutes of 1349, the two rubrics mentioned above were 'A che sieno tenuti e dipintori' (rub. LXXVIII, p. 191), to which there were minor revisions in 1355 and 1356; and 'Delle questioni che vengono per la dipintura de' dipintori' (rub. LXXX, p. 192), which includes the long quotation above: 'Statuito e ordinato è che, se alcuno dipintore dipignerà alcuna sala, camera, palco, o sporto, o muro, o alcun altro luogo, e del pagamento della detta dipintura fusse questione tra 'l dipintore e colui che avesse facto fare tale dipintura, e consoli della detta arte possino, sieno tenuti, e debbino eleggere uno o più dipintori, quali e quanti vorranno; e quali dipintori possino tale questione dicidere e terminare in extimare e dichiarare quello che si convenga a tale dipintore di tale dipintura.'

The new rubric 'Della stima delle dipintura, e contro il brigare per togliere lavori ad altri pittori' was passed on 24 January 1470, while 'Del non dipingere immagini sacre dove si fanno brutture' was approved on 16 December 1506. Both are transcribed by Fiorilli, 1920, docs. 12 and 13, pp. 67–70. The line from the document of 1506, translated above, reads: 'nostro Signore o di nostra Donna o di alcuno santo o santa in alcuno lungo … ove sia usitato pisciare o fare altra bruttura.'

The reforms of 1406 are published in Ciasca, 1922 (see above), pp. 391–4: 'Che i dipintori due volte il mese vadino a sancta Maria Nuova'; 'Che ogni dipintore paghi ogni anno alla compagnia di sancto Luca soldi .x.'; 'Che i messi dell'arte, a petitione de' capitani della compagnia di sancto Luca, constringha quegli della compagnia a pagare.'

As have the statutes of the Medici e Speziali, the vernacular *ordinamenti* of the Compagnia di San Luca have been published several times, most recently in Waźbiński, 1987, vol. 2, pp. 417–20. The version quoted here is from Gaye, Giovanni, *Carteggio inedito d'artisti dei secoli XIV, XV, XVI* (Florence, 1840), vol. 2, pp. 32–6: 'ordiniamo che tutti quelli che venghono o verranno a scriversi a questa compagnia huomini o donne sieno chontriti e chonfessi de' loro peccati, o almeno chon intendimento di confessarsi il più tosto che potrà acconciamente; et che i Capitani o i chamerlinghi quelli scriveranno, si annuntino loro ciò e beni che questa compagnia fa. Et qualunque sia ricevuto a questa compagnia sia tenuto di dire ogni dì cinque pater noster cum cinque ave Maria: et se per dimenticanza o vero per alcuna altra sollicitudine non li dicesse ogni dì, possali dire il dì seguente, o quando sene raccorderà.'

The *primo registro* is preserved at Archivio di Stato di Firenze, Accademia del Disegno, 1, fols. 3r–19r; the *Libro rosso* at Archivio di Stato di Firenze, Accademia del Disegno, 2 (Debitori e creditori e ricordi, libro rosso A, 1472–1520). The entry for Filippino Lippi is on 56v–57r and includes the section translated above: '1503 / Filippo di filippo … Mori addi 18 daprile 1504 e sotterassi i[n] san michele Disdomini idio gli perdoni'. For Verrocchio, see Covi, 2005.

For the deliberation of the Opera del Duomo, 19 December 1408, see Poggi, Giovanni, *Il Duomo di Firenze: documenti sulla decorazione della chiesa e del campanile, tratti dall'Archivio dell'Opera* (Berlin: B. Cassirer, 1909), doc. 172: 'Deliberaverunt quod Nicholaus Pieri Lamberti, Donatus Nicholai Becti Bardi et Nannes Antonii, et quilibet eorum habeat unam figuram et seu lapidem marmoreum pro quatuor Evangelistis deputatis et quarta lapis intelligatur esse concessa illi ex dictis tribus qui melius fecerit eius figuram; cum salario seu provisione per operarios alias ordinanda.'

For the *Libro del pilastro*, see Doren, Alfred, *Das Aktenbuch für Ghibertis Matthäus-Statue an Or San Michele zu Florenz* (Berlin: B. Cassirer, 1906). The contract is at pp. 26–30 and the relevant clause reads: 'Imprima il detto Lorenzo di Bartoluccio promise et per solenne stipulagione convenne a' detti consoli et IIII arroti et operai fare la detta fighura di San Macteo d'octone fine alla grandezza et della grandezza il meno che è la fighura al presente di Santo Giovanni Batista dell' arte de' mercanti, o maggiore quello più che paressi alla discretione d'esso Lorenzo che meglio stare debbi …'

Chapter 5: Patronage Networks

For Filippo Strozzi's son (Lorenzo), see Strozzi, Lorenzo, *Vita di Filippo Strozzi il Vecchio* (Florence: Tipografia della casa di correzione, 1851), pp. 22–3: 'Filippo … essendo per natura inclinato all'edificare ed avendone non poca intelligenza, si messe in animo di fare uno edifizio, che a sè e a tutti suoi in Italia e fuori desse nome.'

For Giovanni Battista Dei, see Luchs, 1975, doc. 27, p. 419: 'La qual Pittura fu fatta in modo molto significante, e misterioso, poichè siccome fu pagata de danari assegnati da Jacopo Salviati per fare il Sepolcro al Cavaliere Jacopo suo Avo, il quale come ne scrisse Alamanno suo figliuolo, ebbe special divozione al Principe degli Apostoli, così torna bene che l'uno e l'altro di detti Santi vi siano dipinti. Chi poi fusse curioso d'osservare in questa Pittura ogni minuzia, vi potrebbe vedere uno scherzo del Pittore, il quale ne due piccoli spazi d'aria che restano tra la sedia della Madonna, e i Santi, vi ha dipinto in lontananza tra certe Casine, il Campanile del Duomo della parte di S. Pietro, e da quella di S. Jacopo il Campanile del Bargello, che torna in vicinanza delle Case de Salviati.'

The location of Tanai Nerli's house is given in the Decima Repubblicana of 1498 as 'una chasa per mio abitare posta in sul

Borgo San Jacopo a popolo Santa Felicita', Archivio di Stato di Firenze, Decima Repubblicana 4 (Nicchio 1498), fol. 361r.

There is considerable confusion in the recent literature on the location of the Capponi chapels in Santo Spirito, and some authors claim that they had four chapels. In fact, the fourth Capponi chapel to the left of the Visitation chapel came to them only in 1731 (Paatz, 1952–5, vol. 5, pp. 142, 156–7). Much of the confusion is cleared up by Westergård, 2007, pp. 176–7 n. 582, and Thomas, 2003, pp. 55–6.

For Palmieri's *On Civil Life*, see Palmieri, Matteo, *Vita civile*, ed. Gino Belloni (Florence: Sansoni, 1982). It is not translated.

The translation of Gino di Neri Capponi's *ricordi* is by D. Kent and F.W. Kent. For the full text, see 'Ricordi di Gino di Neri Capponi', in Gianfranco Folena, *Miscellanea di studi offerta a A. Balduino e B. Bianchi* (Padua, 1962), pp. 34–9.

For Giovanni Rucellai's 'diary', see Perosa, Alessandro, *Giovanni Rucellai ed il suo zibaldone: I. 'Il zibaldone quaresimale'* (London: Warburg Institute, 1960).

For the description of Lorenzo as '*maestro della bottega*', see Benedetto Dei, *Cronaca*, ed. Roberto Barducci (Florence: Papafava, 1985), p. 114.

Chapter 6: The Patronage of Women

For the masses celebrated for Giovanna degli Albizzi at Cestello, see Luchs, 1975.

For the Florentine statutes, see *Statuta populi et communis Florentiae: publica auctoritate, collecta, castigata et praeposita anno salutis MCCCCXV* (Fribourg, 1778), liber secundus, rubrica IX: 'Quod nulla mulier debeat per se, sed per procuratorem agere in causa civili.'

For Alberti's *Della famiglia*, see Alberti, Leon Battista, *Opere volgari*, ed. Cecil Grayson, 3 vols (Bari: Laterza, 1960), vol. 1: 'Rispuose e disse che aveva imparato ubidire il padre e la madre sua, e che da loro avea comandamento sempre obedire me, e pertanto era disposta fare ciò che io gli comandassi.' The treatise was translated by Renée Neu Watkins as *The Family in Renaissance Florence: A Translation by Renée Neu Watkins of I libri della famiglia by Leon Battista Alberti* (Columbia, SC: University of South Carolina Press, 1969), p. 211.

For Alessandra Strozzi's letters, see Macinghi Strozzi, Alessandra, *Lettere di una gentildonna fiorentina del secolo xv ai figliuoli esuli* (Florence: Sansoni, 1877), some of which are translated in an edition by Heather Gregory (Los Angeles and London: University of California Press, 1997).

For Lucrezia Tornabuoni's letters, see Tornabuoni, Lucrezia, *Lettere*, ed. Patrizia Salvadori (Florence: Olschki, 1993). Some of her writings are translated into English: Tornabuoni, Lucrezia, *Sacred Narratives*, ed. and trans. Jane Tylus (Chicago and London: University of Chicago Press, 2001).

Chapter 8: Style II: A Turn to Nature or a Return to the Antique?

For Pliny's *Natural History*, see the H. Rackham translation for the Loeb edition, or *The Elder Pliny's Chapters on the History of Art*, ed. Eugénie Sellers, trans. K. Jex-Blake (Chicago: Ares, 1968).

Poggio Bracciolini's letter to Niccolò Niccoli: Bracciolini, Poggio, *Lettere*, ed. Helene Harth (Florence: Olschki, 1984), vol. 1, no. 79, pp. 195–6. For a translation, see Gilbert, Creighton, *Italian Art 1400–1500: Sources and Documents* (Englewood Cliffs, NJ: Prentice-Hall, 1980), p. 168.

Francesco da Sangallo's letter of 1567 is in Biblioteca apostolica vaticana, MS. Chig. L.V. 178, fols. 104v–105v.

Medieval descriptions of the *Marcus Aurelius* can be read at www.census.de.

Benvenuto da Imola's *Commentary on Dante's Comedy*: 'Ego autem vidi Florentiae in domo privata statuam Veneris de marmore mirabilem in eo habitu in quo olim pingebatur Venus. Erat enim mulier speciosissima nuda, tenens manum sinistram ad pudenda, dexteram vero ad mammillas, et dicebatur esse opus Polycleti, quod non credo, quia ut dictum est Polycletus sculpsit in aere, non in marmore.' Benevenuti de Rambaldis de Imola, *Comentum super Dantis Aldigherij Comoediam*, ed. James Philip Lacaita, 5 vols (Florence: G. Barbèra, 1887), Purgatory 10: 28–33.

Savonarola's *De simplicitate Christianae vitae* was printed in Florence in 1496 and translated into the vernacular by Girolamo Benivieni a few months later. Savonarola, Girolamo, *De simplicitate Christianae vitae* (Rome: A. Belardetti, 1959), p. 192: 'E benché e' paia che le opere dell'arte piaccino agli uomini, nientedimeno, se noi rettamente consideriamo, troverremo che quelle tanto più piacciono quanto più imitano la natura. Onde e coloro e' quali lodono alcuna pittura dicono: "Ecco, questi animali pare che vivino e questi fiori paiono naturali."'

For Quintilian, his *Istitutio oratoria*, IV, ii.63; VIII, iii, 2; VIII, iii. 16.

For Michelangelo's biography: Condivi, Ascanio, *Vita di Michelagnolo Buonarroti*, ed. Giovanni Nencioni, Michael Hirst and Caroline Elam (Florence: Studio per edizione scelte, 1998). There are various English translations, including Condivi, Ascanio, *The Life of Michelangelo*, trans. Alice Sedgwick Wohl (University Park, PA: Pennsylvania State University Press, 1999).

Leonardo's comments on the centenarian on a sheet in the Royal Library, Windsor, RL19027v: 'Ecquesto vechio di poche ora ina[n]zi la sua morte mi disse lui passare ce[n]to anni e che non si sentiva alcu[n] manchame[n]to nela persona altro che deboleza e cosi sta[n]dosi assedere sopra uno letto nello spedale di sca[nta] maria nova di fire[n]ze sanza altro movime[n]to o segnio dalcuno accide[n]te passo di questa vita…

E io ne feci notomia per vedere la causa di si dolce morte la quale trovai venire meno per ma[n]came[n]to di sangue e arteria che notria il core ellialtri me[n]bri inferiori li quali trovai molti aridi stenuati essechi la qual notomia discrissi assai privato di grasso e di omore che assai inpedisce la cognitione delle parte laltra notomia fu du[n] putto di 2 anni nel quale trovai ogni cosa co[n]tra[r]ia a quella del vechio.' *The Literary Works of Leonardo da Vinci, Compiled and Edited from the Original Manuscripts by Jean Paul Richter*, ed. Carlo Pedretti (London: Phaidon, 1977), vol. 2, p. 115, with truncations expanded and some alterations for ease of comprehension. The translation is taken from Clayton, Martin, and Ronald Philo, *Leonardo da Vinci: The Mechanics of Man* (London: Royal Collection Publications, 2010).

For Cristoforo Landino's comments on 'FIORENTINI EXCELLENTI IN PICTURA ET SCULPTURA', see his *Comento sopra la Comedia*, ed. Paolo Procaccioli (Rome: Salerno, 2001), part IV, vol. 1, pp. 240–2.

Chapter 9: Modes of Viewing: Sacred and Secular Art

Gregory the Great's letter to Serenus, Bishop of Marseilles, is translated in Davis-Weyer, Caecilia (ed.), *Early Medieval Art, 300–1150: Sources and Documents* (Englewood Cliffs, NJ: Prentice-Hall, 1971), pp. 47–9.

Aquinas discusses idolatry in the *Summa Theologiae, secunda secundae partis* (second part of the second part), question 94. The quotation relating to the prototype was from the *tertia pars* (third part), question 25, article 3. The *Summa* can be consulted online in Latin and English translation.

For the decree by the prior and chapter of San Lorenzo in 1434, see Ruda, Jeffrey, 'A 1434 Building Programme for San Lorenzo in Florence', *The Burlington Magazine*, vol. 120, no. 903 (June 1978), pp. 358–61.

On corporeal, spiritual and intellectual 'sight', see Augustine, *De Genesi ad litteram* (*On the Literal Meaning of Genesis*), Book XII, chapter VII: 'Primum ergo appellemus corporale … secundum spiritale … tertium uero intellectuale ab intellectu …'

For the wedding celebrations in Pesaro that included a figure of Erato, see *Ordine de la noze de lo Illustrissimo Costanzo Sfortia de Aragonia et de la Illustrissima Madona Camilla de Aragonia sua consorte nel anno* 1475 (Vicenza, 1475). The occasion is also described in a manuscript in the Biblioteca apostolica vaticana, which included the description of '*Venere sancta*' and the swan, and has been published: De Marinis, Tammaro (ed.), *Le nozze di Costanzo Sforza e Camilla d'Aragona celebrate a Pesaro nel maggio 1475* (Florence: Vallecchi, 1946).

The inventory of the cadet branch of the Medici family (Lorenzo and Giovanni di Pierfrancesco de' Medici) was published by Shearman, John, 'The Collections of the Younger Branch of the Medici', *The Burlington Magazine*, vol. 117, no. 862 (1975), pp. 12–27. It included both Botticelli's *Pallas and the Centaur* and the *Primavera*.

For the sources of the *Primavera* mentioned above, see Lucretius, *De rerum natura*, V.737–40; Ovid, *Fasti*, V. 193–222; Horace, *Carmina*, I.xxx; and Seneca, *De beneficciis*, I. iii, 2–10. These texts are all available in both the original and translation in Loeb editions.

Chapter 10: Medium and Material

Giovanni Tortelli's philological excursus on 'horologium' in his *De orthographia* (1449) is transcribed and translated in Keller, Alex, 'A Renaissance Humanist Looks at "New" Inventions: The Article "Horologium" in Giovanni Tortelli's "De Orthographia"', *Technology and Culture*, vol. 11, no. 3 (1970), pp. 345–65.

The documentation from the Cambini account books for the Cardinal of Portugal's chapel was published in Hartt, Corti and Kennedy, 1964. Additional documentation was published in Apfelstadt, Eric, 'Bishop and Pawn: New Documents for the Chapel of the Cardinal of Portugal at S. Miniato al Monte, Florence', in K.J.P. Lowe (ed.), *Cultural Links Between Portugal and Italy in the Renaissance* (Oxford: Oxford University Press, 2000), pp. 183–223.

The inscription over the entrance to the chapel reads: 'ALVAR[US] EP[ISCOP]US SILVEN[SIS] OPUS FACIUNDU[M] CURAVIT QUI TRA[N]SLATO CARD[INALIS] CORPORE ARAM DIVIS / JACOBO VINCENTIO ET EUSTACHIO ASSIGNATA DOTE SACRAVIT XI K[A]L[ENDIS] OCTOBRIS MCCCCLXVI.'

Conclusion: A Self-Conscious Art

For a facsimile and translation of Francesco Albertini's *Memoriale* of 1510: Albertini, Francesco, *Memorial of Many Statues and Paintings in the Illustrious City of Florence*, trans. Salvatore Amato, Waldemar H. De Boer and Patricia Brigid Garvin (Florence: Centro Di, 2010).

The story of Milo's death was narrated by Strabo, *Geographica*, 6.1.12; Pausanias, *Description of Greece*, book VI (Elis II).xiv.8; and Valerius Maximus, *Factorum et Dictorum Memorabilium*, IX.12.ext.9. The description of Milo breaking cords around his forehead is from Pausanias, *Description of Greece*, book VI (Elis II).xiv.7.

Bibliography

References that appear in the General Bibliography or Artists' Bibliography are not repeated in the Select Bibliography for each chapter.

General Bibliography

AMES-LEWIS, FRANCIS (ed.), *Florence* (Cambridge: Cambridge University Press, 2012)

CRUM, ROGER J., and John T. Paoletti (eds), *Renaissance Florence: A Social History* (Cambridge: Cambridge University Press, 2006)

GOLDTHWAITE, RICHARD A., *The Economy of Renaissance Florence* (Baltimore: Johns Hopkins University Press, 2009)

PAATZ, WALTHER, and ELISABETH VALENTINER PAATZ, *Die Kirchen von Florenz: Ein kunstgeschichtliches Handbuch*, 6 vols (Frankfurt am Main: Klostermann, 1952–5)

RANDOLPH, ADRIAN W.B., *Engaging Symbols: Gender, Politics, and Public Art in Fifteenth-century Florence* (New Haven and London: Yale University Press, 2002)

RUBIN, PATRICIA LEE, *Images and Identity in Fifteenth-century Florence* (New Haven and London: Yale University Press, 2007)

—, and ALISON WRIGHT, *Renaissance Florence: The Art of the 1470s* (London: National Gallery, 1999)

Monographs by Artist, Largely in English

DIDI-HUBERMAN, GEORGES, *Fra Angelico: Dissemblance and Figuration*, J. M. Todd (trans.) (Chicago: University of Chicago Press, 1995)

HOOD, WILLIAM, *Fra Angelico at San Marco* (New Haven and London: Yale University Press, 1993)

CARL, DORIS, *Benedetto da Maiano: A Florentine Sculptor at the Threshold of the High Renaissance* (Turnhout, Belgium: Brepols, 2006)

HORNE, HERBERT P., *Alessandro Filipepi, Commonly Called Sandro Botticelli, Painter of Florence* (London: G. Bell & Sons, 1908)

LIGHTBOWN, RONALD, *Sandro Botticelli*, 2 vols (London: Elek, 1978)

SAALMAN, HOWARD, *Filippo Brunelleschi: The Buildings* (University Park, PA: Pennsylvania State University Press, 1993)

BENNETT, BONNIE A., and DAVID G. WILKINS, *Donatello* (Oxford: Phaidon, 1984)

JANSON, H.W., *The Sculpture of Donatello*, 2 vols (Princeton: Princeton University Press, 1957)

KRAUTHEIMER, RICHARD, *Lorenzo Ghiberti* (Princeton: Princeton University Press, 1956)

CADOGAN, JEAN K., *Domenico Ghirlandaio: Artist and Artisan* (New Haven and London: Yale University Press, 2000)

BROWN, DAVID ALAN, *Leonardo da Vinci: Origins of a Genius* (New Haven and London: Yale University Press, 1998)

CLARK, KENNETH, *Leonardo da Vinci* (London: Penguin, 1993)

KEMP, MARTIN, *Leonardo da Vinci: The Marvellous Works of Nature and Man* (Cambridge, MA: Harvard University Press, 1981)

CECCHI, A., *Filippino Lippi e Sandro Botticelli nella Firenze del '400*, exh. cat., Scuderie del Quirinale, Rome (Rome: 24 ore cultura, 2011)

NELSON, JONATHAN KATZ, and PATRIZIA ZAMBRANO, *Filippino Lippi* (Milan: Electa, 2004)

HOLMES, MEGAN, *Fra Filippo Lippi: The Carmelite Painter* (New Haven and London: Yale University Press, 1999)

RUDA, JEFFREY, *Fra Filippo Lippi: Life and Work with a Complete Catalogue* (London: Phaidon, 1993)

JOANNIDES, PAUL, *Masaccio and Masolino: A Complete Catalogue* (London: Phaidon, 1993)

HIRST, MICHAEL, *Michelangelo: The Achievement of Fame, 1475–1534* (New Haven and London: Yale University Press, 2011)

WALLACE, WILLIAM E. (ed.), *Michelangelo: Selected Scholarship in English* (New York and London: Garland, 1995)

WILDE, JOHANNES, *Michelangelo: Six Lectures*, ed. John Shearman and Michael Hirst (Oxford: Clarendon Press, 1978)

GERONIMUS, DENNIS, *Piero di Cosimo: Visions Beautiful and Strange* (New Haven and London: Yale University Press, 2006)

WRIGHT, ALISON, *The Pollaiuolo Brothers: The Arts of Florence and Rome* (New Haven and London: Yale University Press, 2005)

GABRIELLI, EDITH, *Cosimo Rosselli: catalogo ragionato* (Turin: Umberto Allemandi, 2007)

WOHL, HELLMUT, *The Paintings of Domenico Veneziano: A Study in Florentine Art of the Early Renaissance* (Oxford: Phaidon, 1980)

BUTTERFIELD, ANDREW, *The Sculptures of Andrea del Verrocchio* (New Haven and London: Yale University Press, 1997)

COVI, DARIO A., *Andrea del Verrocchio: Life and Work* (Florence: Leo S. Olschki, 2005)

Select Bibliography by Chapter

Introduction

GOMBRICH, ERNST H., 'The Renaissance Concept of Artistic Progress and its Consequences', *Actes du XVIIme Congrès International d'Histoire de l'Art* (La Haye: Imprimateur nationale des Pays-Bas, 1955), pp. 291–307

Chapter 1: Symbols, Saints and Heroes

BROWN, ALISON, 'De-masking Renaissance republicanism', in James Hankins (ed.), *Renaissance Civic Humanism: Reappraisals and Reflections* (Cambridge: Cambridge University Press, 2000), pp. 179–99

BULLARD, M.M., 'Adumbrations of Power and the Politics of Appearances in Medicean Florence', *Renaissance Studies*, vol. 12, no. 3 (1998), pp. 341–56

HEGARTY, MELINDA, 'Laurentian Patronage in the Palazzo Vecchio: The Frescoes of the Sala dei Gigli', *The Art Bulletin*, vol. 78, no. 2 (1996), pp. 264–85

MARCHAND, ECKART, 'Exemplary Gestures and "Authentic" Physiognomies', *Apollo*, vol. 159, no. 1 (2004), pp. 3–11
RUBINSTEIN, NICOLAI, 'Classical Themes in the Decoration of the Palazzo Vecchio in Florence', *Journal of the Warburg and Courtauld Institutes*, vol. 50 (1987), pp. 29–43
—, *The Palazzo Vecchio, 1298–1532: Government, Architecture, and Imagery in the Civic Palace of the Florentine Republic* (Oxford: Oxford University Press, 1995)
WACKERNAGEL, MARTIN, *The World of the Florentine Renaissance Artist: Projects and Patrons, Workshop and Art Market*, trans. Alison Luchs (Princeton: Princeton University Press, 1981)

Chapter 2: Telling Tales: The Story of Florentine Art

BELLOSI, LUCIANO, *Pittura di luce: Giovanni di Francesco e l'arte fiorentina di metà Quattrocento*, exh. cat., Casa Buonarroti, Florence (Milan: Electa, 1990)
BURKE, JILL, 'Inventing the High Renaissance, from Winckelmann to Wikipedia: An Introductory Essay', in Jill Burke (ed.), *Rethinking the High Renaissance: The Culture of the Visual Arts in Early Sixteenth-century Rome* (Farnham, Surrey: Ashgate, 2012), pp. 1–26
CAGLIOTI, FRANCESCO, 'Due "restauratori" per le antichità dei primi Medici: Mino da Fiesole, Andrea del Verrocchio e il "Marsia rosso" degli Uffizi', *Prospettiva*, vols 72 and 73–4 (October 1993 and January 1994), pp. 17–42 and 74–96
RUBIN, PATRICIA LEE, *Giorgio Vasari: Art and History* (New Haven and London: Yale University Press, 1995)

Chapter 3: Writing about Art

BAXANDALL, MICHAEL, *Giotto and the Orators: Humanist Observers of Painting in Italy and the Discovery of Pictorial Composition* (Oxford: Clarendon Press, 1971)
BERTOLINI, LUCIA, 'Sulla precedenza della redazione volgare del "De pictura" di Leon Battista Alberti', in Marco Santagata and Alfredo Stussi (eds), *Studi per Umberto Carpi: Un saluto da allieve e colleghi pisani* (Pisa: ETS, 2000), pp. 181–210
GRAFTON, ANTHONY, '*Historia* and *Istoria*: Alberti's Terminology in Context', *I Tatti Studies*, vol. 8 (1999), pp. 37–68
KEMP, MARTIN, 'From "Mimesis" to "Fantasia": The Quattrocento Vocabulary of Creation, Inspiration and Genius in the Visual Arts', *Viator*, vol. 8 (1977), pp. 347–98
ROCCASECCA, PIETRO, *Filosofi, oratori e pittori: una nuova lettura del "De pictura" di Leon Battista Alberti* (Rome: Campisano editore, 2016)
SETTIS, SALVATORE, '*Ars moriendi*: Cristo e Meleagro', in Maria Luisa Catoni (ed.), *Tre figure: Achille, Meleagro, Cristo* (Milan: Feltrinelli, 2013), pp. 85–108
VESCOVINI, GRAZIELLA FEDERICI, 'Contributo per la storia della fortuna di Alhazen in Italia: Il volgarizzamento del MS. Vat. 4595 e il Commentario terzo del Ghiberti', *Rinascimento*, vol. 5 (1965), pp. 17–49

Chapter 4: Guilds, Confraternities and Competition

BELLANDI, ALFREDO (ed.), *'Fece di scoltura di legname e colori': scultura del Quattrocento in legno dipinto a Firenze*, exh. cat., Galleria degli Uffizi, Florence (Florence: Giunti, 2016)
BLOCH, AMY R., 'Lorenzo Ghiberti, the Arte di Calimala, and Fifteenth-Century Florence Corporate Patronage', in David S. Peterson and Daniel E. Bornstein (eds), *Florence and Beyond: Culture, Society and Politics in Renaissance Italy. Essays in Honour of John M. Najemy* (Toronto: Centre for Reformation and Renaissance Studies, 2008), pp. 135–52
CLIFTON, JAMES, 'Vasari on Competition', *The Sixteenth Century Journal*, vol. 27 (1996), pp. 23–41
FIORILLI, CARLO, 'I dipintori a Firenze nell'arte dei medici speziali e marciai', *Archivio storico italiano*, vol. 78, no. 2 (1920), pp. 5–74
MATHER, RUFUS GRAVES, 'Documents Mostly New Relating to Florentine Painters and Sculptors of the Fifteenth Century', *Art Bulletin*, vol. 30, no. 1 (March 1948), pp. 20–65
MIDDELDORF KOSEGARTEN, ANTJE, 'The Origins of Artistic Competitions in Italy (Forms of Competition between Artists before the Contest for the Florentine Baptistery Doors Won by Ghiberti in 1401)', in *Lorenzo Ghiberti nel suo tempo* (Florence: Olschki, 1980), pp. 167–86
MUNMAN, ROBERT, 'The Evangelists from the Cathedral of Florence: A Renaissance Arrangement Recovered', *The Art Bulletin*, vol. 62, no. 2 (1980), pp. 207–17
SALVESTRINI, FRANCESCO, 'Associazionismo e devozione nella compagnia di San Luca (1340 ca.–1563)', in Bert W. Meijer and Luigi Zangheri (eds), *Accademia delle Arti del Disegno: studi, fonti e interpretazioni di 450 anni di storia* (Florence: Olschki, 2015), pp. 3–17
WAŹBIŃSKI, ZYGMUNT, *L'Accademia Medicea del Disegno a Firenze nel Quattrocento: Idea e istituzione*, 2 vols (Florence: Olschki, 1987)

Chapter 5: Patronage Networks

BORSOOK, EVE, and JOHANNES OFFERHAUS, *Francesco Sassetti and Ghirlandaio at Santa Trinita, Florence: History and Legend in a Renaissance Chapel* (Doornspijk, Netherlands: Davaco, 1981)
BRIDGEMAN, JANE, 'Filippino Lippi's Nerli Altar-Piece: A New Date', *The Burlington Magazine*, vol. 130, no. 1026 (1988), pp. 668–71
BURKE, JILL, *Changing Patrons: Social Identity and the Visual Arts in Renaissance Florence* (University Park, PA: Pennsylvania State University Press, 2004)
CAPRETTI, ELENA, *The Building Complex of Santo Spirito* (Florence: Lo Studiolo, 1991)
—, 'La cappella e l'altare: evoluzione di un rapporto', in Cristina Acidini Luchinat and Elena Capretti (eds), *La chiesa e il convento di Santo Spirito a Firenze* (Florence: Giunti, 1996), pp. 229–38
ECKSTEIN, NICHOLAS A., *The District of the Green Dragon: Neighbourhood Life and Social Change in Renaissance Florence* (Florence: Olschki, 1995)
GOLDTHWAITE, RICHARD A., *The Building of Renaissance Florence: An Economic and Social History* (Baltimore: Johns Hopkins University Press, 1980)
KENT, D.V., *The Rise of the Medici: Faction in Florence, 1426–1434* (Oxford: Oxford University Press, 1978)
—, *Cosimo de' Medici and the Florentine Renaissance: The Patron's Oeuvre* (New Haven and London: Yale University Press, 2000)
—, and F.W. KENT, *Neighbours and Neighbourhood in Renaissance Florence: The District of the Red Lion in the Fifteenth Century* (Locust Valley, NY: J.J. Augustin, 1982)
KENT, F.W., *Household and Lineage in Renaissance Florence: The Family Life of the Capponi, Ginori, and Rucellai* (Princeton: Princeton University Press, 1977)
—, 'Patron-Client Networks in Renaissance Florence and the Emergence of Lorenzo as "Maestro della Bottega"', in Bernard

Toscani (ed.), *Lorenzo de' Medici: New Perspectives* (New York: Peter Lang, 1993), pp. 279–313
—, *Lorenzo de' Medici and the Art of Magnificence* (Baltimore: Johns Hopkins University Press, 2004)
LITTA, POMPEO, *Famiglie celebri in Italia* (Milan: Giusti, 1819), vol. 7 (for 'Strozzi di Firenze')
LUCHS, ALISON, *Cestello* (New York and London: Garland, 1975)
SIMONS, PATRICIA, 'Patronage in the Tornaquinci Chapel, Santa Maria Novella, Florence', in F.W. Kent and Patricia Simons (eds), *Patronage, Art, and Society in Renaissance Italy* (Oxford: Oxford University Press, 1987), pp. 221–50
THOMAS, ANABEL, *Art and Piety in the Female Religious Communities of Renaissance Italy: Iconography, Space, and the Religious Woman's Perspective* (Cambridge and New York: Cambridge University Press, 2003)
WESTERGÅRD, IRA, *Approaching Sacred Pregnancy: The Cult of the Visitation and Narrative Altarpieces in Late Fifteenth-century Florence* (Helsinki: Suomalaisen Kirjallisuuden Seura, 2007)

Chapter 6: The Patronage of Women

APFELSTADT, ERIC, 'Andrea Ferrucci's "Crucifixion" Altar-Piece in the Victoria and Albert Museum', *The Burlington Magazine*, vol. 135, no. 1089 (December 1993), pp. 807–17
BASKINS, CRISTELLE LOUISE, *Cassone Painting, Humanism, and Gender in Early Modern Italy* (Cambridge: Cambridge University Press, 1998)
DEMPSEY, CHARLES, *Inventing the Renaissance Putto* (Chapel Hill, NC: University of North Carolina Press, 2001)
GARDNER VON TEUFFEL, CHRISTA, 'The Altarpieces of San Lorenzo: Memorializing the Martyr or Accommodating the Parishioners', in Robert W. Gaston and Louis A. Waldman (eds), *San Lorenzo* (Florence: Villa I Tatti, 2017), pp. 184–243
KING, CATHERINE, *Renaissance Women Patrons: Wives and Widows in Italy, c. 1300–1550* (Manchester: Manchester University Press, 1998)
KLAPISCH-ZUBER, CHRISTIANE, *Women, Family, and Ritual in Renaissance Italy*, trans. Lydia Cochrane (Chicago: University of Chicago Press, 1985)
KUEHN, THOMAS, *Law, Family and Women: Toward a Legal Anthropology of Renaissance Italy* (Chicago: University of Chicago Press, 1991)
LLEWELLYN, LAURA, 'Art, Community and Religious Women in the Oltrarno, Florence: The Early Visual Culture of the Convents of Santa Monaca, Santa Chiara and the Annalena', PhD dissertation, Courtauld Institute of Art, University of London, 2016
LUCHS, ALISON, *Cestello* (New York and London: Garland, 1975)
MUSACCHIO, JACQUELINE MARIE, *The Art and Ritual of Childbirth in Renaissance Italy* (New Haven and London: Yale University Press, 1999)
PRIETO GILDAY, ROSI, 'The Women Patrons of Neri di Bicci', in Sheryl E. Reiss and David G. Wilkins (eds), *Beyond Isabella: Secular Women Patrons of Art in Renaissance Italy* (Kirksville, MO: Truman State University Press, 2001), pp. 51–75
SOLUM, STEFANIE, *Women, Patronage, and Salvation in Renaissance Florence: Lucrezia Tornabuoni and the Chapel of the Medici Palace* (Farnham, Surrey: Ashgate, 2015)
STREHLKE, CARL BRANDON, *Italian Paintings 1250–1450 in the John G. Johnson Collection and the Philadelphia Museum of Art* (Philadelphia: Philadelphia Museum of Art/Pennsylvania State University Press, 2004)
STROCCHIA, SHARON T., *Nuns and Nunneries in Renaissance Florence* (Baltimore: Johns Hopkins University Press, 2009)
THOMAS, ANABEL, *Art and Piety in the Female Religious Communities of Renaissance Italy: Iconography, Space, and the Religious Woman's Perspective* (Cambridge and New York: Cambridge University Press, 2003)
TOMAS, NATALIE, *The Medici Women: Gender and Power in Renaissance Florence* (Aldershot, Hampshire: Ashgate, 2003)
TREXLER, RICHARD C., 'Le célibat à la fin du Moyen Âge: les religieuses de Florence', *Annales: Économies, Sociétés, Civilisations* (1972), pp. 1329–50
VAN DER SMAN, GERT JAN, *Lorenzo and Giovanna: Timeless Art and Fleeting Lives in Renaissance Florence* (Florence: Mandragora, 2010)
WESTERGÅRD, IRA, *Approaching Sacred Pregnancy: The Cult of the Visitation and Narrative Altarpieces in Late Fifteenth-century Florence* (Helsinki: Suomalaisen Kirjallisuuden Seura, 2007)

Chapter 7: Style I: Perspectives on Space

BELTING, HANS, *Florence and Baghdad: Renaissance Art and Arab Science* (Cambridge, MA: Belknap Press of Harvard University Press, 2011)
CAMEROTA, FILIPPO, *La prospettiva del Rinascimento: arte, architettura, scienza* (Milan: Electa, 2006)
ELKINS, JAMES, 'On the Arnolfini Portrait and the Lucca Madonna: Did Jan van Eyck Have a Perspectival System?', *The Art Bulletin*, vol. 73, no. 1 (1991), pp. 53–62
KEMP, MARTIN, *The Science of Art: Optical Themes in Western Art from Brunelleschi to Seurat* (New Haven and London: Yale University Press, 1990)
MOREL, PHILIPPE, ANDREAS BEYER and ALESSANDRO NOVA (eds), *Voir l'au-delà. L'expérience visionnaire et sa représentation dans l'art italien de la Renaissance* (Turnhout, Belgium: Brepols, 2017)
PANOFSKY, ERWIN, *Perspective as Symbolic Form*, trans. Christopher Wood (New York: Zone Books, 1997)
RAYNAUD, DOMINIQUE, *L'hypothèse d'Oxford: essai sur les origins de la perspective* (Paris: Presses universitaires de France, 1998)
ROXBURGH, DAVID J., 'Kamal al-Din Bihzad and Authorship in Persianate Painting', *Muqarnas*, vol. 17 (2000), pp. 119–46
TRACHTENBERG, MARVIN, *Dominion of the Eye: Urbanism, Art, and Power in Early Modern Florence* (Cambridge and New York: Cambridge University Press, 1997)
WHITE, JOHN, *The Birth and Rebirth of Pictorial Space: A Historical Study of the Treatment of Perspective* (London: Faber, 1967)

Chapter 8: Style II: A Turn to Nature or a Return to the Antique?

DEMPSEY, CHARLES, *The Early Renaissance and Vernacular Culture* (Cambridge, MA: Harvard University Press, 2012)
FISCHER, CHRIS, 'Fra Bartolommeo's Landscape Drawings', *Mitteilungen des Kunsthistorischen Institutes in Florenz*, vol. 32 (1989), pp. 301–42
FUSCO, LAURIE, and GINO CORTI, *Lorenzo de' Medici: Collector and Antiquarian* (Cambridge and New York: Cambridge University Press, 2006)
KEIZER, JOOST P., 'Portrait and Imprint in Fifteenth-Century Italy', *Art History*, vol. 38, no. 1 (2015), pp. 10–37
McHAM, SARAH BLAKE, *Pliny and the Artistic Culture of the Italian Renaissance: The Legacy of the Natural History* (New Haven and London: Yale University Press, 2013)
NICKEL, HELMUT, 'The Emperor's New Saddle Cloth: The Ephippium of the Equestrian Statue of Marcus Aurelius', *Metropolitan Museum Journal*, vol. 24 (1989), pp. 17–24

NUTTALL, PAULA, *From Flanders to Florence: The Impact of Netherlandish Painting, 1400–1500* (New Haven and London: Yale University Press, 2004)

SEYMOUR, CHARLES Jr., 'Some Reflections on Filarete's Use of Antique Visual Sources', *Arte Lombarda*, vol. 18, no. 38/39 (1973), pp. 36–47

Chapter 9: Modes of Viewing: Sacred and Secular Art

ARASSE, DANIEL, 'Entre dévotion et culture: fonctions de l'image religieuse au XVe siècle', *Faire Croire*, vol. 51, no. 1 (1981), pp. 131–46

DEMPSEY, CHARLES, *The Portrayal of Love: Botticelli's* Primavera *and Humanist Culture at the Time of Lorenzo the Magnificent* (Princeton: Princeton University Press, 1992)

GARDNER VON TEUFFEL, CHRISTA, *From Duccio's* Maestà *to Raphael's* Transfiguration*: Italian Altarpieces and their Setting* (London: Pindar Press, 2005)

—, and CIRO CASTELLI, 'La tavola dell'*Annunciazione Martelli* nella basilica di San Lorenzo a Firenze, con uno studio tecnico sulle modalità costruttive del supporto', *OPD Restauro: Revista dell'Opificio delle Pietre Dure*, vol. 26 (2014), pp. 35–52

KESSLER, HERBERT L., 'Gregory the Great and Image Theory in Northern Europe during the Twelfth and Thirteenth Centuries', in Conrad Rudolph (ed.), *A Companion to Medieval Art* (Oxford: Blackwell, 2006), pp. 151–72

NAGEL, ALEXANDER, and LORENZO PERICOLO, 'Unresolved Images: An Introduction to Aporia as an Analytical Category in the Interpretation of Early Modern Art', in Alexander Nagel and Lorenzo Pericolo (eds), *Subject as Aporia in Early Modern Art* (Aldershot, Surrey: Ashgate, 2010), pp. 1–15

Chapter 10: Medium and Material

ARCHER, MADELINE CIRILLO, 'The Dating of a Florentine *Life of the Virgin and Christ*', *Print Quarterly*, vol. V (1988), pp. 395–402

CAMBARERI, MARIETTA, with ABIGAIL HYKIN and COURTNEY LEIGH HARRIS, *Della Robbia: Sculpting with Color in Renaissance Florence*, exh. cat., Museum of Fine Arts, Boston (Boston: MFA Publications, 2016)

CAMPBELL, CAROLINE, and ALAN CHONG (eds), *Bellini and the East*, exh. cat., National Gallery, London (London/Boston: National Gallery/Isabella Stewart Gardner Museum, 2005)

CECCHI, ALESSANDRO, et al., 'The Conservation of Antonio and Piero del Pollaiuolo's Altar-piece for the Cardinal of Portugal's Chapel', *The Burlington Magazine*, vol. 141, no. 1151 (1999), pp. 81–8

EMISON, PATRICIA, 'The Replicated Image in Renaissance Florence, 1300–1600', in Roger J. Crum and John T. Paoletti (eds), *Renaissance Florence: A Social History* (Cambridge: Cambridge University Press, 2006), pp. 431–53

GRAY, EMILY, 'Early Florentine Engravings and the Devotional Print: Origins and Transformations, *c.* 1460–85', PhD dissertation, Courtauld Institute of Art, University of London, 2012

HARTT, FREDERICK, GINO CORTI and CLARENCE KENNEDY, *The Chapel of the Cardinal of Portugal, 1434–1459 at San Miniato in Florence* (Philadelphia: University of Pennsylvania Press, 1964)

HIND, ARTHUR M., *Early Italian Engraving: A Critical Catalogue with Complete Reproduction of All the Prints Described*, 4 vols (London: Quaritch, 1938)

KINGERY, W. DAVID, and MEREDITH ARONSON, 'The Glazes of Luca della Robbia', *Faenza*, vol. 76, no. 5 (1990), pp. 221–4

KOCH, LINDA A., 'The Early Christian Revival at S. Miniato al Monte: The Cardinal of Portugal Chapel', *The Art Bulletin*, vol. 78, no. 3 (1996), pp. 527–55

—, 'The Cardinal of Portugal Chapel: Two Omissions: Response', *The Art Bulletin*, vol. 79, no. 3 (1997), pp. 563–5

LANDAU, DAVID, and PETER W. PARSHALL, *The Renaissance Print: 1470–1550* (New Haven and London: Yale University Press, 1994)

LEVENSON, JAY A., et al., *Early Italian Engravings from the National Gallery of Art* (Washington DC: National Gallery of Art, 1973)

NUTTALL, PAULA, '"Fecero al cardinale di Portogallo una tavola a olio": Netherlandish Influence in Antonio and Piero Pollaiuolo's San Miniato Altarpiece', *Nederlands Kunsthistorisch Jaarboek*, 44 (1993), pp. 111–24

PEPE, ERMINIA, 'Le tre cappelle rinascimentali in Santa Maria di Monteoliveto a Napoli', *Napoli nobilissima*, 37 (1998), 97–116

RABY, JULIAN, 'Mehmed II Fatih and the Fatih Album', *Islamic Art*, vol. 1 (1981), pp. 42–9

STRIKER, CECIL L., 'The Cardinal of Portugal Chapel: Two Omissions', *The Art Bulletin*, vol. 79, no. 3 (1997), pp. 562–3

ZUCKER, MARK J., *The Illustrated Bartsch: Early Italian Masters* (New York: Abaris, 1994), vol. 24, part 2

Conclusion: A Self-Conscious Art

BAXANDALL, MICHAEL, *Painting and Experience in Fifteenth-Century Italy: A Primer in the Social History of Pictorial Style* (Oxford: Oxford University Press, 1988)

BELTING, HANS, *Likeness and Presence: A History of the Image before the Era of Art*, trans. Edmund Jephcott (Chicago: University of Chicago Press, 1996)

POMMIER, EDOUARD, *Comment l'art devient l'art dans l'Italie de la Renaissance* (Paris: Gallimard, 2007)

STOICHITA, VICTOR IERONIM, *The Self-Aware Image: An Insight into Early Modern Meta-Painting*, trans. Anne-Marie Glasheen (Cambridge: Cambridge University Press, 1997)

Index

Page numbers in **bold** refer to illustrations and their captions

Picture Credits

Photographs from Florentine Museums are all © Studio Quattrone, Florence except as listed below. Details of collections are given in the captions. Additional information, copyright credits and photo sources are given below. Numbers are figure numbers unless indicated.

Front Cover © Studio Quattrone, Florence

Fig. 1 Photo © Ben Blackwell / SFMOMA. © Succession H. Matisse / DACS 2019
3 Photo Scala, Florence – courtesy of the Ministero Beni e Att. Culturali
4 © givaga / 123RF
5 © Vincenzo Fontana/Arte & Immagini srl / CORBIS / Corbis via Getty Images
6 Photo Scala, Florence – courtesy of Musei Civici Fiorentini
16 Photo © RMN-Grand Palais (musée du Louvre) / Michel Urtado
17 By kind permission of Lord Leicester and the Trustees of Holkham Estate, Norfolk / Bridgeman Images
21 Photo Scala, Florence
22 © Alinari Archives / CORBIS / Corbis via Getty Images
23 © B.O'Kane / Alamy Stock Photo
24 Photo © John Harrington Photography, Washington D.C.
25 Photo © The National Gallery, London / Royal Collection Trust / © Her Majesty Queen Elizabeth II 2019
26 Photo © RMN-Grand Palais (musée du Louvre) / Tony Querrec
27 © Gabinetto Fotografico, Gallerie Degli Uffizi, Florence
28 Photo © RMN-Grand Palais (musée du Louvre) / Tony Querrec
29 Sailko CC
41, 42, 43 Photo Scala, Florence
47 © Achim Bednorz, Cologne
49, 50 Photo Scala, Florence – courtesy of the Ministero Beni e Att. Culturali e del Turismo
51, 52 © Foto Giusti Claudio
56 Photo Scala, Florence / Fondo Edifici di Culto – Min. dell'Interno
62 © 2017 Photo the Philadelphia Museum of Art / Art Resource / Scala, Florence
63 Photo © RMN-Grand Palais (musée du Louvre) / Jean-Gilles Berizzi
64 Alinari Archives, Florence
65 Museo Thyssen-Bornemisza / Scala, Florence
67, 68 © Victoria and Albert Museum, London
69a © 2017 Photo the Philadelphia Museum of Art / Art Resource / Scala, Florence
70 Samuel Courtauld Trust, The Courtauld Gallery, London / Bridgeman Images
71 Photo Scala, Florence / bpk, Bildagentur fuer Kunst, Kultur und Geschichte, Berlin / Photo: Joerg P. Anders
73 Photo © Ministero dei beni e delle attività culturali e dei turisomo / Biblioteca Nazionale Centrale, Florence / GAP S.r.l Florence
74 Samuel Courtauld Trust, The Courtauld Gallery, London / Bridgeman Images
75 © The National Gallery, London / Scala, Florence
78 © 2017 Photo The Philadelphia Museum of Art / Art Resource / Scala, Florence
80, 82, 85 © The National Gallery, London / Scala, Florence
86 © Roland and Sabrina Michaud / akg-images
88 By kind permission of Lord Leicester and the Trustees of Holkham Estate, Norfolk / Bridgeman Images
89 Photo Scala, Florence – courtesy of the Ministero Beni e Att. Culturali e del Turismo
90 Courtesy Bernardo Gondi
91 © Trustees of the British Museum
92 © Iberfoto / Alinari Archives
93 © 2017 Photo Scala, Florence / bpk, Bildagentur für Kunst, Kultur und Geschichte, Berlin. Photo Elke Estel / Hans-Peter Klut
94 De Agostini Picture Library / G. Nimatallah / Getty Images
98 Photo Scala, Florence / bpk, Bildagentur für Kunst, Kultur und Geschichte, Berlin
99 © Trustees of the British Museum
101 Royal Collection Trust © Her Majesty Queen Elizabeth II, 2017 / Bridgeman Images
105 Photo Scala, Florence – courtesy of the Ministero Beni e Att. Culturali e del Turismo
106 Finsiel / Alinari Archives
108 © Photo Josse, Paris
110 © Finsiel / Alinari Archives
121 Photo Scala, Florence / bpk, Bildagentur für Kunst, Kultur und Geschichte, Berlin
122 © Devonshire Collection, Chatsworth / Reproduced by permission of Chatsworth Settlement Trustees / Bridgeman Images
123 © Araldo de Luca, Rome
124 © KHM-Museumsverband
125 © Trustees of the British Museum
127 © Hadiye Cangökçe, Istanbul
128 © Trustees of the British Museum
129 Cleveland Museum of Art, OH / Bridgeman Images
131 © Trustees of the British Museum
132 Regionální muzeum K. A. Polánka, Žatec. Foto: Jaroslav Holštajn (MS HK 902)
133 Staatliche Graphische Sammlung München, Inv. 174027 D.
134 Photo Scala, Florence / bpk, Bildagentur für Kunst, Kultur und Geschichte, Berlin / Photo Dietmar Katz
140 Museu Nacional de Arte Antiga, Lisbon, Portugal / Bridgeman Images
141 © Trustees of the British Museum
142, 143 Photo © RMN-Grand Palais (musée du Louvre) / Stéphane Maréchalle